P9-CMO-775

DOING RESPECTFUL RESEARCH

DOING RESPECTFUL RESEARCH

POWER, PRIVILEGE AND PASSION

SUSAN A. TILLEY

FERNWOOD PUBLISHING
HALIFAX & WINNIPEG

Copyright © 2016 Susan A. Tilley

All rights reserved. No part of this book may be reproduced or transmitted in
any form by any means without permission in writing from the publisher,
except by a reviewer, who may quote brief passages in a review.

Editing: Nancy Sixsmith
Cover design: All Caps Design
Printed and bound in Canada

Published by Fernwood Publishing
32 Oceanvista Lane, Black Point, Nova Scotia, B0J 1B0
and 748 Broadway Avenue, Winnipeg, Manitoba, R3G 0X3

www.fernwoodpublishing.ca

Fernwood Publishing Company Limited gratefully acknowledges the financial support of
the Government of Canada through the Canada Book Fund, the Manitoba Department
of Culture, Heritage and Tourism under the Manitoba Publishers Marketing Assistance
Program and the Province of Manitoba, through the Book Publishing Tax Credit, for
our publishing program. We are pleased to work in partnership with the Province of
Nova Scotia to develop and promote our creative industries for the benefit of all Nova
Scotians. We acknowledge the support of the Canada Council for the Arts, which last
year invested $153 million to bring the arts to Canadians throughout the country.

Canada   Canada Council Conseil des arts   NOVA SCOTIA Manitoba
         for the Arts   du Canada

Library and Archives Canada Cataloguing in Publication

Tilley, Susan Ann Bernadette, 1956-, author
Doing respectful research: power, privilege and
passion / Susan A. Tilley.

Includes bibliographical references and index.
ISBN 978-1-55266-819-1 (paperback)
1. Ethnology—Research. 2. Faculty advisors. 3. Counseling
in higher education. 4. Mentoring in education. I. Title.

GN345.T54 2016   305.80072'3   C2015-908513-6

CONTENTS

Acknowledgements ix

Preface 1

1   Introduction 4
      Catalyst for Writing This Book 4
      Thinking Back to My Doctoral Studies...5
      Informing the Book: Theoretical Framework...7
      Disrupting the Norms..11
      Creating New Canons..12
      Organizing Themes of the Book...13
            Theme 1: Critical Reflexivity 13
            Theme 2: Distance dynamic..14
            Theme 3: Respectful Research 16
            Intersecting Themes..17
      Choosing and Working with a Research Advisor.......................................17
            Choosing an Advisor...18
            Articulating Expectations 19
            Complexities of the Relationship 21
      Moving On...21
      Annotated Bibliography...22

2   Setting the Parameters...26
      Understanding Qualitative Methodology...28
      Methodology and Method...29
      Researcher Positioning 30
      Planning the Research 35
      Research Focus and Questions...37
      Access and Rapport..40
      Reciprocity 44
      Timelines 45

Collecting Data...46
Interviewing..47
    Focus Group Interviewing...51
Observation 54
Journaling in Qualitative Research 58
Documents as Data...59
Methods Matter..61
What to Do with the Data? 61
The Question of Quality..63
Dissemination 65
Annotated Bibliography...66

3   Research Ethics and Qualitative Research **70**

Introducing Research Ethics 70
Ethics Review of Research Involving Human Participants 72
    Research Ethics Board 73
Constructing an Ethics Application for Review 74
    Delegated and Full Review 75
Multiple Bodies of Oversight..78
Qualitative Research as Risky Business 79
Free, Informed and Ongoing Consent...81
Consent Process 83
Confidentiality 86
Data Withdrawal 89
Ethics and Focus Group Interviews...89
Observations..90
Maximizing Benefits...91
Moving Forward: Permissions in Hand 92
Submitting Ethics Applications: A Beginning Point 94
Annotated Bibliography...95

4   Transitioning into the Field and Collecting Data **100**

First Steps: Finding Participants 101
Applying a Critical Lens to Data Collection 107
    Collecting Demographic Information 108
    Common Data-Collection Methods................................109
Down to the Basics: Conducting Interviews......................................109
Complexities of Group Conversations 114
Observing in the Field 116
Journal Writing: Producing Data 122
Collecting Support Documents..124
Planning for What Might Happen Down the Road................................124
Moving On..126
Annotated Bibliography...126

5 Transcription: Constructing Representations of Qualitative Data ...131

Assumptions about Transcripts and the Transcription Process............133
Focus Groups and Transcription 138
Planning for Transcription: What to Do? 140
Checking Back with Participants: Member Checking 145
Annotated Bibliography...148

6 Data Analysis 152

Making Sense of the Data..152
Documentation of Process 156
Addressing the Complexities 158
Questioning Everyday Knowledge 159
Knowledge of the Past 160
Accounting for Difference 161
Theorizing the Data..163
Illustration 1: Foucault and Surveillance 164
Illustration 2: Theoretical Intersections 166
Illustration 3: Participants Theorizing their Experiences....................168
Questions to Prepare for Analysis 169
Articulating the Findings...170
Educating Ourselves Matters 170
Moving Forward 171
Annotated Bibliography...171

7 Representation: Writing Up/Down 176

Keeping Promises Made...178
Participant Feedback...179
Reasoning Our Representational Choices 182
Using Participants' Words: Quoting as a Problematic Process 187
Representation Across Difference 190
Articulating Research Findings...193
The Final Programmatic Representation: Thesis, MRP and Dissertation 194
Decisions About Writing 194
Annotated Bibliography...197

8 Dissemination: Moving into the Public Domain 202

Required: Constructing and Defending a Final Document....................204
Expectation: Engaging in Reciprocity...207
Desired: Academic and Personal Goals 209
Dissemination Venues 209
Goals for Completing the Program...214
From Presentation to Publication..215
Where to Publish? 217
Authoring with Others...218
Beyond the Book and Journal Article 219
Checking Back Again...220
A Reminder 221
Annotated Bibliography...221

9 Conclusion **226**

Final Reflections 227
A Look Forward 228
Postscript 230

Links **235**

References **236**

**Appendix A: Information Letter and Informed
    Consent Form** **258**

Appendix B: Focus Group Interview Script **263**

**Appendix C: Moving From Transcripts to (Bilingual)
    Transcript Poems (Sample)** **265**

**Appendix D: Response to the Editor Regarding
    Manuscript Submitted for Publication** **267**

Index **274**

ACKNOWLEDGEMENTS

A book is rarely the result of one person and that is the case in this instance. Many others have contributed to the shaping of this text. First and foremost, I extend my endless gratitude to the women I met when teaching and researching in the prison and those who participated in my doctoral research. Their voices contributed greatly to the critique offered in this text. They taught me many things about lives lived, inside and outside of prisons and schools, and about the complexities of conducting respectful research, which I hope are captured on the pages that follow.

Thank you to the students I taught and learned from in qualitative research courses and in my role as advisor; our work together has informed many of the issues raised in this book. I especially thought of your questions and our conversations when making decisions about what content was most important for readers who are beginning or already started on their research journeys. Snežana Ratković and Phil Teeuwsen, doctoral students I have advised and who have been at my side from the initial stages, contributed to the shaping of the text. They read chapters and provided constructive feedback that made its way onto the pages. They also contributed illustrative material connected to their doctoral research to the text. Sandra Starmans provided her perspective as a beginning master's student on the chapters she read in the later stages of the process. She was instrumental in the construction of the final annotated bibliographies that conclude the chapters.

I send gratitude to students who worked with me as research assistants during the period I was writing the book. In particular, a special thank-you to Christina Skorobohacz, who was involved in the early stages of the book construction, conducting database searches and serving as a sounding board as I developed the chapters. She also contributed to writing early versions of annotated bibliographies for the book chapters.

This book was a long time coming. Thank you to Carl James for suggesting I write a qualitative research text and pushing me along the way. My appreciation goes to colleagues in the education faculty and others who joined us for writing retreats over the years. I benefitted from the focused time away from the university devoted to our individual writing projects and the support and camaraderie shared.

Thank you to people who read drafts of chapters and provided constructive feedback, including Nombuso Dlamini, who read early versions of the first three chapters; Ebru Ustundag, who read chapters at the latter stage of the process and was a wonderful source for relevant literature and encouragement; and Cindy Bell, who made contributions to a final edit and the construction of the index. My gratitude also goes to Celia-Haig Brown, who was my doctoral advisor and started me on my academic journey.

I send thanks to my friends who listened to me over the past few years as I talked about the developing manuscript and was trying to write when so many other tasks were calling my name. Finding space and time to write has been the major challenge. Many friends shared writing time with me at my house and in their homes; thank you. We supported each other with conversation, feedback, good wine and food; much appreciated. I send gratitude out to all those people whom I have not forgotten but are too many to name.

I travelled with computer in hand to different locations, including Ontario, Grand Marais (USA) and British Columbia, seeking out time and places to write and to visit my friends. I took my computer home to Newfoundland, where I received love and support from family and friends.

I am grateful for the support Errol Sharpe provided to me from the proposal stage to the final book production stage, a lengthy but worthwhile journey; much appreciated. I also send thanks to all the individuals associated with Fernwood who helped to move the book into the public domain. And finally, thank you to the reviewers of the initial book draft for their critical and constructive comments: their suggestions contributed to this final version.

PREFACE

Although numerous research texts focusing on qualitative methodology(ies) and/or the teaching of specific qualitative research methods are on the market, a need exists for additional texts that emphasize the complexities of the qualitative research process in comprehensive ways. Embedded in the healthy number of books that have been produced to teach students how to conduct qualitative research are philosophical, theoretical and political perspectives, and intersecting discourses that influenced the writing of the texts. The underlying perspective of this text reflects a critical, feminist, postmodern, social justice orientation toward qualitative methodologies and methods, and emphasizes the critical tradition of questioning the privileging of dominant discourses, which play an important role in the education of novice and student researchers.

This book is not written for those looking for in-depth discussions of specific qualitative methodologies; it is for those interested in interrogating the complexities of qualitative research, regardless of the methodology chosen. I do not take up the all-too-familiar debate related to the quantitative/qualitative divide. Such debate has been a part of the historical struggle of qualitative researchers working to gain respect in the academy and to secure funds to do their research. There are many researchers who have taken up this discussion in the past (Lincoln and Guba 1985; see Bogdan and Biklen 2003: 39–41 for a chart summarizing the characteristics of both).

The purpose of this text is to encourage undergraduate and graduate students conducting qualitative research involving human participants to give thoughtful consideration to covert elements of the research process. Instructors of research courses and researchers who conduct qualitative research and serve as advisors for undergraduate and graduate student research will find in this book useful discussions of critical perspectives on qualitative methodology, as well as illustrations of

1

complex issues researchers face regularly when conducting research. Also helpful is the focus on the role of advisor in supporting students through to the completion of their research and on the students' responsibilities to ensure that they complete successfully. The text includes a discussion of the challenges of the dissemination process: some of the avenues open to students to present, publish and go public with their work at various stages in their program of study. Interactions that students might anticipate having with their advisors are illustrated throughout the text.

This book can stand on its own or serve as an important supplementary text to conventional texts required in qualitative research courses in education and disciplines within the social sciences. It includes a number of Canadian sources to illustrate the concepts introduced, and as such will be valuable to individuals who research, teach and study in North American/Western contexts; it is especially appropriate for those of us teaching and researching in Canada. The book explores elements of everyday research practice: choice of research focus and questions; selection of context and participants; collection, analysis and representation of data; and dissemination activities and responsibilities. An emphasis is given to the commonly used methods of interviewing and observation, the primary methods I used in my doctoral research, with additional discussion of various methods that connect with these two. What is significant about the current field of qualitative research is the proliferation of methods available for use, which are impossible to address sufficiently in any one text.

The role that power and privilege play in decisions related to what gets researched, who conducts research, and how data are represented and disseminated is embedded in discussion throughout the chapters of the book.

The book has three central organizing themes that are emphasized in relation to research practice: critical reflexivity, distance dynamic, respectful research. Although all aspects of practice can be examined in light of each of the organizing themes, the text is constructed so that particular areas are highlighted in detail in specific chapters. As well, each book chapter has an annotated bibliography of additional sources that provide a discussion and/or examples of research that are related to the issues addressed in the chapter.

This book is integrally tied to who I am as a researcher and my experiences in the field: a different field, a different researcher, a different book. The critical, feminist ethnographic research I conducted with women in prison, my PhD research experience, was integral to the writing of this book. I turned back to my doctoral research because it was through that experience that I came to develop understandings that I now hold dear in my daily work as a researcher, teacher and advisor to students who also conduct research. The women prisoners taught me many things, research and other-world related, and continue to influence my thinking today.

In this text, I draw extensively from my dissertation to help explain and elaborate on the logistics and complexities of conducting respectful research. Even though the dissertation was published a number of years ago, the questions of methodology and method addressed in that work continue to be relevant in current times as researchers grapple with the complexities of conducting respectful research. In addition to the examples drawn from my doctoral research, the questions that students asked me over the years when they were facing challenges in the qualitative research courses I taught, or addressing the complexities of conducting their own research, inform the text. The students for whom I currently serve as advisor have provided concrete examples related to some of the topics.

My three-year term as graduate program director of an interdisciplinary MA program in social justice and equity studies has also left its mark on this text. During those three years, I interacted with many graduate students and affiliated faculty members across disciplinary boundaries and learned much from them about the program, research and advisement challenges faced, regardless of the faculty or department within which students and faculty members were situated.

As I wrote the chapters, I was aware that language can be used as a tool of exclusion and was careful not to use undecipherable jargon; however, complex ideas often need complex language. I encourage students to engage with the text even if facing challenges with some of the language. Similar to the way students need to write to become better writers, they need to develop and hone their skills in reading to understand particular academic discourse as they work through complex material. Students need to be willing to work with language and build on skills that make the discourse accessible.

This book encourages student researchers who conduct qualitative research to recognize that the research world in the West continues to be dominated by those of us who represent privileged, white, Eurocentric, middle-class perspectives, many of whom were socialized in academic institutions to take up research practice in particular kinds of ways. The effect this influence has had on decisions made about who and what gets researched, and how the research is planned and conducted, is addressed in the chapters that follow. The book works against the *critical*, remaining distanced from the academic arenas in which the researchers themselves are socialized, and possibilities for change are created. Issues discussed in this text can serve to provoke conversations that make their way into educational settings in which many of us teach qualitative research to students who want to continue in the academic realm or who aspire to research within/across community contexts distanced from institutions such as universities, and those who want to become informed consumers of research results.

Chapter 1

INTRODUCTION

CATALYST FOR WRITING THIS BOOK

I walk down the long narrow corridors. At every turn a heavy metal door must be unlocked so that I can pass through. Each time a door is opened it slams shut ominously behind me. The pass-card I've been given only slightly alleviates the sense of claustrophobia as each of the doors locks behind me. I am sensitive to the eyes that watch me, eyes that are parts of bodies not visible to me. These bodies are stationed in front of monitors at the central control block. They watch as I travel through the maze of barriers. I make my way through the rotunda. Women are there, sitting alone or in small groups chatting. They look up to see who is passing. I am familiar to some of the women so they make small, almost imperceptible gestures of acknowledgment. The rotunda is their world and not the place for us to meet and interact. I must wait until they cross over into our space, our meeting place called school. I pass through the final barrier, the locked door that separates classroom from rotunda. Then and only then do I find myself in a place that is familiar, a place that connects with my world outside the prison. (Tilley 1998a: 9–10)

The walk through the corridors described here was an entry in a journal recounting the beginning of my initiation into a heavily secured and guarded context, a prison, which later became the site of my doctoral research. I was hired to work in the prison based on past teaching experience and my connection to a friend of a friend who was already teaching in that context for many years. This work was a way for me to support myself while completing doctoral studies. The rotunda, an area women would pass through as they made their way to their work assignments, a place they could stop and congregate (until forced to move on), was a prison space, understood as outside the realm of the school and the teachers. I taught in the prison with no intention to shift from a teacher to researcher position, but circumstances led me to change my stance and that decision.

THINKING BACK TO MY DOCTORAL STUDIES

Moment 1

I am sitting in my philosophy course listening to a range of students pontificating about what constitutes justice. They make their connections to the philosophical thinkers, attempting (I think) to impress the professor. The class is from 4:00 p.m. until 9:00 p.m., so by the end I am exhausted. I am in the prison classroom early the next morning; we begin with the women sitting around a large table. This is their time to lead the discussion. As we sit there, a student enters the room, slams her fist to the table and asks, "What is justice?" We then have a rich discussion with painful illustrations, and I am lost in the theoretical material contradictions.

Moment 2

I am walking down the corridor at the university chatting with my friend Kathryn. It has been a few months since I began teaching in the prison. I am telling Kathryn about my experiences and lightly declare that I feel like I am finding the freedom to teach in the prison context. We both laugh at the irony of my statement, but as our laughter dies down, I know I have to explore both the naïveté and truth of that statement. How can I feel a freedom to teach in a prison? The freedom I feel contrasts so sharply with the regimented and controlled experience of my public school teaching.

Moment 3

One of my professors is telling me that I should conduct research in the prison. I tell him that I already have my research planned and research context decided. I explain that I don't believe I should conduct research with women living a life of incarceration, a vulnerable population. But pushing in the back of my mind are the women's voices, what they talk to me about during our interactions in the classroom. They tell me they have much to say about what happened to them as they struggled to obtain a public school education. A few have asked why I don't research them; finally they would have someone to listen to what they were unable to say to their teachers and other students before they left and gave up on the possibilities of an education.

The backdrop of memories constructed and shown here refer to a few of the many significant moments, during the initial stages of my doctoral studies, that convinced me to don a researcher lens in the prison context, even though I did not start with that intention. The theoretical knowledge I was learning in doctoral courses was intersecting with my growing knowledge of the women and their experiences of incarceration and struggles for education, both inside and outside of the prison. Through engaging with feminist theories, which emphasized gender as an analytic category for understanding the lives of women and their experiences of oppression, and critical theories that highlighted knowledge/power relations and the hegemonic and subjugated positioning of particular kinds of knowledge, I was able to make sense of the ways in which power was exercised in the context of the prison and in the lives of the women before incarceration. The theories I integrated into the course papers I wrote forced me to think about the gendered/raced/classed/sexed experiences of the women and the circumstances that contributed to their criminalization. As I engaged a critical feminist research praxis, I imagined possibilities for conducting research in the prison, research that could contribute, if only in small ways, to adding the perspectives and voices of women who had experienced incarceration to the academic and media discourse already in place. I was able to imagine a way to proceed and felt an obligation to do so.

My doctoral research served as a catalyst to write this qualitative research book many years later; it has finally settled into its shape after a long period of deliberation and writing. I learned many things from the women who participated in my critical feminist ethnographic study, from those involved in the observations I conducted and the twenty-two women who agreed to take part in in-depth, open-ended interviews; and the teachers, especially Geraldine, who supported my application to teach in the prison and participated in the research. I was very fortunate to be able to gain access to the prison and to the women engaged in schooling in that context willing to participate. Times have changed; education is now privatized in Canadian prisons, and the degree of access I secured to conduct my research would less likely be given today.

While teaching and researching in the prison school, I was exposed to various individual, cultural and institutional differences. Previous to that time, I lived and worked in a small, mostly homogenous province in Canada. I interacted with people who reflected my social locations: white, middle-class, able-bodied and successfully educated in public school contexts. The women I met in the prison taught me how individuals who do not reflect the norms of the dominant population can experience marginalization and oppression in everyday and schooling contexts. I came to understand better how my actions as an individual or as part of the public school institutional machinery and society in general could contribute to (or work against) the oppression and marginalization of others. This book is partial payback of sorts to the women who participated in my doctoral research and who spoke of wanting people to understand what it means to be criminalized and incarcerated and to struggle for an education.

Although few readers of this text will be conducting research in prisons, I expect many will be interested in engaging with antioppressive, emancipatory research that they believe can make a difference in some way to individuals and community populations experiencing various forms of inequities and marginalization. Whether students with programs completed continue on to further studies, decide to make their home in academe, or return to previous or new professions, the research process they experience has the potential to prepare them to question institutional and societal structures and practices, which they previously may have accepted as the well-established, secured and unchangeable norm.

INFORMING THE BOOK: THEORETICAL FRAMEWORK

> We live in both/and worlds full of paradox and uncertainty where close inspection turns unities into multiplicities, clarities into ambiguities, univocal simplicities into polyvocal complexities. (Lather 1991: xvi)

Theories I initially came to know through my university studies (particularly graduate work), critical, feminist, postmodern and poststructural theories taken up as objects of study in courses and later explored as I moved from student to academic, have contributed to the shaping of this text. These bodies of theories, which intersect, contrast and complement each other (Hesse-Biber 2012), are useful for examining the "both/and worlds full of paradox and uncertainty" that Patti Lather (1991) describes. (See Gannon and Davies 2012 for discussion of the points of departure among these perspectives.)

Situated within a critical postmodern framework, qualitative researchers are working with the understanding that research is value-laden, and knowledge is always partial and contestable; that a neutral, objective researcher, interviewer/observer does not exist except in the imagination. Knowledge produced as a result of conducting qualitative interpretive research is not intended to culminate into pronouncements of stable truths, but instead represents multiple realities and readings of phenomena under examination. Such knowledge is understood to be contextually sensitive and influenced by various sources, including researchers, participants and contexts. (See Lincoln et al. 2011 for a comprehensive comparison of inquiry paradigms.)

This book reflects an understanding of the impossibility of "objective" methods and a clinical separation between researcher and researched in qualitative research; a "rejection of the so-called objective all-seeing eye/I of positive research" (Davies et al. 2004: 223); and a concern, that although incompatible with underlying assumptions of critical qualitative methodologies, what Pushkala Prasad (2005: 4) describes in the following quote as "qualitative positivism," continues to hold a degree of influence in the world of qualitative research.

> Qualitative positivism employs nonquantitative methods of data collection such as interviews and observation within conventional positivist assumptions about the nature of social reality and the production of knowledge. Reality is assumed to be concrete, separate from the researcher, and understandable through accurate use of "objective" methods of data collection.

Embedded in the arguments of this book is an emphasis on the critical questioning of researcher intentions and methods, and the taken-for-granted of research practice. As well, the book provides support for student researchers who are interested in developing emancipatory research agendas and conducting research that contributes to social action and change.

Numerous researchers positioned within the academy have interrogated qualitative methodologies (Dehli 2008; Denzin and Lincoln 2005b; Gallagher 2008; Guba and Lincoln 2005; Lincoln and Guba 1985; Roth 2005; Smith 1999; Weis and Fine 2004) and method (Conrad 2004; Ibanez 1997); and explored approaches to, as well as how to *craft*, qualitative research (Hesse-Biber and Leavy 2004; Prasad 2005). Methodological critique was an early practice of critical feminist scholars in particular (Cook and Fonow 1990; Gorelick 1991; Harding 1987; Lather 1991; Reinharz 1992; Smith, D. 1987; Smith L. 1999).

> From the early days of the women's movements of the 1970s, feminists have tried to intervene in the ways social sciences think about and do research. They have tried to transform the methodologies and epistemologies of their disciplines. Central to these projects have been concerns about whether and how customary approaches to knowledge production promote or obstruct the development of more democratic social relations. (Harding and Norberg 2005: 2009)

Critical feminist researchers have a long history of questioning the underlying influences of patriarchy on research that historically marginalized women. They called into question the practice of judging the *validity* of qualitative research using the lens of positivist criteria and the pressure applied to qualitative researchers to embody an objectivity and neutrality — as defined by positivism (Acker et al. 1991; Bakhru 2008; Haraway 1991; Harding 1993; Narayan 1993). Feminist researchers supported and engaged in the questioning of ethics in general, and specifically in relation to the interview context and interviewer-interviewee relationships (Eyre 2010; Oakley 1981; Patai 1994). They questioned the complexities and im/possibilities of respectful representation (Dehli 2008; Henry 2003; Stacey 1988; Wolf 1992) and promoted qualitative methodology as a tool to be used against oppression (DeVault 1999). Feminist researchers acknowledged the need for reciprocity in research, a "give and take," a mutual negotiation of meaning and power (Lather 1991: 57).

The feminist perspective influencing this book, which dates back to my doctoral research when the work of feminist scholars helped me conduct respectful research with women in prison, is comprehensive, recognizing gender as an important research focus and analytic category while also emphasizing the need to factor in and understand difference more broadly. The early emphasis feminist scholars gave to understanding difference fueled the demand for qualitative methodology(ies) and methods to account for the intersecting influences of gender, class, race, dis/ability and sexuality on the research act, stressing how these and other fluid and interconnected socially constructed categories shaped research. Many women of colour were at the forefront of this demand. "As women of colour have made clear, researchers must find an epistemological position and methodologies that can make sense of differences" (Strega 2005: 211). Patricia Hill Collins (2012) reminds scholars and researchers of the roots of intersectionality in early Black feminist politics.

This early emphasis is evident in more current times in the growth of studies across disciplines interested in exploring intersectionality in tandem with questioning local and global inequalities (Bose 2012; Cho et al. 2013; Choo 2012; Dhamoon 2011; McCall 2005). While recognizing the growing emphasis on understanding the influences on and effects of intersections across social locations and subjectivities in the lives of research participants and communities locally and globally, Leslie McCall (2005), Jennifer Nash (2008) and others point out that the methodological challenges to do such work, similar to earlier attempts, remain great.

Feminist literature is replete with theoretical and epistemological debates related to the qualitative landscape (see Olesen 2011 for an overview). Critical postmodern agendas continue to push back against conventional humanist qualitative methodology (St. Pierre 2011). In more recent years, researchers working within transnational feminist perspectives continue this tradition of methodological critique (Dillard and Okpalaoka 2011; Swarr and Nagar 2010).

The influence of Michel Foucault (1979, 1980) on this book's discussion of the ways in which power is exercised through the research act and the multiple intersecting phases of the research process also dates back to my doctoral research. The role of power/knowledge in the re/production and maintenance of dominant institutional policies and structures that marginalize/privilege particular individuals and populations underlies the critique of research practice offered. These institutional structures are steeped in cultural norms and practices that influence research conducted.

The centrality of culture in everyday life, that culture is performed rather than stable, is reflected in this text. Culture is not only a concept applied to those individuals positioned as outside of the mainstream Eurocentric norm, struggling to understand Western cultural capital (Bourdieu 1984; Yosso 2005). Culture also happens on home turf as well as inside/outside territorial borders. Researchers are *culturally* situated individually and contextually, and these positionings intersect and influence the research conducted.

The critical research praxis promoted in this text is influenced by critical feminist perspectives that push researchers to question themselves and the limitation of their knowledge in the hopes of building capacity to conduct research in respectful ways, engaging a praxis that entails "reflection and action upon the world in order to transform it" (Freire 2008: 51). This critical praxis recognizes research as privileged work that brings with it great responsibility.

Qualitative methodologies are interpretive methodologies, and some would argue that "The craft of the qualitative researcher is a hermeneutic craft" (Ezzy 2002: xv). This text leans toward that understanding. Douglas Ezzy defines hermeneutics as "the theory of interpretation. It theorizes the relationship between our own pre-existing interpretations and the interpretation of the texts and people we are studying. Hermeneutic practices are interpretive practices." Researchers come to their interpretive work with various theoretical and experiential frameworks in place (recognized or not), as do their participants. These frameworks are used, built upon and revised in the process of making meaning of data. While engaging with data, researchers pay attention to the perspectives of their participants as well as their own and how they intersect and influence meaning. Interpreting data involves "an ongoing circular process of moving between one's own perspective and the perspective of the other person" (Ezzy 2002: 27). The meanings constructed are historically, socially and culturally situated; they are never absolute truths to be left unquestioned. Multiple and intersecting layers of interpretation are in operation as researchers interact with participants and collect, analyze and represent their data. As they engage their craft, student researchers must question their meaning-making, asking themselves why this interpretation and not another.

DISRUPTING THE NORMS

Critical frameworks create space to question dominant, historical Eurocentric practices embedded in the institutions within which many students learn to be researchers and receive permission and resources to conduct research. Deborah Britzman (1991: 43), while referring to the education canon, writes:

> To counter the dominant view of knowledge as neutral and capable of "speaking for itself," knowledge must be approached as problematic in its social construction, and the problem of representation, interpretation, and meaning — that is, the question, how do we know what we know — must become a central theme in disciplinary studies and in school classrooms. To admit such a theme, the social construction of canonical knowledge and how such material becomes the measure of convention must be interrogated.

Britzman's advice reflects the goals and perspectives of researchers working within critical theoretical frameworks. It is important that students also take up Britzman's call to interrogate the "social construction of canonical knowledge [in connection with conducting research] and how such material becomes the measure of convention" (Britzman 1991: 43). Kari Dehli (2008: 61), in relation to research and methodology, writes of the dominance of a neoliberal governmentality in the education and production of new researchers and the maintenance of methodological regimes:

> Methodology writing and teaching are also about producing and organizing subjects and about specifying the ways in which individuals are to take themselves up, and recognize others as belonging to subject-positions in methodological regimes. In this sense, teaching about and supervising students in methodology are about generating experts who can be trusted to produce truth according to authorized rules and transparent procedures.

Although difficult to work against such governmentality, students' awareness of its influence makes it possible for them to question the sanctioned knowledge that is permitted, supported and transmitted within and across programs, methodology, texts and classes. Such critical questioning can also make visible knowledge that dominant groups disqualify and/or ignore, particularly knowledge related to deep structural inequities that continue to exist in communities both within and outside of academe. As Foucault (1980: 82) suggests, "It is through the re-appearance [or honouring] of this knowledge, of these local popular knowledges, these disqualified knowledges, that criticism performs its work."

Significant critique has emerged from scholars who work against the grain, inter-rogating the effects of mainstream research on individuals and groups marginalized within dominant Eurocentric contexts (Lopez and Parker 2003; Loutzenheiser 2007; McCaslin and Breton 2008; Smith 1999; Stonebanks 2008; Twine and Warren 2000; Tyson 2003). For example, work of Indigenous, critical race and anticolonial scholars brings into full view questions of dominant groups, and often Eurocentric white privilege and the effects of colonization (Battiste 1998; Jordan 2009; Lawrence 2002; Peters 2011; St. Denis 2007; Stanger-Ross 2008; Wilson 2008; Yosso 2006). Marie Battiste (2008: 497) writes: "Unraveling the effects of generations of exploitation, violence, marginalization, powerlessness, and enforced cultural imperialism on Aboriginal knowledge and peoples has been a significant and often painful undertaking in the past century."

Linda Tuhiwai Smith (2014: 58) describes the incompatibility of a Western, dominant Eurocentric research lens on Indigenous contexts and peoples:

> It [Western research] is research that brings to bear, on any study of indigenous peoples, a cultural orientation, a set of values, a different conceptualization of things as time, space and subjectivity, different and competing theories of knowledge, highly specialized forms of language, and structures of power.

The critique offered by these scholars is important for students to understand so they can reflect on their developing methodological knowledge while at least being minimally aware of the multiplicity of contradictory views and ways of *doing* things.

All arguments are positioned within and fueled by political and social discourses. Whether or not students choose to position themselves within a critical tradition while engaging with the questions and issues this qualitative research book illus-trates, they will at least have been part of discussions that make the underlying assumptions of critical traditions and the always/already available historically embedded perspective of Western academic traditions visible.

CREATING NEW CANONS

While recognizing the theoretical backdrop to this text, I also caution against constructing feminist, postmodern and critical theory as the canon from which all else is measured. As Patti Lather (1991: 155) reminds us, poststructuralists argue that "there are no social positions exempt from becoming oppressive to others. Any group, any position can move into the oppressor's role." Even though I clearly indicate my theoretical positioning within this critical feminist framework, I do not suggest that this framework now reflects a master narrative from which all else is measured. Students need to practise a healthy skepticism and to always be "suspicious of totalizing theories and expert prescriptions" (Lather 1991: xviii), including those labelled *post* and *critical*.

In his book about writing ethnography, John Van Maanen (1988: xv) states; "I am conscious, however, that my own argument is also a product of conventions and ideology and is thus caught up in the same problems of which I write. This is unavoidable." I similarly acknowledge that I am a product of particular experiences, education and discourses in the hopes that this declaration will aid readers in their interpretation of what I have constructed as a critical qualitative research text.

ORGANIZING THEMES OF THE BOOK

In addition to the illustrations of the complexities of the research process drawn heavily from my doctoral work, three main themes are embedded in the text: the importance of enacting a critical reflexivity to the design and process of qualitative research, the influence of a distance dynamic on research practice, and the challenges of conducting respectful and ethical qualitative research. These themes are introduced initially in this section and then discussed and illustrated more fully in the chapters that follow.

Theme 1: Critical Reflexivity

> One important aspect of criticality is an ability to reflect on one's own views and assumptions as themselves features of a particular cultural and historical formation. Such a reflection does not automatically lead to relativism or a conclusion that all views are equally valid; but it does make it more difficult to imagine universality or finality for any particular set of views. Most important, it regards one's views, as perpetually open to challenge, as choices entailing a responsibility for the effects on one's arguments on others. (Burbules and Berk 1999: 61)

When qualitative researchers apply a critical reflexivity to their research process, they engage in a deep questioning of themselves as researchers and acknowledge the layers of complexities that are part of the qualitative research process. When student researchers understand, as Nicholas Burbules and Rupert Berk (1999: 61) suggest, that their "views and assumptions as themselves are features of a particular cultural and historical formation" and apply that understanding to the research they design and conduct, they are more likely to factor in how their historical and cultural positionings, their identities, influence their research than those students who move forward in their work with little thought given to such matters. A critically reflexive lens would require (among other things) student researchers to take into account the ways in which their social locations and identities intersect and influence the design and focus of their research, and to examine closely their research praxis, including the macro and micro decisions they make as the research process unfolds. The lens I envision is an intersectional lens that would also recognize the interlocking systems of oppressions that work to marginalize some individuals and privilege others (Collins 1991, 2000, 2012). Most important in the development of a critical lens is the student researchers' ability to question the limitations of their knowledge in relation to the research they are planning and to systematically work against those limitations.

Although articulating a definition of critical reflexivity is a beginning step in the movement toward the development of a critical lens, operationalizing criticality is far from simple. In *Getting Smart*, Lather (1991: 62–63) stated that "the search to operationalize reflexivity in critical inquiry is a journey into uncharted territory." I would argue that what Lather wrote in 1991 still holds true for the most part. The exploration of the research process that runs throughout this book illustrates what critical reflexivity can look like in practice and encourages students to develop critical awareness of how research, even when designed with good intent, can exploit people and contexts.

To hone their critical and reflexive lens, students might begin by engaging in critical questioning of themselves at the initial stages of the research: What are the truths they hold dear in relation to the research focus? Why do they hold such beliefs and assign them such importance? When students adopt critical perspectives, they have an opportunity to begin to understand the research world in all its complexities and how they fit into that world — in various ways dictated by their complex, always shifting, sometimes declared and often ascribed identities. When operationalizing a critical reflexivity, they are attempting to make visible what can remain obscured in the everyday practice of research, from the initial design stage through to the writing up and down of research findings. They will have to be willing to work hard to understand the complexities of language, interpretation and meaning-making embedded in a reflection process connected to the messy world of qualitative, interpretive methodologies, not settling for realist explanations. (See Davies et al. 2004 for a comprehensive discussion of reflexivity.)

Theme 2: Distance Dynamic

Qualitative research is typically understood as an intimate endeavour with the researcher's familiarity with context and participants influencing the research process. The appropriate degree of intimacy varies depending on the methodology and methods; consider the *closeness* necessary in life history research or participatory action research and how that might differ from the distance possible when an individual researcher is conducting an institutional case study or qualitative research generic in nature. The researcher, as a primary instrument in the research process, strives to develop an acceptable level of familiarity. However, agreement on what degree of closeness is acceptable differs from researcher to researcher, participant to participant and context to context.

The concept of a distance dynamic is a useful analytic tool for understanding the challenges and complexities of interpretive research. The Merriam-Webster Online Dictionary (2013) defines *distance* as "separation in time"; "an extent or advance away or along from a point considered primary or original"; or "personal and especially emotional separation." Timeframes are important to many aspects of qualitative research practice. For example, how much time in the context is long enough to develop a credible understanding of that context? What is an appropriate timeline for the research to unfold (for instance, data collection, analysis and dissemination of findings)? How does the passage of time between collection of data and data analysis influence findings? How might timelines be affected when data is collected online? Produced as artistic artifacts?

Qualitative researchers must critically reflect on the ways in which distance between themselves and their research contexts and participants influences the research: What kind of distance can or should be kept between the interviewer and the participant involved in in-depth, open-ended interviews or when researchers are in their participant observer role? The degree of distance between the women prisoners and me was lessened through my positioning as both teacher and researcher. I needed to consider how my identities intersected and influenced the research process. What degree of distance is possible or desirable when the researcher is also the teacher?

The distance dynamic is related to the researcher and raw data and the process of analysis: What degree of distance is acceptable between the researcher and raw data before the credibility of the research is questioned? As a verb, the dictionary (2013) writes of *distance* as the action "to place or keep at a distance"; "to leave far behind." When are student researchers at the point when they make the choice to leave their research behind? The context? The participants? When is this possible? Desirable? What is a respectful withdrawal process?

The distance dynamic operates in qualitative research from the planning stage to the reporting of findings. For example, at the design stage, student researchers make decisions about their research focus, the problems they want to explore and the articulation of their research questions. They need to think about how their degree of familiarity with the research context or community (on- or offline, geographical or technological) will enhance or inhibit their access to a research site.

Overall, there are no simple answers to questions related to the possible effects of the distance dynamic on research endeavours. A student's awareness of the dynamic and how it operates throughout the research process is useful for making the effects visible and for working against those distances that are detrimental to the research process and participants.

Theme 3: Respectful Research

> To look twice is to practise respect. (Absolon and Willett 2005: 108)

> To actively respect what we do not know, or understand, is extremely difficult — I think back to my first walk through the prison, my deeply embedded assumptions, my lack of knowledge, my misinformation. However, the researcher's familiarity with the context does not always guarantee that the research conducted will be any less hazardous to the participants than the research directed by someone stepping in from the outside for a brief encounter. Different risks evolve as researchers and contexts change. (Tilley 1998b: 327)

Kathy Absolon and Cam Willett (2005: 108) suggest that "to look twice is to practise respect." However, the doubled look must be an informed look, a look supported by a critical reflexivity similar to the one introduced previously as a theme. The critical lens that students apply to their research praxis will encourage them to look beyond the everyday and ask questions that can provoke multiple responses, questions that are often more easily ignored than examined. Such a deep and critical gaze is necessary because what constitutes respectful qualitative research and critical research praxis cannot always be fully understood at the initial stages of research; the researcher's knowledge, methodological choices, research focus and participants will influence the process that unfolds.

Currently, student researchers in Canadian university contexts who choose to conduct research with human participants have to complete an ethics tutorial and an ethics review process at their institution before proceeding (TCPS2 2014). When students complete the requirements, they are better informed about the institutional stance on ethical conduct when researching with human participants. However, in addition to understanding the principles articulated in institutional policy, respectful praxis requires a contextual sensitivity on the part of the student researchers. Researchers practising respect will be aware that issues of ethical import cannot be fully addressed through a process that occurs in isolation of the unfolding of the research process and all the unexpected experiences that that process entails (e.g., Eyre 2010; Tomkinson 2015).

In the case of women in prison, they are infantilized; they are no longer permitted to make everyday decisions and lose control over determining what they can do with their lives. When researching in the prison, I needed to be sensitive about not doubly exposing the women to a patronizing gaze through my added lens as researcher. Respect can be demonstrated when student researchers understand the fine line between supporting and enabling participants' rights to make their own decisions and patronizing them. Recognizing this fine line can become especially difficult (as well as very important) when participants fit within institutionally imposed categories of risk and vulnerability, including people with physical and intellectual disabilities, children, students in schools and prisoners.

In the qualitative research courses I currently teach, to encourage students to keep practising respect at the forefront of their work, I ask them to take a moment and reflect on the research they are designing or have conducted in the past. Knowing what they know about the research — the actual process and benefits, the behind-the-scenes view — would they be willing to volunteer to participate? Would they want their children or families or people they love to take part? If the answers are "no," I suggest they need to ask themselves why and to use their responses to help them revise their research plans and process.

Intersecting Themes

The three themes embedded in the text are closely interconnected. It is difficult to address the issue of conducting respectful research without also emphasizing the importance of student researchers developing and using an informed critical lens to ask hard questions of their research praxis. Those hard questions must take into account how the distance dynamic influences researchers' ability to conduct credible, respectful qualitative research. Students are not working alone. Research advisors play a significant role in students' research plans and process decisions. They can be used as sounding boards to help students address questions about how to engage in critical reflexivity, address issues related to distance and make decisions that result in student research being both respectful and ethical.

Although the main thrust of this book is on planning and doing qualitative research, a secondary emphasis is on advisement and the student-advisor relationship. The concluding sections of this chapter (and other sections of the book) emphasize the role of advisors and the complexities of the student-advisor relationship. Although relationships between students and their advisors take various shapes and develop over time, students can play an important part to ensure that the relationship is productive from the beginning to the completion of their research journey.

CHOOSING AND WORKING WITH A RESEARCH ADVISOR

University, discipline, faculty, department and program context-specific practices influence the process in place for students to obtain a research advisor (also referred to as *supervisor* in other contexts) who will work with them to complete the research requirements of their program. Although there are a multitude of differences within and across these contexts related to student programs of research, and the expectations and criteria of advisement, commonalities exist. This section and other discussions embedded throughout this book related to advisement issues attempt to share some useful information and advice about issues related to student advisement. In some programs, students are assigned an advisor before they begin, and in others they choose an advisor after they have been accepted into a program. Those students moving from a master's into a PhD program may do a lot of legwork to choose an advisor to fit their needs, whereas an undergraduate student may have less choice in advisors when completing an undergraduate thesis. At the master's level, a mixture of both occur: Students can use their initiative to seek out an advisor, or the institution might assign the person with faculty member agreement. The length of time the relationship is in place is somewhat connected to the degree program, but it is also related to the research focus and methodology and how well the individuals work together.

The points raised in the following discussion reflect my experiences as an advisor as well as instructor and mentor of graduate students who have had varying experiences of advisement. These points are connected to issues related to students beginning their research journey and developing their initial relationship with their advisors. In later chapters, advisement issues that can emerge as the research process unfolds will be the emphasis.

Choosing an Advisor

An advisor is generally someone students are familiar with, either by way of previous study or through knowledge of the person's research interests and publications. Before approaching faculty members to ask them to consider serving in an advisement capacity, students should find out relevant information about the faculty member and read the individual's university web page and relevant publications to support their argument that the individual would be a good *fit* for the student's research focus and the advisor position. Students should not only look for someone who can potentially help them with their anticipated research goals but also consider how they can contribute to the research and work of the potential advisor. The student-advisor relationship can be long term; if possible, it is best to point to how both can potentially benefit from the relationship.

Based on context and discipline, advisors may have a few or many students to whom they have made a commitment. They will be invested in their students to varying degrees, possibly more invested when mutual benefits are expected to accrue. Be prepared that individuals may not be willing to take on the advisement role for a myriad of reasons, such as already having a heavy load or planning a sabbatical — reasons that have nothing to do with the actual student. Then there are declines based on the specific focus of the research. Students at times might not be willing or able to negotiate their areas of interest. Students need to convince themselves and the faculty member that working together is a good plan, increasing the chances that faculty members will be willing to add them to their advisement rosters.

Students may have already developed an interest in particular qualitative methodologies and methods, which can also influence their advisor choice. They may want to engage in current (and sometimes not so current) newly articulated research methodologies and methods that some faculty may not be well-versed in, support or see as relevant to their disciplinary concerns (Weber 2008). For example, students might be interested in conducting various forms of online research and interacting with participants gathering data via the Internet. A program may be situated within a department that has not yet embraced the growing emphasis on computer-meditated communication (CMC) for research purposes or has no faculty members who conduct online research (or want to engage with the Internet world) available to advise the student. Students may have to search for individuals (and programs) that can work with their choices.

Students are often the ones who challenge the academic boundaries of what is acceptable; sometimes they succeed. When unsuccessful, they sometimes continue to imagine a future when they may have greater flexibility and other opportunities to follow a more desirable pathway. Regardless, it is at the initial stages of finding programs and advisors that students have to decide whether they can work within the normative regulations of their chosen program to secure their degrees.

Articulating Expectations

Whether students made the advisor choice or their advisor was assigned to them, an important first step is to meet and communicate about mutual expectations. Students and advisors have individual styles and work expectations. Before meeting with potential advisors, students need to take an inventory of their learning styles, work habits and needs. Questions to consider include these: What kind of contact do they benefit from most? Face-to-face? Electronic? What kind of feedback or encouragement do they need? What are their areas of weakness and areas of strength? What is their timeframe for completion? What skills do they have that can be of help to the advisor?

There are a number of important questions students can ask of potential advisors during their initial meeting: What are the advisor's expectations? How much contact does the advisor expect to have with students? How much and what kind of feedback does the advisor typically provide? How many students does the advisor currently have? Will the advisor be taking a sabbatical in the near future? If yes, what would that mean for the student's program? How would the advisor assist in putting together an advisory committee, choosing the additional members? The answers to these questions provide background and process information to help students and faculty members make a decision. When students have approached me regarding advisement, I have suggested they speak to students I have taught and/or advised previously before a decision is made.

International students who are first-timers to the country and university context may have a number of challenges, including acclimatizing to the context and culture, university, community and country. It is very useful for these students to seek out other international students who are farther ahead in their studies or who have completed a similar program to discuss advisement possibilities. Support for international students is scattered across the campus, so international students need to use initiative to seek out resources that may not be well-advertised.

Students complete graduate studies with goals in mind specific to their individual situations, including family and finances. At times, they have far-reaching plans when they begin as undergraduate students, knowing that they ultimately will complete a PhD. Others complete an undergraduate degree or master's degree as a final degree and then return to or begin new work positions with no plans to study in the future, although they may have a change of mind after time passes.

A common question that new master's students ask relates to the exit requirement connected to their degree. The criteria are university- and program-specific, but often a choice exists in the research pathway between completing a major research paper (MRP) (or a similar requirement) or thesis. Students who plan to apply later to a PhD program will ask whether taking the MRP route lessens the possibility of being accepted into a doctoral program. There is no simple answer to this question. I expect that there are occasions when institutional decisions about which applicant to choose may be swayed based on the fact that one applicant has completed a thesis and the other an MRP. I also know that students who have completed MRPs have continued on to complete PhD programs. The same can be said for some students who completed course-based MA and MEd degrees. Institutional requirements for graduate admissions are currently more flexible than in previous years. Either of the routes can lead to a PhD. What I tell students is that perhaps there is an expectation for more depth/originality of the research question/s and focus for a thesis than an MRP, and that students are often required to defend their research to a committee including examiners external to their advisory committee. The time commitment is often longer than that needed for completion of an MRP. I also remind students that admission into graduate programs rests on more than the quality of their previous degree. Weight is also placed on the strength of reference letters and the relevant quality and quantity of experiences represented in a curriculum vitae (CV) submitted with the application. I suggest that the most important strategy, no matter the exit route chosen for a degree, is to end on a strong note that reflects a high degree of knowledge and experience that will support a new journey through a PhD.

There are more part-time students at the doctoral level in recent years and some have plans to obtain an academic position similar to those of many of their full-time colleagues. When in discussion with advisors, it is important that students share long-term goals because such goals can be reflected in planning decisions. I have advised full-time and part-time doctoral students when the former were not interested in obtaining an academic position and the latter were very determined to shift into a university position. After taking time to think about their goals and needs, students will be better able to communicate them to a potential advisor. Two of the part-time doctoral students for whom I served as advisor were very clear from the beginning of their programs that they wanted to obtain an academic university position, and we planned accordingly. For instance, among other emphases, we developed strategies to support the students in building the strong CVs necessary to compete in the academic market (see Teeuwsen et al. 2012).

Complexities of the Relationship

The advisor is a key individual for the success of students meeting goals and completing research requirements. While students depend on advisors for guidance, research opportunities (perhaps paid) and networking opportunities, advisors expect students to be independently progressing with their research as agreed and in a timely fashion. Advisors assign grades and eventually write references. Power is always in play in student/advisor relationships. When tensions develop, it may be difficult for students to speak out about problems they are facing. Communication of needs and expectations at the outset of the process can help lessen the multiplying of misunderstandings. At the initial stages, students can ask to establish a pattern of regular communication and meetings, taking the initiative so that they are not communicating with their advisors only during times of crisis and frustration. If all else fails, universities have policies and procedures in place to assist students who are not flourishing in their studies and need someone other than their advisor with whom to discuss their needs. Be informed. Ask questions. Read the pertinent student policies; you may need to access them at a later stage.

MOVING ON

This beginning chapter introduces the doctoral research that was the catalyst for me writing this critical qualitative research text and from which I draw many of the illustrations of the complexities of the research process. This earlier work also influenced the theoretical framework and the three themes embedded in the text and described in this chapter. The exploration of the complex and sometimes precarious student-advisor relationship beginning in this chapter continues throughout the book.

The annotated bibliographies provided at the end of chapters include descriptions of additional sources for students to turn to that relate to the chapter emphasis. These annotations include books, articles, theses and dissertations. Similar to the way the chapters intersect and ideas cross over various research phases, the annotations may connect to multiple chapters, but are placed in only one for reasons of organization.

While recognizing the interconnectedness of all elements of a qualitative research process, I organized each of the chapters in this book to emphasize and illustrate a specific area of the research process. The how-to of process and procedures are discussed but juxtaposed with questions of why and to what purpose and to whose benefit. The hope is that student researchers find this book useful for helping them prepare to conduct qualitative research, ask critical questions of their research plans and process, and make their way along a research journey that in the end will leave them and those involved happy with what they accomplished.

Annotated Bibliography

Barnes, Benita J., and Ann E. Austin. 2009. "The Role of Doctoral Advisors: A Look at Advising from the Advisor's Perspective." *Innovative Higher Education* 33: 297–315.

> *Benita J. Barnes and Anne E. Austin examine how exemplary doctoral advisors understand their roles and responsibilities to their students. Using open-ended, in-depth qualitative interviews, the researchers spoke to twenty-five exemplary advisors from the social sciences, humanities, education and natural sciences, all of whom had a large number of students who successfully graduated under their supervision. Findings show that assumptions held by exemplary advisors about their advisory positions and students varies across disciplines and departments, and their attitudes about their roles and responsibilities are complex rather than formulaic. However, Barnes and Austin found that exemplary advisors generally focused on multiple similar activities in their roles, including assessing students' areas of weakness and strength; fostering professional growth; and helping students negotiate projects, doctoral committees, professional conferences and publishing. The article concludes with recommendations to doctoral students, deans of graduate studies and faculty advisors about how they can ensure that the advising experience is effective and productive for all involved.*

Baumbusch, Jennifer L. 2010. "Conducting Critical Ethnography in Long-term Residential Care: Experiences of a Novice Researcher in the Field." *Journal of Advanced Nursing* 67, 1: 184–192.

> *This study emphasizes qualitative research as a vehicle for social change. Jennifer L.*

Baumbusch, a novice researcher in the field of nursing, explains the goal of critical ethnography as disrupting the status quo and uncovering hidden social and political agendas. She suggests that nurse researchers who conduct critical ethnographies should try to merge their research findings with educational strategies as a means to stimulate critical reflection and change in successive generations of nursing students, thus bringing about transformation beyond the research site.

Brady, Jennifer. 2011. "Cooking as Inquiry: A Method to Stir Up Prevailing Ways of Knowing Food, Body, and Identity." *International Institute for Qualitative Methodology* 10, 4: 321–334.

Jennifer Brady seeks to challenge the "gender politics of academia" by pushing against the more widely recognized boundaries of knowledge production. She provides an example of a nontraditional embodied approach to qualitative research. Specifically, Brady advocates for an embodied practice of social research through a method she terms "cooking as inquiry," which centres on the body and the act of preparing food as legitimate sites of knowledge. Examining the usefulness of this method as a means to explore issues of relational power and identity, Brady outlines her methodological frameworks: collective biography and autoethnography. She concludes with a discussion of potential applications of the method and provides a list of guiding questions to help researchers evaluate the usefulness of this method for their research projects.

Brook, Julia, Susan Catlin, Christopher DeLuca, Christine Doe, Alyson Huntly and Michelle Searle. 2010. "Conceptions of Doctoral Education: The PhD as Pathmaking." *Reflective Practice* 11, 5: 657–668.

Six doctoral students studying education at an Ontario university share their reflections on their collective experience of doctoral studies. Opposing the implicit and explicit expectations of the academy and mandate set by the Ontario Ministry of Training, Colleges and Universities, the authors challenge the view that ideas are individually owned and that learning is a fixed and singular process, disconnected from academic relationships and the conditions in which learning takes place. Instead, they regard learning as "pathmaking," a collective effort crucial to facilitating movement into successive self-claimed paths. The authors argue for a conception of doctoral studies that structures opportunities for students to collaborate in meaning-making and engage in deep reflection on their learning.

Graham-Marrs, H.A. 2011. "Narrative Descriptions of Miyo-Mahcihoyan (Well-Being) from a Contemporary Nehiyawak (Plains Cree) Perspective." Unpublished doctoral dissertation, University of Saskatchewan, Saskatoon, SK.

Although this dissertation does not refer to them specifically, H.A. Graham-Marrs' study illustrates the three key themes of this book: critical reflexivity, distance dynamic and conducting respectful research. The purpose of her research was to identify factors that facilitate positive change in the mental health and well-being of the Plains Cree people of Thunderchild First Nation, of which Graham-Marrs is a member. In the prologue, Graham-Marrs positions herself as a cultural insider and novice mental health therapist questioning her long-standing beliefs about health and well-being. She cites her personal and professional experiences, as well as the impact that colonization and residential schools have had on her immediate family and on her community, as the impetus for her study. In the methodology section of this dissertation, Graham-Marrs justifies her decision to conduct a narrative inquiry as a culturally appropriate method of conducting respectful research with Indigenous peoples, examines historical and ethical considerations when working with vulnerable populations and outlines newly established guidelines for research with Indigenous people.

Kilbourn, Brent. 2006. "The Qualitative Dissertation Proposal." *Teachers College Record* 108, 4: 529–576.

Brent Kilbourn goes into great detail on how the proposal functions as an academic document in its own right. Using examples from numerous proposals, Kilbourn discusses the essential elements of a proposal (introduction, problem, theoretical perspective, questions, literature review, methods, ethics and plan/timeline) and demonstrates how these elements can be addressed to make the proposal's central argument as strong as possible. He does not offer a "map" to completing the proposal, but rather a description of the "terrain" through which students must navigate to successfully argue that their planned research will indeed make an original contribution to the field.

Lorenzetti, Lisa. 2013. "Research as a Social Justice Tool: An Activist's Perspective." *Affilia: Journal of Women and Social Work* 28, 4: 451–457.

Lisa Lorenzetti discusses the history of research as a tool of oppression and questions the control that contemporary researchers have over their participants' stories. She considers the transformational potential of qualitative research in the field of social work. While advocating for a "critical perspective rooted in anti-oppressive praxis" (p. 451), the author reflects on her personal experiences of integrating her identities as a social activist, counsellor and researcher.

McKenzie, Holly Ann. 2012. "The Different Stories of Cree Woman, Daleen Kay Bosse (Muskego) and Dakota-Sioux Woman, Amber Tara-Lynn

Redman: Understanding Their Disappearances and Murders Through Media Re-presentations and Family Members' Narratives." Unpublished master's thesis, University of Regina, Regina, SK.

This researcher's concern for social justice in the case of missing and murdered Aboriginal women is the motivator for her master's thesis research. Holly Ann McKenzie uses a Mestizaje *approach to guide her research, fusing together several feminist theories (feminist poststructuralism, feminist postcolonialism, Indigenous feminism and other Indigenous women's writings), each of which she explains in detail. She explores Indigenous ways of knowing in light of the dominant structures and privileged Eurocentric knowledge. The final chapter of her thesis explains the potential of education and the media for disrupting hegemonic norms and shifting the current culture of newsrooms from one that justifies violence against Aboriginal women to a culture that more accurately represents Indigenous people and is culturally aware and sensitive to their concerns.*

Sethi, Bharati. 2012a. "From a Maid to a Researcher: A Story of Privilege and Humility." *Canadian Social Work Review* 29, 1: 87–100.

Bharati Sethi describes her work as a "critical conscious reflection" (p. 88) on her role as a student enroled in a master of social work program and researcher in a small urban centre. She argues that self-reflexivity enriches research practices, and she shares her personal research journey from multiple subject positions: as immigrant, racialized woman, researcher and someone who has been diagnosed with a mental illness. For her, storytelling and other arts-based methodologies have proven invaluable for disturbing binaries such as us/them and expert/client. Sethi states that self-reflexivity as a method enabled her to unpack the ways in which the "other" is also a reflection of "herself/selves." She concludes that the rethinking of binary categories is particularly helpful when engaging in research that is intended to facilitate social change.

Chapter 2

SETTING THE PARAMETERS

This chapter is an exploration of the early phase of research, including the development of a qualitative research plan. Based on disciplinary positioning, students may be familiar with the language of design. I use *plan* and *design* interchangeably. The research design is not to be confused with the research proposal, which students in most academic programs are expected to develop, submit and often defend before beginning their research. (See Hine 2012 and Kilbourn 2006 for writing research proposals related to Internet research.) Proposals take various forms, are student- and context-specific, and need to be worked out between student researchers and their advisors. There is no agreed-upon version that all disciplines or departments follow; some proposals reflect the linear word-description emphasis taken in this chapter (for the purposes of constructing a proposal, not to represent the research process), whereas other versions may take a nonlinear emphasis and include visual multimodal elements. For the most part, all versions include, in some form, the necessary information for students to construct a viable proposal and move forward with their research. The research plan, which will be discussed in greater detail later, is often initially articulated in the context of the methodology chapter of the research proposal.

The first chapter of a research proposal often serves as an introduction to the research. It includes a rationale for the research (why?) and a description of the purpose (for what ends?). Background to the research, especially historical background, is an important section commonly included. Research problems and questions are articulated in this introductory chapter. What is the problem the student is interested in exploring? What are the questions important to ask in relation to this problem or research focus?

The second chapter of the proposal is often the literature review. This chapter includes a comprehensive (but not complete) review of relevant literature related to the research focus. Texts dedicated solely to the development of comprehensive literature reviews are available for students to use to help them construct a review appropriate to their research focus (see Hart 2009; Jesson et al. 2011). Aspects of the canon of the field (e.g., primary sources) and current literature make up the body of the chapter as well as studies reporting on research similar to what is being proposed. Through this literature review, students demonstrate knowledge of the field. The study's theoretical framework is often constructed as part of the literature review chapter. The theories or body of theories to be used to explore the research problem and questions, and to analyze data, are organized within this framework (see Anfara and Mertz 2006, 2014). The literature review and theoretical framework constructed for the proposal will be further developed as students move into the research context and conduct the research. The data collected often require student researchers to return to the literature and theories to analyze and understand their relevance. Students have to go beyond what they have read and included in this chapter of their proposal to complete the research process cycle.

The third chapter of the proposal is frequently constructed as a methodology chapter, which is the chapter that connects most with the research plan discussed later. Knowledge of qualitative methodology, including more general literature and work specific to the student researcher's particular choice of methodology and methods, is demonstrated in the methodology chapter. The research design is fully articulated and serves to establish that the student is prepared to begin the research.

Constructing a comprehensive proposal takes time and energy. A myriad of decisions have to be made before a research proposal is completed. I remind students I advise that the time and effort they devote to producing a strong proposal will help ensure that they do not flounder unnecessarily when moving forward in their research. Also, a strong proposal provides a robust skeleton for the MRP, thesis or dissertation. Each proposal chapter will have content that can be built upon for the final document. For instance, the methodology chapter will serve as a base that will be fleshed out later when students write about the research process that actually occurred, rather than what was planned. When developing and writing proposals, students are already moving toward constructing their final research documents. (For examples, see University of Texas, Intellectual Entrepreneurship, *Sample Dissertation Proposals*.)

UNDERSTANDING QUALITATIVE METHODOLOGY

To begin planning a qualitative research project, students need a sufficient degree of knowledge about qualitative methodologies and answers to a number of questions, including these two overarching ones: What methodology is best-suited to exploring the chosen area of interest? What methodology will ultimately lead to deeper understandings of the areas under investigation? Methodological decisions are integrally tied to the research problem and questions to be explored, to the methods chosen and to student researchers' identities.

It is generally understood that qualitative researchers frequently generate knowledge to get to deeper meanings of experience while acknowledging the contextual, value-laden character of the knowledge constructed as a result of the research. They want to come to some understanding of data that makes sense in relation to research participants and research contexts, understanding that represents truths that reflect particular moments in time. Within a qualitative framework, researchers are primary instruments for collecting, interpreting, analyzing and representing data; understanding is valued; and research is conceived of as an interpretive and often political act. If the purpose of the research is to better understand the social world and human experience, qualitative methodology is an appropriate choice to make.

Various methodologies exist for qualitative researchers to choose from, many with long histories and others more recently in use. A vast amount of literature is available, including numerous handbooks dedicated to qualitative methodology that can help students build knowledge to make informed decisions about which methodology is the best choice for exploring their research focus (e.g., DeLyser et al. 2010; Denzin and Lincoln 2005b, 2011; Kindon et al. 2010; Kovach 2010; Mutua and Swandener 2004; Patton, 2002; Reason and Bradbury 2006; Seale et al. 2004). In addition to reading about qualitative methodology more generally, students can explore literature focused on one specific methodology/framework, such as grounded theory (Charmaz 2006a, 2011), narrative inquiry (Chase 2011; Clandinin and Connelly 2000; Clandinin 2007), queer methodology (Browne and Nash 2010), Indigenous methodology (Archibald 2008; Smith 1999; Wilson 2008) and feminist methodology (Hesse-Biber 2012; Jaggar and Wisor 2014) to understand criteria unique to their methodological choices.

Although various forms of participatory research involving qualitative methodologies are often the choice of experienced qualitative researchers with emancipatory, social justice goals in mind (e.g., Conrad and Wallis 2009; Kapoor and Jordan 2009; Kindon et al. 2010), they can be challenging for student researchers if the project is not part of a larger research initiative involving experienced researchers (e.g., their advisors or other faculty members). Ultimately, students receive degrees based on completion of their research projects; care must be taken to ensure that they can demonstrate clearly their primary roles as researchers in the research they plan. Participatory and community-based research initiatives have unique challenges that students who are sole researchers in their projects do not face (although challenges exist for all choices made). Such research initiatives may be more appropriate for students completing a PhD and who have accumulated relevant research knowledge and experience rather than those students attaining less-advanced degrees and without the level of support, knowledge and experience needed.

Regardless of choice of qualitative methodology, there will be opportunities for students to shape the qualitative research process in ways that involve participants and community members at different junctures in the research. For instance, at the initial stages of the research, students can create various collaborative spaces in which participants who have the desire can be involved in the research beyond the act of providing data for the project (e.g., contributing to initial discussion of research plan, in-process research decisions, collaborative reporting back sessions).

METHODOLOGY AND METHOD

The research literature provides multiple and sometimes conflicting definitions for *methodology* and *methods* (Carter and Little 2007). At times, discussions shift between articulating explicit differences between the two to blurring the boundaries and using the terms interchangeably. Regardless, methodology and methods are intricately tied together with choices about what data to collect and what collection processes to use decided in relation to the methodology chosen for the study. Hesse-Biber and Leavy (2004: 22) suggest that "the methodological question cannot be reduced to a question of methods; methods must be fitted to a predetermined methodology." When methods (off- or online) are discussed in this text, the focus is on the avenues for collecting qualitative data that sit comfortably within the context of a qualitative, interpretivist framework and the specific methodology chosen, as well as the critical perspective employed by the researcher. Such processes might include interviewing, observing, photographing, videotaping, creating artistic representations, or collecting artifacts and documents. Researchers and participants together might create appropriate ways in which to collect rich data important to exploring their research focus.

Regardless of specific methodology or choice of methods, an important first step for student researchers conducting critical qualitative research is to reflect on the ways in which who they are (their multiple shifting and intersecting identities) and how they are positioned in relation to the research influence the project they have in mind and ultimately the research conducted. In light of this, the next section begins with an exploration of researcher positioning.

RESEARCHER POSITIONING

Student researchers choose a particular research focus for multiple reasons that include but also extend beyond intellectual curiosity. For instance, they might become involved in a specific area because it connects to their advisor's research program. Often, their motives are related to professional and personal experiences and to goals related to their passions. Regardless of the reasons why students choose to research what they do, they need to consider their positioning in connection to the research context and participants when designing their projects. Who are they in relation to the individuals who will participate in their research? How do their multiple, shifting and socially constructed identities intersect with those of their participants or communities? What are their connections to the research context (if any), and how might these connections influence the research? Whether students will be able to gain access to contexts, with the potential participants necessary to conduct their research, will be tied to the types of connections (obvious and not so obvious) they have to people and places essential to their study.

In my doctoral research, my familiarity and my teacher positioning factored into the women prisoners' decisions to become research participants. Many of them indicated to me that my gender influenced their willingness to participate. They would not have done so if I had been male because of their previous, often abusive experiences suffered at the hands of men. Other socially constructed differences that intersected across race, class and sexuality bubbled to the surface as the research progressed. Although I declared in print that I was a white, privileged, middle-class and heterosexual woman, I realized during the research process that recognizing my racial/class identity and my privilege was only a first step to the more meaningful work I had to do to actually factor in the influence of who I was on my interpretive processes, data analysis and my ability to represent the data respectfully.

Considering that in the context of qualitative research, researchers are primary instruments in the research process, it is not surprising that researcher positioning has been discussed in a comprehensive body of literature related to qualitative methodology over the decades. The literature is replete with descriptions of various researcher positionings: researcher as insider, outsider and someone in-between (Acker 2000; Banks 1998; Khan 2005; Paechter 2013; Sherif 2001). Researchers may be viewed as insiders when they are involved in a study that is connected to their workplaces or communities, if they are researching issues with participants who have similar professional identities or conducting research in a community in which they have lived or worked. The insider researcher in online contexts is often a member of the community that is the focus of the research and someone who contributes to postings on the site (Paechter 2012). The researcher who is an outsider is someone unfamiliar to the participants or foreign to the context.

Historically, the outsider in Indigenous communities was the white, Western researcher conducting research *on the natives* (Lawrence 2002; Smith 1999, 2014).

The researcher considered insider-outsider might be someone with connections to a community but not a current member, or someone who has similar professional credentials but no history in the context or connection to participants. Carrie Paechter (2013) describes a dual role and the complexities of being an insider as a long-standing member of an online site with a pseudonym participant identity while also negotiating a location as researcher, a separate identity not connected to her pseudonym personae.

Bahira Sherif (2001: 437) writes of being a "partial insider" and the complexities of her multiple identities. She writes of her struggles "on both academic and personal levels with the dilemmas of establishing rapport with [her] informants while balancing an insider/outsider perspective." She was born in Cairo and was nine years old before leaving with her Egyptian father and German mother. She wrote eloquently of how she found herself "torn between conflicting identities: the American graduate student, the Egyptian daughter, the single woman in her late twenties and the trained anthropologist who was always observing and aware of the process as if from the outside" (Sherif 2001: 440). In my doctoral research, I understood myself positioned as "someone familiar" (Tilley 1998a: 28–29). I was not an insider — that designation had particular meaning in a prison context. Nor was I outsider considering the time I had spent in the prison school context before deciding to conduct research there. I was connected to the prison through teaching there before I asked permission to conduct research. Although this familiarity assisted me in gaining access, it also created complications. For example, I had to give careful thought as to how to enact respectful relationships with research participants in the context of the power circulating within the prison and school context specifically.

Articulations of researcher positioning are also characterized outside of binary constructions, such as the researcher as border worker (Haig-Brown 1992; Haig-Brown and Archibald 1996: 250–251). Michelle Fine (1994) writes of researchers as "working the hyphens," and Patricia Hill Collins (1986) wrote of the "outsider within." In describing her research with lesbian identified women in Hong Kong, Shang Tang (2006: 14) explains the complexities of positioning and ultimately coming to regard herself as an "outsider within":

> More often than not, I found myself oscillating between roles, a researcher, a friend, a festival director, a peer counselor, a workshop organizer and a "foreigner," as someone who has spent years away from Hong Kong. These roles are often linked to my past work or community histories and the current impressions that the interview participants might have had

about me. I look upon these roles as positions that I perceived the interview participants to read me as occupying. The oscillation of roles may
not be from a complete left or right, but more like straddling in-between,
signifying both being hesitant or embracing of the roles that participants
might have allocated for me.

Complicating matters further is that although researchers may see themselves as
positioned in a particular way, in some cases the participants may view the researchers in a different light. Deianira Ganga and Sam Scott (2006: para. 30) describe
entering the field positioned in their minds as insiders because they shared with
participants a similar cultural/ethnic background, but this was not necessarily the
way that participants categorized them:

> To begin with, the older first-generation migrants considered Ganga an
> outsider, and this was only exacerbated when they discovered that the
> research was "official" and was based at the University of Sheffield. Such
> formality, alongside the obvious age difference, obliterated any sense of
> commonality that the investigator and her participants may have had as
> fellow Italians.

In addition to accounting for inconsistencies between researchers' claims to
a particular positioning and participants' views on the matter, assumptions held
regarding the possible effects of a determined position need to be considered. In the
case of the researcher as insider, assumptions that this positioning will contribute to
relationships more easily handled between researcher and participants, complications not so likely to arise because of the close relations are questionable. Although
this assumption may hold true in some circumstances, it is problematic in others.
Research complications may not be more easily handled — the insider knowledge
and connections may actually complicate rather than support the research process.
This taken-for-granted belief that an insider is more able to cope with complications also extends to the similarities across socially constructed identity categories
that make one an insider: ethnicity, race and sexuality, for example. There is no
guarantee that insiders will be better able to conduct research in their communities
than someone who appears visibly or otherwise different. When problematizing
insider positioning in relation to researchers who identify as queer researchers
studying queer youth, Lisa W. Loutzenheiser (2007: 121) writes:

> At the most straightforward level, a researcher is not a youth. One's sen-
> sibilities and points of reference are different, and for example, a queer
> researcher does not belong to the youth and peer culture that is so vital
> to many queer young people. Depending upon the researcher, the types

and frequencies of intersections amongst different axis of similarities across marginalizations, the fact that the researcher identifies as queer may be as complicating as it is advantageous.

In *Decolonizing Methodologies*, Linda Tuhiwai Smith (1999: 5) writes of some of the complications associated with Indigenous researchers conducting research in their communities:

> There are a number of ethical, cultural, political and personal issues that can present special difficulties for indigenous researchers who, in their own communities, work partially as insiders, and are often employed for this purpose, and partially as outsiders, because of their Western education or because they may work across clan, tribe, linguistic, age and gender boundaries. Simultaneously, they work within their research projects or institutions as insiders within a particular paradigm or research model, and as outsiders because they are often marginalized and perceived to be representative of either a minority or rival interest group.

Beverly Mullings (1999: 341) writes of a fluidity in her multiple positionings as "insider," "outsider," "partial insider" and "temporary insider." She conducted research in Jamaica and describes the complexities of her positioning based on her identity in relation to the research context and participants, "the complexities of my own attributes — a black woman of British/Jamaican heritage, from a North American University — made it impossible to be viewed as either an insider or outsider." She described "a constant shifting of the multiple axes upon which [her] identity rested."

Whether single or multifaceted, labels are sometimes mistakenly interpreted as straightforward, when in actuality they are representative of complex relationships. Researcher positioning as represented in binary discourse is problematic especially when taken as is — when naturalized, essentialized and generalized across contexts and participants. International North/South research collaborations are often contexts in which the complexities of researcher positioning, the impossibility of straight binary categories, and the influence of the researchers' multiple and shifting identities on the research process are difficult to dismiss (e.g., Dlamini et al. 2012).

Transnational feminist research involving researchers, participants and contexts across the North and South is reflective of the growing need to continue interrogating positionality and its complexities. Shahnaz Khan (2005: 2022) writes of the predicament of being a "third-world" non-white researcher living and working in a "first-world" site conducting research in a "third-world" context. Although Canadian colleagues assume that she will conduct research in Pakistan and on women (like her) in the third world (and all that implies), she is not "Pakistani enough" for those in Pakistan. Her Pakistani critics point to the fact that she does not bear the risks they do and will return to Canada to write her academic papers while they continue to deal with their patriarchal, misogynist laws. Khan (2005: 2025) writes of the complexities she lives in her life as a researcher:

> Situated as the other of the other, I am reminded that the position of native informant is precarious. The native informant is an authority on third-world women. The authority of my claims, however, is continuously deferred to the western academy for legitimization, identifying once again my complicity in reproducing the master narrative of third-world peoples. Such a process suggests that my research is not relevant to Pakistani struggles.

Understanding and accounting for how researchers' and participants' multiple and fluid identities may actually influence research is complex work. To do this difficult work, students need to give serious consideration to their subjectivities, their socially constructed, multiple identities and social locations and how they intersect under the weight of which all researchers engage in research.

Methodological critiques, often from critical feminist perspectives, have emphasized power relations and the exercise of power in research (Fine 1994; Fine and Weis 1996; Harding and Norberg 2005; Patai 1994). How is power exercised in its various forms in research contexts influencing researchers and participants and research process and outcomes? Valli Kanuha (2000), while acknowledging that she shares cultural and racial locations with her participants, also recognizes the power differential that exists related to her roles as researcher and social worker. I was acutely aware of the power differentials when I asked the women to critique the school in which I operated as teacher and then freely walked away each evening while the women who participated returned to their cells.

Currently the pressure for mainstream researchers to account for researcher and participant/community differences and the power relations inherent in the research act, in meaningful ways, is increasing. More stringent and strategic permission processes that affect researchers' access to sought-after research sites (e.g., Indigenous communities, schools, youth centres) are illustrative of this increasing emphasis on accountability. Doors are not so easily opened to researchers who are without clearly articulated reasons about why they should be trusted to research in the context chosen or without plans in place to ensure that the participants and communities benefit. As a result of this pressure, researchers who are comfortably situated in the academy have begun to acknowledge publicly the differences that exist between themselves and their participants. However, the differences declared in print are often those hard to hide from the naked eye or the critical reader, such as visible race and gender differences.

Not surprisingly, areas of difference often left unexplored publicly in the researcher-researched relationship are those connected to the influences of dominant Eurocentric assumptions and power/knowledge relations that underlie research designs and decisions related to everyday research practice. Linda Tuhiwai Smith (2014: 58) writes of Western scientists/researchers: "The finer details of how western scientists [researchers] name themselves are irrelevant to Indigenous peoples who have experienced unrelenting research of a profoundly exploitative nature."

In the case of critical qualitative perspectives, researchers are understood to be influenced by their world perspectives and sociocultural characteristics instead of objective, apolitical, neutral observers or data collectors. Lorenzetti (2013: 545), writing in relation to social work and the promotion of research as a "social justice tool," states that there is "no apolitical fence to straddle" and that a "qualitative researcher is more encouraged, if not compelled, to step off the fence and to disclose biases and uncover that which has been dismissed as inevitable." The expectation is that student researchers question the normalized ways of *doing* research and be aware of and account for the influence they exert, obvious and not so obvious, over the research process and outcomes. Taking account of the influences of researcher/ participant multiple positionings, intersecting social locations and identities requires a critical reflexivity on the part of student researchers that engages with a level of critique that can unmask and interpret the various degrees and kinds of differences in operation in the research process and context.

PLANNING THE RESEARCH

When students construct plans to conduct research within a critical qualitative framework, particular theories or bodies of theories (i.e., postmodern, poststructural, feminist, intersectional) inform their research. Their plans reflect a questioning of the research process and demonstrate awareness of issues related to privilege, power, knowledge and representation. Plans reflect an emphasis on the development and maintenance of respectful relationships between themselves and their participants from initial stages to completion of their research projects. The messiness of the research process and likelihood of students having to face dilemmas *in situ* will also be reflected in the research plan. The plans often advance outcomes that make a contribution to participant or community needs and social change.

When planning, students make choices about research focus, research questions, methodology, methods and the individuals/groups they will ask to participate in their research. When they critically reflect on their background experiential and academic knowledge, and their assessment of the likelihood of acquiring access to

Figure 1. Research Plan

Research Focus: What, in broad terms, is this study about? What is my topic? What is the research problem?	Questions to Consider: What do I know about this topic? Do I know enough about the topic to conduct respectful research? Is the topic worthy of personal and community resources?
Research Questions: What do I want to know about my research focus? What questions will guide my study?	What makes this research worthwhile? Who benefits? Who might be harmed or upset? Am I designing research for social justice/equity purposes? What is my connection to this topic that I think I might be able to pursue such purposes?
Methodology: What methodology is appropriate for exploring my questions?	How would I answer my research questions at this point? What do my answers tell me about my preconceived ideas and opinions?
Methods: What methods will I use to explore my questions? Are these methods consistent with my methodology?	Am I familiar with the methodology/methods? How does my choice of methodology reflect my understanding of knowledge and research? Who will have access to the data?
Data: What kinds of data will I need? How will I obtain this data?	How am I positioned in relation to the research site? Am I an insider/outsider/someone familiar/occupying a hybrid space?
Research Site and Participants: Where will my study take place? Who will I ask to participate in this study? Will I have access to the research site and the participants? How will I gain access?	How could my positioning impact my ability to find participants? How could this positioning impact my rapport with the participants? How will I enact reciprocity? What role will the participants play in the analysis of the data? Will they see the data before analysis? At what points in the study will I provide feedback? At what points in the study will I ask for feedback? Am I respectfully representing the data?
Analysis: How will I analyze the data? Are my data analysis plans consistent with my chosen methodology?	What steps will I take to enhance credibility? (Including member-checking, time in the field or with data, thick-descriptions, transparency of process)
Writing and Dissemination: Do I write well? Where will I publish my findings? Who will be interested in my findings?	How will I balance my voice and the voices of my participants? Would I let my children or someone I care about participate in this study as it is currently planned?

their desired research site and participants, they may choose to revise their initial plans until they can settle on a design that they envision, with all that they are able to take into account considered, as their workable plan, a plan advisors and ethics board reviewers can also agree is ethically sound.

A comprehensive qualitative research plan includes a discussion of a number of elements of the research process, including articulating research problems and questions, choosing appropriate methodologies and methods, and analyzing data and disseminating findings. The research plan shown in Figure 1 presents an overview. Students will dedicate a lengthy period of time and enormous effort to complete the research they design, so narrowing down to a workable as well as worthwhile research project is an important process. A comprehensive qualitative design sets the parameters for the research to be conducted and is an important tool in the student researcher's hands.

However, in the case of qualitative research, the research plan is never final; it is a fluid working document. As the research proceeds, students and participants live out the plan, so revisions are often needed as a result. The fact that changes are sometimes necessary and that issues not considered at the planning stage arise as the research process unfolds is understandable, considering that the plan is constructed at a particular moment in time and often in isolation of research participants and contexts. This does not negate, however, the importance of student researchers constructing a comprehensive plan before proceeding with their research. Changes made in research plans can cause a ripple effect that is important for students to recognize and address in the continuous assessment of their original plan. A plan *once and for all* is unlikely to be the end result of a student researcher's initial groundwork, a reflection of the ways in which the qualitative research process unfolds over space and time and with people.

RESEARCH FOCUS AND QUESTIONS

Choosing what to research may be an easy decision for students who began their studies with a passion to research a specific area or problem (and continue with that interest throughout their program). Other students may have only a broad sense of what they want to explore or may have too many areas of interest that complicate the process of honing in on an appropriate and doable topic and constructing an effective plan. It is important for students to explore possible areas to research during the early stages of their programs while knowing they may experience shifts in focus as they learn more through coursework and new academic and research experiences. Choosing a research emphasis is a first step.

Research questions, theories, data collection, analysis processes and representation decisions, and other aspects articulated in the research design are intricately tied together, not isolated pieces of a linear and unchangeable plan. Students engaging in qualitative research from critical perspectives, when deciding on problems and research questions, often consider the theories or bodies of theory that will help them explore their research focus. They often question the privileging of particular bodies of knowledge and explore issues connected to dominant group structures and practices that marginalize and privilege different individuals, communities and institutions. Many of these researchers are interested in contributing, even in small ways, to emancipatory goals and social change. They may want to engage in what Kathy Charmaz (2011: 359) describes as "social justice inquiry":

> When I speak of social justice inquiry, I mean studies that attend to inequities, and equality, barriers and access, poverty and privilege, individual rights and the collective good, and their implications for suffering. Social justice inquiry also includes taking a critical stance toward social structures and processes that shape individual and collective life.

The focus for my doctoral study evolved through my interactions with women in the prison and a self-reflexive critique of my public school and prison school teaching. I was interested in understanding the women's experiences of secondary school contexts, schools similar to ones in which I taught, and in exploring the women's educational experiences in the prison school, both contexts in which particular kinds of knowledge were present, absent, invisibly there. I wanted to explore the possibilities for incarcerated women to engage in education while experiencing the punishing regime of a prison. I was questioning the promise of education as a means of rehabilitation for women in prison and as a way to prepare them to re/enter the workforce and secure gainful employment when set free again. I was witness daily to the falseness of such claims. I wanted to understand the freedom I felt when teaching in the prison context that was often missing in the public school contexts in which macro and micro systems of control were also in place. Qualitative methodology was best-suited for the focus of my study, and a critical theoretical framework was useful to the analysis of data collected and to the critique of the research process that my participants and I experienced.

Articulating appropriate and specific research questions tends to be more of a challenge than choosing the research focus. The broad problem or focus that is of interest to the students and is contributing to their decisions to conduct research provides a basis for the shaping of their research questions. There may be one overarching question and then subquestions, or one question in general. Sometimes students who intend to collect interview data confuse interview questions with research questions, and although related, they are rarely the same. A study's research questions are broadly (but not too broadly) stated. It is important for students to be flexible and to play with producing and finalizing their questions. Research questions may also emerge through the researchers' collaborations and connections with communities and participants. During initial data collection, students may create additional or rearticulated research questions as a result of interactions with participants.

It helps to brainstorm ideas and share questions with other students, friends and family if those individuals have an interest. Writing questions in multiple ways is useful for finalizing the most effective construction. Care needs to be taken to ensure that the questions are not too broad or too narrow. Avoid questions that can be answered quickly with a *yes* or *no*. Students also need to contemplate whether their research questions are worth exploring from their perspective as well as the perspective of the field. Various research texts address research questions, including the logistics of formulating questions that are well-constructed and appropriate to the research focus (Agee 2009; Alvesson and Sköldberg 2009). Students will find taking time to turn to these and other texts to learn more about the work of articulating specific research questions very useful.

Students have to not only construct strong, focused questions related to their research interest or research problem and that are possible to explore but also consider whether they have the background knowledge and expertise to ask the questions and conduct the research they are planning. In the case of online Internet research, which is becoming more popular in traditional university contexts, students may have well-articulated questions, but not fully understand the implications of being positioned in cyberspace or have expertise and experience related to that research context (see Hewson et al. 2003; Hine 2012).

Advisors can help students to demarcate a reasonable research area and articulate questions. Even though advisors may not agree on the degree to which a research topic is worthwhile (a student's passion for the topic area may differ from the advisor's), they must at least understand why the student believes it to be worthwhile and see the possibilities for the research to make a contribution. The contribution of the research may vary based on the level of study: undergraduate, master's or PhD. What is essential for students deciding on the research topics and questions they will explore is to have a well-supported rationale for expending both personal and community (university and otherwise) resources on the research they are planning, remembering they will have to live with their decisions for an extensive period of time. Are they appropriately invested?

When constructing a critical qualitative study, students also need to apply their critical reflexivity to their planning, asking themselves questions related to the researcher/researched relationship and the ways in which power and privilege might operate in the research process. A student I advised, who was completing her master's degree in education while making final decisions related to her thesis topic and research questions, chose not to pursue her initial interest related to the experiences of students from other countries studying in Canada. She came to realize that she would be focusing what she had come to understand as her privileged white lens on the culturally different Other. Applying her critique to her research plans, she decided to focus her research on Western white teachers who choose to teach ESL in *foreign* countries. The participants reflected her background in terms of class and racial identity. She was able to gain access to other teachers partly because of her researcher positioning, social locations and ability to develop rapport with participants. She designed her research using her experiential knowledge acquired through years of teaching in similar contexts, contributing to a literature that was and continues to be in need of development (Powick 2004).

Before the final touches on their official research questions, which are a sign of the end of a time-consuming process and the beginning of another level in the planning, students may want to consider the following questions:

- Will they be able to maintain their interest in the research focus they have chosen for a lengthy time period?
- Do they have, or can they acquire, the necessary knowledge to design a credible study in their area of interest?
- Is their research focus or research question(s) too broad or too narrow?
- Considering their research focus and questions, do they see the possibility of accessing an appropriate research context and/or potential participants?
- Will their research make a contribution to the literature? Fill a needed gap?
- Do their questions or designated problem areas reflect the level of degree program they are completing: undergraduate, master's, PhD? Or are they taking on too much or too little?

When students plan research that explores aspects of the social realities of marginalized populations or vulnerable groups and/or the power relations that support dominant hegemonic practices that oppress particular individuals and populations, they need to pay special attention to what may be the politics of gaining and maintaining access in addition to constructing appropriate and respectful questions.

ACCESS AND RAPPORT

When students plan research with individuals and populations, especially those marginalized within the dominant societal structures with whom they have no prior connections, the plan constructed may theoretically be a reasonable plan, but not possible to put into action for a number of reasons. Geraldine Pratt, in collaboration with the Philippine Women Centre of BC and Ugnayan ng Kabataang Pilipno-Canadian Youth Alliance (2010: 93), explains why Filipino activists at the Kalayaan Centre refused to develop research partnerships, seen as falsely constructed collaborations, with outside "self-designated" researchers who wanted access to Filipino women who were located at the centre:

> These failed encounters [refused collaborations] display commonly held assumptions about who has methodological expertise, and the capacity to think and write creatively ... the self-designated experts aimed to abstract and re-tell these [womens'] stories on and in their own terms. The benefits from collaboration seemed to flow in one direction: away from the Filipino activists to the professionals who approached them.

Outside researchers are often not trusted, and sometimes for good reason. Both gatekeepers and potential participants need to see value in research participation and believe they and their data will be treated respectfully. Students may have great enthusiasm and passion for their research, but they must also ascertain the likelihood that an appropriate research site will be accessible and that successful recruitment of participants is likely. A level of trust is necessary before access is granted.

Gaining access may mean gathering multiple institutional permissions (e.g., hospitals, schools, prisons). Students who want to conduct research in schools must be willing to work through the institutional processes of the university ethics board and school boards to gain approval. Sometimes permission is eventually given, but this is not always the case. Students may choose to work through required changes when asked to revise plans to gain access originally denied, particularly if a specific research focus is very important to the student researcher. On occasion, students will gain access to research contexts only to find a lack of willingness on the part of individuals to participate. I requested and was given multiple institutional levels of permission (provincial government, prison institution, local college) to conduct research in the prison, but these permissions did not guarantee that I would find willing participants.

Important questions for students to consider at the planning stage include these: What is the likelihood that they can access the context imagined? Can they create and sustain effective communication lines with key people who may ultimately participate, or influence others whom they might ask to participate in the research? For example, after lengthy discussion with a student asking me to serve as advisor, I declined because of her research focus and unwillingness to reshape her emphasis. I could not support a non-Indigenous student planning to research in an Indigenous community with no previous connections or knowledge and experience in the area, on the basis that she wanted to do something *good* for the community. She may have chosen this participant group with the best of intentions without knowledge of or exposure to the critique that such rationale smacks of paternalism, as well as assumptions that this community needs or desires such assistance from researchers or others. For the student to assume that she would be given access was foolhardy at the very least.

Conducting respectful research with marginalized and often minority populations may be possible for researchers situated within the dominant and often privileged population. However, they step on *tricky ground* (Smith 2005) and need to be willing to be educated and work in collaboration (Battiste 2008; Styres and Zinga 2013). Student researchers need to understand, at least to some degree, the complexities of conducting respectful research involving individuals and communities who continue to experience the effects of colonialism, racism and marginalization embedded in dominant social and institutional systems.

Gaining access can also be challenging for student researchers who want to conduct research online. Students need permission to conduct online research when the cyberspaces and the people participating there are used as the focus of study. For instance, online discussion groups of interest to a student researcher may have no interest in being researched. Carrie Paechter (2013: 77) describes using her insider position as a means of gaining entry to her online research site:

> I made full use of my insider position as a respected member of Wikivorce, both because it enabled me to know whom to contact, and because my posting history established my bona fides as someone committed to the site as a whole. I emailed the gatekeeper, the owner and founder of the site, explaining who I was, identifying myself as a longstanding member, and asking his permission to carry out the research. This was granted, and we then agreed on a process through which I would formally enter the site as a research field.

Many relationships are forged at the early stages of the research process, including those among the researchers and authority figures who are connected to research contexts, and individuals who will ultimately agree or not to participate in the research process. Developing a respectful rapport with individuals connected to the research will contribute to gaining access and finding individuals willing to participate in the research. Rapport is about talking and (more importantly) having a proficiency in listening/hearing. Attitude and presence will affect student researchers' abilities to engage in positive communications with those in authority over research contexts and later with participants.

When students create plans to research in specific communities, often they will have developed relationships along the way. The community/participants themselves may have identified the research problem and contributed to the generation of research questions. The student researcher may have been invited into the community to conduct research that reflects the concerns of its members, but also of interest to the student.

Before recruiting people to participate in their research, students need to seriously consider the possible impact on participants, individual and/or community. Who will benefit from the research? Incur the costs? Researcher/institution/participant/community?

> Research with human subjects involves inevitable costs to them. For these and other reasons, it is important to make carefully reasoned decisions not only about the costs and benefits of undertaking research, but also about the distribution of these costs and benefits, i.e., to consider who incurs the costs and who enjoys the benefits. (Jaggar and Wiser 2014: 498)

The plan should reflect the researcher's consideration of what costs participants may incur and the ways in which they can benefit, as well as whether the intended participants are part of an over- or under-researched population. In research initiatives that emphasize participatory elements, which is often a goal of critical qualitative research, the discussion of costs and benefits can be part of the researchers'/participants' communication and decision-making processes.

Groundwork for positive communication is connected to the credible, well-written research plans that student researchers construct that address the criteria that people and institutions have set for involving themselves or others, under their purview, in research. The following are some access tips to remember:

- Have sufficient contextual and background knowledge when making connections with those in charge (including online context).
- Possibly visit the site to become aware of the conditions and contexts for collecting data. Plans need to make *common sense* to those they will be asking to participate.
- Know the context well enough that what is being asked is reasonable — especially true when involving institutions such as schools, hospitals, prisons and community centres.
- Create timelines that make sense in the bigger picture, in research contexts and for participants.
- Produce well-written research plans and applications in terms of substance and grammar. The plan is moving into a public arena and is a representation of one's identity as a researcher.
- Be able to articulate an understanding of responsibilities as a researcher (i.e., knowledge of ethical requirements, to do no harm).

RECIPROCITY

Reciprocity, a giving back to participants and communities on the part of researchers, is an important consideration for students in the planning stage of their research. Students will receive their degrees based on a successful completion of their research projects. The shape reciprocity takes is research- and context-specific and may be realized over the life of the study or at its conclusion and beyond. Careful thought needs to be given to what can serve as a form of reciprocity to participants and communities; participants and communities may have their own suggestions on what benefits should accrue for them.

Here I describe a request from Anna, one of the participants in my doctoral research, which illustrates the unpredictability of reciprocity and its complexities:

> This afternoon before I left, Anna came back to look for me. She asked if she could have her [interview] transcript before February 27 because she was going to court and she wanted to give it to her lawyer. She thought it might be helpful because she had talked about her background, her schooling and things that had happened to her. My first thought was that this was a possibility for reciprocity, that Anna herself would have gained something "material" from doing the interview. My next thoughts were trying to remember what was in the transcript that Anna might not want any of the guards or anybody else to see. I could always bring the transcript to her. She could read and give it back to me in the school. I could send it to the lawyer if she wanted to make sure nobody else read it. (Fieldnote, Tilley 1998a: 36–37)

Researchers are not in control of how participants and communities might benefit (or be disadvantaged) from participating in research. It is important to strive beyond the initial plans for benefits outlined at the research planning stage, which often serve as "minimal reciprocity" (Lather 1991), and to respond to possibilities emerging for reciprocity when researchers are situated in the research context and the research process unfolds. In contrast, student researchers must also be aware of the wrongs that can be committed as a result of acts of reciprocity that researchers propose, especially during the initial stages of the research when the researcher is in the beginning stages of understanding participants and their contexts in relation to the research focus (e.g., providing benefits that are seen by participants to be unfairly distributed and disturb established relationships among participants and communities as a result). If the researcher is uninformed when constructing plans for reciprocity, benefits may ultimately make little contribution or (more concerning) contribute to deterioration of participant and community relations.

TIMELINES

A variety of deadlines exist that student researchers have to be aware of in terms of their program; they need to educate themselves about those dates to ensure that they meet their time limits. Deadlines related to the research component of their program will inform the timelines that students construct for research completion. However, there is no clear path to research completion. Students have to overcome a number of challenges along the way, both personal and academic; many that cannot be foreseen. Creating a timeline and revisiting it periodically is a useful strategy. With advice from advisors, students can develop a preliminary timeline for the bigger picture goals and then shorter timelines for meeting the smaller objectives that ultimately make completing research possible.

Where to start? Plan backward. Students can start with the date they want to graduate and then fill in the tasks that have to be completed as they consider backward travel. If they want to defend their thesis by a particular date, what has to be completed earlier? Make a list, starting with completion of courses. Students need to be reasonable, remembering that research with human participants is time-intensive; participants have their own goals and responsibilities (this also applies to students' advisors and committee members).

As a result of constructing a reasonable timeline, students might choose to change their focus and/or methodology, or choice of research requirement. For instance, completing a master's-level MRP requires less time than a thesis. A thesis is more comprehensive, and a defence process can add time in terms of the logistics of organizing the meeting for the defence (a possible three months at my institution). Students might choose not to conduct research with human participants because of the loss of control related to timelines. A university research ethics review process can add two or three months (or more) to research timelines based on the individual institutional processes. If other institutional permissions are sought, timelines may stretch even longer. Better for students to change research focus or methodology at the initial stages rather than later in the research process.

The process of setting the wheels in motion to begin conducting research will influence timing (e.g., gaining access can take longer than anticipated). These uncertainties are often eventually resolved, and the research then progresses as requested (sometimes with agreed-upon changes). Students' willingness to be flexible and shift focus to other aspects of their work while waiting for plans to move forward is very important. Timelines are curious things. Although planning and preparation may take a lot of time, if done well, they often save time in later phases.

Students need to revisit their timelines regularly over the length of their research program, officially renegotiating with advisors when major changes need to be made or deadlines are no longer reasonable.

COLLECTING DATA

An effective qualitative research plan includes a comprehensive description of the types of data to be collected and the data-collection process envisioned. The main emphasis in this text is given to two methods, interviewing and observing, with other methods introduced in relation to these two. (Although data collection is introduced in this chapter, the complexities of student researchers moving into the field and collecting their data are discussed at greater length in Chapter 4.)

With the growing emphasis in arts-based research (e.g., Cahnmann-Taylor and Richard Siegesmund 2008; Knowles and Cole 2008; Lafreniere and Cox 2013; Rolling 2013), visual (Prosser 2011; Rose 2007; Weber 2008), participatory performance research (e.g., Conrad 2004; Gallagher 2007, 2008; Goldstein 2008; Walsh and Brigham 2007), research online (e.g., Hewson et al. 2003; Hine 2012; Mann and Stewart 2000; Markham 2005) and hybrid methodologies (e.g., Gallagher et al. 2013) come a multiplicity of methods available to collect qualitative data useful in critical qualitative research projects connected to emancipatory, social justice goals. Many of these methods incorporate interviews and observations of various sorts, as part of their collection process.

Within an interpretive, qualitative paradigm, researchers have used interviews and observations extensively in the past and continue to use them when conducting research involving human participants in social sciences and education. They are the primary methods I used to collect data with the women in prison who participated in my doctoral research and are the methods that produced much of the data I draw upon to illustrate discussion points and critical issues raised in the chapters that follow.

A research plan may require a single set of primary data or multiple data sets that can include both primary and secondary data. Such labelling may give the false impression that secondary data do not play an important role in the research. However, such data are often essential to the study. As well, data-collection plans can shift as research proceeds, and what was originally designated to be secondary data can become primary, and vice versa.

The amount of data to be collected for a study must be considered in light of the purpose and type of research. Collecting too much or too little data can pose problems for student researchers. For instance, students can be overwhelmed with data that take them beyond the intention of their research focus and questions. In relation to online research, Hine (2012) and Paechter (2012) warn researchers to be aware of the vast amount of data that is available electronically and to limit the collection of data to what is essential for the study. Whether collected on- or offline, if too much data are collected and as a result never analyzed, the excess data do little to contribute to the research; plus, the process consumes researchers' and participants' valuable time, which is better spent elsewhere.

On the other hand, too little (or *thin*) data are also a problem. In the case of too little data, student researchers might find themselves without the data necessary to address the research questions at the centre of the study or to complete the study with credible or useful findings. Although one *right* answer does not exist in terms of planning how much data to collect, student researchers need to give this issue serious consideration at the design stage. Of utmost importance is that students have an organized plan to keep track of their data-collection and analysis process, descriptions of which will ultimately become part of the methodology chapter in their final research documents. Students working with their advisors can create reasonable expectations for this phase of the research process.

INTERVIEWING

Andrea Fontana and James H. Frey (2000) write of the interview society and describe how many individuals have participated in interviews of various forms over the years. People experience interviews in their everyday lives: online surveys, telephone surveys, entrance interviews, and commercial or focus group interviews. As a result of their exposure to interviewing, student researchers may come to their work with many unacknowledged assumptions and possibly an overconfidence in their abilities to conduct interviews. Before embarking on a qualitative study that has interviewing as a data-collection method, students need to assess their knowledge and assumptions of the interview process and whether they have or need to develop interview skills.

Standard descriptions of interviewing as a qualitative research method are available in a substantial body of literature dedicated to this method (e.g., Fontana and Frey 2000, 2005; Fontana and Prokos 2007; Gubrium and Holstein 2001; Jackson and Russell 2010; Kvale 1996). In the case of critical feminist research, interviewing as a research method has been commonly used as well as critically examined (Kirsch 2005; Oakley 1981; Patai 1994). In the case of computer-based technologies and data collection, a growing literature specific to the topic is available to students to help them prepare to conduct interviews online (Hewson et al. 2003; Hine 2012). Interviewing is also used in visual and arts-based research projects in conjunction with other methods (see Irwin and Springgay 2008, a/r/tography; Prosser 2011, photo-elicitation and photo-voice).

The student researcher's perspective and the underlying philosophical assumptions of the methodology and the study's theoretical framework will influence and shape the decisions students make related to interviewing. A typical classification of types of interviews might include structured, semistructured, unstructured (Olson

2011); open-ended-in-depth; gendered and postmodern interviews (Fontana and Frey 2005). The differences across various interview types are often reflected in the role of the interviewer and participants and the format of questions addressed in the interview session.

Structured interviews reflect underlying assumptions of positivism, including the need for an objective interviewer-controlled process to capture the truth. In structured interviews, researchers have a list of questions constructed prior to the interview that they intend to ask the participant. The interviewer is distanced from the interviewee, attempting to remain objective and to have no influence on the participants' responses, believing this to be a possibility. The characteristics of this type of interview are often diametrically opposed to the expectations of the more unstructured, postmodern versions of interviews in qualitative research projects (see Fontana and Prokos 2007; Kamberelis and Dimitriadis 2013).

A semistructured interview moves somewhat away from the formalized positivist version and allows for and acknowledges that an interviewer may not be able to remain distanced from the interaction and may have a role, although restricted, in the interview conversation. Interviewees do more than provide the interviewer with answers to *a priori* questions — some questions are not decided before the interview takes place, but arise in the moment as a result of the interview conversation. A step away from the structured version, this semistructured interview often reflects a postpositivist stance that keeps the interviewer, theoretically at least, in control at the centre.

Unstructured, in-depth and open-ended interviews are often the choice of researchers situated within a critical postmodern framework. In this version, interview questions may be prepared and shared with the participant before the interview, with the expectation that these questions are to initiate a conversation between the interviewer and interviewee; some questions may never be answered, and new questions often emerge through the conversation to which both the interviewers and interviewees contribute. Researcher-interviewers acknowledge having a role in the conversation: "Interviews are seen as negotiated accomplishments of both interviewers and respondents that are shaped by the contexts and situations in which they take place" (Fontana and Frey 2005: 716).

Multiple truths may be discovered as knowledge is constructed through the interview conversations. The interviewer has no hold on power; power is understood as circulating within the interview context, not as a static entity. Interviews can reflect elements common across the various types (e.g., both semistructured and in-depth/open-ended may preplan questions, but not to the same degree). However, unstructured, open-ended, in-depth postmodern interviews are possibly the type situated furthest away from the traditional structured positivist version (see Fontana and Prokos 2007).

In the prison research, I conducted in-depth, open-ended interviews because I wanted to provide a context in which women could speak to their schooling experiences. An open-ended version made it possible for participants to guide the conversation to issues they felt important to discuss in relation to the research focus or were otherwise important to them. I provided an interview schedule prior to the interview to encourage participants to give some thought to the guiding questions as well as to provide them with some idea of what avenues the interview might take, knowing that there was no guarantee of what the content of the conversation would be. The in-depth, open-ended format interview was a data-collection method that was well-suited to the critical feminist ethnographic research I was conducting.

Differences will cut across interviews when a specific qualitative methodology is chosen. For example, a researcher conducting a life history may choose an unstructured process that encourages participants to dig deep into the past to study a specific phenomenon or to explore an individual's or community's life trajectory. The process might entail interviewing one person multiple times and providing fewer guiding questions, possibly starting with one question, "Tell me about your life." Whereas someone conducting an action research project with the purpose of developing new curriculum and implementing change in a specific educational context may interview multiple individuals fewer times and create guiding questions specifically related to curricular issues.

When conducted online, interviews may reflect a variety of types of interviews. Student researchers may choose synchronous and asynchronous processes. Online interviewing is sometimes used when participants are located at a great distance from the student researcher. Travel and other monies needed to conduct multiple interviews at various geographical locations make online interviewing attractive to researchers. As well, when the focus of the research is related to a sensitive topic, individuals may feel more comfortable being interviewed online or by telephone, not visible to the researcher. Students might also choose to conduct a combination of both offline and online interviews if crossing these contexts enhances the possibility of collecting rich data (see Davis, M. et al. 2004; James, N. and Busher 2009).

Decisions regarding whether a few participants will be involved in multiple interviews or a larger number of participants involved in a single conversation will be made based on the research focus and methodology. The order of interviewing is also a consideration. For example, when conducting two interviews per participant, students can choose to have a round of interviews with all participants and then return for a second interview with each individual in the same order as the first interviews. This particular ordering system is often beneficial because students can build their knowledge over the first set of interviews and return to participants with questions that arose based on their first interviews, but also as a result of the other interviews conducted. Sometimes the best decision is to interweave interviewing with observations and other data-collection methods.

When researchers use visual- and arts-based participatory research methodologies to conduct research, data can come in various forms: artifacts; photographs; art; collage; and performance-, participant- and/or researcher-produced (Goldstein 2008; Rose 2007). Still photographs, found and researcher- or participant-produced, have served as primary data that document the lives of individuals and communities, presenting historical and cultural perspectives (Rose 2007; Wiebe 2013). The pictures may be newly created or part of those already in existence. It is not unusual to have the photographers or those connected to the photographs (in the photograph or knowledgeable of the content of the photograph) to be interviewed as part of the data-collection process. The interview is often used to contextualize, interpret, analyze and at times make decisions on the representation and dissemination of the visual data.

During the last few decades, the popularity of photo-voice as a data-collection method has gained momentum in critical participatory research projects. Participants involved in this data-collection method document their perspectives and experiences through the lens of a camera. Youth and others belonging to marginalized communities, in particular, have taken to photo-voice, engaging with the technology and the opportunity to have their perspectives represented in ways that they choose, to make their voices heard from the margins (Moletsane et al. 2007; Power et al. 2014; Walton et al. 2012). In the case of community-based participatory research (CBPR), participants are often engaged in multiple aspects of the participatory research project, including planning and analyzing, and contributing to decision-making related to the representation and dissemination of images produced. These decisions include what images will be disseminated and whether, how and when they will be available to the public (see Hergenrather et al. 2009 for a review of studies using photo-voice).

To varying degrees, arts-based methodologies also incorporate interviewing as part of their research process (Schroeter 2013). For instance, when conducting research using popular theatre with the main emphasis on the performance, Diane Conrad (2004) included, near the end of the project, an informal interview with students who volunteered in the final stages.

The following questions are helpful for student researchers to consider when developing their research plan and deciding whether interviewing will be used as a data-collection method. What assumptions do they have about interviewing? How comfortable are they conversing with others? What are their strengths and weaknesses related to interviewing — lots of experience or none? What do they most need to learn about interviewing to do it well: types, techniques or both? Do they understand how to incorporate interviewing with other more-participatory methods (e.g., photo-voice)? Do they understand the specifics of online interviewing, the technology? Will interviewing (whatever shape it takes) provide rich data that support the exploration of the research questions and/or the participants' needs to address critical social issues? These are the types of questions that students can discuss with advisors at the beginning stages; the responses will influence the shaping of their plans and proposals.

Regardless of whether students are using interviewing in conventional ways or in conjunction with postmodern arts-based and visual methodologies, they need to consider their knowledge about interviewing and their abilities to engage in interviewing in respectful and productive ways. Most important is that students understand the differences and possible uses across types of interviews to decide which fit their methodology and best serve their purposes and those of their individual and community participants.

Focus Group Interviewing

Historically, focus group interviews have been used for myriad reasons, including collecting information on the public's views on saleable products, monitoring effects of advertising on product sales and gaining information on political views to inform would-be and practising politicians and political parties (Frey and Fontana 1991). The *focus* of focus group interactions was researcher-driven (often corporate/government-supported), and the process was researcher-controlled. Participants were expected to reveal certain truths about the research focus to the interviewer. These group interviews reflected the positivist leanings of structured versions of one-on-one interviews. More currently, George Kamberelis and Greg Dimitriadis (2013: 13) position the focus group "as a methodological strategy with its own historical and theoretical specificity" taking various shapes that include the use of traditional interviewing styles to "collective conversations."

In academic contexts, focus groups continue to be used for multiple purposes and take a variety of shapes. Qualitative researchers use focus group interviewing to collect primary data (Davison 2007; Haley 2006) in conjunction with other data-collection methods. Focus groups can provide secondary data that supports or informs data sets collected through other methods used in the study — for example, in conjunction with interviews with individuals, observations or the production of video, artistic/visual data. When individuals who participated in one-on-one interviews engage in focus groups, they have an opportunity within the group to experience and respond to the research focus and questions in a different way than when individually responding. In the case of sensitive research, individual participants may be better able to engage with the issues when interacting with the responses and ideas of others, building conversation together instead of in a one-on-one, interviewer-interviewee context.

The body of literature that addresses focus group interviewing emphasizes procedural and technical challenges as well as the complexities of capturing and interpreting group interactions. Frey and Fontana (1991: 175) remind readers "that the characteristics of the group (e.g., size) and the background of members (e.g., leadership style) can impact the interaction and response patterns within the group." Anthony Onwuegbuzie and his colleagues (2015) provide a comprehensive review of the central issues associated with focus group interviewing and a lengthy and useful list of sources that address issues as well as logistics: duration, number of participants, sampling strategies, researcher roles, structure and organization, data sources and analytic procedures. George Kamberelis and Greg Dimitriadis (2005: 887) "explore the complex and multifaceted phenomena of focus group research", and Fernando J. Bosco and Thomas Herman (2010) emphasize a critical approach that moves away from an emphasis on the logistics.

In the past few decades, a distinct turn has occurred toward consideration of focus group research that reflects an emphasis on postmodern, poststructural orientations well-suited to critical qualitative methodologies. David Morgan and his colleagues (2008) write of emergent options for focus groups that move away from more traditional formats and positivist orientations; the research/moderator creates a context in which participants have the opportunity to shape the content of the focus group as well as the process.

Although challenges exist, focus groups (when conducted effectively) provide a unique context in which multiple participants can contribute important data to a study. Focus groups allow more perspectives to be addressed and opportunities for individuals to think through responses in relation to what others have to say; data are constructed in a participatory milieu (see Rosell et al. 2014). In a focus group interview, a broader representation of people are involved in data production, a process that can serve as a venue to construct agreed-upon plans for needed action. When multiple people are involved, unique perspectives may find visibility in the collective conversation rather than be left unsaid. Kamberelis and Dimitriadis (2011: 545) describe focus group research that exists at "the intersection of pedagogy, activism and interpretive inquiry" and as holding great promise for research agendas with critical orientations and a concern for research contributing to social justice.

Focus groups can happen on- or offline. One of the many challenges of online focus groups that researchers continue to face is creating manageable interactions (Morgan et al. 2008). Video can be used to document focus group conversations to capture voices and also physical dimensions of group conversations (e.g., gestures, facial expressions, physical reactions to individual contributions to conversation). (See Heath et al. 2010 for a comprehensive discussion of video research.)

Focus groups are also used to collect data in international cross-cultural contexts. In the case of large research studies, experienced researchers often have the resources available to hire appropriate individuals to assist in the collection of data — for example, a moderator to implement the focus group discussion who works in the language and culture of the participants and/or individuals to translate the recorded or visual data (Hennink 2007). However, this will rarely be the case for student researchers. Students have to assess carefully whether they have the knowledge and skills to conduct focus group research in international and/ or cross-cultural contexts before deciding to do so. When international students choose to return to their home countries to conduct their research, although they may have the language skills and cultural knowledge to implement focus group research effectively, they must also have the necessary resources.

Focus group research creates ethical challenges unique to the process — for example, the impossibility of any promise of confidentiality for the participants. (Ethical issues connected to collecting data through the use of focus groups will be addressed more fully in Chapter 3, which focuses on research ethics.)

Before choosing focus groups as a means of collecting data, student researchers have to decide whether the method is compatible with their methodology and research focus. Is a focus group interview(s) an avenue to collect relevant data for their research project? Will the process contribute to creating rich data helpful for understanding the phenomenon under study? When used in conjunction with other data-collection methods, is focus group interviewing contributing useful data? Student researchers also need to consider whether they have the skills to facilitate group discussions, skills that are different from those needed for interviewing individual participants.

At the planning stage, students may want to consider whether they have the skills or can develop the skills to do the following:

- Serve as moderator of a group interview situation
- Observe group dynamics: who talks and who is silenced
- Keep the group on track — connected to the research focus
- Intervene when needed in ways that do not interrupt or derail the conversation
- Unravel power relations operating and diminish their influence on data
- Access appropriate audio- and/or visual equipment
- Use the technology
- Control the amount of data collected
- Transcribe the audio and/or video material collected (see Chapter 5).

OBSERVATION

As a method of data collection, *observation* has a long history in social science research, and current practices reflect those past traditions to various degrees. Ethnographic fieldwork, with a heavy emphasis on observation, was an early practice of anthropologists who travelled to *foreign* lands to study cultures, at times spending years in the field (Malinowski 1961; Mead 1923; Wolf 1992). Observations occurring over lengthy time periods contributed to the building of cultural knowledge and a thick description of the world and people under study (Geertz 1973). Students studying within the disciplines of anthropology and sociology, especially at the doctoral level, may be following suit and conducting fieldwork abroad or at home using observation as a primary data-collection method, but perhaps for shorter time periods than their predecessors. Observation continues to be a popular method of collecting data in various qualitative methodologies and in contemporary spaces beyond its more traditional use in the fields of anthropology and sociology (see Angrosino and Rosenberg 2011; Yon 2000).

Researchers conducting observation from critical postmodern perspectives critique assumptions that informed earlier observational practices, in particular, the possibilities of achieving a positivist-oriented objectivity. Michael V. Angrosino and Judith Rosenberg (2011: 467) suggest that "the potency and persuasiveness of the postmodern critique of traditional assumptions about objectivity have led some qualitative researchers to rethink and revise their approaches to observational methods." From a postmodern perspective, researchers, participants and contexts are understood as intersecting and influencing the observation process and what is ultimately seen/interpreted, recorded and analyzed. Regardless of the qualitative methodology, researchers' identities and those of their participants and the knowledge and experience they each bring to the research context shape the observation process and ultimately the meaning derived from the data. As Charmaz (2006b: 15) reminds readers: "Neither the observer nor the observed come to a scene untouched by the world."

When engaging in a critical research praxis, researchers consider their epistemological and ontological beliefs and their knowledge about the act of observing and what is produced as a result of that act and the influence of their positioning on their observation process and decisions. The assumption that *the truth* will be captured and that power is static and held in the hands of the observer is as problematic in regard to observations as it is in the case of other data-collection methods (e.g., interviewing). Angrosino and Rosenberg (2011: 469) reflect on power in the "classic" approach to observation:

> Although rarely acknowledged at the time, the classic approach was based
> on a model of interaction in which power resided in the ethnographer

[researcher] (who set the research agenda and implicitly represented the more generalized power of elite institutions); power is now [understood as] more clearly shared.

From critical postmodern perspectives, power is understood as shared, circulating in the process of observation rather than *held* in the hands of the researcher-observer who is in control of the observational situation. This power sharing takes many shapes, but is particularly made visible in critical participatory research projects when participants are active in various aspects of the research process, from initial stages to the research conclusion.

Student researchers have to make many decisions regarding the logistics of observation as a data-collection method that will be articulated in their research plans, including which strategies they will use to conduct their observations. Michael Quinn Patton (2002: 265) explains important distinctions differentiating observational strategies that are used in ethnographic studies and in qualitative research methodologies more broadly:

> The first and most fundamental distinction that differentiates observational strategies concerns the extent to which the observer will be a *participant* [emphasis in text] in the setting being studied. This involves more than a simple choice between participation and non-participation. The extent of participation is a continuum that varies from complete immersion in the setting as full-participant to complete separation from the setting as spectator, with a great deal of variation along the continuum between these two end points.

The location on the continuum where student researchers situate themselves will fluctuate, but it ultimately is decided in relation to the research focus, methodology and goal for data collection.

Student researchers may choose to engage in multiple strategies based on their methodologies, the amount of time they plan to be in the field/culture/context and the amount of data required. Within one study, researchers may at some points be positioned as distanced, unobtrusive observer/spectator or full participant, and at other junctures have various degrees of involvement. During the prison study, I conducted direct unobtrusive observations (while understanding my presence as influencing the scene to varying degrees), recording by hand what I was seeing and interpreting. I also conducted participant-observations while attempting to research and teach simultaneously. Researchers also observe across multiple settings to build understandings of participants and their interactions. Daniel A. Yon (2000: 23) conducted participant-observations across various settings during the school ethnography he completed for his doctoral research. He explains:

> I undertook participant observation in a wide range of settings including classrooms, the library, the hallways, the cafeteria, the drama studio. The art studio, the music room and, when the weather made it possible, in the parking lot and in the playing fields. I also spent time with the students in the nearby shopping mall.

He spent one academic year (averaging four days per week) in the school being immersed in the culture.

Advances in technology have made it possible for student researchers, who have the desire and academic support, to collect data in the virtual rather than material world, including through observation (Hewson et al. 2003). Observations may be aimed at understanding online interactions, cyberspace community life or various aspects of life on the Internet. Studies may include online observation as a primary and/or secondary data-collection method or in combination with data collected offline.

Although student researchers face challenges when conducting observations in virtual spaces similar to those that occur when researching on the ground in private and institutional locations, they also need to address unique complications that arise in CMC. For instance, Angrosino and Rosenberg (2011: 473) suggest that "deeply nuanced subtexts may be missed in superficial meanings of typed words." When involved in Internet and online projects, researchers cannot observe faces, gestures or tone of voice in the ways they can in offline conventional settings. Participants can disguise their identities, shed old ones and construct new ones. Angela Garcia and colleagues (2009) explored the challenges that online ethnographers face moving from conventional settings to online sites, including the ethical implications of online research. Although occasions may arise when an ethics review process is not necessary for data collection in a virtual world, permissions are often required when researchers are interested in conducting observations online that involve individuals and communities, similarly to research conducted elsewhere. The distance from the material to the virtual world is not as far as is sometimes imagined, and *real* people and communities are at the centre of the virtual worlds that students are often interested in researching.

The ways in which observations are documented vary along a continuum, with choices that include pen and paper; word processing and computers; and visuals such as artwork, photographs and video. Student researchers may choose to use a combination of techniques to record what they observe during the data-collection process. Whatever their choice, they need to consider how being positioned as observer (degrees of involvement) affects the observation process. Kathleen Gallagher and Isabelle Kim (2008: 107) write about the complexities of using digital video methods to collect data in high school drama classrooms: "Like its predecessor the still camera, the presence of the video camera is anything but neutral: it affects that which it films, including, in this case, our relationships with the research participants and their relation to each other and their space."

When using cameras and video equipment to document observations, researchers need to have the technology capable of capturing as much as possible what is being observed as well as the technological skills to deal with process issues that arise in the research context. Gallagher and Kim (2008: 109), writing from a postpositivist perspective about digital methods in participatory research, emphasize the importance of negotiating the research relationship and the space for participants to not only be viewed through the lens but also to be able to direct the cameras and to return the gaze when desired: "A primary challenge for postpositivist researchers ... who choose to use video in their research, is to negotiate the research relationships in order that research participants are not merely testing and being tested/critiqued, but *con*testing [in original] and returning the gaze."

Historically, documentation of observations in ethnographic research have taken the shape of fieldnotes (Emerson et al. 2001; Sanjek 1990). These fieldnotes were "intended to provide *descriptive* accounts of people, scenes and dialogue, as well as personal experiences and reactions" (Emerson et al. 2001: 353). From an anthropological perspective, Roger Sanjek's (1990) collection of edited chapters illustrates multiple forms and uses of fieldnotes, as well as underlying theories and assumptions that influence the fieldnote structure and content.

At the initial stages of research, when students are constructing their plans and deciding which data-collection methods to choose (observation or otherwise), skill level and access to resources need to be part of their consideration. Although changes may be made in the way observations are conducted (online or offline, video or the physical eye) — logistical changes as the research proceeds — the design provides the important guidelines for the procedures.

The following are important questions for students to consider when making research plan decisions:

- Does the student researcher have the skills to conduct observations, or can those skills be developed within the timeframe of the program?
- Are the plans for observation suitable and doable for the intended context and participants?
- How will observations be recorded: by using pencil and paper, constructing diagrams or other visuals, filming using digital video cameras?
- Is the student researcher familiar enough with the equipment to be used?
- Is the student researcher knowledgeable enough to observe via the Internet in chat rooms and other cyberspace gathering places?

- To what degree will the student researcher be immersed in the context/ field?
- How will the student researcher address researcher positioning in relation to the research and the influence on data collected?
- Will using observation as a data-collection method enrich the study and be time well spent?

JOURNALING IN QUALITATIVE RESEARCH

Maintaining a research journal over the life of a research project is a method of data collection that is useful in qualitative inquiry. A research journal can be organized in multiple ways, based on the researcher's preferences. If the material collected is to be considered data, it must be organized, consistent and actually analyzed at some point. Yvonna S. Lincoln and Egon G. Guba (1985: 327) write of a reflexive journal that provides information about self and method:

> With respect to the self, the reflexive journal might be thought of as providing the same kind of data about the *human* instrument that is often provided about the paper-and-pencil or brass instruments used in conventional studies. With respect to method, the journal provides information about methodological decisions made and the reasons for making them.

Their suggestion for three sections to be included in the journal is still useful in more current times:

1. The daily schedule and logistics of the study
2. A personal diary that provides opportunity for catharsis, reflection upon one's values, interests and growing insights
3. A methodological log: decisions and rationales for methodological choices.

Valerie J. Janesick (1999: 513) describes the benefits of journal writing in qualitative studies, suggesting that participants as well as researchers can engage in the process and enrich the project's data bank:

> Journal writing allows one to reflect, to dig deeper if you will, into the heart of the words, beliefs and behaviors we describe in our journals. It allows one to reflect on the tapes and interview transcripts from our research endeavors. If participants also keep a journal, it offers a way to triangulate data and pursue interpretations in a dialogical manner. It is a type of member-check of one's own thinking done on paper.

Dan Mahoney (2007: 580) writes of maintaining a fieldwork journal, which he describes as more than a tool for documenting research practices and decision-making:

> It [a fieldwork journal] taught me: (a) how to value and be more transparent about the tools and sensibilities I brought to the research context; (b) how to articulate my emotions, empathy, and feelings towards my study collaborators; and (c) how this emotional context was an important analytical tool for the promotion and success of the research project.

The research journal is a place to document aspects of the research process that are not included in other data sources. Students can decide what the contents of their journals will include (e.g., words, visuals, relevant artifacts) and what process is used to capture the narratives intended (e.g., handwritten, electronically recorded). They can dialogue with participants about the participants' willingness to write/construct journal entries, deciding together for what purpose and in what shapes.

Students' research plans will include a description of the purpose to which they will put the research journal, organizing their documenting processes so that what they construct will provide useful data for the study. They need to be consistent so that what they include systematically covers the duration of the research process. Entries will take a variety of shapes and may at times happen *in the moment*. In addition to the sporadic entries, students should develop timelines for purposeful, consistent entry writing (e.g., record and entry at the same time each day), eventually experiencing the writing moments as habit.

DOCUMENTS AS DATA

Documents are useful data for a number of reasons, including what they can offer researchers in terms of historical and/or contextual knowledge related to their research context and participants. When the appropriate documents are collected and analyzed, researchers have the opportunity to understand the discourses intersecting with their research focus from an historical perspective. The range of documents that student researchers can draw on to inform their investigations of particular phenomena, experiences or processes can include public documents of all sorts, institutional policies, curriculum documents and media reports, both off- and online. Historical documents might include historical policy and program documents, and geographical and institutional maps related to a research contexts and communities. Students need to have developed effective search skills to find and access relevant materials.

Documents in the form of agendas and meeting minutes (e.g., Farrar 2004); and various public and private documents such as evaluations, reports, proposals, contracts, e-mail, letters and mission statements (Harper 2006) can serve as data. Christina Skorobohacz (2008) included "take-home activities" for participants to complete that were connected to their identity and role negotiations in graduate school. The participant-generated texts created and subsequently analyzed included identity mappings, written reflections, object and metaphor identifications, and lists.

Documents can take the shape of visuals, camera or physically produced. As part of the research process, participants might produce materials as additional representations of their experiences (e.g., artwork, personal journal entries, poetry). To serve as data, materials have to be collected/constructed, but also analyzed.

Documents can also contribute to too much data. Current technologies present the opportunity to access a vast number of documents. If too much time is given to document collection, time for analysis lessens and documents are left by the wayside. I collected newspaper accounts that connected to women in prison over a four-year period, planning to conduct a discourse analysis, but ultimately they fell to the wayside because I was overwhelmed by the data mounting over the course of the research.

It is important for students to return to their research questions often to consider whether their document collection moves too far beyond what is required for the study. The following questions are important to consider:

- What documents are essential?
- How can a search be organized to ensure that the appropriate documents are accessed?
- Are the documents retrieved and analyzed helpful to the research (e.g., do they help the researcher to understand better the research context or participant experience)?
- How will documents be organized to ensure that they contribute to the research as much as possible?
- Will the documents collected and analyzed contribute to the researcher's understandings of other data or provide a fuller picture of the research context and participants' responses and/or behaviours?
- Will the documents contribute to the construction of useful findings?

Based on students' plans for the future, they may store the documents for a later time when they can focus on the analysis in relation to other or similar research questions.

METHODS MATTER

Students need to understand their method of choice, study the method, practice the method and understand analysis in the context of the method. They must decide what methods can be most useful and ethical in relation to the research context and individual participants, community participants and otherwise. As I became more familiar with the women and prison context, I was better able to understand the complications of producing such data. To use video to observe in the prison was an additional intrusion into a space that was built on a foundation of surveillance. Photography made the women uneasy; they did not want to have their images captured and used in unintended ways. One woman who participated in the research had drawing skills, and she produced a detailed map of the school, the rooms and the objects in them. I was not permitted to include the map in my dissertation, although I did use it to create fieldnotes of micro and macro descriptions.

Even when permission is easily given, student researchers still need to apply their critical lens to the process and ask whether their choice of methods is respectful of the participants and community contexts.

WHAT TO DO WITH THE DATA?

The analysis process should not be seen as a distinct stage of the research; instead, it is a reflexive activity that should inform data collection, writing, further data collection and so forth. Analysis is not, then, the last stage of the research process; it is also a part of the research design and of data collection. The research process, of which analysis is one aspect, is a cyclical process (Coffey and Atkinson 1996: 6).

Basic questions about what data, how much data and how researchers will systematically analyze data are essential to consider before the research begins. Thinking through the logistics of analysis can influence students' plans for data collection and their decisions on the best data-collection methods to use. Care needs to be taken to not collect too much or too little data for the study; the former leads to data not being analyzed, and the latter requires the researcher to return to the field for more data sources.

Although analysis occurs at various points as the research progresses, there will be an often lengthy time period when students, with participant involvement or not, are consumed with the logistics of analyzing their data. This focused period of time will be used to engage in what can be considered the four Cs of analysis: the process of coding, collapsing, categorizing and (re)constructing that is often described, with context-specific nuances, in qualitative research texts. The ways in which researchers choose to engage with the concentrated emphasis on analysis dictate the depth of analysis achieved and influence the text that ultimately unfolds

in the form of MRP, thesis or dissertation. Although conventional analysis procedures are important for student researchers to use (Coffey and Atkinson 1996;
Dey 1993; Ezzy 2002), additional analysis strategies unique to a research project
may only be imagined during data collection or its aftermath and at other points
in the research process.

Student researchers need to develop a systematic analysis process that is
congruent with their qualitative methodology (e.g., grounded theory: Charmaz
2006a; narrative inquiry: Daiute and Lightfoot 2004) and appropriate to the type
of empirical data collected (see Altheide and Schneider 2013). Ultimately, the
research conducted and the data actually collected will shape analysis decisions.
When student researchers have a rich database at their fingertips, analysis can be
fruitful and interesting work that leads to findings that are deemed credible, but
students need to ensure that they do not become too enamoured of their original
research plan and be blind to necessary changes. Whatever the strategies used, the
analysis needs to be consistent and systematic and described in research documents
for a more public eye to examine. Most important, students should not leave plans
for analyzing their data until after the data have been collected. Paul Atkinson and
Sara Delamont (2005) provide a comprehensive chapter addressing analytic perspectives and related themes that reflect the arguments in the field. It should not be
surprising to anyone that there is more than one *right* way of analyzing qualitative
data (see Chapter 6 for a discussion of the complexities of analysis and the role
theory plays in student researchers making meaning of data).

Both the data-collection and analysis processes that student researchers engage
in and describe in their research documents will contribute to (or work against)
their findings being judged as credible. When asked, students need to be able to
argue the legitimacy of their analysis procedures to participants and the broader
research community. At the planning stages, students (with the assistance of their
advisors) can work out the specifics of their analysis process, ensuring that choices
made are suited to the research focus, theoretical positioning, methodology and
plans for data collection, while recognizing that the specifics may change as a result
of the research process that ultimately unfolds.

Questions of representation have been a major emphasis in developments in
qualitative inquiry in past decades (Clifford and Marcus 1986; Denzin and Lincoln
2005b; Fine et al. 2000). Along with making plans for data analysis, student
researchers also have to consider issues of representation. The critical and ethical
stance they take will influence those decisions. What representations of data/find-
ings will be made public and documented in the research texts and other accessible
spaces? Power relations embedded in the researcher/researched relationship will
complicate decisions related to data representation based on the analysis. Although
analysis and questions of representation intersect and influence each other as part

of a cyclical research process, each is discussed in great length in separate dedicated chapters for organizational purposes (see Chapters 6 and 7, respectively).

THE QUESTION OF QUALITY

When planning their research, students need to consider the question of quality. Upon completion, will the research hold up to the scrutiny of a variety of audiences, including advisory committee, external examiners, participants, community members and audiences of presentations or reviewers of manuscripts submitted to journals? Will the process reflect the agreements made with ethics review boards and participants (i.e., promises made in regard to keeping confidentiality, providing reciprocity)? A large body of literature exists, covering historical and contemporary discussion of what constitutes *quality* qualitative research, including what criteria should be applied to judge quality and what procedures employed to assess whether criteria have been met (Hammersley 1992; Lincoln and Guba 1985; Patton 2002; Schwandt 1996; Smith and Hodkinson 2005).

Students should be informed about the conversations and arguments in the field so that they can make decisions and follow procedures that will convince audiences that their research is worthy of attention. The time they expend on developing a comprehensive review of methodological literature is time put to good use, not only because such knowledge will strengthen a student's research but also because a review of methodological literature needs to be included in the initial proposal and later is revised and incorporated into final research documents.

Research quality can be demonstrated in various ways (e.g., consistency in data collection, member checking). First and foremost on a macro level, the question of quality is deeply connected to the paradigm within which the research is situated. The expectation is that the paradigm's epistemological and ontological foundations and the theoretical framework chosen to explore the research focus shape the research process. In light of the orientation of this book, the quality criteria reflect a critical, feminist, postmodern orientation. Student researchers must be clear on their positioning — where they stand — before they can argue why their research process and data (and ultimately their findings) should be trusted. Credibility will be connected to the degree to which the researcher demonstrates an ethical stance that permeates the researcher-researched relationship and decisions related to the research process. Consistency on a grand scale — research questions and process suited to the methodological framework chosen — is needed.

The quality criteria emphasized in this book reflect the themes introduced in the first chapter. For example, to support claims to credibility, student researchers need to demonstrate in their final documents that they have applied a critical reflexivity throughout the research process. Procedurally, they might use research journals to systematically record the critical methodological decisions they make and the reasoning behind their choices. Micro considerations of quality at the level of data collection require evidence that data-producing methods were consistently employed and that the necessary depth of analysis was achieved through the use of appropriate analytic strategies. The findings must be supported by the data analysis described. In qualitative research, transparency of method is extremely important. Students need to construct a process that will achieve a level of transparency to convince an audience that their research is trustworthy.

Judgments of quality of research are also greatly influenced by the actual public representation, the writing that includes research process and ultimate findings. Choices that researchers make about what to include and what not to make public affect credibility judgments. In qualitative theses and dissertations, the researcher's positioning is taken into account as the research process is moved forward. Questions of quality can emerge when student researchers have not troubled the research process, but present it as a linear unproblematic unfolding without dilemmas. The written representation should reflect some of the methodological dilemmas that Gallagher (2008: 2) argues student researchers are often forced to hurry through to move the research forward but at a loss with the foreclosure of "inventiveness and curiosity":

> Sadly, in graduate studies across disciplines, students are increasingly hurried through their methodological dilemmas; the details should not stand in the way of a study well-completed. But these dilemmas cloud our certainties for good reason; they compel a philosophical spirit and underscore the difficult work of knowledge production. Our counsel to graduate students to resolve their dilemmas and drive through the ambiguities of their projects may diminish the experience of research and, in the worst cases, foreclose inventiveness and curiosity.

It is good to remember that writing style can capture the readers' attention or lead to them putting the work down and never finishing it. Whatever the content included in the final representation, written text, artistic work, photographs or video clips, the product produced will need to be coherent, consistent and convincing.

In the chapters that follow, students will be encouraged to apply a critical reflexivity that helps them turn their lens inwardly to ask questions of themselves as researchers and of their positioning in relation to the research context and participants. They will be encouraged to question their analytic moves and decisions related to representation, as well as to consider whether they are engaging an ethical stance acceptable in light of the research participants and context, and to question how the research they conduct will make a contribution.

DISSEMINATION

Students begin their studies with goals in mind that are connected to the level of study (undergraduate, master's and PhD). Many opportunities are available for them to participate in the research community in their institutions and across academic contexts, and these opportunities vary based on the degree level of study. Exceptions are also made for students who take initiative and seek involvement not usually available (for example, an undergraduate student participating in writing for publication). Students may work with their advisors on the advisor's research agenda and be part of the research/presentation/publication cycle. As well, they may work as research assistants (RAs) with faculty members other than the advisor and be involved in dissemination activities based on their employment. When students are involved in presentation and publication activities before completion of their research projects, these experiences can serve as useful preparation for the dissemination of their own research later.

Dissemination activities can occur at various points in a student's program, not only at the completion of the research component. Early dissemination can involve a variety of activities, including research presentations made in classes, online interactions, blogging, virtual presentations at conferences, video clips, physically presenting papers at graduate student conferences or discipline-based conferences focused on beginning elements of the research. When they reach the stage of involving human participants, students must ensure that the dissemination activity meets the ethical requirements agreed to with the research ethics board (REB) and any other institutional or community review process completed. When constructing timelines, students should consider how they want to shape their graduate student experience. Do students want to participate in other activities, work as RAs, present and publish, build teaching experience working as teaching assistants (TAs)? All these rich experiences are often available now to both master's and PhD students and sometimes to undergraduate student researchers. If students do choose to involve themselves extensively in the research community, they must factor this into their degree completion timelines. Involvement in these activities usually means longer overall timelines for program completion.

Students' degree of involvement in such activities has to be discussed with their advisors. Advisors agree to work with students based on an approximate timeframe for students to complete their program. When students do not engage the advisor in such discussions, relationship tensions can develop. Most advisors are happy to see their students willing and able to engage in the research community (e.g., as part of training and building experience), but not when engagement evolves into long periods of time that interfere drastically with students' time to completion. Students need to remember that their advisor is likely busy with several other students, teaching classes, administrative responsibilities and research endeavours.

The main task for students to complete at the initial stages of research is to construct a workable plan. As demonstrated in this chapter, each piece of the research design has an impact outside of its own domain (e.g., data collection and analysis). Students need to continuously apply their critically reflexive lens to the construction of their plan, going back and forth and fine-tuning each component while moving forward. When the comprehensive plan is complete, the student researcher can take one last look from beginning to end and hopefully decide that at this point in time, this plan is the *best* plan with which to move forward, knowing that it has to be lived out, changed and rearranged as the research proceeds. Advisors and committee members will also decide on the student researcher's readiness to begin the research based on the plan articulated.

Chapter 3 is designed to help students who have constructed their research plans to complete an ethics review process (university or other institutional/ community) and to successfully gain the necessary permissions to begin research. Within the Canadian context, universities follow a national policy, the *Tri-Council Policy Statement: Ethical Conduct for Research Involving Humans* (tcps2 2014), but universities interpret and implement the policy individually. The discussion in Chapter 3 is general enough to provide students with support for completing institutional applications, regardless of the university they attend. The chapter addresses the complexities of conducting respectful research with human partici-pants, which extends beyond initial official processes before the research begins, to emergent issues that arise, *in situ*, in context with participants as the research process evolves over time. With the successful completion of the ethics processes, students are ready to move into the field, the emphasis explored in Chapter 4.

Annotated Bibliography

Agee, Jane. 2009. "Developing Qualitative Research Questions: A Reflective Process." *International Journal of Qualitative Studies in Education* 22, 4: 431–447.

   Jane Agee describes the dynamic process involved in articulating qualitative research questions. She takes the reader through the stages of question generation, explaining that a researcher may revisit, refine and shift questions in situ as the research study unfolds. Agee identifies the makings of a "good" question: the need for specificity and careful consideration of context. She also discusses the identification of a clear focus, set of objectives and manageable scope. Agee also highlights the value of eliciting feedback from multiple sources. Her article includes examples from actual studies that illustrate the complex interplay between research questions, theoretical framing, and mode of inquiry. She discusses the need for an ethical and reflexive lens, particularly when one decides to conduct research with vulnerable populations.

Avni, Anoosha E. 2012. "Skilled Worker Immigrants' Pre-Migration Occupation Re-Entry Experiences in Canada." Unpublished doctoral dissertation, University of Alberta, Edmonton, AB.

Students seeking an exemplar of a traditional approach to qualitative research may find the methodology section of this dissertation particularly helpful for planning and organizing their own research projects. By way of interpretive inquiry, Anoosha Avni, a doctoral student in educational psychology, gives voice to the skilled immigrant workers who have succeeded in finding work in their premigration occupations in Canada. She clearly outlines many of the aspects of qualitative research: researcher positioning, research focus and questions, and participant recruitment. Additionally, Avni outlines the specifics of the interview process and her use of a research journal as data. Also included are clearly articulated procedures for evaluating the quality of data and research generated.

Boote, David N., and Penny Beile. 2005. "Scholars Before Researchers: On the Centrality of the Dissertation Literature Review in Research Preparation." *Educational Leadership* 34, 6: 3–15.

David N. Boote and Penny Beile challenge a view of the literature review as a chore that must be tolerated as part of the completion of a doctoral dissertation. They suggest that the literature review be viewed as genuine scholarly work in its own right — scholarship that analyzes the research field and seeks to locate educational research firmly in that field. To be effective, the literature review, like the research itself, must be generative and capable of facilitating further study. The authors offer a rubric for determining the quality of a doctoral literature review, including criteria addressing the following areas: coverage (criteria for what should be included in the review), synthesis (pulling together the literature), methodology (discussion of methodologies used in the literature), significance (discussing the significance of the research problem relevant to the literature) and rhetoric (the quality of the writing that supports the claims made in the review). The authors discuss their original research, in which they apply this rubric to doctoral dissertation literature reviews and conclude that although their criteria are high, it is not unreasonable to ask for such quality work, given the scholarly importance of the literature review.

Lau, Sunny Man Chu, and Saskia Stille. 2014. "Participatory Research with Teachers: Toward a Pragmatic and Dynamic View of Equity and Parity in Research Relationships." *European Journal of Teacher Education* 37, 2: 156–170.

Drawing on principles of critical ethnography and participatory action research, these two university-based researchers highlight the participatory aspects of their collaborations, focusing specifically on the complex issue of establishing parity and equity among academic researchers and teachers when working together in educational settings. Although Sunny Man Chu Lau and Saskia Stille acknowledge the challenges and extra demands collaborative processes may entail, they conclude that this type of research can benefit all stakeholders, provided that there is flexibility in obligations and responsibilities of both parties; and that as an act of reciprocity, school-based participatory research ultimately supports teachers in meeting their individual learning and professional goals

Raynor, Margaret E. 2012. "Salves and Sweetgrass: Singing a Metis Home." Unpublished master's thesis, York University, Toronto, ON.

Margaret E. Raynor's thesis, chosen as a winner of the Canadian Association for Curriculum Studies award, is grounded in Metis epistemology and framed within the tradition of testimonio. *Raynor explores her experiences as a Metis student and teacher with the goal of identifying factors for her personal success as well as best teaching practices. Her methods of inquiry include the use of ceremony, memory, reflection, prayer, dreams and vision; as well as discussions and interactions with elders, family and friends. Raynor organizes her study into two parts. The first section, which she defines as "performance," is developed based on various data, including journals, poetry, correspondence and exchanges with the parents of past students and relatives, family photos and historical records. The second section provides detail on Raynor's chosen methodology and methods, ethical considerations, findings and a summary of her research.*

Sinner, Anita, Carl Leggo, Rita Irwin, Peter Gouzouasis and Kit Grauer. 2006. "Arts-based Educational Dissertations: Reviewing the Practices of New Scholars." *Canadian Journal of Education* 29, 4: 1223–1270.

In this article, Anita Sinner and her colleagues review and explore arts-based educational dissertations and trace the origins of a research practice described by the authors as "the methodology of a/r/tography." They use the following questions to guide their review: What do arts-based methodologies/methods consist of? What is the range of arts-based methodologies/methods applied in this collection? And what is the relationship between arts-based methodologies/methods and social science methodologies/methods? This article includes a summary chart of all the arts-based dissertations completed at the University of British Columbia between 1994 and 2004, along with the methodological practices they used.

Wright, Lisa L. 2009. "Leadership in the Swamp: Seeking the Potentiality of School Improvement through Principal Reflection." *Reflective Practice* 10, 2: 259-272.

> *In the first part of her article, elementary school principal Lisa L. Wright describes how she reflects on and analyzes moments of tension in her professional role. She contemplates possibilities for moving forward and offers connections to her familial history as a source of knowledge and mechanism for strategy development. In the second part of her article, Wright details her involvement in a board-wide project on reflection with principals. She negotiates multiple roles throughout this process, including that of "learner," "facilitator," "critical friend," "research assistant" and "researcher" (2009: 262). Sharing key excerpts from her "researcher journal," she documents her struggles and emerging questions. Throughout her article, she encourages researchers and practitioners (e.g., principal-researchers) to be "reflective" and "reflexive." She incorporates useful figures and accompanying questions to stimulate critical, reflective thinking. She documents her connectedness to and involvement in various communities, and wonders how participants will be affected when details of their experiences are included in her findings.*

Zhou, Ally A. 2004. "Writing the Dissertation Proposal: A Comparative Case Study of Four Nonnative and Two Native-English-Speaking Doctoral Students of Education." Unpublished doctoral dissertation, University of Toronto, Toronto, ON.

> *Ally A. Zhou's dissertation is useful for graduate students both in terms of its focus on dissertation proposal writing and in the ways that transcription and analysis are explored. Interview data from six native and non-native English speaking doctoral students and their five professor-mentors, along with written texts (the students' dissertation proposals and other written documents produced by the students and their mentors) were analyzed for their textural features and how they were produced. Key findings from the study suggest that variations in the process of proposal writing are more likely to occur based on the individual students and their chosen discipline, more so than whether they are native or non-native English speakers.*

Chapter 3

RESEARCH ETHICS AND QUALITATIVE RESEARCH

Student researchers who have research plans completed are ready to construct their applications to REBs and other bodies with oversight of the contexts and people they want to involve in their research projects. At Canadian universities, researchers cannot begin their research until they have successfully completed an REB ethics process and have garnered permissions from other institutions, communities or individuals with relevant oversight. The purpose of this chapter is twofold. First, it assists students who are planning to conduct qualitative research with human participants to understand the ethics review process and to complete the ethics applications required by their institutions. Second, the chapter sensitizes students to the complexities of ethical issues — those considered in the plan and those that arise after institutional approvals have been given and students have begun their research. When turning a research lens on human participants, student research- ers need to understand what constitutes ethical praxis in light of their goals, the knowledge being produced and their responsibilities as researchers. Although the good intentions and integrity of the researcher cannot ensure that harm will not be done, they are paramount in strengthening the official protection offered.

INTRODUCING RESEARCH ETHICS

In this chapter, an emphasis is given to the concepts of consent, confidentiality and risk, which are central in the overall ethics review process, whether consid- ered individually or as interlocking. Chapter 3 of the *Tri-Council Policy Statement: Ethical Conduct for Research Involving Humans* (TCPS2) explicitly outlines the general principles of free, informed and ongoing consent (TCPS2 2014). Along with explaining the principles, the document describes aspects of the application process and other important details (e.g., what needs to be included in information given to potential participants).

Although discussion of the complexities of research ethics and *in situ* ethics issues begins in this chapter, an emphasis on this area is woven throughout the book, a reflection of the interconnectedness of research praxis and questions of ethics in qualitative research (i.e., ethics in relation to data analysis, representation and dissemination).

Institutional reviews multiply when student researchers' chosen context has a process in place to oversee research conducted within its jurisdiction. For example, many school boards in Canadian contexts are formalizing review procedures for research applications to conduct research within their jurisdiction (Tilley and Ratković 2009). In the case of First Nations communities, historical and continuing concerns with exploitation and voyeurism have culminated in a number of these communities developing research protocols. Battiste (2008: 498) describes the Mi'kmaw Ethics Watch that has been assigned the task "to oversee research processes that involved Mi'kmaw knowledge sought among Mi'kmaw people, ensuring that researchers conduct research ethically and appropriately within Mi'kma'ki (Mi'kmaq Nation territories)." When students need approvals to begin their research, in addition to those obtained through universities (e.g., hospital, school board, community bodies), they need to take the time to understand the expectations of the additional review bodies to gain access to the research site and participants.

Although faculty members have a responsibility to ensure that the students they advise successfully complete the ethics review process, the more informed students are about the policy and procedures in place in their specific university contexts, the less likely they will experience difficulties obtaining the necessary approvals. Completion of strong applications requires students to commit substantial thought and time to the process. In Canada, students are required to complete a university online ethics tutorial as a condition for submission of an ethics application (TCPS2 2014). If not required in other contexts, students may still be able to access such resources as available.

The discussion that follows is helpful for providing students with an historical background and basic knowledge of the requirements of the ethics review process common across Canadian and North American universities and that also reflect university requirements in other countries (i.e., institutional review boards in the United States).

ETHICS REVIEW OF RESEARCH INVOLVING HUMAN PARTICIPANTS

The *Tri-Council Policy Statement on Ethical Conduct for Research Involving Humans* (TCPS) was first implemented in Canada in 1998 (there was an updated version in 2010 and most recently in December 2014). This policy statement, which was a joint initiative of the three federal granting agencies (the Canadian Institutes of Health Research, the Social Sciences and Humanities Research Council and the Natural Sciences and Engineering Research Council), is applicable to all disciplines of research. As a result of the implementation of the policy, Canadian universities established REBs "to review the ethical acceptability of all research involving humans conducted within their jurisdiction or under their auspices, that is, by their faculty, staff or students, regardless of where the research is conducted, in accordance with this Policy" (Article 6.1; TCPS 2014: 69). The purpose of the REB is to consider the ethical implications of research proposed not to make judgments on quality, except in cases in which quality issues intersect with ethics concerns. The approval of an REB ethics application does not, in itself, equate with approval for the research to commence; other factors outside the purview of an REB may impinge on research proceeding (e.g., other required institutional permissions not given). Researchers in Canadian universities conducting research with human participants (which requires ethics clearance) are not eligible to receive funding from any of these three federal granting agencies unless an REB has favourably reviewed their ethics application.

Students planning to conduct critical qualitative research should be aware of the debate related to ethics review and qualitative research that has emerged and continues to unfold in academic contexts. Researchers, many of whom conduct qualitative social science and education research, are concerned about university review boards' application of policies and procedures that they perceive as increasing (often inappropriate) oversight of academic research (Eyre 2010; Fitzgerald 2005; Grayson and Myles 2005). They are concerned about the audit culture and what K.D. Haggerty (2004) characterizes as an "ethics creep" that he argues is advancing in institutional contexts, including universities (see Lewis, M. 2008, "ethics drift"). Ethics creep "involves a dual process whereby the regulatory structure of ethics bureaucracy is expanding outward, and colonizing new groups, practices, and institutions, while at the same time intensifying the regulation of practices deemed to fall within its official ambit" (Lewis, M. 2008: 394). Over the last few decades, the intensification of oversight applied to research conducted within schooling contexts, much of which in earlier years was considered inquiry within a "zone of accepted practice" (Zeni 2001: 158) and as such not under the auspices of an REB, can in some instances reflect this ethics creep.

An extensive body of literature is available that points to what many qualitative researchers consider the incompatibilities between interpretive research and university ethics review policies and procedures (Conn 2008; Patterson 2008; Tolich and Fitzgerald 2006; van den Hoonaard 2002, 2011). An historical and continuing criticism aimed at university review boards in Canada and beyond is that an ill-fitting lens is being applied to qualitative research. Critics argue that the TCPS was originally developed from a biomedical perspective on ethics more suited to positivist quantitative research and policies not easily or credibly applied to qualitative methodologies (Ells and Gutfreund 2006; Owen 2004). At times, experienced qualitative researchers have complained that addressing institutional ethics review requirements can affect the integrity of their interpretive research designs (Eyre 2010; Parnis et al. 2005). The researchers from Canada and around the world who attended the Ethics Rupture Summit in 2012 and signed the *New Brunswick Declaration of Research Ethics*, indicated their commitment to "enhancing ethical research practice, and supporting innovative alternatives to the regulation of research ethics that might achieve this end" (van den Hoonaard and Tolich 2014: 94).

Over the past few decades, changes have occurred that somewhat address researchers' critique of the troublesome aspects of the original TCPS (1998) to qualitative interpretivist research (TCPS2 2010; TCPS2 2014). One example is the addition of a section addressing qualitative research specifically. Researchers across Canada who were troubled by the TCPS and ethics review process contributed their voices to promote such changes (see Social Sciences and Humanities Research Ethics Special Working Committee 2004, *Giving Voice to the Spectrum*). Whether the critique from social science and education researchers will be lessened as a result of the more recent changes will be known in the years that follow. Understanding the historical and continuing arguments in the field will not only help student researchers construct applications that meet the requirements of REBs and other institutional review boards but also prepare them to take part in a dialogue that is expected to continue into the future.

Research Ethics Board

Faculty members, student representatives and community representatives external to the university are commonly part of a university review board. In Canada, TCPS2 2014 outlines the criteria for establishing an REB in Article 6.4. In addition to an REB having a minimum of at least five members (including both men and women):

a) at least two members have expertise in relevant research disciplines, fields and methodologies covered by the REB;

b) at least one member is knowledgeable in ethics;

c) at least one member is knowledgeable in the relevant law (but that member should not be the institution's legal counsel or risk manager). This is mandatory for biomedical research and is advisable, but not mandatory for other areas of research; and

d) at least one community member who has no affiliation with the institution. (TCPS2 2014: 72)

The membership of the REB usually exceeds the minimal requirements. In current years, a concerted effort has been made to include individuals who represent disciplines across the universities and who have knowledge and experiences of diverse methodologies, as well as individuals with expertise related to Indigenous cultures and knowledge. Students are often welcomed to sit on the board. External community members who are at arm's length from the university are included as members of the REB (e.g., previous research participants, individuals working for community outreach initiatives, Aboriginal Elders). Members regularly serve three-year terms and bring varied expertise and experiences to their work on the review board (Tilley 2008).

CONSTRUCTING AN ETHICS APPLICATION FOR REVIEW

After developing their research plans, students will have already thought about their research questions, methodology, potential participants, data-collection methods and plans for dissemination; and have the extensive information required to complete their ethics application. If their research plan is well-written, they can transfer content from that document to the ethics application. Issues related to risk, consent and confidentiality need to be addressed in the application. Recruitment materials that include information letters, consent forms and data-collection instruments must be submitted with the application (see Appendices A and B). Templates for recruitment documents are often posted on university websites to help student researchers develop personalized versions.

Important questions for students to consider when preparing to complete their ethics application include these: What are the foreseeable risks of the research to participants? What ethical issues might arise because of the choice of research questions, context and participants and due to methodological choices? How will ethical issues be addressed? The institutional review process, while maintaining oversight, also serves an educational function, with the potential to make ethical concerns explicit to student researchers and to prepare them for dealing with some of the complicated ethical *in situ* demands. Students can also take ownership of their own education and become familiar with ethics board requirements. They can locate and read the policies and then discuss the process and issues with their advisors. They can take advantage of methodology courses, asking ethics-related questions (if not already included in course content). As a result of this work, students will build knowledge invaluable to them not only in the completion of the application but also in their research contexts as they conduct their research.

International students who are conducting research in Canada follow the same processes as their Canadian counterparts. Matters become more complicated when students want to travel back to their countries to collect data, a situation that is becoming more common with the rise in numbers of international students and the technology available to communicate across continents. In this case, as part of the conditions of the REB process, students have to complete ethics review requirements in place in their country of choice, which might not reflect the North American processes (Gormley 2006). Most important is that before planning their research, students should assess whether they have the support they will need to conduct their research at a distance and to face all the challenges that researching at a distance may entail.

Delegated and Full Review

In the Canadian context (and other North American contexts), university review boards often have at least two levels of review applied to research applications, based on assessed level of risk to participants of the proposed research. In Canada, these levels are referred to as *delegated review* and *full review* (TCPS2 2014: 79).

Research assessed as within the range or below minimal risk is most likely assigned a delegated review; when deemed a high level of risk, research applications often require a full board review. Although language for these processes may differ across institutions and countries, assessment of risk level often determines the review procedures to be applied. In the area of social sciences and humanities, many ethics applications are given delegated (in earlier times referred to as *expedited*) reviews (see Oki and Zaia 2006; Tilley et al. 2009). Delegated review procedures follow (more or less) the process described in the following sections.

An application is submitted, and the REB delegates the ethics review to individuals from the REB membership. A minimal number of board members and sometimes the chair of the board are involved in the review of delegated applications. For example, the application may be sent to one or two board members who are seen as having the expertise necessary for the review. They review the application and send a report back to the chair, who identifies any additions or revisions deemed necessary to fulfil review criteria. University ethics boards' decisions cover a number of possibilities, including some version of the following: *Accepted* indicates approval of the ethical acceptability of the research; *Clarification/Revision Required* indicates that revisions are necessary to the application before ethical acceptability can be determined; *Resubmission Required* indicates concerns on the part of the reviewers and a need for substantive revisions. *Full Board Review* may be required when the application is resubmitted.

When clarification is required, the expectation is that student researchers will respond and submit revised documents, showing that the required changes have been made and/or issues in the feedback have been addressed. A decision will be made as to whether the concerns listed in the original response to the student were adequately addressed. If yes, students receive approval of the ethical acceptability; if not, further clarification may be required. Although applications are deemed in need of full review or delegated review at the initial stage of the review process, an application that is given a delegated review can sometimes be deemed in need of a full review as a result of the delegated review process.

A full review procedure, which is often assigned when the level of risk is deemed high, requires approval from the majority (if not all) of the board members who review the application. The student researcher will receive a response based on reviewers' comments. In some university contexts, students (and sometimes their advisors) will be asked to attend a board meeting, during which they have an opportunity to address the queries of the board. After the meeting, the student will receive advice regarding possibilities for revision of research plans that allows the board to make a positive determination of the ethical acceptability of the research. In some cases, this process may result in a request for application resubmission.

A significant amount of time is necessary for student researchers to complete an ethics review process and to gain approval for the research they are proposing. Students can make reasonable estimates of the time their portion of the work will entail, but they must also factor in university-estimated timelines for application processing. REB time estimations should be accessible to students on university websites. Although time estimates are not guaranteed, they are helpful in students' projection of deadline goals to complete the process and begin research.

The care taken to address the application requirements will contribute to a more timely response from the review board and a lessening of frustrations for students at the latter stages of the process. When extensive clarification is required, the time to receive approval of the ethical acceptability of the research and the time to begin the research are lengthened. In some circumstances, the timeline extension is an appropriate response to an underdeveloped ethics application that proposes a questionable design with ethical implications. Student time is better spent in carefully constructing a comprehensive application at the front end of the process rather than revising the application based on a requested clarification. Students may want to consider the following suggestions to help facilitate the processing of their ethics application:

- Complete the ethics application after constructing the research plan. The necessary information needed will be available at that point.
- Factor reasonable timelines into the research plan to complete the ethics

review process (e.g., time to complete the comprehensive application and also the wait time for board response, possibly four to six weeks). Factor in the timelines for other institutional/community review processes necessary in addition to those of the university.

- Carefully read the university documents that outline the procedures of the ethics review board and the principles upon which the requirements for a positive decision are based.

- Complete the online tutorial well in advance of constructing the ethics application. The tutorial may provide ideas to enhance the research plans in regard to ethical consideration and otherwise. Complete a tutorial if available, even if not required (e.g., the Tri-Council tutorial available from <pre.ethics.gc.ca/english/tutorial/>; York University's academic integrity tutorial available from <yorku.ca/tutorial/academic_integrity/acaddishforms.html>).

- When applicable, use the templates provided by the review board to complete the application.

- Ensure that applications and attachments are written effectively in terms of both structure and content. Although university review boards are focused on assessing the ethical dimension of the research planned, sloppily constructed paragraphs and sentences — lack of grammatical correctness — can interfere with the reviewers' understanding of the research and signal a lack of seriousness with which the student is addressing the task. Consistency across all aspects of the application form and additional attachments is necessary (i.e., information letter, consent form, interview schedule). For example, an application might have a clearly articulated research focus, but the interview schedule does not reflect the emphasis described, resulting in a request for clarification. Although making the requested modifications to applications that the REB requires may be easily accomplished after the problems are made evident, the time it takes to do so could be better spent moving the research forward.

- Indicate in the application that there is an awareness and sensitivity to the ethical issues related to the planned research. For example, if recruiting a vulnerable group to participate in the research, be explicit about the strategies in place to ensure that the individuals are fully informed about what is being asked of them (e.g., Mishna et al. 2004; Parr 2010). Describe how multiple explanations of the data-collection process will be provided by using various venues to ensure that participants are clear on what is expected of them.

- When the research planned is *sensitive*, emphasize explicitly in the application that there is an awareness of the degree of sensitivity necessary that is taken into account in the planning (see McCosker et al. 2001; Parnis et al. 2005). For example, in the case of research focused on exploring areas related to heterosexism and homophobia and collecting data through interviewing, students should indicate that attention has been specifically paid to structuring interview questions that are respectful of the participants' sexual orientations.

- If proposing research that crosses international boundaries, clearly indicate an understanding of what is expected from the review processes in place in the country/context involved and an acceptable level of knowledge of the research context and participants, possibly connections already in place. Indicate that there will be ongoing communication between the student researcher and the advisor.
- If conducting research online, be aware of the ethical implications of conducting research in cyberspace, which are often similar to requirements for research offline (Paechter 2013).

My experiences as an REB member over a three-year term, as well as conducting interviews with REB members about their experiences reviewing research applications and analyzing reviewer responses to research applications, have shown me that reviewer irritation intensifies when written documents that student researchers submit are incomplete, inconsistent, generally poorly constructed and/or reflect an overall insensitivity toward the ethical issues implicit in the research planned. Such applications create reviewer frustration, often resulting in requests for clarification and extended timelines for researchers moving forward with their research (Tilley 2008; Tilley et al. 2009).

MULTIPLE BODIES OF OVERSIGHT

Gaining access [to the prison] as a researcher involved obtaining various permissions from a complex network of authorities. I contacted the administrator at the college responsible for the prison education program. He was supportive of my request, informing me that I would have to obtain additional permission from the college's Ethics Review Committee, which I did at a later date. In terms of prison administration, I explained my research plans and provided a copy of a proposal to the local prison administration and permission was granted. After sending similar materials to Victoria, I received permission from the provincial authorities. The final permission I received was from the university's Ethics Review Board. I was officially authorized to conduct research with the women who attended the prison school and had the papers to prove it. (Tilley 1998a: 33)

Although students receive approval from the university REB, indicating that their plan reflects ethically responsible research, additional institution, agency and/ or community permissions may be needed before the research and participant recruitment can begin. Many of these authoritative bodies have policies and procedures in place for people requesting permission to conduct research within their jurisdiction. Sometimes, the institutional applications for clearance are submitted simultaneously with university review board applications. At other times, one institution might require evidence of clearance from the other institution before reviewing applications (e.g., a hospital board or school board might require that REB clearance be given before an application will be reviewed). Students need to spend time learning about the requirements of the institutions or communities in which they want to conduct research. The reviews those institutions apply may consider other dimensions of the research proposed that extend beyond those related to ethical considerations (e.g., school contexts, concerns for disruption of regular teaching). Hospitals and prisons, other agencies and communities within or outside Canada may decide against giving permission based on criteria that are beyond the student researchers' control, so having a back-up plan is a good idea. There may be times when researchers need to shift their choice of desired site or reshape their focus because they cannot gain the access required to conduct the research as planned.

QUALITATIVE RESEARCH AS RISKY BUSINESS

A main concern for ethics review boards is related to the degree of risk that research poses for participants. TCPS2 (2014: 22) defines minimal risk in the following way:

> "Minimal risk" research is defined as research in which the probability
> and magnitude of possible harms implied by participation in the research
> is no greater than those encountered by participants in those aspects of
> their everyday life that relate to the research.

When assessing applications, reviewers consider the degree of risk associated with the research proposed. However, in the case of interpretive research, the task of identifying risk involved is not always straightforward. Although they provide a road map of the research plan, qualitative research designs may require change as the research proceeds. Student researchers might quite tidily describe respectful participant recruitment and ethical online or offline data collection, interview or observation processes, but they cannot reveal all matters *up front* because of the emergent quality of their research designs. Although review board members may be well-versed in interpretive methodologies, this is not always the case. Student researchers may not take risk seriously enough for the purposes of the review board.

For the most part, the research that students propose will fall within the range of minimal risk; if they address risk in comprehensive ways in the application, being proactive in addressing questions that might arise due to the nature of the research described, they will face fewer complications as part of the review.

Risk and *vulnerability* are interconnected. When potential participants are individuals or groups considered vulnerable, reviewers assess the degree of risk in light of the vulnerability of participants:

> Vulnerability is often caused by limited capacity, or limited access to social goods, such as rights, opportunities and power. Individuals or groups in vulnerable circumstances have historically included children, the elderly, women, prisoners, those with mental health issues and those with diminished capacity for self-determination. Ethnocultural minorities and those who are institutionalized are other examples of groups who have, at times, been treated unfairly and inequitably in research, or have been excluded from research opportunities. (TCPS2 2014: 8)

When minors are asked to participate, multiple consents, including institutional and individual, may be required. For schools, parents or guardians and sometimes the minors (when age-appropriate) may be required to indicate consent. When consent for a child to participate is gained from an authorized third party, researchers must ascertain the child's assent. However, whether the minor is freely participating may not be easily established. For example, pressure from parents and/or other adults may consciously or unconsciously be applied, or participation may be more about pleasing the researcher/teacher/parent than a desire to participate. In such cases, it is essential that student researchers applying for ethics approval indicate in their application that they are aware of the complexities of obtaining free and informed consent from participants in their specific research context, vulnerable and otherwise; and that they have created as many ways as possible to support their participants to freely choose to participate or not (e.g., asking permission at various times and in multiple ways). Risk may actually develop as the research proceeds and conditions change, and students need to indicate that they are sensitive to that possibility. For example, it may only be in the latter stages of the interview that a researcher recognizes that a parent has coerced a child to participate. The student researcher will have to find a way to respect the child's right not to contribute data while also ensuring that the child is not put at risk by ending the interview, which would indicate to the parent that the child did not comply with his/her wishes.

It becomes difficult when reviewers overestimate the level of vulnerability and become guardians of individuals who are able to make informed decisions (see Tilley 2008). Janice Morse (2005) is concerned that vulnerable populations

— those with serious illnesses in particular — will be unable to participate in qualitative research when REBs overestimate levels of vulnerability. She agrees that a layer of protection is needed, but that protection must be balanced with individuals' rights to make their own informed decisions about participation.

In the prison context, I became aware of the impact that my limited knowledge of the participants and research context had on the possibilities of respectful research praxis. My application passed REB scrutiny (and additional scrutiny of other institutional bodies), but I did not fully understand some of the risks related to my researcher choices. Interviewing in the prison involved some unknown (to me) risk. For example, on occasion I was asked by prison authorities to shift my interviews from the visitors' area to a meeting room adjacent to the women's cell units. I was not aware this was a problem until one of the participants explained that she preferred not to be interviewed in that room because other women could see her through the glassed enclosure and may think that she was reporting on them — positioning her as a prison informer rather than research participant.

No guarantee exists that REB members or other reviewers will understand the risks 100 percent when they are unfamiliar (or even familiar) with the context or participants, or have a surface knowledge of qualitative methodology(ies) in general. However, reviewers' assessment of risk may be very helpful to student researchers who do not have the knowledge and experience to understand the dangers of what they propose. It is the responsibility of the students (with the assistance of advisors — and/or community members in the case of participatory research) to construct a plan that convinces the institutional bodies that before the student researchers proceed, they are prepared as much as possible to conduct ethical research.

FREE, INFORMED AND ONGOING CONSENT

Respect for Persons implies that individuals who participate in research do so voluntarily, understanding the purpose of the research, and its risks and potential benefits, as fully as reasonably possible.... Equally, Respect for Persons implies that those who lack the capacity to decide for themselves should nevertheless have the opportunity to participate in research that may be of benefit to themselves or others. Authorized third parties acting on behalf of these individuals may decide whether participation would be appropriate. (TCPS2 2014: 25)

At the research design stage, students decide who will be asked to participate in their research and what shape the recruitment process will take. These details must be included in the ethics application. The review board will be assessing whether an appropriate recruitment process is in place and whether the recruitment materials provided in the application ensure that the individuals asked to participate will be fully informed. Chapter 3 of the TCPS2 (2014) document explicitly outlines the general principles of free, informed and ongoing consent that students need to consider in relation to the research they are proposing.

The individuals recruited will influence the process taken in arriving at informed consent. In the *straightforward* case in which adults are being asked to participate in research that is within or below the range of minimal risk, the researcher is not in a power position over them and the focus of the research is not considered sensitive, the likelihood of approval is increased if the constructed application demonstrates that this is the case. The proper construction of recruitment documents will enhance the chances of an uncomplicated review process: for example, the necessary information is in all documents and matches, in substance, the templates the review board provides and the information included is consistent across all documents. In the majority of cases, a signed informed consent form indicates that the participants are aware of the implications of their involvement in the research and are voluntarily participating. When children and other individuals who are considered a vulnerable population are required as participants, multiple individuals may have to give consent: possibly family members, parents and/or medical personnel. Consent forms should be crafted specifically to the participants (they are different for children and parents). If researchers are English-speaking and participants are not, materials are expected to be translated. If potential participants' level of literacy interferes with their understanding of the intent of the research and the work their participation requires, other strategies must be in place to ensure that the participants are fully informed (e.g., people on hand to translate).

Plans for audio recording interviews are often given less scrutiny than plans for using visual media (videotaping, photography, artistic works) that capture participant images on film or in visuals that can serve to identify them and be shared across time and space (see Gallagher and Kim 2008). Sandra Weber (2008: 50) writes of visual images in connection to ethics:

> Not all images are equal or equally effective or valid. Images, like words, can be used to twist and distort and mislead. Ethical issues (what is a responsible use of images of other people, who owns or controls them, loss of anonymity, and so on) can be very thorny and complicated.

When videotaping or filming to collect data, a detailed explanation of the process and use of data will be needed. Student researchers have to explain the purpose and use of the images. Are they for researcher analysis only or will others have access to them (e.g., clips shown at public forums, community gatherings)?

If participants are from a designated vulnerable group, more scrutiny is applied. Demonstrating that participants are fully informed and agree to the planned use of the visual materials will assuage reviewers' concerns about what might be considered an intrusive method.

In the case of critical qualitative research, the research focus is often on what might be considered by many as *sensitive* issues (e.g., research on homophobia, schools and racism), participants involved categorized as vulnerable or marginalized/oppressed (children, prisoners, refugees and immigrant populations), methods participatory and participant-driven. It is important that researchers not be too easily dissuaded from proposing and conducting critical research for fears of being faced with a complicated ethics review process. They must prepare their applications knowing and addressing the challenges they may face.

CONSENT PROCESS

When constructing their processes for gathering consent, student researchers must ensure that they meet the criteria the TCPS2 outlines. Article 3.1 states the following:

a) Consent shall be given voluntarily.
b) Consent can be withdrawn at any time.
c) If a participant withdraws consent, the participant can also request the withdrawal of his/her data or human biological materials. (TCPS2 2014: 26)

Student researchers must also provide "prospective participants, or authorized third parties, full disclosure of all information necessary for making an informed decision to participate in a research project" to ensure that consent is informed consent (TCPS2 2014: 28). Key documents that researchers construct and reviewers assess to ensure that participants are giving free and informed consent are the information letter and consent forms (often combined) (see Appendix A for an example). To ensure that participants are informed, the expectations tied to the interview process must be stated clearly in the consent materials. What is the purpose of the interview? What exactly is the participant required to do? What are the rights of participants? What are the benefits that participants or communities might accrue? How will participants be protected from potential harm? Will data be kept confidential? Include sample questions on the consent form that provide the participants with some indication of what to expect in the interviews. Logistics of the interviews are explained in the participant information and consent documents. How many interviews? How much time is required? Where will they take place and for how long? Who will be present? The aftermath of the actual data-collection process, what is expected of the participant, needs to be articulated in the consent process. For instance, after an interview, are the participants asked to read transcripts and respond? If yes, how does this process unfold? Depending on the number of interviews and transcripts, participants have to dedicate an amount of time to this activity.

Qualitative research is often designed to explore the experiences of human participants, so interviewing that encourages participants to reveal aspects of their experiences that they may not plan to talk about during the interview is not uncommon. Such interviews are often of the in-depth, open-ended version, which researchers regularly choose when working within a critical qualitative interpretive framework.

Interviewers may have a schedule of questions to which they refer, but the nature of the in-depth, open-ended interview supports an interviewer/interviewee dynamic that is interactive and moves beyond a script. Such interviews allow for deep exploration of the phenomena under study. REB reviewers may pay special attention to studies that student researchers propose when in-depth, open-ended interviewing is the method of choice for collecting primary data because of the potential risk involved when participants unintentionally reveal information. REB members may want some assurance that students are prepared to address complications that arise as a result of the interview/interviewee exploratory conversation. Students can indicate their sensitivity to this concern by articulating ways in which they might address this issue if it arises in the research context. In the application, for example, students might outline their willingness to make decisions to not include data that were clearly part of recorded conversation, but not intended for research purposes. They might choose to include an extensive member-checking process in their research design that encourages participants to participate in member-checking processes that provide an opportunity for them to see and comment on how their data are being used.

When the focus of the research is considered a sensitive area, reviewers' perceptions of the intrusiveness of the questions asked may provoke additional scrutiny. The fact that the student researcher makes clear on the consent form that all participants do not have to answer questions they deem too intrusive is helpful in the quest for clearance. In their applications, students may want to highlight their efforts to ensure that the participants are clear on this point and to illustrate to the reviewers that the researcher has given this area serious consideration. Student researchers also need to indicate that they understand that consent is not a *one-moment-in-time* decision; it is a continuous process that requires student researchers' attention throughout the research process to ensure that participants (or those who agreed for them) are fully informed, especially when any modifications have been made to what they were told and are expecting (changes made to initial research plans may require a request for modification to the review board).

Individuals and communities selected for the participant pool will influence how free and informed consent is obtained. In the Canadian context, the TCPS2 outlines alternative procedures for cases in which signed consent forms may not be appropriate:

> Where consent is not documented in a signed consent form, researchers may use a range of procedures, including oral consent, field notes and other strategies, for documenting the consent process. Consent may also be demonstrated solely by the actions of the participants (e.g., through the return of a completed questionnaire). Where there are valid reasons for not recording consent in writing, the procedures used to seek consent must be documented. (TCPS2 2014: 46)

A consent-gathering process can be digitally recorded. Researchers record their explanation of the research process and state the details normally included in a written consent form, and participants provide verbal agreement that they understand and agree to participate. Such a process may be particularly useful when the research is of a sensitive nature and individuals do not want a record of their signatures kept (e.g., a closeted lesbian teacher). The complexity of informed consent will also be framed in relation to cultural and community norms and procedures (Piquemal 2001; Schnarch 2004). Researchers arguing for more culturally relevant processes for gaining consent are becoming more common, particularly for Aboriginal participants and communities. When is the permission of a community required? (See Longboat 2008 for a discussion.) When does the participation of an individual who has given permission also affect the community that has not done so? What are the community protocols that need to be recognized, acknowledged and followed when research is conducted? Students can access a comprehensive discussion about the ethical conduct of research involving First Nations, Inuit and Metis peoples (Longboat 2008; TCPS2 2014: 109–137).

In cases of written consent being "culturally unacceptable," it is the student researcher's responsibility to be familiar enough with the research context to argue for a process that is acceptable to the participants and possibly their communities. During her doctoral research at a Canadian university, Louise Gormley (2006) faced many challenges keeping within the guidelines articulated in the TCPS when working with participants in a small Mexican town in which asking participants to sign consent forms (even if written in their first language) actually created participant suspicions (Tilley and Gormley 2007).

In response to feedback from First Nations communities and researchers, including qualitative researchers across Canada (Battiste 2008; Schnarch 2004; Social Sciences and Humanities Research Ethics Special Working Committee 2004), university review policy and procedures have changed somewhat to better reflect an awareness of the problems of the influence of Western, Eurocentric positivist norms that originally influenced the development of the TCPS (see Chapter 9, TCPS2 2014). However, there continues to be pressure to push the change agenda forward so that the institutional ethics review is suited to and supportive of research in the social sciences, humanities and education (Tolich and Fitzgerald 2006; van den Hoonaard and Tolich 2014).

CONFIDENTIALITY

When reviewing research applications, university boards are guided by principles that cut across research contexts and methodologies. However, the methodology of choice will influence how these principles are applied in practice. A core principle common to institutional ethics review policies is the protection of human dignity that entails, among other things, a respect for participant privacy:

> Privacy refers to an individual's right to be free from intrusion or inter-ference by others.... Individuals have privacy interests in relation to their bodies, personal information, expressed thoughts and opinions, personal communication with others, and spaces they occupy.... An important aspect of privacy is the right to control information about oneself.... The ethical duty of confidentiality refers to the obligation of an individual or organization to safeguard trusted information.... [It] includes obligations to protect information from unauthorized access, use, disclosure, modification, loss or theft. Fulfiling the ethical duty of confidentiality is essential to the trust relationship between researcher and participant, and to the integrity of the research project. (TCPS2 2014: 57–58)

When assessing research applications, review board members will consider whether a clear plan to protect participant privacy is articulated, which includes keeping the confidentiality of participant data. In particular, they will consider whether issues related to anonymity and data confidentiality are sufficiently addressed as part of the research plan. At times, student researchers confuse these two concepts, promising anonymity when the research design does not support that possibility. Anonymity means that the identities of the participants are not known to anyone, including the researcher. For example, in studies for which data are collected through surveys with no identifying information included, the researcher cannot identify who completed each individual survey. However, in the case of interviews and observations, the researcher will be able to identify the participants. Data is confidential as long as no one other than the researcher and participant (and others to whom the participants agree can have data access) can connect the participants to the data.

Whereas research cast within a positivist quantitative framework often includes primary data that are anonymous (not even the researcher knows for sure!), in the case of qualitative research, data are often identifiable (e.g., data connected to interviewing and observation, visual data). Students conducting qualitative research must ensure that the data collected, while not anonymous, are kept confidential unless given participants' free and informed consent to do otherwise.

To avoid requests for clarification related to anonymity and confidentiality issues, student researchers can employ a number of strategies:

- Assign pseudonyms

  To ensure that data cannot be connected to specific individuals, assigning pseudonyms is a common practice. Participants are often invited to choose the pseudonyms they want to use. Researchers construct a list that matches the pseudonyms to the participants' real names, and they are the only ones who have access to this list. This process is limited in its effectiveness if care is not taken to ensure that data are not connected to individual participants in other steps of the research process, which may happen if identifying information finds its way into written documents or oral reports. Such identifying information might include the name of the town in which a participant lives, details of institutions that lead to readers recognizing the research context and possibly the individual participants involved.

  When participants ask to be identified, care needs to be taken that other individuals who do not want to disclose their participation are not identifiable as a result of including other identities in the representation of data or final documents.

- Contact potential participants

  Logistical decisions are made in the process of setting up interviews and returning transcripts that might compromise the promise of confidentiality without a little foresight on the part of the student researcher. An example is a student researcher sending a general e-mail to all participants rather than individually (e.g., a general feedback form).

- Choose appropriate interview sites

  The place chosen to conduct an interview has potential to interfere with confidentiality — for example, conducting interviews in a teacher's classroom or an individual's office. If people know that an individual is taking part in the research, they might also be able to connect what is reported in the findings to specific individuals. In many cases, participants may not be concerned about their identity being known or whether they can be personally connected to specific data. However, this issue must be discussed as part of the researcher-participant informed consent process to ensure that the participant is making an informed decision regarding confidentiality needs.

- Consider access to data

   Give careful consideration about the individuals who will need access to the raw data or identifying representations of data, so they can be named explicitly during the consent-gathering process. For instance, advisors may want access to data to be able to assist students with their projects. Student researchers and advisors might listen to digital recordings or view videotapes and/or photographs, and look over transcripts. Although pseudonyms may be assigned, the taped conversation may reveal identifying information. To ensure that confidentiality promises made to participants are not broken in this way, students can include a line in the consent form, indicating that the advisor (and other relevant individuals) will also have access to data.

- Return transcripts and other documents representing data

   If there is agreement that data will be kept confidential, transcripts and other documents must be protected and kept secure by the researcher (e.g., in a locked cabinet or office). When member checking using transcripts is part of the research plan, procedures need to be in place to ensure the safe passage of transcripts from researcher to participants that does not interfere with promises of confidentiality. For instance, an agreed-upon process suitable for the individual participant situation must be worked out. In the case of the prison research, I wanted to return transcripts, but was also aware that if the women kept the transcripts in the prison, they might not have control over who would ultimately read them. In this case, I arranged for them to read the transcripts when I was present, but I kept the transcripts in my care, removing them from the prison when I left for the day.

   If data are sent electronically, they must be sent password- and/or otherwise protected (see Kanuka and Anderson 2015 for "e-learning" research and reliability of electronic correspondence and threats to security). Care must also be taken when disseminating findings that identifying information is not leaked into documents going public.

   Keeping data confidential takes foresight; students need to engage their critical reflexivity, paying special attention to questions of ethics at the planning stages and when constructing their ethics applications.

DATA WITHDRAWAL

The consent process must include direction to participants for data withdrawal. Although it is the hope of all researchers that they not be faced with a participant's request to withdraw data, they must be prepared for that eventuality. Participants are informed that they have a right to refuse to answer any questions they perceive as too intrusive and a right to withdraw their data at any time during the study. What this means in practice is that the researcher promises to destroy the participants' data upon request. Reviewers will assess applications to see whether this information is explicitly outlined in the consent form and/or process.

Data withdrawal is not possible in all circumstances, however. The student researcher must be able to isolate and identify the data. For example, if too much time has passed, the data may be embedded in theses that are ready for defence or have already been defended. Articulating the limitations of the possibility of data withdrawal is an important piece to explicate in the consent process.

The ethics applications that student researchers construct proposing qualitative research have to pass the scrutiny of university institutional ethics review boards and any other institutional and community bodies that have jurisdiction over the research context. Being explicit about the logistics of data-collection plans is essential.

ETHICS AND FOCUS GROUP INTERVIEWS

When students complete ethics applications that describe focus group interviewing as a data-collection method, they must address ethical issues specific to group interviews in addition to those common to individual interviews. For example, in the case of focus group interviews, individuals being recruited must understand that the researcher cannot guarantee confidentiality. Participants involved in a focus group interview may choose to disclose information outside of the interview context. Students need to demonstrate in their applications that they understand the ethical issues related to focus group interviews and have addressed those issues as much as possible. For example, consent forms will clearly state that confidentiality cannot be guaranteed in the focus group context (see the Focus Group Interview Script in Appendix B).

Recruited individuals will decide whether a guarantee of confidentiality is a necessary criterion for them to agree to participate. They may determine that the interview focus and potential interview discussion are unlikely to provoke conversation that they would be concerned about keeping confidential. Janice Haley (2006) describes a number of strategies she used to ensure that possible risks of the focus group settings were understood. With the focus group participants, she discussed consent multiple times and talked about addressing sensitive matters. She created a context in which the individuals in the group contributed to constructing guidelines for procedures.

The following are a few suggestions for students to consider when constructing their applications and describing their plans for focus group interviews:

- Include a step in the research plan before the interview commences to reiterate the limitations of confidentiality in the focus group interview with the participants involved.
- Include a procedure that requires participants to sign a confidentiality agreement that asks participants to respect confidentiality after the focus group interview is completed.
- Send a synopsis of the researcher's interpretation of the conversation (possibly taking excerpts from the transcript to support the points made) instead of a complete transcript of the focus group interview to individual participants. In this way, a paper copy of the taped interview will not be available to possibly contribute to diminishing the degree of confidentiality achieved.

In their ethics applications, students can emphasize the ways that the focus group experience is a context in which reciprocity can be experienced. For example, participants involved in research exploring immigrants' experiences of returning to their professions in a new country might benefit greatly from the group interview experience in terms of understanding the experiences of others and making connections that may be continued outside of the research context (Ratković 2014). The benefits of individuals engaging with other participants involved with the research may outweigh any concerns participants might have about confidentiality.

OBSERVATIONS

Under the microscope of the ethics review process, observation is often understood as a method that is more intrusive than interviewing. Participants are captured in context — the details of their lives are recorded for research purposes. Through a research ethics lens, what is important is that enough information is provided to individuals being asked to participate to ensure that they understand, as much as possible, the implications of being observed. Recruiting materials must explain the form in which observations will take. Logistical details are important to ensure that participants understand the process. What kind of observation? How many observations? How long will the observations be? How are the observations documented? What visuals will be produced? How will visuals be used?

Individuals who plan to conduct research in a context in which they are observing nonvulnerable adult participants and writing fieldnotes to document their observations, a seemingly uncomplicated and straightforward process, may find their ethics applications easily processed. However, as the recording procedures become more sophisticated (e.g., plans that indicate filming or photography, production of visual data), risk levels may be perceived to have escalated. As in all cases, the observation process needs to be detailed explicitly in the recruitment material, with special attention paid to ensuring that potential participants understand what will be produced as a result of the observations.

The following guidelines may be useful for students to follow when they are asking permission to conduct qualitative research that entails observation:

- Pay special attention to constructing a consent process that highlights the purpose and procedures in use for collecting data through the observation.
- Clearly articulate the means by which confidentiality is achieved.
- If individuals (participants) shift in and out of the research context, propose a plan that ensures that newcomers are informed or why it is problematic for them to be informed.
- Occasions arise when researchers have permission to observe only certain bodies in a room, so they must find ways to keep the lens from straying. Construct a diagram that indicates where individuals to be observed are situated.
- Explain plans to deal with cases in which what was observed was not the intended focus. Possibly alert the participant and request permission to use the data or not include the data in the study.

When data collection and dissemination involve artistic representations or visuals that have identifying elements, similar worries related to confidentiality will surface. Students need to clearly articulate how they are ensuring confidentiality for participants in all cases in which this is an expectation.

MAXIMIZING BENEFITS

When completing university ethics review applications, student researchers are asked to describe the benefits of the research. A common general response given is that the research will contribute to "society and the advancement of knowledge." Sometimes there is a direct benefit to the research participants described (e.g., a medical benefit, educational benefit). In the case of students, the benefit to the student researcher's learning may be addressed. Benefits take shape in multiple ways, dictated by the specific participants and research contexts. Who the researcher is might also influence both the degree and kind of benefits appropriate (e.g., academic researcher, undergraduate, master's or doctoral student). Access to research sites may be directly related to how those involved, individuals and communities, perceive direct (rather than more elusive) benefits accruing from the research experience.

When students proposing qualitative research shape their studies to maximize the benefits that participants and research contexts accrue as a result of the research, a balance may be achieved across risks and benefits. However, it is important to remember that potential benefits, similar to risks, can never be known definitively before research commences. For example, when I submitted my REB application to conduct research in the prison, I wrote of benefits in very general ways: the findings would contribute to a scarce literature and inform teachers and prison administrators. Additional benefits, forms of reciprocity, emerged over the life of the research (e.g., women prisoners understood their rights as research participants). In critical feminist methodological literature, benefits are often subsumed under a discussion of reciprocity, the intentional shaping of research to ensure that there is some giving back to the research participants and research contexts (Lather 1991). Reciprocity or benefits, however, should not be confused with incentives, which at times can lead to undue influence and coercion:

> Where incentives are offered to participants, they should not be so large or attractive as to encourage reckless disregard of risks.... In considering the possibility of undue influence in research involving financial or other incentives, researchers and REBs should be sensitive to issues such as economic circumstances of those in the pool of prospective participants. (TCPS2 2014: 27)

University ethics boards, while having no standard definition applied to all cases of what constitutes coercive incentives, have an expectation that researchers articulate arguments for their choice of incentive for their specific participants and research context in their applications.

MOVING FORWARD: PERMISSIONS IN HAND

> The official protection afforded imprisoned women by corrections' administration and/or university ethics review committees is not sufficient.... The researcher must be critically reflexive, considering the potential of both harm and good possible from the research act, always keeping in mind who benefits from the research. The good intentions and integrity of the researcher are no guarantee that harm will not be done; however, they are paramount in strengthening the official protection offered. I now understand more fully how the degree

of respect for participants and the level of exploitation depend greatly upon the individual researchers. The words of Popol Vuh, quoted in the book *I Rigoberta Menchu* [Burgos-Debray 1984: 139] come to mind when I consider the responsibilities of those individuals who become involved in conducting such research: "Don't wait for strangers to remind you of your duty, you have a conscience and a spirit for that." (Tilley 1998a: 35)

When student researchers conduct their research from critical perspectives, an ethical, respectful research praxis is an expectation; they cannot wait for strangers to remind them of their duty; they need to "have a conscience and a spirit for that."

Qualitative researchers conducting research embedded in critical frameworks continuously engage a reflexivity with the objective of uncovering underlying problems with their research design/decisions that may not have been visible or understood at the initial stages, understanding that ethical issues emerge *in situ* and often without warning. Marilys Guillemin and Lynn Gillam (2004: 278) describe the process of being reflexive in an ethical sense:

> Being reflexive in an ethical sense means acknowledging and being sen-
> sitized to the micro ethical dimensions of research practice and in doing
> so, being alert to and prepared for ways of dealing with the ethical ten-
> sions that arise. As we have stated, reflexivity does not prescribe specific
> types of responses to research situations; rather, it is a sensitizing notion
> that can enable ethical practice to occur in the complexity and richness
> of social research.

Student researchers will need to remain vigilant about assessing the respectfulness of their research processes as they move forward, sensitized to the possibilities of ethical issues coming to light as they become more involved in the research context and interactions with participants multiply.

In tandem with complying with REB requirements, researchers are engaging a critical reflexivity that questions the institutional processes in place and recognizes the dangers of overdependence on institutional procedures and policies to provide all the necessary guidance on what constitutes ethical research. Complex issues can be addressed *in situ* if students have a willingness to ask difficult questions of their research process and to make revisions to their plans when changes benefit participants and/or research contexts, but may interfere with the students' progress as planned. The following list illustrates strategies students might consider when practising an ethical stance:

- Develop a familiarity with the research context and participants to the degree that you can foresee at least some of the ethical concerns that could arise. Understand the historical context as much as possible.

- Be aware of limitations (i.e., knowledge limitations in terms of methodology, theory, culture).
- Ask questions. Let the advisor know when guidance is needed.
- Be observant of the process and the implications of the decisions made. When something does not feel right, there may be a good reason.
- Listen to the participants.

After applications have been processed through the university review board and approved as ethically sound, and all other necessary permissions are garnered, students can move forward. They should be pleased to have successfully completed the ethics review process and excited to begin the actual research.

SUBMITTING ETHICS APPLICATIONS: A BEGINNING POINT

The need to submit an application for ethics review can serve as a catalyst for getting students to finally complete their research design and move forward in their program. The process calls for decision-making on the part of students who may be wavering on questions of design. To complete the ethics application successfully, students must know the minute details of their research plan.

Ethics review can be conceived of and experienced as an instrumental exercise in completing forms and adjusting to the expectations of the review process. Ethics application forms and templates do not necessarily reflect the interrelatedness of aspects of the research process. When students think of a research ethics review as a front-end paperwork activity rather than a continuous process, they may place too little weight on preparing for and continuing to address ethical issues that arise in the research context. I had various levels of permissions to conduct my doctoral research in the prison, but for the most part I was inadequately prepared to think/act ethically in the prison context. I learned much at the hands of my participants. Although the integrity of researchers can make the difference in whether research is respectfully conducted, this integrity is tied to researchers' capacity to be critically reflexive and willing to question the limitations of their knowledge and systematically work against those limitations.

Students can turn to many resources to prepare their ethics applications, especially those available in their specific institutions (e.g., policy and procedure documents, ethics tutorials, online resources and samples of consent materials). When they have completed their legwork and given their applications some thought, they can turn to their advisors for contributions to the task. Ultimately, advisors sign off on student applications, indicating their support for the documentation and research plan and an agreement to monitor any ethical complications.

When students remain in communication with them, advisors can help students identify and work with ethical issues as they emerge if the students are unable or unsure.

The completion of an ethics review process (including a tutorial) serves as an educational tool that enhances the student researchers' knowledge about ethical conduct. Many students may not have considered research ethics in any depth until faced with documenting their research plan and applying for ethics approval from the REBs.

Ensuring respect for human dignity in the research endeavour is a core principle central to a university ethics review that must guide all aspects of the research process. In practice, adhering to such a principle requires researchers to pay attention to the aspects of the research that are context- and participant-specific when making initial design and research-in-process decisions. Student researchers need to take responsibility for understanding their research contexts and participants in ways that make it possible for them to conduct ethical research and for being informed about the challenges that go hand-in-hand with accomplishing such a goal. They are fortunate to find people and places willing to be a central focus of their inquiring minds for even a minimum amount of time and need to always keep in mind that research is a privilege that carries great responsibility, not a right given to individuals carrying or acquiring academic degrees.

Chapter 4 will focus on students moving into the field, bringing life to their plans for conducting research with human participants. They will need to apply the knowledge of ethics they have learned, and will continue to acquire, to the dilemmas that evolve as the research they plan unfolds, often with twists and turns not initially imagined.

Annotated Bibliography

Bell, Kirsten, and Amy Salmon. 2011. "What Women Who Use Drugs Have to Say about Ethical Research: Findings of an Exploratory Qualitative Study." *Journal of Empirical Research on Human Research Ethics* 6, 4: 84–98.

This study examines female drug users' experiences of research and what they understand to be ethical and respectful engagement. Despite the relationship the researchers had with the community partner agency, women sensed that the interviewers who conducted focus groups were not hearing what they had to say. When describing their experiences, participants talked about feeling "dehumanized." Kirsten Bell and Amy Salmon consider issues of confidentiality, informed consent and the ethics of monetary payment for research participants who are considered to be part of a vulnerable population.

Burles, Meredith. 2010. "Negotiating Serious Illness: Understanding Young Women's Experiences through Photovoice." Unpublished master's thesis, University of Saskatchewan, Saskatoon, SK.

> *The ethical implications of dying patients serving as research participants are explored in great detail in this master's thesis. Meredith Burles designed her study with ethical treatment and care of her participants at the centre of her research. Drawing from phenomenological assumptions about the social world, Burles incorporates four key feminist principles that create the framework for an ethical methodology that focuses on the women and their experiences from their gendered standpoint. Her open-ended interviews allowed for flexibility and tailoring to individual participant's emotional needs. In addition, Burles explains in her thesis the measures she took to avoid causing participants unnecessary harm, which included but were not limited to the use of a graduated consent form that allowed participants to choose a level of confidentiality they were comfortable with, extra caution to ensure protection of participant privacy in relation to visuals produced related to photo-voice, and a consideration of the moral responsibilities researchers have to their participants not only during the research process but also when disseminating findings. Burles addresses the role of reflexivity underlying the ethical principles of her study.*

Carnevale, Franco A., Mary Ellen Macdonald, Myra Bluebond-Langner and Patricia McKeever. 2008. "Using Participant Observation in Pediatric Health Care Settings: Ethical Challenges and Solutions." *Journal of Child Health Care* 12, 1: 18–32.

> *Franco Carnevale and his colleagues argue that participant observation as a method of data collection may elicit data and foster insights more effectively than structured interviews and quantitative methods. They examine ethical issues specific to pediatric settings, such as balancing risks and benefits, and obtaining informed consent when using participant observation in research involving young patients and their families. Although the authors recommend that ethical norms be operationalized, they also stress that REBs guard against the uniform application of ethics standards rooted in quantitative methods. Instead, they suggest that the risks and benefits related to any given study that uses participant observation should be examined independently and the consent process be tailored accordingly.*

Castleden, Heather, Vanessa Sloan Morgan and Christopher Lamb. 2012. "I Spent the First Year Drinking Tea: Exploring Canadian University Researchers' Perspectives on Community-based Participatory Research Involving Indigenous Peoples." *The Canadian Geographer* 56, 2: 160–179.

This article discusses human research ethics and REBs. The authors explain the tenets of community-based participatory research (CBPR) as "a process by which decision-making power and ownership is shared between the researcher and the community involved; bi-directional research capacity and co-learning are promoted; and new knowledge is co-created and disseminated in manner that is mutually beneficial." Yet despite sound egalitarian principles, the authors found that individual research-ers' interpretations of these principles varied widely. Given the destructive effects of colonialism and imperialism on Indigenous communities, the authors argue for the adoption of a "partnership paradigm" and clearly articulated ethical guidelines for research involving Indigenous peoples in Canada.

Damianakis, Thecia, and Michael R. Woodford. 2012. "Qualitative Research with Small Connected Communities: Generating New Knowledge While Upholding Research Ethics." *Qualitative Health Research* 22, 5: 708–718.

This article addresses the issue of confidentiality when conducting research in small communities where members may be closely connected to one another. More specifi-cally, Thecia Damianakis and Michael R. Woodford focus on the ethical challenges, conceptual and practical, that may arise in this type of setting. They include a visual map that outlines various ethical considerations at multiple stages of the qualitative research process when working with small communities in which people are closely connected, along with suggested actions to take at each stage.

Maiter, Sarah, Laura Simich, Nora Jacobson and Julie Wise. 2008. "Reciprocity: An Ethic for Community-Based Participatory Action Research." *Action Research* 6, 3: 305–325.

Sarah Maiter and her coauthors offer an extensive discussion of reciprocity, includ-ing what it is, what it looks like and how it is embedded in ethical practice. They document multiple forms of reciprocity evident throughout various phases of a CBPR project. Relationship building remained at the core of this research endeavour as diverse people, institutions, organizations and groups engaged in an "exchange of information and culture sharing" (2008: 313). From their participation emerged fruitful ideas for community actions and events that various groups began to plan and execute on their own. Participants experienced mutual benefits through opportunities to develop skills, connect with others, gain new knowledge as well as publish. Yet the authors note that challenges may follow because universities often devalue this type of work, and not all expectations are ever fulfiled. They note that reciprocity involves continuous hard work.

Morrison, Zachary J., David Gregory and Steven Thibodeau. 2012. "'Thanks

for Using Me': An Exploration of Exit Strategy in Qualitative Research."
International Institute for Qualitative Methodology 11 4: 416–427.

> *This article addresses the aftermath of data collection in interview-based research projects. The authors argue that looking ahead to the end of the data-collection phase and planning an exit strategy that considers the participants first is just as important as establishing trust and rapport in the initial stage of the interview process. Based on Zachary J. Morrison's personal experiences of disengaging from his participants (a vulnerable population of obese adolescent boys), the authors argue for a reframing of the typical researcher-participant relationship. They suggest a "participant-researcher" paradigm to help resituate vulnerable participants as foremost in such relationships. The authors call for established protocols to guide how research relationships are ended within the context of qualitative methods, particularly with respect to vulnerable populations who have been part of the research project and therefore may have developed close relationships with the researcher over an extended period of time.*

Rivière, Dominique. 2011. "Looking from the Outside/In: Re-thinking Research Ethics Review." *Journal of Academic Ethics* 9: 193–204.

> *Based on earlier experiences as the principal investigator of a multisite qualitative study whose project was delayed eighteen months due to several rounds of clarification required by an ethics review board, and drawing on her later expertise as a member of the same review board, Dominique Rivière shares her reflections on the ethics review process from both her "outsider" and "insider" perspectives. Specifically, she examines recent changes to the TCPS as she questions policies around regulating research, and challenges current understandings about the relationship between language and power when it comes to obtaining informed consent from participants. Finally, Rivière reflects on the research review process as a practice or a "performance" in which consent forms served as a cue to remind her of her role as a researcher whose responsibility it is to maintain the trust of her participants so that the research will be carried out ethically.*

Tilley, Susan A., Kelly D. Powick-Kumar, and Snezana Ratković. 2009. "Regulatory Practices and School-Based Research: Making Sense of Research/Ethics Review." *Forum Qualitative Sozialforschung/Forum: Qualitative Social Research* 10, 2, Art. 32.

> *Susan Tilley and her coauthors explore the research ethics/review practices of a specific Canadian university REB and a school board research review committee (RRC) in Ontario. The authors analyzed 312 REB applications and ninety-four applications submitted to a school board RRC, and conducted sixteen in-depth,*

open-ended interviews with REB *and* RRC *members. The article discusses the foci of research being conducted in schools, institutional board decisions (especially requests for clarifications) and suggests that more empirical research on* REB *and school board review committee policies and practices is needed.*

Townsend, Anne, and Susan M. Cox. 2013. "Accessing Health Services through the Back Door: A Qualitative Interview Study Investigating Reasons Why People Participate in Health Research in Canada." BMC *Medical Ethics* 14, 40: 1–11.

This article explores ethical issues around research participant recruitment in the field of health research. Specifically, Anne Townsend and Susan M. Cox examine how participants involved in health research seek reciprocity in the form of access to health services that would otherwise not be available to them. The authors highlight the tension between the standard wording of informed consent policies and the subtle coercion of vulnerable participants who are motivated to engage in these types of studies because of concerns related to their own health. The authors call for a "more cautious consent process" (2013: 9), particularly when obtaining informed consent for clinical drug trials for the profoundly ill. They conclude with important questions about recruitment and informed consent policies that need to be asked.

Chapter 4

TRANSITIONING INTO THE FIELD AND COLLECTING DATA

Chapter 2 focused on the construction of a critical qualitative research plan and introduced methods used in qualitative research projects. Chapter 3 explored research ethics, outlining policies and procedures related to the ethics review of qualitative research and describing the challenges of conducting respectful research. This chapter emphasizes student researchers' preparation and movement into the field, a field broadly understood to include physical/geographical space, cyber- and Internet space, and space more generally — the places and spaces where researchers interact with their participants. The complexities of data collection in the context of critical qualitative research and researchers' attempts to enact respectful research praxis are explored. I draw from my doctoral research to illustrate the quandaries that arose for me in the field, some of which I addressed appropriately; others I learned from and continue to question in light of my research experiences since that time.

Inevitably, students I advise tell me how excited they are to begin their data collection, which indicates that they are entering a new phase and making progress. The excitement is attached to the *doing* of research, not so much to the preparation. I remind them that whether they are adequately prepared to collect their data ultimately influences the numbers and kinds of challenges they face when interacting with participants in the research context. The degree of success that students experience is also connected to their willingness to make adjustments as the research process unfolds. The timelines they initially constructed as part of their designs need to be carefully monitored and, if necessary, reconfigured as data collection progresses.

In general, students need to prepare to collect their data when necessary, building on the skills they have or acquiring new skills if possible; they need to exhibit a confidence in their abilities as researchers. It will be difficult to gain access to a research site and recruit participants if students do not exude at least a reasonable level of confidence in their abilities and an awareness of the possible challenges they might face. The effort they extend to building their knowledge and skills will contribute to their heightened confidence.

FIRST STEPS: FINDING PARTICIPANTS

Time and energy are needed to actively recruit participants who fit criteria established for a research project. Even when all the institutional permissions are in place, no guarantee exists that the individuals and communities that researchers hope will agree to participate will do so. Recruitment poses less of a problem when students already have some degree of familiarity, and people and communities are supporting the research they are proposing. This is particularly true of situations in which student researchers have been invited into the context to research initiatives that are community or institutionally identified. However, maintaining access over the research period may at times be difficult, similar to projects in which researchers had no prior connections. As part of the recruitment process, students are responsible for ensuring that potential participants have the correct and full information and are making a noncoerced decision. Ultimately, they will choose whether to participate based on the information provided by the researchers (e.g., information letter, consent form) and personal reasons specific to them, which they may not necessarily explain to the researcher.

A number of recruitment strategies for use in qualitative research are described in detail in the literature. Students have to decide which strategies are most useful for accessing the appropriate people for their research. Common strategies include opportunistic sampling (see Johnson and Clarke 2003) and purposive and convenience sampling. In the case of interviewing, T. Rapley (2004: 17) explains: "The actual 'problem' of recruitment can vary dramatically. When accessing potential interviewees you have to follow many trails, often relying initially on friends and colleagues and then on contacts given by other interviewees." Interacting with one person connects you to another and it repeats, creating a snowball effect. Monique M. Hennink (2007) has written a chapter dedicated to recruitment of focus group participants. When trying to locate people, students can use various hard copy and electronic forms of advertising: flyers, posters, websites, blogs and Twitter.

In general, having some degree of familiarity with the research context and potential participants can be extremely useful for recruitment. In particular, a key supporter connected to context and people can play an instrumental role in assisting student researchers to find participants (Hole 2007a). This is especially the case when other recruitment strategies have failed to produce willing individuals and communities. In the prison context, Geraldine, one of the experienced prison teachers, was a key person. Without her support, I would not have been able to position myself as a researcher in the prison school or collect the comprehensive data I collected. Geraldine assisted me in arranging interviews and dealing with the institutional personnel who interfered at times in micro details of the research process. She helped remind students, new and otherwise, that I was conducting research, observing and writing fieldnotes. She also participated in weekly lunchtime meetings during which I recorded conversations about our work. I was very fortunate. There may be individuals who have a keen interest in the research students are proposing and who can provide student researchers with the support they need to identify individuals to participate. During the initial contact stages, students can search out individuals who may serve in this capacity.

The research focus will influence people's willingness to participate when they are faced with making a decision. In qualitative research, participants are often asked to reveal details about their personal and/or professional lives and experiences. People may be hesitant to do so. Potential participants may be willing to be interviewed, but not so willing to be the subject of observation, considering the process much more of an intrusion, doubly so when a camera is the documentation tool or various visuals are used as data. Women agreed to participate in the research I conducted in the prison because they were very interested in the research focus. They had much to say about schools and education — some said that their children were having similar experiences to the ones they had in schools and they were fearful for their children's future. I was familiar enough to them that a level of trust was established, and they were willing to share their experiences with me. And although I was observing, it was not through the lens of a camera.

If student researchers cannot recruit in the ways they planned, they have to be creative and develop new strategies while ensuring that they follow an ethical process. If they make substantial changes to their recruitment strategies, they may need to submit a modification to the institutional bodies that gave them clearance. Luckily, a request for modification is usually not as comprehensive and time-consuming a task as the initial application.

Recruitment success is necessary to begin the research, but individuals who agree can always have a change of heart. Students will need to develop rapport with participants, a relationship that supports effective communication, which helps sustain participants' engagement with the research, a process that often extends over a lengthy time period. When asking children or adolescents to participate, students may have to extend the rapport to parents, family members and the participants' broader community members, or to agency personnel when the research is focused on a vulnerable population. Students may be able to encourage individuals to participate, but they also have to be as confident as possible that a commitment exists to see the research to completion. Better to choose wisely in the beginning than to regret choices made at a later date. For example, individuals who are willing but very hesitant in the beginning stages or are having difficulty committing to dates for data collection might indicate that they are unlikely to complete their participation. Ultimately, researchers cannot be assured that individuals will remain committed to the conclusion of the project, but keeping communication lines open with participants might help ward off the loss of individual participants as the research proceeds.

Research with individuals from marginalized, vulnerable populations is regularly conducted. As discussed in Chapter 3, institutional permissions that researchers acquire may not provide enough guidance or oversight in areas related to *in situ* ethics. In the bigger picture, the research may be beneficial to those in authority (which is why permission was given), but less helpful to the vulnerable population. In the prison context, women were often being asked to participate in research. They taught me many lessons about respectful research as I bore witness to their experiences with other researchers before my project began. Maggie's description of her participation in research was particularly compelling.

> The women spoke of previous research projects authorized by prison authorities and ethics review committees. They described receiving letters requesting that they take part in interviews, for which they would be paid. Maggie explained to me her participation in a project conducted by a researcher who came from the outside for the sole purpose of conducting research with women in prison. Maggie needed the $10.00 the researcher offered her so she signed the consent form and showed up for the interview at an arranged time. Set up in the room was a video camera, not a tape recorder as she had expected. The consent form had said "taped," not videotaped. The interview focused on personality traits, but shortly into the interview Maggie was questioned about her charges and her experiences of abuse and incest. She told the researcher she was uncomfortable answering questions about those things and that she didn't like being filmed. The researcher's response was to tell her she need not be nervous and to suggest they take a short break, after which they continued, with camera equipment running. Maggie was devastated by a process that forced her to re-live some of her worst nightmares. (Tilley 1998b: 320)

Although women in prison are included in the vulnerable category, they are usually judged to have the capacity to make the decision about whether to participate in research. The authorities knew videotaping was intended, but the participant did not. The intention of focusing on the women's experiences of incest was camouflaged with the more general statement of interest in how women made attachments. It is hard to understand this as anything other than blatant deception through omission to encourage participation and as unethical behaviour on the part of the researcher — tolerated in a prison, but perhaps not in a different context.

It is often difficult to understand the degree of vulnerability from a distance. When in the field, even after gaining participants' permission, student researchers need to continue to ensure that participants understand what is being asked of them and what might possibly happen as a result of them having participated in the research.

Even when participants are committed to involvement in the research, they may change their minds and not continue if they have a negative experience, particularly if they feel researchers have deceived them. Such an experience can lead to an individual's departure and also have a ripple effect that ends with the withdrawal of other participants. The researcher described here had to change her plans because Maggie withdrew and told others; women who had signed up demanded there be no video camera involved or they would not participate.

It is often difficult to gain access to social institutions that have historically made (and continue to make) decisions that affect the lives of those who experience marginalization and inequities and to research participants who are in powerful positions that affect the lives of those not similarly privileged, conducting research described as *studying up* in the literature. (See Kezar 2003 on elites and interviewing; and Aguiar and Schneider 2012 for recent work related to studying up.) Corporate CEOs, administrative bodies of medical schools and government departments, school superintendents and lawyers, for instance, are steeped in cultural capital (e.g., knowledge of research processes and outcomes) that might make them question participating in research, particularly emancipatory, social change–oriented research focused on critiquing systems of which they are members (see TCPS2 2014 for a discussion of the category of critical inquiry). Even if there is an awareness of the need to research those in powerful positions, gaining access and permissions can be difficult. If students are designing research that involves participants and institutions fitting elite categories, they need to recognize the complexities of the situation and find ways to gain and maintain access. For example, their recruitment strategies may include a less than fully transparent description of the purpose. However, the research itself poses no more than minimal risk to the participants; it does not interfere in any way with the participant's right to dignity. When operating without full disclosure conducting critical inquiry, student researchers will have to demonstrate in the institutional ethics review process that the lack of disclosure is necessary for research purposes (see TCPS2 2014, Article 3.7A for a comprehensive discussion of departures from general principles of consent).

Students wanting to conduct research with particular individuals or populations need to ensure that potential participants understand the value of the research to themselves and their communities or for social change in general, as well as from the researcher's perspective of what is to be gained. As discussed in Chapter 2, if research is designed with an emphasis on reciprocity, institutions, communities and individuals may be more willing to say yes when asked to participate in the research. Commitment to reciprocity is demonstrated when research plans include attention to opportunities for the research to also benefit those outside the academic community.

Reciprocity is an expectation built into various qualitative traditions that emphasize the importance of research being reciprocally beneficial. For example, in the case of participatory action research (PAR), reciprocity is an expectation. Participants often contribute to the design of the research and may be involved in data collection and analysis as well as other aspects of the process, as invested in the project as the *outside* collaborating researcher(s). When writing about CBPR, Sarah Maiter and her colleagues (2008: 305), suggest that "the notion of reciprocity — defined as an ongoing process of exchange between parties with the aim of establishing and maintaining equality between parties — can provide a guide to the ethical practice of CBPAR."

In critical qualitative research, reciprocity can take many shapes. Intentional plans for reciprocity can include giving back expertise to the research participants and their communities, and disseminating materials that will benefit the community in very concrete ways (e.g., translate into additional funding for programs or resources). Although plans for reciprocity are articulated at the design stage, the shape that reciprocity ultimately takes may be influenced by what happens in the field as the researcher's knowledge of individuals and context develops. In the prison context, a process was in place for women to move back slowly into the community after a long sentence was served. I trained as a citizen escort, a person who could take the women nearing release out on daily and overnight visits. I have pleasant memories of spending two Christmas holidays taking a woman who was completing a prison term home to her family. Participants in my doctoral research also learned a great deal about their rights as research participants through their participation in my study. Neither of these instances was described in the research plan or REB application as a way to give back to the participants, but emerged as important benefits over the life of the study and beyond.

In some cases, individuals agree to participate to be helpful while also strategically benefitting directly from the research. This is common when research is focused on postsecondary contexts, and the students participate as a way to build their own research skills and knowledge in anticipation of conducting their research in the future.

Individuals are often willing to participate in qualitative research that relates to issues close to home, both personal and/or professional. If the research question is meaningful to them, they may more quickly agree to participate than individuals who are distanced from the research and feel little if any investment. When recruiting individuals, in addition to reaching out to those with extensive knowledge and experience in the research topic (e.g., medical issues and illness, children's reading difficulties, program or institutional change), researchers also need to account for the investment factor. Individuals who feel some degree of investment are less likely to decline to participate (even after consenting) or to withdraw data at a later stage in the project.

Although researchers can never know for sure all the ways in which they may give back to their participants or share in a collaborative and beneficial research relationship, they can from the beginning embed a serious consideration of reciprocity into their planning. If not possible sooner, they can provide opportunities later to hear participants' views on the matter and create possibilities for reciprocity in the moment.

To enhance the success of the recruitment process, student researchers may want to consider the following list of questions:

- Is the research designed in ways that will encourage individuals to want to participate?
- Have participant and community voices been listened to? Will those who invited student researchers into their context still want to participate or encourage others to participate?
- Is there a persuasive rationale for institutional authorities, community leaders or other individuals to agree to participate in the students' research?
- Is the amount of time participants will have to commit to the study reasonable? Is too much being asked of them?
- Based on what student researchers have learned through the recruitment process, are adjustments needed to their research plans? Do such adjustments require a submission for a request for modification from the REB or other authorities that gave approvals for the research in the first place?
- Are explicit forms of reciprocity built into the research design that may be beneficial to the individual and communities being asked to participate?

APPLYING A CRITICAL LENS TO DATA COLLECTION

When research is conducted from critical perspectives using qualitative interpretivist methodologies, issues related to data collection are considered broadly, not limited to the logistics of the process. The methods selected and the collection process planned and enacted will reflect the philosophical, epistemological and ontological assumptions undergirding the methodology chosen. For example, student researchers informed by critical feminist perspectives will factor in the influences their identities and social locations have on the data-collection processes in which they and their participants are involved (e.g., interviewing, observing, filming, producing artistic expressions) and the kinds of data collected. They will be willing to question the limitations of their researcher eye in understanding what it is they have observed, interpreted and documented. Their responsibilities will be more visible as they become less distanced from the participants and can no longer claim the same innocence with regard to details of participants' lives or research contexts. They will understand that their identities and those of their participants (including the ways in which they are socially constructed by race, class, gender, sexual orientation and dis/ability) can influence their choices, decisions and ability to collect data.

Working within this critical framework, researchers will engage in a respectful praxis that provokes them to question how they operationalize their methods and pay attention to the complex ways in which privilege, power and resistance are implicated in the data-collection process. They should also be willing to change plans when necessary but not required if it is to the benefit of participants, communities and research contexts. In the prison context, I considered and questioned the fact that I was a teacher in the only place participants felt a degree of safety. How could interviews and observations affect their safe space? Influence their willingness to participate? Affect the degree of resistance they felt to speak the *truth*? The challenges that students will face when attempting to conduct respectful research will emerge in full force as they move into the field and attempt to translate their research plans into action. This translation requires turning attention and critique to the logistics of the process, which is the emphasis of the sections that follow.

Although finding contexts and individuals willing to participate in research might have been challenging for student researchers, data collection can begin once the participants are in place. The depth and breadth of the data that students collect will be connected to their research questions, methodology and level of degree they are completing (undergraduate/master's/PhD). Working with advisors at the planning stages will help students ascertain the appropriate amount and kinds of data needed.

Collecting Demographic Information

The extent of participant demographic information and personal details to be collected will differ across research contexts. Demographic information, individual or community, provides necessary information and context for the researcher and can influence the data-collection plans. The information required will be directly related to the research focus. When interviews and observations serve as primary data, this information may be gathered when students first meet their participants. In online contexts, demographic information can be accessed during the first virtual interaction.

Demographic information can also be abstracted from representations of data that are already constructed (i.e., interview transcripts, documentation of observations, visuals), during interactions with participants who are producing data (arts-based research and visual data) and through the conventional use of a standard form with questions. The depth/amount of demographic and personal life detail needed to inform a study is not always apparent at the initial stages. Student researchers need to be careful not to overstep when asking for information and intrude in ways participants are not expecting because they might hinder future communications. A straightforward solution is for students to ask for the information that can be easily understood as important to the study and to explain clearly to participants why other information not so explicitly connected is important to obtain.

In some circumstances, researchers may understand exactly what information they need only at (or after) the conclusion of their study. They may be able to return to participants or communities to gather information that they find they need at a later stage of the research, but this is not always possible. Although gathering demographic information may seem straightforward, there can be complications. I found this to be the case in the prison:

> I gathered the majority of the information about the women interviewed through a background information form.... and by culling individual transcripts and extracting personal details given in conversation. At the beginning of the research project, I consciously decided not to push for information about charges and previous incarceration experiences. I believed by not forcing the disclosure of that information, I was being respectful of the participants. In hindsight, I realize the limitations of the demographic information I collected. More information would have contributed to the limited statistical information available on women in prisons (Johnson, H. and Rodgers 1993: 96). I was assuming a matronizing stance, deciding for participants whether or not they would want to contribute that information if asked. Upon reflection however, I wonder

how soliciting information about previous criminal charges would have affected interviews. The participants were informed of the intent of the study, that I was interested in exploring schooling experiences. Probing for more personal information about charges and criminal records may have affected the dynamics of the interviews. (Tilley 1998a: 20–21)

Student researchers may need to gather demographic information from individuals and communities to explore their research questions. Participant resistance may surface due to fears that information collected will compromise confidentiality or result in negative outcomes for an individual or community (i.e., Indigenous population and concerns with use made of information collected through the Canadian census). Student researchers must communicate clearly their purpose for asking participants for such information.

Common Data-Collection Methods

Although it is impossible for student researchers to be prepared for every eventuality when collecting data, being as organized as possible is an achievable goal. Students should not take for granted that they have the innate abilities (although a few may) to collect data without spending time educating themselves about the intricacies of their methods.

DOWN TO THE BASICS: CONDUCTING INTERVIEWS

Many decisions have to be made in preparation for conducting interviews, regardless of type of interview, including those related to what might be considered mundane details. Students who address such details at the initial stages will help to ensure that data collection proceeds without foreseeable problems arising. For instance, they need to have basic supplies (i.e., pen, pencil and paper; laptop; electronic equipment) close at hand; they should not have to search for supplies as interviews begin. Equipment needs to be in place and checked to see whether it is in working condition. In terms of interviews, this means acquiring and testing digital recorders, microphones, and camera and video equipment before interviews begin. If students choose to collect data using sophisticated equipment, they need to be fully trained in its use before moving into the field. In the past, students I advised reported not being aware that equipment was damaged until after the interview had taken place — for example, a video camera rolling but not recording. Good practice includes checking equipment prior to and sporadically through the collection process. Taking a break five or ten minutes into the interview or observation to see that the conversation and actions are recorded is a prudent practice. Backup equipment, which runs simultaneously with the primary recording device during the interviews, is sometimes used to ensure that data is captured.

Student researchers need to think ahead to be prepared. They should bring a minimum of two hard copies of research documents to the interview sessions, including consent forms, information letters and interview schedules: one for the researchers' records and the other for participants to keep. Students should not assume that participants will bring such documents, even when participants had copies sent to them before the interview session. Electronic versions of documents can be referred to at the time of online interactions.

The decision of where to conduct interviews is important; although it is addressed in the research plan, it is most often determined when students move into the field. Although the location needs to be convenient for participants, the *most* convenient location for the participant may not be conducive to a productive interview or an appropriate site. Such locations include participants' kitchens, dining rooms and other house sites, in which possibilities exist for participants to continue with home life tasks while the interview is recorded, including answering the phone and dealing with requests from children and family members. Interviews conducted in more public spaces, including popular coffee shops, can result in the production of noisy and inaudible recordings and may lead to concerns related to confidentiality as people move in and out of the context and participant voices are unintentionally heard by others in addition to the researcher.

Such locations may work at times if participants (and researchers) are aware of the possible complications and the location is structured in ways that honours the need for a focused time and place devoted to the interview. When children are participating in interviews, more naturalistic contexts might be the best choice of locations. Lori Irwin and Joy Johnson (2005: 826) describe the complications of conducting ethnographic interviews with primary-aged children at a home site and conclude:

> We need to tailor the interview space to the expressional style of the child, and in doing so, we need to think beyond the traditional spaces that are often associated with high-quality interviews. Some children might best be interviewed as they walk, play, or are enjoying outdoor spaces, in what we refer to as kinetic conversations. Although kinetic conversations can be technically challenging, our experiences to date have been successful; these interview contexts yield more complete and more naturalistic expressions of children's experiences for some children.

While trying to honour a participant's last-minute site change, a student explained to me that she moved the interview to the teachers' lounge in the school, where she and the participant sat in the corner recording their conversation. The problems with such a location are multiple. Even though it was after the school day ended, teachers continued moving in, out and about the room. The individual who was participating was in plain view, and the noise in the room affected the condition of the data recorded. As well, the location may have influenced what the participant was willing to say. Ultimately, the student regretted agreeing to the change of location because the conversation recorded represented stops and starts, disjointed conversation that was difficult to make sense of when listened to and represented on the transcript. The participant had trouble clarifying meaning during the member-checking process. *In situ*, students may have to negotiate a change of space that is not only based on participant choice but also makes sense in terms of interview quality and resulting data. Participants may not always have an adequate understanding of the problems of their preferred location and be quite willing to work out an alternative plan once given an explanation.

The decisions students make related to the interview process will reflect the researcher positioning and methodology. After working in the prison before conducting the research, I was positioned as someone familiar. The in-depth, open-ended interviews were useful for gathering extensive data related to the experiences I was exploring with the women. I provided preliminary guiding questions to the participants prior to the interview date. I wanted them to have time to think about the research focus and consider the questions. In addition to other subjects, they would be asked to discuss their memories of secondary school experiences, which for many of the participants had happened a number of years prior to the interview. Some of the participants indicated that they were a little nervous about the interview, afraid they would not be able to answer questions. I wanted to alleviate their concerns. I was not attempting to access a grand narrative, but to explore with them the memories that remained from those years of secondary schooling. Providing guiding questions beforehand gave the women time to think back and formulate responses that we could expand upon during the interview session.

If not experienced in interviewing, students should practise the method for preliminary preparation. Preparatory interviews may mean convincing a student colleague, friend or relative to serve as a substitute participant, so that student researchers hone their skills. Some students may conduct a pilot study as a way to develop their interviewing skills. At the least, practising with the recording device and interview schedule is essential. For those students who have never participated in research or interviews, agreeing to participate in interviews might be useful as preparation. They will gain some experience of what it feels like to be a participant/interviewee.

When he was interviewed about his transcription work connected to a research study, Ken describes his experience, and what he learned, by shifting to a participant position from that of person paid to transcribe research recordings:

He [Ken] was able to relate to the original research participants' experiences after shifting into that position [of participant] himself. An empathetic tone replaced the original judgmental stance that he initially acknowledged. He referred to some of his comments in his notes [related to his transcription work] as "snarky comments" but not "viciously snarky." Ken played a role in the judging, of which he suggests, the participants were wary. Through a shift in positioning, Ken was able to develop a more informed perspective. At one point he stated, "I think I understand the ladies [participants in the study] a little better now." After reading his transcript, Ken also commented on the ways in which the words recorded may not have reflected the ideas he was trying to convey during his interview even though he agreed they were the words he had spoken. (Tilley 2003a: 16–17)

Conducting interviews with a vulnerable group can be more challenging than with other participant categories (see Cotnam-Kappel 2014 regarding youth participants). It is especially important for researchers to continue to ask themselves if what is happening, even when part of the plan, is respectful practice. As Daphne Patai (1994: 31) states: "The personal interview is ... a particularly precise locus for ethical issues to surface — unless, that is, we are (as indeed we often are) suppressing our awareness of these issues."

When I first began interviews with the women in the prison, I carefully explained that we would start with the first question, but we did not have to follow in any predetermined order; the questions provided were being used to get the conversation started and to provide direction so that the interactions were relevant to the research focus. I was very sensitive to the fact that these women had had difficult life experiences, but planned to focus on school experience, keeping a distance from their life troubles. At the time, I believed this to be a way to have at least a limited control over the conversation:

Anna's interview reminds me of how amiss I was in believing that I could control what happened in the interview. In public schools, there is an attempt to create an appearance of separating school life and what I refer to as "real" life. I was operating with a false belief that the women could separate out their school experiences from their life experiences. I decided I would focus on their memories of schooling and not their memories of childhood and in particular abuse. However I attempted to constrain the route questions took, it was impossible to limit the extent to which they led into descriptions of Anna's experiences of abuse. I again had to face the realization that no matter how respectful I was trying to be, as I conducted my research, I may be responsible for opening up wounds the women were trying to heal. (Tilley 1998a: 47)

Although understanding that I was conducting in-depth, open-ended interviews, I was holding on to positivist assumptions that fuel beliefs that the researcher/ interviewer holds the power in the interview context as the individual taking and keeping control. Michel Foucault (1980), whose work informed the theoretical framework of the prison research, helped me to understand why I could not control the interview in ways I had planned. He explains power as a circulating force — not static and captive in any one individual's hands. In the case of qualitative interviewing (including the structured version), it would be naïve to think that one individual, including the interviewer, holds power throughout the process. Participants make other choices and will decide what and how much information to give in response to questions.

In many instances, I needed to adjust the dates and times of the interviews I scheduled. Even though I scheduled appointments for interviews that suited the participants and sent reminders the day before, often circumstances changed and I found myself alone in the room with equipment in hand. An institutional complication may have occurred that kept the participant away, or it might have been a personal matter. The women continued to want to participate, but the choice was often out of their hands.

Decisions about the timing of interviews will be made throughout the data-collection process. Sometimes changes occur as a result of a participant's request and sometimes they are a complication of the researchers' making. Student researchers need to prepare for the eventuality that such changes happen in context. When interviews are rescheduled, the daily research timelines are affected, as well as the overall project timelines, which is why it is important not to have an overly tight time schedule. I have heard student researchers speak disparagingly, at times from a place of arrogance, of their participants not following the assigned data-collection schedule. I remind them they must practise respect and try to find a way to complete the data collection that can work for their participants.

I kept notes documenting my experiences before, during and after interviews. These notes contained logistical matters. I contextualized the interview act as well as recorded descriptions of the interview process. I elaborated upon what would not be captured on the audio recordings, including the impressions made through the visual aspects of the process. I explained to participants my purpose for note-taking, including jotting down questions prompted from what they were saying so that I would not forget the connections I wanted to make or disrupt their train of thinking when they were speaking. I inserted the thoughts and questions I had noted into the conversation after the participant finished speaking.

Student researchers need to continue to strengthen their skills and expand their knowledge about interviewing as they conduct their research. As they apply their critical reflexivity to their research processes, they will engage in a questioning that will send them back to the literature to explore possible solutions. As well, when students keep in close communication with their advisors, the advisors can be easily consulted on issues that occur as a result of the interviewing process experienced.

COMPLEXITIES OF GROUP CONVERSATIONS

Although similar logistics need to be addressed in the case of both individual and focus group interviewing, the latter has specific needs related to the use of groups (Bloor et al. 2001; Kreuger 1994). As mentioned in Chapter 2, these needs reflect various aspects of group interviewing: group size, number of focus group sessions needed (one or multiple), homogeneous or heterogeneous groupings and degree of direction from the moderator (student researcher) to participants.

The number of participants will affect the interview experience for all those involved and the resulting data. There can be too many or too few participants. In the case of too many, there can be challenges regarding the interaction patterns; not enough time or space to engage the voices of all the participants or the complexities of the group dynamics as the numbers of participants increase. There may be those who are uninhibited and speak freely, and others who will be reticent to voice thoughts because of others participating in the interview. Although student researchers will have more difficulty paying attention to the influence of group dynamics as the number of participants increases, too few participants may result in limited conversation and ultimately thin data that is not useful to the researcher. Choosing the most suitable number of participants is an important decision that requires some thought on the part of the student researcher (see Onwuegbuzie et al. 2015).

For all interviews, researchers should ensure that the equipment is in working order before starting and during the interview. Before focus group interviews, students will need to make *technical* decisions that are different from those relevant to interviewing individuals. In the case of face-to-face focus group interviewing, microphones need to be placed strategically in the room to ensure that all voices and contributions are recorded. The degree of familiarity the researcher has with the participants and their voices influences the process undertaken. At the beginning of the focus group interview, each participant can speak a few words and identify him- or herself; this will help to create a base from which the researcher can identify who is speaking as conversation continues. Asking participants to identify themselves each time they speak may work, but it can be disruptive to the flow of conversation, and often participants will forget to declare themselves and then have to be stopped and reminded. Student researchers also need to consider the logistics of transcription when preparing for focus group interviews (Barbour 2007; Tilley 2003a). Focus group interactions are more difficult to transcribe because of the multiple voices and interactions recorded (see Chapter 5 for a full discussion of transcription).

In the context of the focus group interview, students will have to decide the role they will play as moderator in contexts that can vary from requiring direct question and response interaction to open and collaborative conversation. When working within critical perspectives, students will most likely choose a process closer to the latter. In collaborative participatory research, the researcher/moderator may function as a group member, contributing fully to the conversation.

The moderator will have to be skillful and observant, able to direct and redirect the conversation to encourage individuals to contribute to the conversation while trying to manage the amount of talk from participants who overpower the interactions and to assess when dominant discourses are silencing differing perspectives. It is important to always be aware of the power in play among the participants themselves and among participants and the moderator that influences the conversation dynamics and ultimately the data.

Focus groups can serve different purposes and add varying amounts of value to a research project. David Morgan and his colleagues (2008: 195) describe the importance of using focus groups in different ways to produce useful research data. They suggest the benefits of an emergent design: group conversations organized for different purposes based on what happens when participants are brought together as designated group members and as connections are made across and within groups. This degree of openness can lead to prospective useful reorganization and change to the focus group process that better suits the research purpose. They write of repeated focus groups instead of a single meeting. Repeated focus groups can help you gain insight into the "ways in which belief systems and ... interaction styles are revealed through interactions."

Focus group conversations can be organized around stimulus and projective techniques such as to provoke and support ongoing conversation (Morgan et al. 2008). When the researcher is open to making decisions *in situ*, data collection can be modified as needed based on what is learned in initial interactions. Overall research goals should be factored into decisions of what kinds of focus groups are required.

In preparation for conducting focus group interviews, student researchers might consider the following questions:

- What size and mix of participants will work best in relation to the research focus?

- What preparations have been made to allow for the complexities of group dynamics in the focus group situation to be observed?
- What strategies will be employed to ensure as equal participation as possible across individuals?
- What strategies will be used to manage the power relations embedded in the group dynamics?

OBSERVING IN THE FIELD

Similar to planning for interviewing, a number of logistical decisions need to be made when choosing to collect data through observation: the *what* and *how* of observation need to be decided. Students will have already articulated many of the *what* decisions in the early stages of designing their research, understanding that changes in plans may be necessary as the collection process progresses (refer to Chapter 2). Plans for observations will be reflective of the methodology, connected to research focus and questions, and context-specific; what is possible in one research context may not be in another. The challenge for students is to engage in a critical process that will produce the data needed.

When situated within a critical postmodern framework, student researchers are aware that their researcher positioning and social locations will influence what they are able to observe, similar to an interview conversation. What they see/perceive will be interpreted through the critical research lens they apply. Alan Peshkin (2001: 242) writes of individuals accessing a "sweep of alternative lenses" that are often working in tandem, through which they can observe research contexts and participants, the phenomenon under study:

> I offer a sweep of alternative lenses for consideration: patterns, time, emic, positionality, ideology, theme, metaphor, irony and silence. Each one invites researchers to perceive in a certain way. They are not mutually exclusive ways of learning or exhaustive of the ways of perceiving. Moreover, we do not use easily one lens at a time, because just as we begin to see things in one way, other things come into focus and get connected, so that we move away from our starting point.

In addition to a "sweep of alternative lenses," student researchers have a variety of observational strategies that fall on a continuum from which they can choose. For example, they may take a distanced perspective by directly observing and having no intentional interactions with people and context, or choose a degree of involvement as observer-participant who is partially or more fully involved in the context (Patton 2002). In the prison, I observed from a distance as well as when positioned as participant-observer and at times observed simultaneously while working in my role as teacher in the classroom. I was aware that wherever I was situated on the observation continuum, my body contributed to shaping the context (see Reid et al. 1996).

Conducting observations can be tricky, even when the logistics have been dealt with to student researchers' and advisors' satisfaction. For example, individuals who agreed to be observed may not have fully understood (even though details were explained) the impact of the process on them personally (i.e., the feeling of being under another's gaze) or professionally (i.e., the influence of the added gaze on their professional practice) and then decide against participating after experiencing the process.

The most dramatic and uncomfortable reaction I remember when I was observing was from Irene during one of our morning meetings in the prison classroom. I was explaining the research process to the group because a number of new students were in attendance. Clearly Irene (who was not a new addition) had been uncomfortable with my role as observer:

> I talk a little bit about the research. Geraldine asks if the new students have been noticing me taking notes and Irene says, "I'm beginning to think you're a cop." After she speaks there is silence. I am shocked and ask Irene when she first started thinking that. She says, "Well, the last couple of days. You are always writing. Maybe you could be an undercover cop." I ask her if there are any other reasons she thinks that and she says "No." There is dead silence again so I ask, "Do you think Geraldine would let me in here to do this if I was a cop?" After a few moments Irene says, "Well, no, I don't think so, of course not." Geraldine picks it up there and laughs. She says, "No, I don't let cops come in here." (Participant observation, Tilley 1998a: 40)

Sometimes I was sitting or standing away from the participants recording observations; other times I wrote notes about an interaction that was happening or just completed. The women were used to seeing me writing things down. My heart sank upon hearing Irene's accusation. I had spent enough time in the context to know that once trust was broken, it was next to impossible to regain. It was important to face Irene's accusation the moment it was voiced. Geraldine, who was held in high regard by Irene and others, fortunately did not hesitate to tell the women that I was who I said I was, not an undercover officer; otherwise, I may not have been able to continue the research. The loss of a research participant and possible closing down of a project is rare after access and permissions have been given, research has begun and data are in the process of being collected, but it is not unheard of. Unanticipated events can influence the outcomes of a study if *in situ* complications are not dealt with immediately. It is hard to prepare for unexpected and troubling interactions beyond recognizing the possibility and thoughtfully responding in the moment.

Discussions of how to document observations through the use of fieldnotes and various forms of note-taking are addressed in the literature (Sanjek 1990; Tjora 2006; Walford 2009). Students will have included processes for documenting their observations in their research plan. However, in the research context they may have to be inventive, finding alternatives that serve their purposes better. I constructed fieldnotes based on participant observation and the observations I recorded from my distanced and uninvolved stance. I recorded significant events as well as the mundane of classroom life and my reactions to both. I used pencil and paper to write jot-notes and constructed diagrams to keep observation records. I used these notes to produce more comprehensive fieldnotes, fleshed-out versions of my interpretations. I also kept a book in the classroom, in which I included jot-notes of what I was documenting. Women were invited to consider what I had written and add commentary of their own. However, after reading the notes, few chose to make any additions.

As observations became more time-intensive, I started jotting down words and phrases that I elaborated upon later. Even with the shortened version of note-taking, I realized I was interrupting the flow of interactions as I turned my mental notes into writing, "even if inscription is simply a matter of, as we say, 'making a mental note,' the flow of action and discourse is interrupted, turned to writing" (Clifford 1990: 51).

Although many students will start with different skill levels and observation experience, they will hopefully gain greater capacity as they conduct their research. They will need to factor in their skill development as part of their data analysis (i.e., recognize the limitations of the earliest observation data on analysis performed later). Although students will likely recognize their lack of skill immediately and move to improve quickly, the more subtle challenges of the data-collection method may take longer to piece together.

I found that observing took tremendous concentration and I was concerned that I could not capture all the details needed, especially during the initial stages. At one point in the study, I carved out a six-week block during which I was a participant-observer fully interacting in the context while observing. This strategy was more challenging than the more distanced positioning. At that time, I decided to add an additional step to my observation and documentation process.

> [I] recorded key words and phrases to use as a reminder of what had happened. During lunch hour I taped a description of the morning

activities. I would use the pieces of paper I had been jotting notes on and verbally expand on them using the recorder. I did the same after school was dismissed. I would go home and immediately record the afternoon's happenings using my jottings as a guide. It was important to record my observations as soon as possible so that the interactions, my observations, were still fresh in my mind. (Tilley 1998a: 188–189)

The downside of such a process was the number of recordings that accumulated to be transcribed later. I stopped recording when I reached what I considered the point of data saturation — after what I documented, based on my observations, became repetitive with no new data added.

Currently, when multiple technologies are available to use when conducting observations, students with the necessary knowledge and resources may choose the technological route. However, although technology offers many possibilities, it also has a downside, and students must be familiar with its limitations. For instance, when student researchers use the commonly used video camera, which is useful as an observation tool, they must not forget that the tool is in their hands; they choose the direction in which the camera lens is pointed and ultimately interpret and construct the meanings of the actions and talk recorded.

Jo-Anne Reid and her colleagues (1996: 88) describe a project in which there were multiple human observers and video and audio technology to "counterbalance a reliance on observer judgment" when observing classroom interactions. However, the technology introduced further complications for understanding the observations:

> The problem of inconsistency of "seeing" was quickly compounded. While the observers would not always agree on what they were seeing, their observations could not necessarily be supported *or* [emphasis in original] discounted by evidence on the videotapes. The audiotape recorder was similarly unhelpful. These machines were apparently "seeing" and "hearing" the same people and events quite differently from us — and from each other.

The camera provides an additional eye for the researcher, and as such, also contributes to the production of partial, contestable and multiple truths (see Gallagher and Kim 2008; Heath et al. 2010). A belief that technology can help the researcher capture truths better is connected more to positivist assumptions than postmodern critical perspectives.

Choice of participants and research contexts will determine, at least in part, the appropriateness of technological assistance as well as the ethical issues that might ensue as a result of technologies used. For me, using cameras and video equipment, filming or producing visuals was not a consideration. I was researching a marginalized group who already lived under an authoritative, often punishing gaze of cameras. During the research, women told stories of previous times when their faces had been captured on camera and of the repercussions that followed:

> Part of the regular school day was an early morning meeting from 9:00 a.m. until 10:00 a.m. when students and teachers met as a group. As the research project progressed, questions about the process and discussions about ethics and rights of participants surfaced and were discussed during those meetings. Women described past experiences of research and media investigations. Deidre, who had had multiple experiences of being video-taped and photographed, told of how an old news file that included a picture of women in prison, with her face up front, was re-circulated three years after it was taken. She had not disclosed her history of incarceration to her employers. The day after the picture was reprinted, she was fired from her position. (Tilley 1998a: 37)

Deidre had secured employment and worked in her job during that three-year period without disclosing that she had been incarcerated. Someone in the community recognized her in the picture and reported it to her employer. Even though she had been a dedicated and respected worker, Deidre was subsequently fired. Although she was legally compelled to disclose her past on her application, she was fearful she would never find employment if her prison history was divulged. Visuals such as photographs and film images have a long lifespan, extending the possibilities of a reappearance.

In the prison context, I sometimes played the role of observer and teacher simultaneously. I wrote notes, aware of the limitations of what I was able to capture related to the broad exchanges I witnessed and when focused explicitly on a specific incident happening. I questioned the possibilities of being both teacher and observer simultaneously. What might be lost or gained? How was the teaching and learning changed as a result of me observing? The moment described here provides an illustration:

> During a writing exercise, I am conversing with Lorna. She begins critiquing her experience of being an incarcerated woman and I decide that what she is saying is important to record. I want her words on paper so I pick up my pen and start to jot down some things. I continue to keep eye contact as much as possible even to the point of letting the pen scratch along the page without the assistance of my eyes, hoping the end result will be legible. I notice her start to hesitate and falter a little. This note-taking is intruding into our conversation [and the writing lesson]. It influences

what is and will be said. The documenting act changes the experience for both teacher and student. (Participant observation, Tilley 1998a: 188)

Although I had accumulated much knowledge about the school, teachers and participants, it did not mean that I interpreted Lorna's hesitations accurately. What was clear in the exchange was that teaching and observing simultaneously had the potential to interfere with student learning. When the students' learning might be detrimentally affected, my teaching responsibilities took precedence over my role as observer. Based on my in-the-moment reflexive critique of my work as observer, I stopped my note-taking on that occasion, delegating my observation activity to secondary standing.

When applying a critical reflexivity to student researchers' data-collection experience, student researchers will hopefully be better able to understand their process. When I began conducting my observations, I did not fully comprehend the *below-the-surface* disruptions of what I was doing. I understood the impact on the women more clearly when Marjorie, a participant, described to me how she felt each morning upon her arrival to the classroom, the only location in the prison without cameras:

> She knew that once she crossed the border between rotunda and the classroom the all-seeing eyes of the cameras could not follow her every movement. Her description prompted me to reflect upon my own camera-eye, as researcher. In the prison school, I was observing the observed. I was adding to the glare, a new set of eyes, albeit a different kind, adding to the ones the women already lived with. As researcher, as participant-observer, I felt I disrupted their safe place, unobtrusively remembering scenes, words, voices. Throughout the process, I was led to question the respectfulness of that added glare. (Tilley 1998b: 321–322)

Observation (technologically sophisticated or otherwise) is complicated. The degree to which researchers/observers will disrupt research contexts and the lives of participants can only be prematurely estimated at the planning stages. Whether data collection comes to a successful completion will be connected to researchers' willingness to negotiate a process that takes on a life of its own once begun.

Although the adage "practice makes perfect" may not hold true in all or any cases, certainly practice can contribute to improvements. I prepared to conduct observations in the prison by reading about ways to observe and practised observing in my everyday world (in qualitative research courses and independently), hoping to develop the level of skill required. Ultimately, my learning was deepened through the research process. As students prepare to begin conducting observations, they may want to consider the following questions:

- Will multiple perspectives be combined to enhance observations?
- Will the role that silence might play in the research context, the complexities of the silences be addressed? (See Mazzei 2003 for a discussion of categories of silence.)
- Will attention be paid to what is not seen as well as what is within the range of vision?
- What strategies will be in place to film participants in situations where others located in the research context need to be excluded (e.g., classroom, drug rehabilitation centre)?
- How will participants be encouraged/supported not only to begin but also to continue to participate in the observations?
- Is there a backup plan in place that can be implemented when the desired number of observations outlined in the research plan are not permitted/conducted?

Observation is a data-collection method that can be time-intensive and can introduce a host of complications. When designing their studies, students need to be careful that they do not underestimate or overreach the requirements for data collection in relation to their degree program (e.g., understand what is appropriate for undergraduate, master's or doctoral programs). For example, conducting a series of observations may be more suited to master's- or doctoral-level research rather than an undergraduate research requirement. Some undergraduate and master's (and possibly doctoral-level) students may not have had the needed time and experience to develop the observational skills and experience required, or the time allocated for the research component of the degree may be too limited. Advisors will help student researchers construct a plan that outlines a reasonable data-collection process that suits their skills and research focus. Based on my experience of advisement, it is more likely that students will have too little time allocated for data collection than too much. In the case of the latter, it will not be a burden for students to end their study well within time limits; however, the former situation will create problems later in the process.

JOURNAL WRITING: PRODUCING DATA

The research journal introduced in Chapter 2 can serve as a space in which students write about important aspects of their research experience. They can record critiques of the research process, including the choices and decisions they make that ultimately influence the outcome of the study. Journal entries can provide a view into the research context. When practising their critical reflexivity through the data-collection process, students need to ask the question *why* consistently. Why do I believe this and not that? They also need to regularly question the appropriateness of the decisions they make. Why am I making this decision and not that one? Asking why is a way to uncover beliefs and assumptions that are influencing the data-collection decisions. Their responses to such self-questioning can be recorded in their research journals and used later in the students' explanations, contributing to a transparency of process. This line of questioning can shape the data-collection process *in situ*, at times creating a need for a change in the initial research plans.

Students can decide on the most appropriate organization of the journal to suit their purposes, whether their entries will be recorded electronically or by hand. The pen-and-paper method may be somewhat outdated, but it is convenient when one wakes up in the middle of the night with a great idea, and the computer is in another location. The suggestions of Yvonna S. Lincoln and Egon G. Guba (1985: 327) for structuring a research journal continue to be useful: the journal consists of three separate sections, which include the daily schedule and logistics of the study, a personal diary that provides the opportunity for catharsis and reflection, and a methodological log. Whatever the sections included, student researchers need to be organized and consistent with entries, dating each as written. Students may want to refer to their original entries as they continue and experience challenges/ contradictions in the research process planned.

Journals can be used as a form of data construction/collection in the early stages of research, before students enter the field to interview or conduct observations. The journal is a tool useful up to the completion of the research; when well-organized, it contains data to explain aspects of the research process, which can be used in isolation or to provide fuller explanations in conjunction with other data. The documentation of the research process in journal entries can play an important role when used in the writing of the methodology chapter in the thesis and dissertation: building data that help provide a grounded understanding.

In the qualitative world, journals are used extensively for a variety of purposes. Rachelle D. Hole (2007a) used journaling to explore the ways in which her privileged positioning affected the research process. She used pivotal moments recorded in her journal in her analysis of the complexities associated with identity issues, reciprocity and reflexivity. Journal entries provide space for researchers to make sense of their data and research process, as well as to understand researchers' reactions to data content, particularly when the data is connected to sensitive topics (e.g., see Sinding and Aronson 2003 about end-of-life care). Mahoney (2007: 580), who maintained a fieldwork journal, identified its utility as much more than a mere tool for documenting research practices and decision-making. Researchers and participants can engage individually or together in producing journal entries for use as data.

Journal writing takes organization, energy and persistence; researchers are often exhausted during the data-collection phase, and writing in their journals can easily be relegated until later.

Entries might include visuals representing the research process: artistic representations, photos, diagrams and maps; some of these entries will never be seen outside the journal, but are helpful to the researcher constructing a fuller picture of the research process.

The opening excerpt at the beginning of Chapter 1 of this book was an entry I initially wrote in my research journal and later included in my dissertation. I did not know at the time of writing that I would use the entry in my dissertation; it was available because I documented aspects of my experience and developing understandings early in my studies.

COLLECTING SUPPORT DOCUMENTS

Researchers can search for documents of various sorts (official or otherwise) that can be useful in their research projects. They will be familiar with databases and library resources to search for documents useful to the exploration of their research questions and to assist them in developing comprehensive understandings of historical, cultural and contextual knowledge related to their research. Government documents and archives can also be useful.

Documents come in various shapes and forms, public and private, historical and current, and may serve as primary or secondary data. When discussing textual analysis, Charmaz (2006b) writes of elicited texts and extant texts. Found photographs can be used as documents to construct narratives of historical and social phenomena, and community and personal lives (Mitchell and Allnut 2008; Rose 2007).

In educational research, the formal curriculum and program guides, and government local/provincial/federal policies pertaining to education are often included in the documents analyzed. For her doctoral research, *Teachers Without Borders: Experiences, Transitions and Identities of Refugee Women Teachers from Yugoslavia*, Snezana Ratković (2014) created a database of documents that included a variety of sources, including the Canadian Charter of Rights and Freedoms, the Canadian Council for Refugees, Citizenship and Immigration documents and Ministry of Education and Ontario College of Teachers publications.

Student researchers will need to decide which documents (if any) will serve as data in their study based on their usefulness to their context-specific research and questions and to take time to explore possibilities.

PLANNING FOR WHAT MIGHT HAPPEN DOWN THE ROAD

Even though student researchers have a research design with a beginning, middle and end, the research process is not linear but circular, with a continuous doubling back as the process evolves. Students have to be willing to adjust their plans to successfully move the research forward. For various (unforeseeable) reasons, participants who agreed to a process and have given their consent may change their minds. This may mean that a participant, who is seated with an interview about to begin, requests a change from a digitally taped interview to a conversation the researcher records by hand, or a participant's short notice of a withdrawal from particular aspects of the process (i.e., is no longer willing to be part of the focus group interview or observations previously planned). Student researchers need to be able to work through the unexpected challenges, remembering always that although they may be 100 percent invested in the completion of their research, participants are often committed to a much lesser degree.

When student researchers move into the field to collect data, they need to strategize ways to ensure that they keep connected to their advisors and the supports available through their programs and university contexts. They need to maintain communication lines while they are in the field, which may mean taking the initiative to book regular meetings to check in with their advisor. It is too late to ask advisors questions related to data collection when data have already been collected. Students can access their advisor's expertise to help them complete their data-collection process successfully. For example, it is useful to ask the advisor to listen to the first interview recorded and read the resulting transcript to give advice on aspects of the interview and transcription process that will help in the interviews that follow; a similar activity can be followed in relation to initial observation.

Undergraduate and master's-level students need to consider the timelines of the program and what can be accomplished within that period. Rather than building a research plan within a particular methodology, such as ethnography or PAR, they often plan generic qualitative research projects (Caelli, Ray and Mill 2003), collecting primary data through interviewing and/or observation or other data-collection methods, but not following all the criteria of specific qualitative methodologies. Students completing PhD studies may make very different choices, having longer timelines and previous research experience and extensive methodological knowledge.

It is important for students to be flexible as they move from being planners to conducting research and collecting their data. It is almost a given that many things will happen for which students have not prepared. Giving some thought to possible alternatives to their research plans will be useful prior to collecting their data:

- Include more than a minimal number of participants from the beginning. It is not unusual to have someone withdraw from a study for a variety of reasons, personal and otherwise.
- Be prepared for participants needing to change agreed-upon dates and times for data collection. Have enough leeway to be able to reschedule.

- Remember to plan exiting the field/context, ensuring that participants are not surprised that the researcher is leaving. Caution is needed, especially in the case of vulnerable populations such as children.
- Before completing the data collection and leaving, student researchers need to discuss with participants what kinds of communication might continue afterward. Researchers may have to postpone the departure if participants are having difficulty ending the relationship.
- Remember that student researchers will have earned a degree as a result of the research, which is a great incentive to work through the challenges that emerge. This is not the case for the participants who have contributed time and energy to the student researchers' research endeavour.

MOVING ON

After data are collected, students must find ways to analyze what they have accumulated. Some data will be analyzed in raw form — for example, artistic works, visuals and poetic creations. For data collected through interviewing and observation, transcripts are often constructed for the purposes of analysis.

Chapter 5 provides an in-depth discussion of transcription, a process commonly used in qualitative research, but rarely addressed in comprehensive ways in the qualitative research literature. The chapter emphasizes the questioning of assumptions influencing the work of transcription and highlights transcription as much more than the mundane process most often described.

Annotated Bibliography

Barrett, Margaret S., and Janet Mills. 2009. "The Inter-Reflexive Possibilities of Dual Observations: An Account from and Through Experience." *International Journal of Qualitative Studies in Education* 22, 4: 417–429.

Margaret Barrett and Janet Mills document their use of "dual observations" as an important part of their ethnographic case study that explores teaching and learning music. Data were collected through interviews (small group and individual) as well as observations. Barrett and Mills recount their reflexive process of merging their two perspectives as a way of mutual sense-making, which allowed for deep conversations regarding the disparities in their renderings and rememberings. Central to their conversation was the way in which their backgrounds, identities, expertise, experiences, role negotiations and connections to the topic under study influenced not only what they noticed and why but also how they came to understand and experience both co-investigator- and researcher-participant relationships.

Breidenstein, George. 2007. "The Meaning of Boredom in School Lessons: Participant Observation in the Seventh and Eighth Form." *Ethnography & Education* 2, 1: 93–108.

> *Researcher George Breidenstein recounts his study of students' daily lives and their enactments of boredom. Using participant observation, video observations, and interviews in two different school settings, he explicates some of the challenges associated with doing this type of research, including a) his limited experience with the phenomenon under study, particularly at the time of the investigation; b) realizations that he has been gravitating to action-oriented individuals perhaps at the expense of others (the more quiet and unassuming students); c) a growing awareness of the ways in which researcher presence may alter students' behaviours; and d) difficulties deriving "verbal" and "collective" understandings of the phenomenon. It is not until he gets involved in classroom life and sits at a desk among the students that he can get a glimpse into boredom through his own and others' experiences.*

Cook, Catherine. 2011. "Email Interviewing: Generating Data with a Vulnerable Population." *Journal of Advanced Nursing* 68, 6: 1330–1339.

> *This article addresses the recruitment and interviewing of participants online as opposed to traditional face-to-face research participation. In her study, Catherine Cook uses online recruitment methods as a means to gain access to potential participants who might otherwise be excluded from research. She argues that hurdles such as "geographical distance, incompatible time frames, clinicians' 'gate-keeping' and participants' desire for anonymity for physical or emotional reasons" (2011: 1130) may be eliminated through online methods. Cook outlines the details of her recruitment process; data collection; and the feminist, poststructuralist approach she chose to analyze e-mail exchanges, along with ethical considerations specific to this method of data collection. She concludes that rich data may be gathered through e-mail interviews; however, to ensure the ethical care of participants, empathic communication skills on the part of researchers is paramount for executing a successful study.*

Herron, Rachel, and Mark Skinner. 2013. "Using Care Ethics to Enhance Qualitative Research on Rural Aging and Care." *Qualitative Health Research* 23, 12: 1697–1707.

> *Rachel Herron and Mark Skinner discuss their use of feminist care ethics when conducting research with a vulnerable population: senior citizens living in a rural area. The authors argue that framing their research through "an alternative framework for theorizing justice that understands all social relations as contextual, partial, attentive, and responsive" (2013: 1697) enhanced the integrity and desired*

outcomes of their research, strengthened their reflexive practice and allowed for a more inclusive understanding of the vulnerability of older rural populations. The authors also discuss the logistics of gaining access. Herron describes how she was able to connect with potential participants by using her personal experiences of growing up in a rural area, and how this kind of insider position may ultimately impact the results of the study.

Holt, Amanda. 2010. "Using the Telephone for Narrative Interviewing: A Research Note." *Qualitative Research* 10, 1: 113–121.

Amanda Holt describes her use of telephone interviews as a viable strategy for conducting narrative research with parents of young offenders. She explains that although some researchers tend to discount the use of the telephone as a legitimate and ideal interviewing instrument, she does not agree. Holt identifies both the challenges and opportunities associated with telephone interviewing. On one hand, individuals potentially lack familiarity and comfort with this approach, so they may desire ongoing prompting and feedback from the researcher. On the other hand, telephone interviewing might offer a way to transcend geographic and time restraints while facilitating flexibility, privacy and future textual analyses. She urges researchers to contemplate the appropriateness of telephone interviewing while taking into account issues such as research context, focus and participant demographics.

James, Carl, and Leanne Taylor. 2013. "'Talk to Students About What's Really Going On': Researching the Experiences of Marginalized Youth." In Tricia Kress, Curry Malott and Brad Porfilio (eds.), *Challenging Status Quo Retrenchment: New Directions in Critical Qualitative* Research (pp. 147–167). Charlotte, NC: Information Age Publishing.

Carl James and Leanne Taylor critically reflect on a qualitative research project that sought to learn about at-risk youths' experiences with and perceptions of school discipline, police and the legal/justice system. Building on critical theories, including critical race theory and critical youth studies, the authors suggest that research that is equitable, respectful and responsive to youths' social, cultural, political and educational realities must apply a range of qualitative methods that are relevant to the youth and to their communities. In particular, they share how they involved youth as consultants and co-facilitators in the research; offered them important resources such as legal advice; and used nontraditional methods, including hip hop workshops. Throughout, the authors identify the ways they needed to constantly negotiate their identities, power and positions as researchers as they attempted to respond to students' needs, build trust, honour the community and collaborate with youth through all stages of the research process. The chapter underscores the importance of reciprocity, flexibility, creativity and collaboration in data collection, and research with racialized and marginalized groups.

Kuoch, Phong. 2013. "Hip Hoe to Hip Hope: Hip Hop Pedagogy in a Secondary Language Arts Curriculum." Unpublished doctoral dissertation, Simon Fraser University, Burnaby, BC.

Phong Kuoch contextualizes his research focus by situating it in an interpretive epistemology. He rationalizes his choice of case study methodology and then, consistent with this method of inquiry, provides extensive detail about the setting in which the study takes place: the school he teaches in: Mosaic High in British Columbia. He provides readers with detailed profiles of the student and teacher participants and describes how he recruited participants from poetry slams, dance teams and rap groups, as well as others who were interested in hip hop more generally. The data-collection techniques Kuoch used include focus group interviews; one-on-one interviews, observation; and artefacts such as blogs, dance team programs and YouTube clips. His document is very useful for its detailed methodology and analysis sections.

Morrison, Connie. 2011. "Avatars and the Cultural Politics of Representation: Girlhood in Social Networking Spaces." Unpublished doctoral dissertation, Memorial University, St. Johns, NL.

This dissertation, which was later published in book form, provides students with an example of "new ethnography" with participant recruitment, data collection and observation for the study, all taking place in the virtual space of an online social networking site. In this study, Connie Morrison uses a feminist poststructuralist lens to explore "the cultural politics of representation" of girls who construct online identities through self-created, personalized avatars. Morrison kept her fieldnotes in an online journal and adapted her interviewer role to serve as a moderator for the online discussions her participants took part in and which made up the bulk of her data. Students who are similarly interested in conducting research with newer technologies may find this innovative study helpful for inspiring other technology-based research ideas of their own.

Plett Martens, Vonda L. 2007. "Moving Between Opposing Worlds: The Moral Experiences of White, Anti-Racism Educators in Saskatchewan." Unpublished doctoral dissertation, University of Saskatchewan, Saskatoon, SK.

Vonda Plett Martens carefully situates her own experiences, positioning and understandings in relation to her research focus. She thoughtfully explains how the key areas for discussion in her interviews emerged from guiding themes in the literature, while noting a central tension, that of "balanc[ing] the need for as non-directive an interview as possible, with [her] curiosity to explore these many specific dimensions of experience" (2007: 71). Her tactic for negotiating this tension involved implementing two different types of interviews (open-ended life-history interviews and semistructured interviews). Plett Martens describes the distinctiveness, unique purposes and separate foci of the interview types within the context of her study, illustrating how she used them in a complementary and cumulative fashion that supported her ability to get at different yet related kinds of information and experiences within each.

Schroeter, Sara. 2008. "Theater in My Toolbox: Using Forum Theatre to Explore Notions of Identity, Belonging and Culture with Francophone Secondary Students in a Context of Diversity." Unpublished master's thesis, York University, Toronto, ON.

Sara Schroeter outlines the challenges she faced executing her study on the effectiveness of teaching theatre techniques as a means to facilitate a sense of belonging among refugee students attending secondary education in a minority language school. She describes overcoming such obstacles as the collaborating teacher suddenly becoming unavailable to work with her, not having met the classroom teachers whose students would be participating in her research and unexpectedly having to lead the collaborative drama workshop on her own. Schroeter demonstrates the value of remaining flexible and open to change while maintaining a focus on research goals. This thesis also provides an explanation of the tenets of critical and social justice-based theories and research practices such as critical pedagogy, PAR, ethnography and practice-based research.

Wilson, Dana H., and Nancy A. Ross. "Place, Gender and the Appeal of Video Lottery Terminal Gambling: Unpacking a Focus Group Study of Montreal Youth." *GeoJournal* 76: 123–138.

This article may be especially helpful to students who want to learn more about the use of focus group data, one of the main objectives for the study. Dana Wilson and Nancy Ross (2009: 125) respond to recent calls in the literature "to analyze focus groups as an interactive group process, rather than as a collection of individual responses, and to establish rigour in the analysis by explicitly making the data-collection process and positionality of the researchers transparent." As a result of their efforts, this paper includes extensive explanations and procedural details about focus groups and the data they generate.

Chapter 5

TRANSCRIPTION: CONSTRUCTING REPRESENTATIONS OF QUALITATIVE DATA

Although boundaries have been pushed to construct innovative ways to produce and collect qualitative data, interviewing and observation remain popular methods in the work of students conducting qualitative research. The data collected through these methods are often processed before a formal data analysis phase occurs. On occasion, student researchers analyze interviews or observations close to their raw form; for example, observation video analyzed using viewing procedures or interview conversation analyzed while listening to digital recordings. Often, however, students transcribe what they have heard/viewed on the recordings to some form of representative transcript, a process that creates a degree of distance between raw data and what is ultimately represented and used for analysis purposes.

Historically, an emphasis has been given to transcription in linguistics- and language-focused research in relation to conversation and discourse analysis (Edwards and Lampert 1993; Mishler 1991; Ochs 1979; O'Connell and Kowal 1999; Psathas and Anderson 1990). Judith Lapadat and Anne Lindsay (1999: 82) argue that the process is theory-laden and complex, involving interpretation and analysis:

> It is not just the transcription product — those verbatim words written down — that is important: it is the process that is valuable. Analysis takes place and understandings are derived through the process of constructing

a transcript by listening and re-listening, viewing and re-viewing.…
Transcription facilitates the close attention and the interpretive thinking
that is needed to make sense of the data.… Transcription as a theory-laden
component of qualitative analysis warrants closer examination.

More recently, a growing body of research is available that explores transcription
from the broad perspective of interpretive, qualitative research and methods (see
Davidson 2009 for a review of transcription literature; Hagens et al. 2009; Mero-
Jaffe 2011; Skukauskaite 2012). Although the growing interest in transcription
— its technical, theoretical, interpretive and analytic relevance in the production
of data representations — is evident in the literature, it is not so clear that student
researchers are exploring transcription in any depth in research courses or other
contexts. Consider the lack of emphasis given to transcription in texts used in
qualitative research courses or in handbooks addressing various forms of qualitative,
interpretivist research that involve data being transcribed (Clandinin and Connelly
2000; Denzin and Lincoln 2011). When describing her transcription experiences
while conducting doctoral research, Cindy Bird (2005: 247) points to her lack of
preparation and the struggles she dealt with when left to learn by doing:

> My experience of transcribing and my subsequent reflection on that
> process provided me with learnings gained outside of one institution's
> prescribed graduate training framework.… I do feel that much frustra-
> tion could have been avoided and time saved if I had been given some
> swimming lessons before being thrown in the pool — lessons on tran-
> scription … the various formats and structures of a produced transcript,
> and conventions already in use within certain research methodologies;
> then moving to more of the theoretical perspectives and issues involved
> in the transcription process and act itself. Perhaps I would have stopped
> dreading [transcription work] sooner had I grasped the concept of tran-
> scription as a key phase of data analysis, as an acknowledged and integral
> part of my data interpretation.

For the most part, transcription remains an underemphasized piece of the
research process in the everyday institutional context. The comprehensive discussion on transcription that follows is meant to encourage students to take the work
of transcription seriously, perhaps if not emphasized in courses, to ask questions,
push the agenda. My hope is that student researchers who understand the complexities of transcription will be better able to make informed decisions about
how to construct meaningful and respectful representations of their research data.

ASSUMPTIONS ABOUT TRANSCRIPTS
AND THE TRANSCRIPTION PROCESS

In terms of experience, although some students may have been involved in transcription as part of previous research activities, including paid work as an RA, many students are first introduced to transcription when faced with transcribing recordings of data they collected themselves.

Transcribing someone else's recorded data is different from transcribing one's own, although there is much to learn from the former experience that can influence the latter. In a study focused on graduate student RA experiences of transcription work, I explored the complexities of transcribing interview data (see Tilley and Powick 2002). In the study, many of the RAs were completing paid work, transcribing individual or multiple recordings, and distanced from any other connection to the research project. Their advisors or other faculty members had hired them to complete the work. One participant spoke of receiving "hallway tapes"; after conversing with a faculty member in the hallway, he agreed to transcribe the researchers' recorded interviews, but little guidance was provided beyond the initial agreement.

> There are absolutely those situations where as a grad student, you know you need some money and you start canvassing professors in the hallways or wherever you can like, "Do you have any tapes available?" I've [even] e-mailed them [faculty researchers]. So definitely I've done a lot of external transcription. (Tilley and Powick 2002: 303)

RAs in the study faced many challenges in completing their tasks. Some were not given much direction, possibly a reflection of the assumption of the straightforward nature of the task that holds strong in many academic contexts. Most RAs spoke of transcription from a positivist framework, positioning themselves as reproducing the truth of the recording, often transferring verbatim conversation to text as the goal. The degree of investment in the work was reflected in the level of involvement the RA participants had with the research project. The RAs who indicated connection greater than the responsibility for transcription alone (i.e., as a member of a research team and in an interviewer/observer role) spoke in ways that reflected a degree of investment in the success of the project:

> The internal ones [recordings related to larger projects in which the participant is involved] definitely make a world of difference, to be what I term "invested and committed" to the project. I think I take the transcription much more seriously. I'm more meticulous.... I'm less perfunctory about it and lackadaisical about the whole project. (Tilley and Powick 2002: 303)

Although RAs participating in the study reported the logistical challenges they faced to understand what was recorded, make punctuation decisions and survive the boredom of the task, they also spoke of the emotional response, especially those RAs who felt invested in a larger project. They described being pulled in by what they heard in the data recorded. Ironically, although some of the RA participants interviewed were describing the quest for objectivity and dismissing the role that interpretation played in their work, they also described being drawn in by the participant narratives, making judgments as they transcribed. Here, Nelson's comments provide an example of this thinking:

> If somebody is describing something so harrowing, you know you are making all kinds of judgments of that subject, of even the interviewer, of the whole process. I remember distinctly being troubled by transcribing this one tape because, you know I couldn't help but have this feeling that how could she [the participant on tape] have been so passive, you know to have taken such a, to have been subject to so much discrimination without fighting back and doing something. So the process of transcribing it's, it's really messy with all these kinds of histories, anxieties that I feel when I'm listening to the stories. (Tilley and Powick 2002: 299–300)

Rather than mundane tasks, the findings of this study spoke to a number of areas, including the logistical challenges of transcription, RAs' interpretive work, and complex interactions with data that RAs experienced as they transcribed (see MacLean et al. 2004 for a discussion of transcription when outsourced beyond the student body). Students transcribing data they have collected for their own qualitative research projects will be less distanced from the raw form than those hired to complete the work for others. However, they will have many of the same struggles as those who are paid, but the investment in the work will often be much greater. Hopefully, the high degree of investment translates into student researchers practising care and caution when engaging in the transcription process and making decisions about procedures.

Before beginning transcription work, students might benefit from considering a number of basic questions, including the following: What are their assumptions about transcription? What are they doing when transcribing? What does the process entail? How can they best produce a transcript that represents the data collected as much as possible?

A productive place for student researchers to begin to think about transcription is to consider the assumptions they hold and knowledge they have about the process:

- Transcription is a mundane task

Student researchers' limited understanding of the transcription process and frustration with the time consumed completing transcription work have contributed to the characterization of transcription as a mundane task. Based on the type and amount of data collected, transcription can be a time-intensive task that can cause frustration by seeming to hold student researchers back from more important pieces of the research process (i.e., analysis). Although there may be an element of the mundane to the work of transcription, the characterization misrepresents the complexities and the significance of the process to the research. When students construct transcripts, they are engaged in work that enhances their intimacy with and knowledge of the data, so the process has implications for data analysis and trustworthiness. As well, transcription work provides opportunities for preliminary analysis, which falls outside the time dedicated to a formal analysis period that is often relegated to a later time in the research process. This preliminary analysis can inform the collection process and aspects of data analysis, including coding and categorization, and the construction of themes that can become central in students' findings. However, this does not happen by accident, but by plan.

Students need to be prepared to pay attention and understand that what they are doing when transcribing is much more than transferring words and actions from recorded material to text. Plans for transcription need to be considered at the beginning stages of research and articulated in the research design to ensure that students recognize and take into account the complexity of the process.

- Transcripts equal raw data

The interviews and observations that student researchers conduct produce raw data that are interpreted and represented as transcripts and materials constructed for the purpose of analysis. What is important to remember is that the transcripts produced are at least twice removed from the actual conversations recorded and interactions observed. It is not unusual to hear student researchers refer to transcripts as if they are equivalent to raw data. This misunderstanding may contribute to students rarely returning to audio/video recordings or accounting for the differences among the original conversations, recordings and constructed transcripts. This problem is not just a question of semantics. When students conceive of transcripts as raw data, they can dismiss too lightly the effect that the distance between raw data and transcripts has on the understandings they develop of their data. In the case of graduate student research, the general expectation is that students are researchers-interviewers-observers combined and produce the transcripts representing the data they collected (although there are exceptions; see Tilley 2003b). Whether student researcher–produced or otherwise, representations constructed of recorded words and images (the products) are not raw data.

- A transcript captures reality

> Acknowledging transcription as representational avoids the mistake of taking the written record as the event and opens the transcription process for examination of its trustworthiness as an interpretive act. (Lapadat and Lindsay 1999: 81)

Transcripts are based on student researchers' interpretative work, not the *whole* truth of an interview or observation, or capturing an objective reality. An assumption that reality has been captured, and a one-to-one correspondence can be achieved between recording and text when the person transcribing maintains an objective stance, is more reflective of positivist rather than interpretivist assumptions of what is achieved through the production of transcripts. The drive for accuracy between what is recorded and its representation is often misdirected. As Blake Poland (1995: 297) states: "The very notion of accuracy of transcription is problematic given the intersubjective nature of human communication, and transcription as an interpretive activity."

There is a distance, both temporal and physical, between the actual interview/observation and the students transcribing it as they relive the experience they are interpreting through listening/viewing the recorded material while removed from the research context. What is most important is not the verbatim process followed, but that the transcripts represent participants' intended meanings. When the focus is on technical accuracy, which often gets translated into capturing every discernable utterance and action, including the minutiae of space fillers — *umms* and *ahhhs*, the interrupting utterances that hold no meaning — the intended meanings may actually be lost to the reader, even when that reader is the participant.

Julie A. Carlson (2010: 1107) describes a participant's reaction after reading the carefully constructed verbatim transcript of her audio-recorded interview that Carlson constructed and sent back to her to read and then to provide a response.

> Abigail was an ideal and enthusiastic participant. Admittedly, I felt quite proud of my inquiry skills, that is, until she received my transcriptions in the mail. I did not hear from her for about three weeks, and so I called to inquire if she had received the transcripts and had any questions. There was an uncomfortable pause before she shared

that her language in the transcripts was so riddled with poor grammar that she did not know how I had ever been able to transcribe the tapes in the first place. She suggested that we could conduct a new interview and she would be sure to do better next time. I assured her that the interview we had was just fine, and there was no need for another one. Still, she was overcome with embarrassment and soon after withdrew from the study, apologizing that she had made a mess of my research.

Although there may be occasions when verbatim transcription is the most appropriate method, there are other ways to proceed (e.g., partial transcription, editing for clarity before returning to participants), which Carlson was unfamiliar with at the time of her research (reflecting the lack of emphasis given to the topic in her research training). As she indicates later in her discussion of member checking, the outcome may have been different if she had informed the participant of what to expect upon receiving her transcript and what the role of the participant was in providing feedback, which was to ensure that the researcher had achieved the goal of capturing the participant's intended meanings.

- Transcripts should be polished texts

> Transcripts are decontextualized conversations; they are abstractions, as topographical maps are abstractions from the original landscape from which they are derived. (Kvale 1996: 165)

Complicating the desire for accurate text is the goal of producing a *polished* text. No matter how polished, transcripts (as Kvale [1996] suggests here) are abstractions from the original conversations. Individuals who transcribe often feel pressure to tidy up the *messiness* of conversation and to produce a polished text that, although nice to look at, may not reflect the original conversation captured during an interview or the talk recorded during an observation, or reflect participants' intended meanings. A transcript is a specialized text produced to serve a specific purpose. A major complication in its production is the required translation of oral conversation into written text. In the case of recorded conversations, whether part of a video-taped observation or interview, live talk is being reproduced as skeletal text based on the interpretation, and sometimes analysis, of the person transcribing.

When people are engaged in conversations, they are involved in a thinking-as-speaking process that is difficult to replicate in text. Most important is that transcripts reflect the participants' intended meanings, but this does not necessarily equate with achieving a polished text. For example, in the case of polishing, difficulties arise as punctuation decisions are made that influence how talk/conversation is represented in text, which has implications for the assignment of meanings.

The following excerpt is taken from an interview I conducted with Ken, who was involved in transcribing focus group audio recordings for a large study, to explore his experiences of transcribing research tapes of focus group conversations. During the interview, Ken described decisions he made about punctuation that connected to issues of translating talk into text and were influenced by his interpretations and analysis of the data recorded:

> Ken: Talk about judgment. Deciding where to put in a period, a comma, or an ellipsis. When somebody stops speaking is a complete judgment for each person for each speech that they make. And I'm sure it affects the finished product. And it makes one person look decisive. It makes one person look inconclusive. And just developing a coherent method to do that, that was a whole set of thoughts that I had to go through. Try this out. No, it just doesn't sound like a comma, and you go back and change all of the "ohs" to ellipses now. No, no, that makes them all sound like, you know, somebody keeps, you know, throwing water on them or something. It doesn't sound like they're having a conversation anymore. (Tilley 2003a: 758)

Writing about the complexities of representing speech as text, Elliot G. Mishler (1991: 261) states that "there are an endless number of decisions that must be made about re-presentation of speech as text, that is, as a transcript, which, although apparently mundane, have serious implications for how we might understand the discourse." Ken was making decisions about how to construct *clear*, easily read texts that reflected, as much as possible, his interpretations of what was recorded. He made *in situ* decisions on how to transcribe that made sense to him as he became more involved in the process, but that went beyond initial directions I had given him.

FOCUS GROUPS AND TRANSCRIPTION

Although individuals transcribing audio-recorded focus group interviews experience similar challenges as those transcribing one-on-one interview conversations, focus group interviews create their own unique challenges for the transcription process (Frey and Fontana 1991; Scott et al. 2009). Group dynamics complicate the work of transcription: the reticent or overly talkative participant, multiple voices speaking over each other, voices being lost, interviewer taking too much control of the situation. The group dynamics come through on recordings as individual identities play out in conversation. Individuals speak over each other; some contribute more to the conversation than others; individuals are silent or silenced by others. Here I use excerpts from interviews with Ken to illustrate the complexities of the process involved when transcribing conversation across multiple participants.

> Ken: You can see it in my software, because on the soundtrack, the sound wave is a little thing that goes half an inch above and half an inch below the zero point. And then all of a sudden it takes up my entire monitor. The size of the sound wave goes from nothing to massive in a jump. And there were actual points I couldn't figure out a way to put it into the transcription other than to constantly put the word interrupts there. I decided not to do that. Where there were five people speaking at once ... they sound like a competition, trying to decide who's going to get the floor now.... Those things, those sections made the entire job really difficult, not to mention they completely defeat [laughs] my voice recognition software. (Tilley 2003a: 755)

Even with the help of software, Ken struggled to capture the multiple voices and what was being said. Ken also struggled to identify individual participants as they spoke, sometimes confusing the voices, especially Ann who "seems to be the teacher of a thousand voices":

> Ken: On the first tape, I despaired after a while of being able to tell Monica and Kate apart.... That was very hard. On the second tape, it took me a long time to recognize ... Ann's voice. For some reason, she sounds like everybody else [laughs]. Whoever spoke before her, she sounds just like that. You can hardly tell when she starts talking and somebody else is finished. I'm not sure why that is, perhaps she just unconsciously inflects other people's tone. But she seems to have, she seems to be the teacher of a thousand voices and it's just impossible to pick her out. (Tilley 2003a: 756)

To deal with the challenge of correctly identifying the speakers, Ken created his own system, a flagging system, to identify the various participants' and researchers' voices:

> Ken: You make detailed notes about what people's voices sound like. So ... Monica trails off a lot. She's got a sort of rumbling sound in her voice. She says the word like and you know a lot, which are good flags. And everybody in the group had these flags. That's what I ended up calling them. (Tilley 2003a: 756)

The person transcribing is interpreting what is heard/seen and constructing the representation. Very telling was Ken's description of highlighting certain voices over others. He untangled waves of talk making the seldom-heard voices more prominent over those who spoke continuously:

> Ken: OK, you [Susan, the researcher] asked Dorothy a specific question about her methodology and whether the introduction of [this new program] has changed her methodology [pedagogy] for the better or not.... And she gets about six words into it and then Monica comes through like a steam train and every time Monica tries to interrupt her, I basically forced her off to the background. I left out half of the words she actually used in some cases, because she trails off into the distance anyway. And it's so hard to pick those things up, but mostly it's because I thought, "Dorothy hasn't gotten a chance to answer this question yet. She has to answer this question or she's of no value in this transcript."... So I put her entire answer together and I minimized the interruptions and I put all the interruptions in a list afterwards. So when you listen to that part of the tape, it doesn't correspond exactly, the tape. And it can't correspond exactly to the tape. (Tilley 2003a: 762)

Ken's emotional involvement with the voices captured on the recording (similar to the emotional responses that the RAs described in the study discussed earlier) influenced the final transcripts. He made the voices he favoured more prominent, either by accident or intentionally.

Ken's responses illustrate the interpretive, analytic and theoretical work that can occur in the process of constructing transcriptions to represent raw data. Although Ken was a paid worker, not a student researcher, and was only involved in this explicit task related to the larger research study, he took his job seriously. Students will deal with similar issues when transcribing focus group data they collect. Being as informed as possible about the complexities of transcription will help them to prepare.

PLANNING FOR TRANSCRIPTION: WHAT TO DO?

Researchers may choose to transcribe data material in full, partially or not at all, based on the focus of their research and research questions as well as their research method: "There may be no single 'approved' approach to transcription, divorced from the context and aims of the research project" (Poland 1995: 300). Whether data are primary or secondary may influence this choice. For example, an oral history study may involve one participant in many extended interviews to allow a complex history to unfold, and the researcher may choose to transcribe full recordings to construct transcripts that *capture* the historical content articulated. A researcher conducting PAR may systematically transcribe sections of audio/ videotape that are connected to specific research foci. PAR participants may involve themselves in this phase of the research process. In the context of focus group interviews, some student researchers may choose to take systematic notes in addition to digital recording and not transcribe the recordings verbatim.

Students collecting data through video need to decide how to construct a transcript that will best represent their data. Besides displaying the words recorded, transcripts may also include visuals of various sorts. Connecting transcription to analysis, Sigrid Norris (2002: 105) suggests that "developing multi-modal video transcription methods of video data are a prerequisite to any adequate multi-modal analysis." He provides examples of multimodal and image-based transcription for the readers' consideration (see Heath et al. 2010 for a discussion of video transcripts and visual representations).

When student researchers design their research and make decisions about whether to ask multiple participants to participate in one interview or observation, or ask fewer participants to be involved in multiple interviews and observations, they must factor in issues related to transcription. For instance, when individual participants are involved in a single interview, students might transcribe immediately after the individuals contribute data or wait until all interviews have been completed.

For multiple participants involved in two or more interviews or observations, the student researcher may want to organize in rounds: first, second or third round. Collect the data for the first round and then transcribe before moving into the second round of data collection. This process makes it possible to return to the participants multiple times to ask them questions that emerged as a result of the participants' previous interviews and the various interactions the student researcher has had with other participants.

Timelines will affect process decisions. Perhaps an interview participant is available only at a time the student researcher scheduled for transcribing previously collected data, or a participant is available for a second-round interview before all first-round transcriptions have been completed. When gaining consent, it is always useful for researchers (even when the plan is for only one interview or observation per participant) to tell participants that at the end of the data collection, student researchers may want to check back with participants for a short conversation to address questions or issues that have emerged late in the research process.

Students can organize so they reap the benefits of doing the transcription work. For instance, transcripts can be useful tools for students to use to critique and develop their skills for interviewing: a moment to step back and think about the actual interview process. A close analysis of a transcript can provide answers to multiple questions. Does the transcript reflect the criteria of the type of interview or observation conducted? For example, a structured interview transcript will look different from an open-ended interview transcript: the former with a systematic back and forth indicated, and the latter with a flexible ordering with additional questions emerging as a result of the unfolding of the conversation, both interviewee- and interviewer-influenced. Are too many of the lines documented the interviewer's, not the participant's? Are there moments when the interviewer might have engaged the interviewee, or the participant-observer might have engaged the observed in more productive ways, pulling them back to the research focus? Is there too much interviewer silence in the open-ended interview? Is there too much interviewer talk in the structured version? Can meanings be assigned to the silences? Is there too much participant-observer interaction in the context of the observation? Have students successfully captured the images intended?

Students can use the first transcript as an opportunity to examine with their advisor the interview or observation process and outcomes; these and other considerations can be discussed before students move on to collect more data. Interacting with advisors at this stage is especially important for students who have not had much hands-on research experience and are relying mostly on what they have read about interviewing and observing. When communication lines are open between students and advisors, always an important consideration, conversations regarding aspects of the research process, including transcription, can be easily arranged.

Although changes (especially micro changes in the data-collection process) can be expected, students need to have well-thought-out plans for producing their data representations before starting the data-collection process. Following an established transcription plan will guard against students being faced with not having paid sufficient attention to the implications of transcription to the research process or not having the necessary time allotted to prepare the data for analysis at the end of data collection. When transcription is taken seriously at the research design stage, it will be evident in the logistical plan that is in place. Before starting transcription work, students need to revisit the plans they initially made and make any revisions necessary, based on how the research process unfolded.

The quality of data recordings influences the quality of representations constructed as conventional or multimodal transcripts. If voices are too low, external noise interferes and/or actions are not clearly captured, the recording will be difficult to transcribe. Students need to pay attention to the quality and condition of recording equipment (e.g., microphones, video camera).

Just as students need the proper equipment to record interviews and observations, they can also benefit from the help of equipment and technical supports to transcribe recorded data. For instance, digital files can be directly fed into computer software programs that ease the work of transcription. An old-fashioned foot pedal is still available if needed. Voice recognition software (VRS) can be useful in some cases, but students need to factor in the time to learn about it and train on the software program. The amount of data collected and the benefits accrued from using the software might not warrant the time needed for training. For focus group interviews, VRS may require more time and energy to learn than one-on-one interview transcription. (Lynne MacLean and his colleagues [2004] discuss voice recognition programs: the pros and cons; strengths and limitations.)

It is important that students have a consistent process for transcribing that is documented. Descriptions of process and related decisions contribute to a transparency of method and are important to include later in the methodology chapter of students' theses or dissertations. The following are additional process points to consider:

- Develop a list of transcription conventions

  A list of transcription conventions that make sense in relation to the research focus and data collected is useful to follow when completing the work of transcription. Conventions will indicate the basis of the decisions made for translating the data recorded into textual representation, including decisions about punctuation, repetitive words or phrases, hesitations in talk, emotion in expressions and various kinds of silences. Students can create a convention list suited to the purpose of their research or adapt those that other researchers have developed (see Bird 2005; Heath et al. 2010 for video transcription; Tilley and Powick 2002). Even though research transcripts are rarely made public, developing and following transcription conventions will provide a degree of transparency of process and support claims to consistency.

- Document shifts to analysis in research journal or log

  Transcription involves interpretive work and often preliminary analysis. Students need to be prepared to document the analytic thinking that can occur while transcribing. It is important to record their thoughts, as they transcribe, in a section of their methodology journal; or insert comments in the transcript as they document the ideas and questions that may later be transformed into codes, categories and themes. Tone? Laughter? Intuitive thoughts ... what words keep reoccurring in the conversation? Are there particular instances when the participant resists explanation? In terms of the process, student researchers might want to record how they are interpreting different kinds of silences. They may begin at this early stage to theorize their understandings of the recoded data. Document this early theorizing!

- Ensure adequate time for the process

  Time is an important resource to have when dealing with the work of transcription. Students need to plan carefully to ensure that they have set aside the time needed to transcribe. For example, for those with average typing skills, six or more hours may be needed for a one-hour recording of an interview (it has taken me longer). The complexities of recorded data affect the time needed. A reasonable estimate needs to be made at the design stage. Although time is a factor, and students want to move on in their research process, they need to keep in mind what is achieved during this phase of their research. As discussed in earlier sections, students are becoming more familiar with the data and analysis flows from the process. The writing they do while documenting their transcription experience will likely find a place in their thesis or dissertation in the methodology chapter.

- Make a final check

  As a means of maximizing transcription quality and reducing errors, a final useful check is to read the completed transcript while simultaneously viewing or listening to the recording. During this process, the student is focused more on full text and clumps of meaning rather than the individual word or image emphasis, a different experience that may prompt changes to the transcript.

- Keep confidentiality

  Students have a responsibility to maintain the confidentiality agreed to when gaining clearance and participant permissions. When transcribing data, they need to take care that they are the only ones within earshot of the conversations and that the recorded interactions are seen only by them. Using earphones can help with issues of confidentiality regarding the voices recorded, and finding secure space for viewing video material will help keep visuals private.

- Prepare transcripts for analysis

  If using a transcript as written text for analysis, prepare the hard copy with large side margins. Space will be needed to record codes and categories and comments. Christian Heath and his colleagues (2010: 71) suggest that when transcribing visual material, "it is useful to include a large margin on one side of the page where observations can be recorded alongside the transcript itself. In some cases, it can also help to accompany the transcript with a series of still images."

CHECKING BACK WITH PARTICIPANTS: MEMBER CHECKING

> Credibility is a trustworthiness criterion that is satisfied when source respondents agree to honor the reconstructions. (Lincoln and Guba 1985: 328–29)

Including member checking as a part of the research process (Lincoln and Guba 1985) is appropriate to qualitative research within a critical framework that understands the role of interpretation in the research act and also the importance of respectful representation and dissemination of data and research findings, all of which are intricately tied to transcription work. Member checking may occur at different junctures in the research process, but is likely to be part of the data-collection and analysis process. While serving as a check on whether the researcher's representation of data reflects the participants' intended meanings, the member-checking process also contributes to the continued communication and rapport built between researcher and participants that is hopefully maintained over the life of the study.

Based on the research design, member checking can take a variety of forms. In the case of interview data, it most often means returning transcripts to participants at some point in the research process. Although member checking is an established practice of many qualitative researchers, it is context-specific, so it is conducted in various ways across research contexts. Many decisions will be made during the process of constructing texts and visuals that are representative of interview and observation data. Ultimately, though, the materials produced need to convince interested audiences that the representations and the findings are credible.

Researchers who send data representations in the form of texts and visuals to participants for member checking must be clear on their expectations. Individuals (or communities) who are first-time participants may not know what to do when asked to read and respond to a transcript; it is important to give directions. Participants can fill in missing pieces, correct words, elaborate on points and ask questions of the researcher.

I have learned through experience that participants are often surprised when they receive their transcripts and are sometimes dismayed at how their contribution is represented. When reading her transcript, a participant in my prison research cried inconsolably as a result of seeing herself in text, and I was left feeling that I had in some way betrayed her trust. Teachers I have interviewed have been embarrassed by the lack of coherence they see as they read verbatim text of their talk captured in print. They see the text as a reflection of their identities, regardless of whether they can be connected to the data. Returning transcripts to the women in the prison was not straightforward. Although I wanted to return the transcripts to them and have them respond, I was concerned about leaving the documents in the prison, where others may have access to what was recorded in the interview.

When engaged in research involving multiple languages, member checking can play a vital role. Snezana Ratković's (2014) doctoral transnational feminist research reflects the challenges that student researchers face as they work across languages. Like Ratković, the participants spoke Serbo-Croatian as well as English. She constructed representations of data in the form of transcript poems, reflecting the multiplicity of language choices, which she sent to participants for member checking (see Appendix C).

If initiating a member-checking process, researchers must be prepared to take participant feedback seriously and make the necessary changes requested. Difficulties may arise, however, when participants want to make changes that go beyond points of clarification. Researchers may be hesitant to use a member-checking process if there is a possibility that participants who see their words in text may choose to withdraw the data they contributed to the study. Here, Ratković (2014: 96–97) describes her hesitations about member checking connected with her doctoral research:

> I felt that the power for producing knowledge circulated away from me, especially on those occasions when I was sending transcripts, transcript poems, interpretative stories, and personal experience narratives to participants for member checking. Opening participants' e-mail responses made me anxious that the participant would not agree with my interpretations or would find those interpretations offensive. Although I had my researcher agenda, I was aware that participants had the power to support or to resist our collaborative production of knowledge, the power to tell or withhold their stories, the opportunities to member check and inform my data interpretations, and the right to withdraw their data and their participation at any point in time without consequences.

On occasion, participants who see their words in print may regret, for various reasons, something that takes on new life in hard copy. The request for changes that cause concern are less likely to happen when participants understand the member-checking processes and purposes from the beginning, and the researchers have taken the time and energy to build a high level of trust with their participants.

However, although member checking and transcript sharing with participants have become more common in critical qualitative research praxis, concerns with such processes, some of which I have previously detailed (e.g., participants' embarrassment) are discussed in the literature (see Mero-Jaffe 2011 for discussion of four dilemmas). In Victoria Hagens's and her colleagues' (2009) discussion of the "interviewee transcript review" (ITR) process, they suggest a number of disadvantages that include the loss of primary data when an interviewee requests removal of important material.

As a result of my doctoral work, I explain transcription and the member-checking process to participants in great detail when I conduct research. I encourage the students I advise to explain the process at the initial stages of data collection, not at the conclusion (which sometimes is months from when the data were first collected). Before participants receive the transcripts, the students need to explain that the transcripts produced are an attempt to turn talk and conversation into written form and are not to be compared to polished written text. In the case of visual data, the participants need to be reminded about what the images will be used for, including whether clips of video or other images will be used in public discussions of the research.

Participants need to be assured and reassured that confidentiality will be kept during the process. Even when the participants know they will not be identified, they want to be portrayed respectfully. This can mean editing quoted material for clarity purposes and standard English grammar. In the early stages, it is important for student researchers to emphasize to participants the role the participants play in member checking, and that researchers are very interested in participants' thoughts on whether their intended meanings are represented accurately. In the course of member checking, participants can also point to places where confidentiality may be compromised because of the identifying details embedded in the text that the researcher might be unaware of, even when paying close attention.

Sending participants a preliminary synopsis with transcripts for member checking can be helpful to them. The synopsis can vary in type and style, may include visuals and possibly kept to a page or two not to overwhelm the participant; most important is that the synopsis reflect some of the key issues central in the data and point to the kinds of interpretations that student researchers are making based on the data they have collected. At times, students may quote directly from the transcript or include visuals to illustrate what data actually led to their researcher interpretations. Synopses provide participants with some understanding, albeit a limited one, of the ways in which the student researcher has interpreted their words and actions and may represent their data in formal research documents. In the case of focus group interviews, students might choose to send the synopsis only, with access to the transcript provided to participants in a one-on-one process with the researcher (refer to Chapter 3 for a discussion of ethics and focus group data).

If the researcher takes member checking seriously and indicates its importance to participants, it is more likely that the participants will do the actual work of member checking rather than ignore a request for their additional participation. When students systematically implement an appropriate member-checking process, they provide a degree of participant engagement that will contribute to convincing readers (advisor, committee members, external examiner, participants and any other interested parties) of the trustworthiness of the data and credibility of their findings.

In addition to recognizing "transcription as representational," as Lapadat and Lindsay (1999) suggest, students need to think carefully about their procedures and how they fit the research methodology and focus. When student researchers conduct their own research, the level of investment is high. If they understand the complexities of transcription beyond questions of logistics (e.g., in relation to analysis and credibility), they may take transcription more seriously — working through moments of impatience with completing what at times may feel a very challenging and time-consuming process.

The next chapter moves from the construction of transcripts as representations of data and the process of member checking to an emphasis on the work of analysis. Although research is far from a linear process, and analysis happens at many intervals as the research moves forward, at some point students move into a formal analysis stage to focus extensively on analyzing their data.

Annotated Bibliography

Bailey, Julia. 2008. "First Steps in Qualitative Data Analysis: Transcribing." *Family Practice* 25, 2: 127–131.

Julia Bailey describes the transcription of audio and video data as an interpretative process that involves judgments about what level of detail to choose and how to construct meaningful representations of recorded data. The article provides a guide to methodological and theoretical considerations for novice researchers. The author gives data examples to illustrate the decisions that must be made when transcribing or assigning transcription to others. She emphasizes the impossibility of capturing the complexity of human interaction in transcript form and recommends that researchers return to the original recordings of data as part of the transcription process.

Bird, Cindy. 2005. "How I Stopped Dreading and Learned to Love Transcription." *Qualitative Inquiry* 11, 2: 226–248.

Cindy Bird recalls her graduate school experiences with transcription as part of her coursework and involvement in research projects. She notes that she did not recognize the importance of transcription until she engaged in this process firsthand. She drew on her rich understandings of the contents of the research tapes to elucidate her transcription process and decision-making. Complex, critical and reflexive thinking emerged as she gained increased experience transcribing tapes of various content (e.g., interview, focus group and observation). Over time, she devised a detailed transcription strategy that integrated synopses, as well as comments regarding points of clarification, speech patterns and tape quality. For her, this process was inherently analytical. Dilemmas quickly arose, including a mismatch between text and tone. She thoughtfully began to consider how "methodological," "ontological" and "epistemological" positionings, along with representational goals, shaped her transcription process. Bird's initial dislike of transcription was later replaced with enthusiasm as she came to recognize its significance.

Carlson, Julie A. 2010. "Avoiding Traps in Member Checking." *The Qualitative Report* 15, 5: 1102–1113.

Julie Carlson addresses the concept of member checking in qualitative research, using five vignettes of personal research experience to explore the challenges of the process. She discusses member checking and its role in increasing the trustworthiness of narrative inquiry. She also makes recommendations for "avoiding the setting and triggering of member check traps" (2010: 1102) that can occur as a result of miscommunication between researchers and their participants.

Doyle, Susanna. 2007. "Member Checking with Older Women: A Framework for Negotiating Meaning." *Health Care for Women International* 28: 888–907.

Susanna Doyle suggests that although member checking has received some attention in the qualitative research world, little is known about how to conduct the member-checking process in research contexts. In this article, Doyle describes a pilot study during which she developed a "methodology for conducting member checks that is consistent with the participatory approaches and the active negotiation of meaning inherent in this [qualitative] paradigm" (2007: 1096). Her comprehensive discussion and illustration of member checking will be useful to other qualitative researchers.

Markle, D. Thomas, Richard Edward West and Peter J. Rich. 2011. "Beyond Transcription: Technology, Change, and Refinement of Method." *Forum Qualitative Sozialforschung/Forum: Qualitative Social Research* 12, 3, Art. 21.

D. Thomas Markle and his colleagues discuss methodological shifts in qualitative research and argue that the qualitative research community is currently experiencing a shift in the transcription of audio and video data. The authors encourage researchers to include multimedia data in their research reports to allow for greater accuracy and trustworthiness in the process of data analysis and representation. The challenges emerging from such an approach and suggestions for possible improvements are discussed.

Prendergast, Monica, Peter Gouzouasis, Carl Leggo and Rita. L. Irwin. 2009. "A Haiku Suite: The Importance of Music Making in the Lives of Secondary School Students." *Music Education Research* 11, 3: 303–317.

> *In the first part of this paper, Monica Prendergast and her colleagues explain a new method of poetic inquiry called poetic transcription/representation. They argue that this method not only evokes emotional responses from the reader but it is also effective in reconstructing and confirming "the lived experiences of others while challenging researchers to learn about their abilities to communicate qualitative inquiry in a different way" (2009: 305–306). In their study of secondary school students enroled in a music program in British Columbia, the researchers specifically use the poetic form of haiku, although they also acknowledge the effectiveness of other forms of poetry as a process of inquiry, as data and as data representation. The article contains a "Development of the Results" section, which includes poetic transcriptions represented as a suite of haiku poems. The authors conclude the article with a discussion of the benefits of affective empirical research techniques such as poetic transcription/representation.*

Tessier, Sophie. 2012. "From Field Notes, to Transcripts, to Tape Recordings: Evolution or Combination?" *International Institute for Qualitative Methodology* 11, 4: 446–460.

> *Contributing to ongoing debates about the relationship between transcription processes and technology, Sophie Tessier presents two distinct points of view. In the first, she discusses the use of technology through an "evolutionary narrative," a perspective that views qualitative research methods as having evolved from fieldnotes to transcripts to tape recordings in an effective effort to improve data management. In the second perspective, technology is presented as a "combination narrative" in which technologies are thought to have evolved to a point where they can combine the strengths of older methods. Tessier explores which of these data-collection methods are most effective in terms of reliability, cost and loss/retention of data. She concludes that combining the advantages of fieldnotes and transcripts, and working from tape recordings without accumulating each method's disadvantages, is possible because of new technology such as OneNote and SmartPen, which are available to today's researchers.*

Tilley, Susan A. 2003b. "Transcription Work: Learning Through Co-Participation in Research Practices." *International Journal of Qualitative Studies in Education* 16, 6: 835–851.

> *Susan A. Tilley explores the complexities of the transcription process when it involves someone other than the researcher, including the ethical implications when*

the participants are a vulnerable group. Tilley uses Jean Lave and Etienne Wenger's (1991) concept of legitimate peripheral participation to explore the experiences of a person she hired to help her transcribe various data collected through fieldnotes, observations and interviews during her doctoral studies. Tilley conducted interviews with Debbie during the period Debbie transcribed and at the completion of the work. The article points to the learning Debbie experienced in relation to conducting respectful qualitative research and to understanding the lives of women in prison.

Witcher, Chad S.G. 2010. "Negotiating Transcription as a Relative Insider: Implications for Rigor." *International Institute for Qualitative Methodology* 9, 2: 122–132.

This article may be of interest to students who are considering conducting research in remote or rural settings and/or with populations that use nonstandard language such as regional dialects. Chad Witcher first presents a brief review of the literature on transcription, highlighting its important role as a means to ensure quality, rigour and trustworthiness of interview data. Drawing on his personal experience as a researcher/transcriptionist, Witcher, who positions himself as a "relative insider" in relation to the community in which he carried out his study, describes the challenges he experienced when conducting and transcribing interviews with senior citizens from rural parts of Newfoundland and Labrador, where the inhabitants speak using a distinct regional dialect. Although Witcher concedes that his researcher's position as a relative insider had its challenges, he believes that the advantages outweigh the disadvantages for the transcription process, especially as he felt his insider positioning allowed him "to remain faithful to the aural record" and present interpretations of the data that were trustworthy and reliable (2010: 129).

Chapter 6

DATA ANALYSIS

Although preliminary analysis intersects with various aspects of the qualitative research process as student researchers interpret and try to make sense of data, the time comes when students have to focus specifically on analysis work. In addition to the philosophical and theoretical framework of the study, the knowledge students gained through the research experience up to the point of formal analysis will inform the meanings they derive from the data. Qualitative researchers who engage in critical analysis of data are not claiming positivist objectivity, but rather critically questioning the implications of their subjectivities in relation to their interpretive and analytic work.

In the same way student researchers need to prepare to move into the field to collect data, they must also prepare to begin data analysis. This preparation includes organizing for the logistics of the work as well as developing understandings of the complexities of analysis that move beyond the *how-to*. This chapter is mostly concerned with the latter. It begins with a short discussion of logistics and then shifts to a consideration of analysis and the complexities the task entails. I draw from my doctoral experiences to illustrate issues discussed.

MAKING SENSE OF THE DATA

Data analysis is the process of bringing order, structure, and meaning to the mass of collected data. It is a messy, ambiguous, time-consuming, creative, and fascinating process. It does not proceed in a linear fashion; it is not neat. (Marshall and Rossman 1989: 112)

> For the purposes of this [Ellingson's] chapter, analysis of data or other
> assembled empirical materials will be understood as the process of sepa-
> rating aggregated texts (oral, written, or visual) into smaller segments of
> meaning for close consideration, reflection, and interpretation. (Ellingson
> 2011: 595)

The plans for data analysis that students articulated during the design stage may still be appropriate or may need revisions at the formal analysis stage. It is difficult to estimate the time necessary for analysis before data have been collected, although reasonable estimates can be made. Methods used and the amount of data ultimately collected will influence the time needed. Advisors can assist students in re-evaluating the analysis plans constructed earlier and help them to make informed decisions on how to proceed. Better safe than sorry.

Students at this stage may feel they have lived through the data-collection phase and (in many cases) the challenges of transcribing their data and are nearing the end of their research; they can become impatient. They need to take care not to rush through this important step of the research process and to remember that analysis is directly linked to credibility claims and will inform the study's findings.

There are myriad ways to analyze data (i.e., content, discourse or narrative analysis), and student researchers may choose one or multiple methods of analysis to make meaning of their data. Their decisions will be tied to their methodology and methods, data type and purpose of the research. Research projects might also have idiosyncratic elements that lead researchers to create analysis procedures that are useful in their context-specific situation. Whatever the process, analyses must be completed in systematic and transparent ways to ensure that findings are seen to be credible responses to the research questions.

A large body of work that explores procedural elements for comprehensive qualitative data analysis is available for student researchers to assess to help them plan their analysis procedures (Altheide and Schneider 2013; Dey 1993; Ezzy 2002; Silverman 2012). Particular methodologies and methods can require specific procedures for researchers to follow; for instance, constructivist grounded theory (Charmaz 2000, 2006a, 2011), narrative inquiry (Daiute and Lightfoot 2004) and analysis of data collected online (Hine 2012; Paechter 2013). In addition to what students have learned in research courses or working as RAs on research projects, they can turn to the comprehensive literature to help them make decisions about the appropriate procedures for their specific research project. Although feeling overwhelmed at the analysis stage is not an uncommon experience for students, the level of anxiety will be determined (at least partially) by the degree to which they have prepared for understanding the analysis process.

Qualitative data analysis software (QDAS) of various kinds is available for analysis purposes (see Davidson, J. and di Gregorio 2011 for a comprehensive discussion of QDAS). Students have to decide whether software will be useful for analysis in light of their methodology and their specific research context. Although software was available, I chose the by-hand route to analyze my doctoral research data. Many advances have been made since that time. Debates on the usefulness of software programs for qualitative data analysis continue in the field. The discussion has moved from the possibilities of software distancing researchers even more from the raw data and intruding on and influencing analysis in unproductive ways (software possibly being more suited to positivist than interpretivist methodologies), to the advances being made in the software world that have produced software products that lend themselves well to the analysis of qualitative data.

Whether qualitative software programs (e.g., ATLAS.ti, Nudi*Ist, NVivo, Ethnograph, HyperResearch, Kwalitan, QDAMiner, XSight) will be useful for the data-analysis process needs to be decided with consideration of the type and amount of data (see Heath et al. 2010 for video data). For much student research, analysis by hand is often the most appropriate choice because of the small amount of data students need to collect and analyze to meet their degree requirements; this is especially true of undergraduate projects. Master's- and doctoral-level research require the collection of more extensive data, so students may choose to use software for analysis. However, the time for learning the software program has to be factored into the process and it can be a lengthy period. For participatory research studies, software assistance may be a good choice, especially if multiple people need access to the data for analysis purposes; software can provide quick access across people and contexts.

Students need to decide the pros and cons of software use before making a decision. Will the software contribute to a more efficient storage and organization of data, more possibilities to conduct a comprehensive critical analysis? Is the student already familiar enough with the software so that the time needed to understand the program is not too great? Maybe there is a mix of uses related to the types of data involved; is the software more suitable to some of the students' data but not appropriate for other data they have collected? Is the software useful for video data? Student researchers will need to articulate a rationale for their choices and provide an explicit description of their software use, which will be included in their thesis, MRP or dissertation.

Generally (and simplistically) speaking, common logistical first steps of qualitative analysis can be distilled down to making decisions on ways to code for units of meaning, constructing categories based on those codes, and deciding what overarching categories and themes can be developed based on the coding and categorizing activities (Coffey and Atkinson 1996; Ellingson 2011; Freeman 2000; Miles and Huberman 1994). Analysis is best achieved when student researchers apply their critical lens to the process, asking questions of their decisions and being continuously aware of the messiness and lack of linearity in the qualitative research process.

Although the analysis process needs to be a good fit with the types of data collected, other factors might influence the researcher's decisions on procedures. For instance, a research goal that was important to me for my study was to maintain the centrality of the women's words/voices in the data analysis. With that intention in mind, I chose to start my formal content analysis (with a view to the discourse represented) on the interview transcripts rather than observation data or a combination of the multiple data sets.

The logistics I followed to analyze interview transcripts included the following procedures. I systematically listened to all interviews with transcripts in hand to check recording against hard copy. After completing this checking process, I analyzed transcripts in groups of four based on chronological order, beginning with the application of *a priori* codes I developed from the research and interview questions and relevant literature. I attached emergent codes to the transcript as they developed. My lists of codes grew as I analyzed the database of interview transcripts.

After one round of analysis, I returned to the earliest transcripts to concentrate on the emergent codes that developed based on transcripts analyzed later in the process to consider what I might have missed in the early stages. I considered the commonalities across the coding language and collapsed similar codes. I also returned to the transcripts to contemplate the conversations/words I had not coded to ask why I made those decisions, to ensure that I had not dismissed important outlying data. After all codes were recorded, collapsed and sometimes reconfigured, I created categories based on the final codes and constructed themes related to the categories developed. At the completion of this process, various themes were captured on paper, and I was left with additional questions to explore and consider in connection with the analysis of other data collected.

While analyzing the interview transcripts, I also highlighted sections when the women described experiences particularly relevant to the research focus and later quoted some of those words directly in my dissertation document. The women's stories of schooling remained central in my process, informing additional steps in the analysis process. Observation data represented in the form of handwritten fieldnotes, transcripts of audio recordings of expanded notes and my research journal were analyzed in a similar systematic fashion; they were used to develop codes, categories and themes. For me, the analysis stage, although exciting, was also when a number of questions surfaced, especially at the initial stage of the process.

Data tangentially connected to the research is often produced when student researchers veer away from the research focus when interviewing and observing in the research context. Many interesting things will be heard and observed that are not necessary to the research focus or meant for a more public eye. Students will need to decide what data to analyze before they spend too much time analyzing materials that do not move their research forward. In some cases, outlying data may actually add to the richness of the study, so students should not cut data without giving them serious consideration. In some cases, students may choose to leave data not explicitly connected for future research, dissemination and publication endeavours, especially if completing graduate programs. To make decisions on what to include, they will need to consider whether/how the data align with the broader research questions. I remind students to continually return to their research questions to keep them on track and moving forward in the *right* direction.

DOCUMENTATION OF PROCESS

Regardless of the analysis processes in place, student researchers must keep in mind the role that analysis plays in judgments that others will make about the credibility of the research. In the case of qualitative, interpretive research, in which the student researcher is understood as human instrument, an important step is to document in detail the analysis process that unfolded in terms of the logistical procedures as well as the complexities addressed.

I used my research journal to record my analysis decisions and to document emergent questions as I moved through the process. This tool helped me think through the multiple possibilities for how I might proceed and provided a level of transparency of process important for those interested in my research findings:

> I have to make numerous decisions as I continue the process of analyzing the data. I have transcripts of interviews, participant-observations, and fieldnotes. Do I consider pieces of each? Compare/contrast as I go along? Do I focus on one set of transcripts like the general fieldnotes and leave the others until later? In the end, the researcher makes the decisions, justifies them and moves on. However, I am always left wondering if I am informed enough to make the best decisions. Are there "best" decisions (or just other decisions) equally important to the exploration? (Tilley 1998a: 53)

Whether using one set of data or multiple sets of primary and secondary data, students need to illustrate in their writing up that they have analyzed the data they claimed to have collected. What was the process for each data set? Were data compared and contrasted? At times, students conducting research that involves multiple data sets, interviews, observations, documents and other forms will describe the collection of the various data and claim triangulation. Patton (2002: 247–248) describes four basic types of triangulation that Norman K. Denzin (1978) earlier identified: data triangulation, investigator triangulation, theory triangulation and methodological triangulation useful in consideration of qualitative analyses processes. In the case of student research, the claim is often related to data triangulation specifically. Although arguments related to the appropriateness of triangulation as basis for judgments applied to interpretivist research have been discussed in the literature (Atkinson and Delamont 2005; Brannen 2004; Coffey and Atkinson 1996), claims of triangulation are commonly made in qualitative studies.

It is not enough for student researchers to declare that data triangulation occurred; they also have to illustrate instances of triangulation and the resulting findings in the text. The individual sets of data need to be analyzed in systematic and appropriate ways, as well as considered in relation to each other and how they intersect, and are useful for exploring the research focus and questions. As well, the analysis description provided must emphasize the multiple sets of data and not focus only on what might be considered the most *interesting* or primary data. Remember that there were reasons for collecting the multiple sets of data, and students need to fulfil their responsibilities to the participants, including conducting a respectful analysis of the data participants contributed to the study. I have noticed over time that theses and dissertations often include direct quotes from interviews and representations of observations, but no signs of in-depth discussion of other data sets described in the study, especially secondary data.

During my doctoral research, I collected various data to understand better the research context, participants and their experiences, as well as to meet the ethnographic criteria of thick description (Geertz 1973: 9–10). The data sets were considered individually as well as in relation to each other as a way for me to develop more comprehensive understandings than are possible with the consideration of data sets in isolation. I analyzed data through the critical feminist lens I had developed and was continuing to develop.

At the analysis stage, the contradictions that emerged when I considered a single data set could be examined in the light of the intersections across data sets. I was better able to understand the *big* picture, the prison school and individual participants while considering interview transcripts, fieldnotes, observations and various data sets together.

> I realize the importance of the participant-observations, the fieldnotes. They contribute to creating a fuller picture. I remember comments Pamela made realizing now that they occurred outside the context of the interview. The transcripts sometimes seem contradictory — Pamela disliked the fact that she never felt she belonged in the school but at another point suggests she enjoyed being able to interact with the other students. Snippets pulled from the texts [transcripts] appear contradictory. But I remember those conversations and know she felt those conflicting

feelings.…. The way that I can work with the information she provided is to place it over-under-in-between her thoughts presented in the multiple data. (Journal entry, Tilley 1998a: 54)

Data related to Pamela came through various sources. She was observed in the school as well as interviewed. The multiple sources analyzed and considered together supported a rationale for the contradictions that surfaced.

Historically, researchers moved out of the field and away from participants to focus on analyzing data. Although this remains the case for many researchers, participant involvement in research has changed over time and across methodologies, and extends beyond activities of member checking. PAR and community-based research are illustrative of such cases (Maiter et al. 2008; Sethi 2014). As well, many Indigenous methodologies involve the *researched* in various stages of the research project (Battiste 2008; Schnarch 2004).

Many student researchers who conduct research as part of degree requirements are working in isolation during the analysis stage. Even if students want more involvement on the part of participants, these participants often have tangential interest and are not invested in a way that they are willing and/or able to continue participation after data are collected. Student researchers may continue contact with participants after data collection as a means of reporting back on findings or fulfiling agreed-upon activities related to reciprocity; others will have said their good-byes.

ADDRESSING THE COMPLEXITIES

Besides understanding logistics, students need to be sensitive to the complexities of analysis work and able to apply a broad critical cultural lens to the process, ultimately complicating their work. I use the verb *complicate* in the context of writing about analysis because it captures the complex, contradictory, sophisticated process that culminates in comprehensive understandings of research data. In particular, researchers operating within a critical framework need to be open to a continuous process of sensitization that will assist them in understanding meanings that emerge when they engage with data, especially data that contradict the embedded assumptions they carry forward into the research context.

The three main themes intersecting throughout this text are a) the importance of student researchers enacting a critical reflexivity; b) the influence of the distance dynamic on the research process; and c) the importance of conducting respectful research; all three themes are intricately connected to the analysis process. Student researchers enacting a critical reflexivity will make sense of the research process *in situ*, applying their critical lens to the decisions they make as the research unfolds. Those researchers intent on conducting respectful research will turn their critical lens inward to help them problematize their research process, including their interpretive and analytic moves and the documentation of the process.

An important question for student researchers to reflect on at this stage of the research process is this: "What do I need to know/understand to analyze my data in respectful and productive ways?" The research questions, contexts and participants will influence the answers individual researchers find to address this question. Student researchers need to draw from critical, theoretical and contextual knowledge to inform their analysis — and continually adjust their knowledge requirements based on the data collected. The appropriate knowledge needed to inform their analysis will be directly tied to the researchers' identity, research focus and research questions.

QUESTIONING EVERYDAY KNOWLEDGE

Student researchers come to their work with various kinds of knowledge and experiences that inform their research process. They have accumulated disciplinary knowledge based on the faculties and degree programs in which they are situated. They also have access to the specific knowledge and expertise their advisors have accrued within the academy and through their continued research initiatives. This knowledge is part of a bank of knowledge that supports their data analysis and critical research praxis.

The women in the prison taught me the importance of questioning the role that taken-for-granted knowledge plays in the practice of research, including the assumptions and stereotypes people hold dear and often remain unquestioned. After a month in the prison, my unarticulated assumptions and stereotypes I held about women in prison began to surface. I wondered why the women I had imagined were in prison, the *hard-core bad* women I saw represented in the media, did not match well the women with whom I was working. My naïveté was stark against the backdrop of the prison institution.

Although student researchers may not be able to understand their assumptions until they are situated within a research context, they can develop a critical questioning stance if they recognize and acknowledge from the beginning that they will have assumptions to uncover. To make their assumptions visible, they need to find ways to strategically question their everyday thinking. For example, students can start by asking "What is it I know about my participants and the research context?" They can then follow with "How do I know what I know?" Their research journals can provide a space to record the moments they find themselves surprised and answer the question "Why am I surprised?"

Within a qualitative, interpretivist paradigm, researchers recognize the impossibilities of separating self from research and the importance of recognizing and accounting for the *bias* that does exist, to ensure that credible research is conducted. Students must be prepared to critique everyday knowledge, knowledge that is often left unquestioned but ultimately informs their critical research praxis.

KNOWLEDGE OF THE PAST

Researchers' degree of historical knowledge in relation to the people, place and broad research context informs the analysis stage of the research process. Students will have to consider whether they have sufficient historical knowledge to understand the data in relation to the context. Is their knowledge adequate enough for them to do a credible job of analyzing the data? Are data pushing them to ask questions related to the research context and/or past history? When student researchers do not have enough background knowledge, they risk engaging in an historical analysis that produces surface readings of the data collected. When, researchers *listen* closely to data, they can build a deeper understanding of the histories and contexts foreign to them, but related to the data; however, they may also be made aware of the need to return to the literature and/or participants to help them in their meaning-making. Acquiring additional historical knowledge of context, participants and sometimes methodology will contribute to a researcher's ability to engage in respectful analysis.

When I conducted interviews in the prison, rather than focusing immediately on the interview schedule and questions, participants who identified as Aboriginal spent time elaborating on their individual and community histories. Originally, I thought this was a strategy that they were using to settle in and feel more comfortable in the interview context and with me in my researcher role. At the analysis stage, I realized the significance of the information they offered in providing context and helping me to understand the data I was collecting. My observation of their persistence in fighting authorities to gain greater access to Elders and to organize Indigenous cultural events in the prison connected to their narratives at the beginning of the interviews, when they talked of the past, the possibilities of survival in the prison and hopes of rehabilitation.

When analyzing data collected from Aboriginal participants, I found myself questioning to what degree I understood the effects of colonization and residential schooling specifically on the women's lives and schooling experiences. Although only one participant had actually lived in a residential school, others had parents who had had that experience. Their interview data contained conversations related to their experiences of being Aboriginal in the Canadian context and of the effects of colonization. The historical impact of residential schools influenced their educational experience. Robina Thomas (2005: 239) writes in her thesis of the continuing legacy of the residential school:

Although the school has been since torn down, the memories of it remain. The thesis was undertaken to shed light on the devastating and catastrophic legacy of the residential school system in Canada. Residential schools have been the single and most devastating event to affect First Nations peoples since contact. Day-to-day, many former students continue to live out the horrific impact of these schools.

The women's data pushed me to reflect on my schooling history as student and teacher, a schooling past that occurred in a context in which the slaughter of the Beothucks happened. The curriculum I learned and taught represented the beautiful Indian princess Shanawdithit while an ugly history of colonization and annihilation was hidden (see Dion 2009 for a recent exploration).

Analysis is a stage in the research process during which students need to understand and work against their limitations and consider returning to the literature (and other sources) in hopes of building historical and contextual understandings when needed. They have to take care not to continue with imperialist colonizing practices when their research involves Indigenous and/or marginalized individuals and populations.

ACCOUNTING FOR DIFFERENCE

Layers of interpretive work have contributed to the data representations that students use for the purposes of analysis. Student researchers are not working with the grand truths they have captured in the process of collecting their data, but are applying an informed critical eye (informed by their identities and social locations, as well as their knowledge and experience) as they make sense of data that ultimately are reconfigured into findings that they hope will speak, in meaningful ways, to audiences that include the participants.

In the case of critical research with social justice goals in mind, participants are often recruited from vulnerable populations that are marginalized by dominant norms and structures. It is not uncommon for multiple intersecting differences — in terms of class, race, gender, sexuality and dis/ability between student researchers and participants — to exist and to be reflected in researcher and participant life experiences. How these differences might influence analysis is an important question for students to keep in mind. In recent years, the influence of identity differences has sometimes been accounted for in researcher/participant interactions. However, the influence of difference in relation to analysis work has often been undercontemplated.

Many of the women participating in my doctoral research identified as visible minorities, including Black, mixed-race and Aboriginal, and were from working-class backgrounds, in obvious contrast to my white, Anglo-Irish,

Newfoundland-Canadian middle-class identity. They left public schools in junior and senior high. I was responsible for understanding the narratives of their school experience in light of my identity and my past as a public school teacher.

When analyzing the women's stories of school experiences, I had to reconcile what the women spoke of with my past teaching experience. Elements of their narratives disrupted my memories of teaching and my identity as *good* teacher.

Data that Irene contributed, although invaluable to my understanding of her stories of schooling, made visible to me my past failure to understand and work against the institutional whiteness and racism embedded in the schooling system and to address the individual racist acts of both students and teachers and to which I contributed. Although Irene's data were hard to *hear*, I had no grounds to argue for a different reading of what the data presented:

> Irene: I wanted to learn but that year I was going to a white school. That's where I found it was racist. They were racist. They thought it was funny an Indian kid going to a white school. My cousin and me were the only two that were there.… I quit school end of Grade 8 because the kids used to push me around in school. I'd get angry and push them back and after school I'd beat them up.… I was in fights and I'd beat them up after school for pushing me around in school. The teacher and the kid's parents went to my dad. The cops went to him saying, "Your daughter is fighting with the kids at the school, you should talk to your daughter." I'd be sitting there listening to what the cops were saying to my dad. My dad would say, "Well, what are they doing to her at school for her to want to beat them up?" And they would say, "Just tell your daughter not to be beating up on kids in school." (Transcript, Tilley 1998a: 143–144)

I wrote my interpretation and analysis of her words and narrative in my dissertation, making connections to my past teaching experiences:

> Irene spoke of bearing the weight of racism as a child in school and not being safe in that white environment. She was punished for responding and protecting herself, while her tormentors were not held responsible for their acts. Descriptions of memories of experiences of blatant racist acts were woven into the incidents First Nations women described to me of their public school experiences. When told to me, Irene's description brought back memories I had of the only First Nations student I had taught in a public school, a context with an almost totally white school population, teachers and students included. The student stayed for half a year sitting quietly in a desk at the back of the room and then he left. After listening to Irene, I began to consider what might have been happening

to that student after school, and in the school outside my range of vision. I began to wonder what might have been happening to him within my range of vision that I was unable to see and to which I contributed. (Tilley 1998a: 152)

I was learning from the intersections of theory and women's narratives, and my experiences inside and outside the prison. During data analysis, I questioned my understandings of my past practice, my work with students who were not representative of the dominant group as well those who were. Data informed explanations for the past scenes I found myself having to unravel.

At the time of the research, I did recognize, at least to some degree, the privilege I lived in every day as well as in the context of the prison. I understood that power circulated within the research context and power relations were embedded in my interactions with participants. I was aware of the challenge I faced to do a critically sensitive read of the research context and data, but was never certain I was moving in the right direction. Student researchers need to understand that there is no one right direction. The important piece is to continuously question what influences the interpretive and analytic path they have taken and to seek/build new knowledge as needed.

THEORIZING THE DATA

Varied theoretical perspectives exist that can be applied to the same research focus or questions. Researchers decide which theories will contribute best to exploring their research questions. Researchers addressing the same research questions may apply different theoretical frameworks. In the early stages of the research, students draw from various bodies of knowledge, based on experiential, conceptual, academic and other sources, to construct a theoretical framework that they include in their thesis, MRP or dissertation document. The analysis stage is often the stage when student researchers find that their theoretical framework needs adjustments. Based on the data they analyze, students may decide that they need to move beyond the theories chosen in the earlier stages of the research and return to the literature to acquire more/new knowledge to help them analyze the data actually collected.

When researchers are engaging a critical lens, critical theories will be central in the framework they construct. There are a vast number of theories that can fall under the broad umbrella of critical theory. In my case, for my doctoral research I needed to access theoretical knowledge that could help me understand the prison/school institution and the life lived within its walls, as well as the participants' schooling experiences inside and outside of the prison context. I looked to critical theories that emphasized questioning of dominant ideologies; institutional, political and social structures; the marginalization and privileging of particular bodies and communities; the intersections across oppressions and knowledge/ power relations.

When students theorize their data, they use formal theory to ask critical questions, pushing beyond a surface analysis that rests on description, interpretation and explanation. The result of their theorizing needs to make sense to them in relation to their knowledge of context and participants, and they need to be able to justify their analysis (surface or otherwise) to those interested, including advisors, committee members, external examiners, public audiences and participants.

In the sections that follow, I provide three illustrations of theorizing data from my doctoral research project. What is represented is the outcome of the theorizing activity, not the extensive work that needed to occur as I struggled to make sense of the data, considering all the possible alternative readings and settling on what I thought was the most supported and credible analysis. The struggle to understand data is hard to capture after the fact, but students should be aware that they open themselves up to challenging work when their goal is critical, nuanced analysis.

The first illustration draws on the work of Michel Foucault (1979, 1980) and demonstrates its contribution to the analysis. The second reflects the ways in which theories intersect as Foucault and Hill-Collins (1991) together influence my understandings of data. The third illustration points to the need for researchers to be open to participants' theorizing of their own experience and the contribution this theorizing can make to the researcher's analysis and meaning-making. Foucault, Collins and other scholars contributed to my theoretical framework and analysis at the time of my research; students will need to decide which theorists are best-suited to help them analyze their research data.

ILLUSTRATION 1: FOUCAULT AND SURVEILLANCE

An important emphasis of critical ethnographic research is the development of an understanding of the research context; physical institutional structures; and institutional cultures, regulations and practices. Foucault's critique of prison and school institutions, and theories of surveillance and power/knowledge relations were central in building my understanding of the prison institution (and schools) and the data women contributed to the study. Foucault compared the apparatus of prisons and schools and the power circulating in both those contexts. Schools were physically shaped in ways similar to prisons, with familiar disciplinary apparatus. Foucault's application of Bentham's panopticon to his theorizing of surveillance fit with my experience of the physical prison and informed my data analysis.

Foucault (1980: 155) describes the benefits of the panoptic architecture of the prison and its role in the control and surveillance of its prisoners:

> There is no need for arms, physical violence, material constraints. Just a

gaze. An inspecting gaze, a gaze which each individual under its weight will end by interiorising to the point that he is his own overseer, each individual thus exercising this surveillance over, and against, himself. A superb formula: power exercised continuously and for what turns out to be a minimal cost.

The guards had access to space on each floor and at the very top of the prison structure that provided an all-seeing view to areas prisoners occupied below them — they applied the "inspecting gaze." The tiny cameras embedded in the walls and ceilings throughout the prison intensified that gaze. To travel from one area to another, prisoners had to connect to the invisible person/s in the control area through an intercom system. They may or may not be given permission. Prisoners could be seen, but could not see their surveyors. Even though the women understood that the gaze could not always capture everyone's every action, the fact that the possibility existed influenced their decisions. They interiorized the gaze and exercised surveillance over themselves during their twenty-four-hour daily existence.

When I compared observational data collected related to women interacting in the rotunda and data from their individual interview conversations, I had to account for what appeared to be contradictions. Women described friendships and connections to other women in the interview data that did not reflect the interactions I observed when they were present together in the rotunda. However, with Foucault's (and later the participants') help, I was reminded that what I observed in the rotunda were the actions of women who knew they were under surveillance. Guards and cameras collected information as they observed the women's interactions. Women made strategic decisions on what could be viewed in that location, decisions reflecting the ways in which, although limited, they had some control over how they were documented, a moment of resistance even as they practised internalized surveillance over their actions. They did not want these friendships, their connections or their sometimes bitter relationships to be part of the accumulated institutional knowledge that could be used against them later. However, the friendships and dis/connections with others were discussed openly with me in the interview conversations.

While theorizing the data, I could not dismiss the fact that although I was a teacher I was also part of the prison structure and part of a surveillance system, which ultimately might also influence the data collected and my analysis. This became clearer to me after the decision was made that teachers would carry a tracking device for safety reasons, the same devices that the guards always carried previously and we had argued against using. The institutional authorities wanted us to blend in more with the context and the surveillance apparatus, ignoring the exaggeration of risk and categorization of women as dangerous offenders this additional equipment represented.

ILLUSTRATION 2: THEORETICAL INTERSECTIONS

Critical theories included in a theoretical framework intersect and inform analysis. To enact a critical analysis, I needed to be aware of and account for the larger matrix of domination (the prison institution and structures) that Foucault articulated, while also understanding what Collins (1991: 230) described as the "interlocking nature of oppressions ... which are part of a larger matrix of domination." Although race, class, gender and sexuality are often singled out as individual factors in oppression, Collins emphasizes how they intersect and fuel the oppression and marginalization of women. The women lived their gendered/classed/raced/sexed lives within the institution as they did in the outside world before becoming incarcerated.

Within the prison context, prisoners were categorized based on criteria that included federal and provincial prisoner status. Women under protective custody were a different category from others in the general population. The women attending school on a regular basis were not happy when teachers spent time with women who had been charged/found guilty of an offence involving children and were housed in protective custody. They judged these women with little empathy:

> The talk turns to the woman who's actually in the prison for killing her son. Social Welfare didn't step in, even though they were aware of the abuse for a while. Taylor tells us, "I have seen a picture of that boy and it broke my heart." Penny says it makes her sick when they go to visits and the woman is in there with her boyfriend. ... Geraldine explains that there were twenty-six different times that doctors had seen the child, but they said there wasn't enough evidence to notify anyone. Social Services eventually went to visit, but decided it would do too much damage to the woman. There was no real reason to take the child away. Lena says, "There's something wrong with the system that didn't take him away." Tonya talks about how she does one thing wrong and she has the cops and Social Welfare at her door and here's this woman doing all those other things and nothing's happening. Leslie talks about when her cousin, who she had a really big argument with, called Social Welfare. Tonya's 7-month old baby was taken away from her because of her cousin's complaint. There's real disgust around the table as we talk about this woman. Deirdre who's sitting beside me is letting out these big sighs. ... They're all reacting and contributing to the conversation. They make it clear that they don't want to be associated with this particular woman. (Participant observation, Tilley 1998a: 66)

I wrote my interpretive and analytic take on the observation in the dissertation:

> Protective Custody is an institutional practice justified on the basis that it provides safety for these women. Many women in the classroom have children of their own and are living a forced separation. Many have been abused themselves as children. They have been treated unfairly. However, they are fixed in their position; hurting children is a crime not easily forgiven. Separating out particular women from the general population creates, for the "regular" prisoner, a focus for hostility and relief; relief to know that within the prison itself, there are still those less worthy, more hated, than she. Eaton (1993), in her study involving ex-prisoners, writes of Terry who experienced "double exclusion." While incarcerated, she was excluded from society as well as kept separate from the general prison population under Rule 43: Her offence involved her child's death so she was put under protective custody, "In prisons there is a pecking order and Rule 43s are right at the bottom." (Terry in Eaton 1993: 61). Students in the prison school illustrate how "those [individuals] who themselves are controlled by the system become part of that system in controlling others. Hierarchies are reproduced and the status quo is preserved." Teachers work with the various institutionally assigned categories of women dealing with the complexities of schooling created by the prison institution. (Tilley 1998a: 66–67)

A surface analysis of the observation might remain focused on the content of the women's comments. Women declare their compassion for the child and an unforgiving stance toward the mother. They point to the ways in which authorities control them through their children, able to have them taken away without the weight of evidence against them. Regardless, the fact that a mother can harm a child is not to be forgiven. Although Lena included an institutional critique, the blame remained centred on the individual woman. The women speaking are not connecting themselves or their circumstances to the protective custody prisoner, although many circumstances, including their gendered and classed experiences, may be similar. They have described in other spaces their living a life in periods of poverty, enduring violence and abuse from partners and family members and doing things they regret, but understanding how their past influenced those decisions. They discuss this woman with only prison gossip to understand her charge/ crime or situation.

The implication of the process of "double exclusion" provides a nuanced perspective on the situation. The participants are already housed in a multimillion-dollar, security-driven institution when only a small percentage can be seen as dangerous.

Similar to Terry in Mary Eaton's (1993) description, the woman in protective custody was twice removed: first from general society and then from the community inside the prison. The system worked to isolate her for her crimes while also contributing to a doubled emphasis on *regular* prisoners being dangerous women.

Within this hierarchical structure, prisoners turn their gaze and surveil those in protective custody; they administer their own punishments when possible (e.g., trying to convince teachers not to work with those prisoners) to women who act in shocking ways, harming a child, stepping outside the normal behaviour expected of a woman. Their actions reflect the gaze of the guards and institutional disciplinary apparatus that they themselves regularly critique as harsh for a prison that is supposedly advancing the goal of rehabilitation. Collins, Foucault (and others) provided the theoretical backdrop to help me make sense of this participant observation.

ILLUSTRATION 3: PARTICIPANTS THEORIZING THEIR EXPERIENCES

Not only did I gain an understanding of the data through applying the Big T theories, intellectual theories included in academic studies, but also through the theorizing the participants did of their own experiences. Pamela, who had a long history of incarceration in prisons across Canada, explains one of her struggles:

> Pamela: I had an experience the last time I was here. Someone told me, "Blacks hang with blacks and whites hang with whites and natives hang with natives." Well, I'm Heinz 57, so where am I supposed to hang out? I've had the black women say I'm not black enough for them and I'm not white enough for others. It is very hard to be black anywhere. Like especially when I was in prison in another province. I was the only black person in prison with [all those women].
>
> Susan: The only one.
>
> Pamela: Only one! It's hard trying to make people understand. It's different things, different needs, even material things. I can't use the same kind of cream as you use. I need special cream.... People like to throw things back at you, like other women saying I think I should be allowed privileges. These aren't privileges. These are necessities. I find a lot of people here don't see colour and then there's a lot of people that do. You have to be either on the white side or the Native side and that makes tension.... And that's where the tension comes from being black because you don't know where you fit. (Transcript, Tilley 1998a: 168–169)

Previous to the recorded conversation, I heard Pamela refer to herself as a "Heinz 57" [a mix of races] in passing, but paid the comment little attention. The complexities of race, racism and various forms of privileging and their material effects on specific bodies were made explicit in that conversation, as well as during numerous other interactions. I also observed the institutional structures that supported and sometimes created the divides across race in the daily practices of the prison. I interpreted the complaints against racialized minority women who were requiring privileges against my new understandings of how privilege and whiteness operated within the confines of the prison, which reflected similarities to how they operated beyond the confines of the prison walls/structures.

Pamela understood how race influenced her ability to find a place that was comfortable among the other prisoners. Her theorizing of her situation and experience of racial tension and discrimination were reflective of the critical theory I applied to the data. I made meaning of the data based not only on the application of my building theoretical knowledge but also with the help of participants' analysis of their own experience, which I learned to value highly.

QUESTIONS TO PREPARE FOR ANALYSIS

Questions that researchers ask at other stages of the research process are also useful to ask at the analysis stage, in addition to questions directly related to analysis work. Although standard definitive answers are not possible for many questions, practising a critical reflexivity helps students address questions and shape their work with critical issues in mind. In preparation for analyzing their data, I encourage students to consider the following questions:

Questioning the Logistics

- Is the student's logistical plan for analysis workable? Suited to the methods and methodology?
- What have students learned through courses and research experience to help with data analysis? What is left to learn?
- What knowledge counts when analyzing data through a critical-feminist-postmodern lens?
- Are student researchers familiar enough with the data to analyze them appropriately?
- Has all the data collected been analyzed? Why or why not?
- Is the analysis process documented in a way that is transparent to others?

Questioning the Self

- Who are the student researchers in relation to their research focus, participants and research context?

- How might their cultural, historical and contextual knowledge impede or support respectful data analysis?
- How might being an insider, an outsider or someone familiar colour their analysis?
- Is there too much or too little distance between participants and student researchers?
- Is the analysis as deep and nuanced as possible, considering the differences between the student researcher and participants (e.g., adult researcher versus child participant)?
- How might the knowledge that student researchers have, based on the intersecting elements of their identities, enrich the analysis?
- What can student researchers do to enhance their analysis when they are aware of identity influences?

ARTICULATING THE FINDINGS

With the results of their analysis, student researchers construct the findings of the study. What have they learned as a result of the analysis process? The coding, categorizing and constructing of clusters of meaning and themes are turned into findings reported in their research documents, including theses and dissertations.

The findings will emphasize emergent knowledge that relates to the research focus and questions. Findings will often contribute new knowledge to the field and support what has been already established. They may make original, conceptual, theoretical and/or methodological contribution to the field of study. Expectation will reflect the degree level — fewer original, nuanced findings at an undergraduate and master's level versus those to be found as a result of doctoral studies. Research findings make a contribution to the literature whether in their support of established knowledge or as a contradiction to what is already present. Some findings will be more important than others, and it is up to the researchers to ensure that they make prominent the findings that are relevant to the field and the research participants.

EDUCATING OURSELVES MATTERS

As discussed earlier in this chapter, student researchers need to have an organized plan in place and make informed decisions on analysis logistics. They need to decide what data will be analyzed and what analysis methods will be employed based on their methodology, research focus and data collected. They need to document their analysis procedures, ensuring that the process is transparent and can be captured in the documents prepared in the final stages to represent the research they conducted.

The comprehensiveness of the literature review developed and the usefulness of the theoretical framework constructed will influence the researcher's ability to enact a respectful and informed analysis. Students must be willing to return to the literature when the theoretical, historical, methodological and experiential knowledge they have is too limited; and sometimes they should return to their participants if they need to deepen their understandings of the data. They will need to understand and acknowledge the bigger picture of Eurocentricism, power, privilege, socially constructed differences and cultural complications that influence interpretive research traditions.

Students can seek out alternative perspectives that are not offered in the curricula of their graduate courses, including the methodology courses they take, remembering that they are learning to conduct research within institutions that exercise power, in various ways, that influence how the study of methodology, qualitative or otherwise, ensues. When suggesting that "methodology itself can be viewed as a form of governmentality," Dehli (2008: 61) states that "teaching about and supervising students in methodology are about generating experts who can be trusted to produce truth according to authorized rules and transparent procedures." Students need to critique their institutional experiences and how they influence the ways in which they take up their identities as researchers, applying their critical reflexivity to the knowledge, processes and procedures they experience while engaged in learning about and conducting their qualitative research projects.

MOVING FORWARD

Qualitative, interpretive research is not linear; researchers return, revisit and refocus on aspects of the research process at various points as the research is conducted. However, following data analysis is a time when researchers emphasize questions of representation. What data will be represented in the findings and documentation, and how will that data be represented? The next chapter explores issues of representation.

Annotated Bibliography

Doucet, Andrea. 2008. "From Her Side of the Gossamer Wall(s): Reflexivity and Relational Knowing." *Qualitative Sociology* 31: 73–87.

In this article, Andrea Doucet presents a unique means for conceptualizing reflexivity and rethinking "everyday knowledge": a metaphor of three gossamer walls. She explains that the first "wall" through which researchers construct knowledge is the relationship to self, including past experiences that continue to haunt researchers in the present. The second gossamer wall is the relationship between the researcher and the respondents, and the third and final wall is between the researcher and the audience. Doucet argues that this metaphor, which invokes the sheerness of gos-samer with the solidity of walls, allows researchers to a) consider transparency in their knowledge production; b) recognize the limits to their knowledge of subjects; c) focus on personal motivations for conducting the research; and d) explore the "spatial quality of reflexivity" that emphasizes different sets of near and distant relations between the researcher, respondents and research community (2008: 84).

Duggleby, Wendy. 2005. "What About Focus Group Interaction Data?" *Qualitative Health Research* 15, 6: 832–840.

Wendy Duggleby considers the complex data that can emerge from focus groups, with particular attention to interaction patterns within the group (e.g., behaviours, language and nonverbals). She takes up the existent challenges involved in ana-lyzing, integrating and representing this multilayered data. The article contains a useful chart to which novice researchers can refer that identifies a variety of articles on focus groups and the strategies used by the researchers to analyze individual, group and group interaction data. In particular, the common analytic strategies that emerge include description, integration into the transcripts, and analysis in light of the given methodology. The author explains that each approach has particular opportunities and limitations. She outlines multiple ways of reporting or represent-ing the findings, which include descriptions or the use of data excerpts. In each case, she emphasizes the importance of relating analysis and representation strategies to one's overarching research objectives and theoretical framework.

Fraser, Heather. 2004. "Doing Narrative Research: Analysing Personal Stories Line by Line." *Qualitative Social Work* 3, 2,:179–201.

Heather Fraser articulates the challenges and opportunities associated with the application of narrative methodology for studying issues in social work settings. She identifies possible ways of collecting and analyzing data, while maintaining that there exists variability across approaches based on the purpose and goals of one's study. More specifically, Fraser describes numerous interconnected strategies for analyzing narrative data that she hopes researchers will find useful. These strategies involve (but are not limited to) using active listening by carving out a space to react to what happened and what was said; transcribing, which facilitates closeness to the data and the emergence of novel insights; striving for a deeper understanding by examining components of the stories, carefully reading the transcripts, looking for relationships and incongruities, and considering both words and actions; attending to sociocultural dimensions as related to self and others; making connections to theoretical perspectives and broader societal issues or conversations; accounting for convergences and divergences across data sets; and constructing an interpretation while acknowledging a multiplicity of views. She offers guiding questions that might prompt researchers to prepare for and move forward with analysis.

Loppie, Charlotte. 2007. "Learning from the Grandmothers: Incorporating Indigenous Principles into Qualitative Research." *Qualitative Health Research* 17, 2: 276–284.

Charlotte Loppie, an assistant professor at Dalhousie University in Halifax, Nova Scotia, reflects back on her doctoral research with Mi'kmaq women, noting that a single methodology or generic approach would fail to do justice to the complexity of the research topic and intricacies of participants' experiences. She is openly aware of the limitations of her knowledge while striving to conduct research in a way that demonstrates reverence toward participants' cultural backgrounds and understandings. She determines that what is necessary is a fusion of multiple methodologies ("Western" and "Indigenous" approaches) and finds ways to negotiate contradictory moments by remaining adaptable and open, as well as bringing together stakeholders. Participants were involved in all facets of the research in ways comfortable to them, and Loppie received ongoing "cultural" training from insiders to support her ability to do this research. She recounts the necessary time involved in establishing relationships and describes keeping "two journals" (one "public" and one "private"). By employing multiple analytic strategies and asking for input on preliminary findings before moving forward, she became prepared for subsequent levels of analysis involving an immersion in multilayered data, which required energy to venture beyond the surface. She reveals that conducting this research had a profound impact on her.

Mosselson, Jacqueline. 2010. "Subjectivity and Reflexivity: Locating the Self in Research on Dislocation." *International Journal of Qualitative Studies in Education* 23, 4: 479–494.

Jacqueline Mosselson describes moving away from her positivist orientations and teachings toward an embracing of interpretivist practices when conducting doctoral research with Bosnian women refugees. Integral to her emerging understandings and sense-making was a carving out of both a space and a way to integrate herself more fully into the project. "I found that including my positionality, personal artifacts, emotional responses to the participants, and the data could enhance the research process" (2010: 480). When analyzing words, Mosselsen also considered the communicative exchange and her accompanying reactions. She wondered how her background, experiences, motivations, familial history and upbringing influenced her curiosities and concerns. Upon careful and ongoing reflection, she recognized important connections and recurring themes. Through her use of critical questions such as "How am I reacting and responding to the participants and the data? What do these reactions and responses teach me? How can these lessons be incorporated into the analysis?" (2010: 488), Mosselsen was able to interact with and analyze the data in thoughtful ways while expressing some lingering regret over not taking her analyses back to her participants.

Palys, Ted, and Chris Atchison. 2012. "Qualitative Research in the Digital Era: Obstacles and Opportunities." *International Institute for Qualitative Methodology* 11, 4: 352–367.

Students who are interested in using digital software programs and other new technologies to collect, manage and analyze data in their research projects may be interested in this article because it outlines the implications for recruitment and sampling; and for gathering, transcribing and analyzing qualitative data. Ted Palys and Chris Atchison outline the benefits that they perceive new technologies are bringing to the field of qualitative research and they discuss what they see as the underused potential of older programs such as NVIVO. The authors also consider the ways in which digital technologies and the Internet are impacting qualitative research, highlighting ethical concerns such as confidentiality and security, particularly when researchers use cloud-based technologies to store their data.

Power, Elaine M. 2004. "Toward Understanding in Postmodern Interview Analysis: Interpreting the Contradictory Remarks of a Research Participant." *Qualitative Health Research* 14, 6: 258–265.

Elaine M. Power describes the complexities involved in conducting analytic work. She draws on her doctoral research with mothers on social assistance living in a small impoverished community in Nova Scotia, Canada, to explain the challenges she faced in understanding a woman's contradictory statements within an open-ended interview. Drawing on concepts from Pierre Bourdieu's work, along with notions of "distance," "reflexivity" and perspective-taking, she explains that "Listening to understand a participant's logic of practice leads the analyst to look beyond, between, and underneath the participant's words, to understand the social space in which the participant is located and in which the interview took place" (2004: 860). Accounting for a) contextual information, b) "tone," c) expressions, d) emotions, e) enduring questions, f) subsequent behaviour and g) significant events transpiring in participants' lives becomes useful in informing possible analyses. She compares and contrasts words, expressions and messages, noting how expectations of others might have influenced the participant's responses and portrayals.

Quint-Rapoport, Mia. 2010. "Open Source in Higher Education: A Situational

Analysis of the Open Journal Systems Software Project." Unpublished doctoral dissertation, University of Toronto, Toronto, ON.

In this Canadian Society for the Study of Higher Education award-winning disser-tation, Mia Quint-Rapoport uses a relatively new methodology called "situational analysis" to theorize the data and explore the impact of Open Journals Systems on knowledge production and dissemination in the academy. She describes this analytical approach as a means "to take research beyond simply the words and statements of participants in the project; to consider their locationality and other elements with which they interact" (2010: 90). Unlike grounded theory, the goal of situational analysis is not to look for commonalities and derive a theory out of the patterns that emerge from the data, "but rather to create an interpretive analysis of a situation and it is the situation that is the object (or subject) of analysis." Thus, in place of Clifford Geertz's "thick description," researchers who choose to theorize their data using situational analysis seek "thick analysis" (2010: 90).

Rallis, Sharon F. 2010. "'That Is NOT What's Happening at Horizon': Ethics and Misrepresenting Knowledge in Text." *International Journal of Qualitative Studies in Education* 23, 4: 435–448.

Drawing on some of the critical incidents that transpired during a research project on innovative schools in which she was peripherally involved, Sharon Rallis describes researchers' limited knowledge and skills as significant impediments to their ability to conduct thoughtful analyses and construct multidimensional representations. She surmises that in this case, "the researchers were unable to scrutinize and interrogate their data in light of the context from which the data were collected. They thus failed to examine reflexively the knowledge they produced in their written representations" (2010: 435). Serious consequences transpired as researcher-generated analyses failed to resonate with participants, and issues of trustworthiness were called into question. Rallis identifies the importance of reflexivity; an examination of one's self, stance, actions and contextual awareness (or lack thereof), with careful considera-tion as to how these dimensions factor into the analytic process. She reiterates the need for researchers to acknowledge multiple perspectives within their analyses.

Chapter 7

REPRESENTATION: WRITING UP/DOWN

Forming representations will mean rendering intelligible accounts of analyses, such as through construction of themes or patterns; transformation of journal entries or transcripts into narratives; or explication of an individual account using a particular theoretical lens. Of course, the processes of analysis and representation overlap throughout the duration of a qualitative project; for example, the production of ethnographic fieldnotes involves both selection of details of an encounter or setting to document (i.e., analysis) and generation of a representation of that analysis (the written notes). (Ellingson 2011: 595)

In tandem with and following analysis, student researchers make decisions in relation to the representation of data, including how to represent research data in meaningful ways and what data to make public. Questions relevant to representational issues are asked at a micro level; for example, "What will I represent from an hour of observation conducted on the hospital ward?" At the macro level, a student researcher might ask, "What is the meta-narrative I will tell in the body of my thesis, dissertation and/or other forms of publication?" After completing the formal analysis stage, student researchers construct, craft and compile representations as texts, visuals, photographs and artistic expressions to communicate their findings to interested audiences. Producing these representations is a step toward *going public*.

Issues of representation have been central in debates in ethnography and in the qualitative, interpretivist research world for decades (Clifford 1988; Clifford and Marcus 1986; Denzin 1997; Stacey 1988; Wolf 1992). Questions of subjectivity/ identity, gender, race, class, researcher reflexivity and neutrality in connection to representation have been a focus in what has been characterized as a crisis of representation (Denzin and Lincoln 2000). Stuart C. Aitken (2010: 57) writes: "This was not just a representational crisis that pointed out the problems of qualitative attempts to capture lived experience; it was a legitimation crisis whereby several axioms of science — validity, generalizability, reliability — were called into question."

In the context of critical qualitative research, the connection between data and their representations are understood to be complicated, fraught with researcher and participants' interpretive and analytic moves, partial and value-laden. Researchers working from a critical, feminist, postmodern perspective acknowledge the degree of interpretive and analytic work involved in producing what ultimately serve as data representations and factor into their work a consideration of the challenges involved in respectfully representing the data analyzed. Student researchers will need to engage a critical reflexivity when making decisions related to questions of representation. An important part of the researcher's considerations is the potential repercussions, for participants and research contexts, of researchers producing data representations and making them publicly available.

Research methodology and methods will influence representational decisions that researchers make. Specific qualitative methodologies may be explicit in terms of the expectations of how data are represented in final research documents, and the credibility of the work will be tied to following the expectations of the methodology (e.g., the shaping of the narrative based on data of personal and professional accounts of experience in narrative inquiry). In the case of ethnography, a common expectation is that the research context be represented in great detail, a "thick description" (Geertz 1973) allowing readers to gain an understanding of the physical space, cultural norms and practices. Van Maanen (1988: 1) describes an ethnography as "a written representation of a culture (or selected aspects of a culture.) It carries quite serious intellectual and moral responsibilities, for the images of others inscribed in writing are most assuredly not neutral." Regardless of the methodology of choice, the representations produced and made public are not neutral, as Van Maanen suggests. When conducting respectful research, questions of representation become front and centre. How do researchers respectfully represent their participants, research contexts, data and findings? How does the work of representation relate to the credibility of the research, the findings? As always, answers to such questions are context-specific. Based on personal choice or methodology, research participants may be very involved in deciding the ways in which data will be represented (e.g., participatory action research, community-based research), totally isolated from the process or have various degrees of involvement.

KEEPING PROMISES MADE

Student researchers who are engaged in constructing data representations and crafting the final research documents through their writing are often distanced from the research context and participants. They need to remember the agreements they made in their ethics applications and the information they gave to participants during the continuous consent process. They also have to think critically about the *in situ* moments when ethical issues emerged that were not accounted for through the institutional process; these issues have implications for decisions made regarding representations moving into the public domain.

When representing data in the documents that will be introduced into a public venue (including the publication as a thesis, MRP or dissertation), students need to ensure that they continue to honour the promises they made in relation to keeping data confidential. At this late stage, they may be better able to distinguish what are or are not identifying details and information. Although data may be extremely useful to the study, the data must be excluded if possibilities exist for their inclusion to breach ethical respectful praxis.

The degree of vulnerability of participants involved in the research would have been considered when the students completed ethics review processes; however, in the latter stages of research, students are better informed as to how to protect their participants, and earlier decisions may have to be reversed at this stage of the research process. Questions that students may want to consider as they construct their data representations include the following:

- Are the promises that were made being upheld in the decisions about what will be made public?
- Is there specific contextual information provided that helps identify a participant?
- Is confidentiality compromised in any way by the details included?
- Are pseudonyms so close to the participants' names that they may be identified in and connected to what is written?
- When juxtaposing data from multiple participants, is identifying information formed?
- Can the findings disseminated have a negative impact on participants?
- Does the risk to an individual outweigh the benefits of reporting the data?
- To whom are findings being reported and are they *safe* audiences?

Student researchers may have to turn to strategies used historically in qualitative research to protect confidentiality (i.e., changing demographic-sex of participant, geographic information) to include the data they judge as important to the research or draw on creative strategies (see Angrosino 1998; Inckle 2010; Orbach 1986). Kay Inckle (2010: 30) describes how she was "confronted with a dilemma of how to represent the fullness of their [her participants'] experiences, their struggles and dilemmas without doing harm to them." She used ethnographic fiction as a method of representation because "through their form and content; ethic and orientation, ethnographic fictions offer a means to research and represent the complexities of embodied experience in ways which are ethically salient and which produce manifold possibilities of transformation and change" (Inckle 2010: 39).

In most studies, even with a solid data-collection plan in place, data collected may not be used for a number of reasons, including the lack of connection to the research questions or the usefulness to the research overall. It is important that in the early stages, student researchers explain to participants the uses that may or may not be made of the data and how the data are used cumulatively to explore the research questions. For instance, they can explain that the data used may not be visible in individual form (for maintaining confidentiality and other reasons), but can still make an important contribution to the study. Such a discussion is possible when a respectful rapport has been developed between student researchers and participants. Even when data are included, participants may be disappointed that what they have contributed to a study is not visible to them in the final documents (e.g., individual quotes from their transcripts).

During the construction of my dissertation, I was always aware that prison officials might read the contents. In fact, they were an intended audience. I was able to provide a critique of a system that those closest to it would not be able to do, even if they had the desire. As an outside researcher leaving the context, and having followed a credible and transparent qualitative research process, I had few fears of how those in authority might be displeased by my findings. The fine line I had to walk continuously was in constructing representations of data and articulating findings in ways that those who contributed could not be held responsible. Although researchers can never be sure of what may follow in the steps of completing a research project, they can fulfil their responsibilities to make the most informed decisions to ensure, as much as possible, that their participants have been protected.

PARTICIPANT FEEDBACK

When student researchers are working with designs that are participatory, individuals connected to the research context will often also be involved in making decisions related to issues of representation. There will be a built-in communication line between the student researcher and the community and/or participants. When the research is solely student-initiated, the student researchers need to build avenues through which participants can provide feedback and researchers can interact with participants to inform their decisions regarding data representations.

Student researchers can use a number of methods to check in with participants when constructing their documents (refer to Chapter 5 for a comprehensive discussion of member checking). During my doctoral research, after I analyzed data and was in the process of writing, I scheduled reporting-back sessions in the hopes of receiving feedback on my work from participants. In one session, I described how I was incorporating participants' data into the dissertation, specifically the representations constructed from interview transcripts and observations. We talked about the ways in which the women (themselves included) were represented in what was written and the flavour of my writing. I read aloud sections of draft chapters. The following response was to a section I had written critiquing media discourse on women in prison:

> Lena: I think the more people represent incarcerated women as thinking, caring, hurting women with hurts, needs, concerns, women that are real and not sensationalized, the better it is for us.
>
> Fran: And intelligent too, because there are some really highly intelligent girls.
>
> Colleen: That we are not these little demons from hell.
>
> Lena: And I think it's [breaking that stereotype through this work] very important. That was the reason that I took part in an interview with you in the first place. I think I probably expressed that to you before the interviews began. That reasoning hasn't changed in any way even though my situation has changed a lot in a year. (Tilley 1998a: 38)

As part of the checking-back process, I also gave draft chapters of my dissertation to Geraldine, the teacher who most supported my work and participated in recorded conversations and an interview. She was very interested in the research from the beginning. The following conversation highlights differences in participant and researcher thinking about what might ultimately be represented in final research texts going public:

> Geraldine and I met after she read the first four chapters. She told me she was surprised I hadn't focused more on the writing group. She said that that was what she would have done. I explained to her that I didn't think of the morning meeting as a writing group. I tried to explain to her that I saw the morning meeting as much more than a time for focused writing. I described how in another chapter I focus on the educational moments I felt played out during some of those meetings, sometimes involving writing sometimes not. She commented on my detailed descriptions

saying that she puts a lot of that out of her mind. She tries to forget she's working in a prison. She really enjoyed the discussion of the interruptions/disruptions. (Tilley 1998a: 58)

Geraldine was also a graduate student completing a master's degree with a focus on teaching writing (outside the prison context), so I was not too surprised when she expressed disappointment that a more comprehensive focus on the writing group was not included. During the meeting, we talked about our different perspectives and interpretations of what was most important to be represented, and in what ways, in my dissertation. However, after our discussion and upon further reflection, I was still comfortable with the degree of emphasis I had given to this area. I understood how keeping a lot of what happened in the prison and classroom "out of her mind" and focusing on the positives of the women's writing activity was one of Geraldine's survival tactics. She was remaining in the school long after I departed. Geraldine was not in disagreement with anything I had written. She particularly liked my scrutiny of the prison context, the critique I offered.

Checking back with participants at the latter stages of the research process can also introduce complications, particularly when participants are unhappy with the choices that researchers are making or have made. Researchers live with the fear that participants may decide to withdraw their data late in the process. I once conducted a research project with faculty members situated at multiple universities. After some time passed since the interviews were conducted, and I returned the transcripts and synopses of my interpretations to participants, a participant contacted me and requested that I not use her data. She had contributed important data, the withdrawal of which would have been a loss to the study. I decided to contact the person regarding her decision, a decision I was not expecting based on previous communications. While making it clear to the participant that the data would not be used as requested, I asked whether she would be willing to leave the data as-is if I initiated a more vigilant checking-back process with her. We agreed that I would forward any texts I planned to publish that included her data in isolation of other data (e.g., directly quoting from her interview transcripts), and she could decide whether she wanted the data removed before the material was submitted for possible publication or presented in a public venue. She agreed, based on trusting that I would keep our new arrangement. If strong communication lines and an effective rapport had not developed previously, her answer to my request may have been different.

When student researchers have a positive rapport with participants and keep communication lines open throughout the research process, any unexpected withdrawal of data is less likely to happen. However, when faced with a request for withdrawal, students might consider alternative processes they could offer that might be acceptable to participants, suggesting such options only after the student researchers have made it clear that they will withdraw and destroy the data as requested if that is the participants' final decision. When withdrawal is the ultimate decision, students need to make the best of the situation, critiquing and learning from the experience and perhaps including a discussion of the challenges of the experience in their methodology chapter.

REASONING OUR REPRESENTATIONAL CHOICES

> As researcher, I worked between what was told and left invisible. While I analyzed transcripts, themes that I was able to imagine emerged, while others lay unearthed. Similarities of the women's experiences were illuminated as well as the differences. With the authority afforded the researcher who, ultimately, is in control of what is written, I created dilemmas and made my choices of what would or would not appear in print.... I was concerned about re-presenting women in a way that did not create the essential female prisoner, while recognizing that in some instances using essentialist claims in strategic ways might benefit particular groups of women (Spivak 1993: 4). As I wrote with the women's voices in the background, I wanted to emphasize the differences between them rather than the similarities. I made my choices and wrote, understanding that "it is the ethnographer who lays her fingers on the keyboard to play the final note in the chorus of voices" (Stack 1996: 106). (Tilley 1998a: 58)

As the doctoral research process unfolded, I was made more aware of the power of the social world outside the prison to shape people's understandings (and had shaped my understandings) of who was imprisoned and what lives were lived in that context. I wanted to combat the typical representations of women prisoners and stereotypes that I had consumed through the media discourse and the entertainment world. This goal influenced my choice of which data would be most prominent in the texts I constructed. I carefully chose details of the prison context abstracted from fieldnotes and other data to provide insight into life in prison that reflected my interpretation of the realities of the everyday lives of the women participants while hopefully making visible the misinformation that supported the stereotypical and essentialized image of female prisoners.

To ensure that others, including those like me — part of the dominant privileged, white, Western-educated, middle-class norm — would have an opportunity to develop a more informed understanding of incarceration and prison outside of media representations, I included data that spoke to the ways in which surveillance operated to control, manage and infantilize women who were no danger to society, but were locked up in a multimillion-dollar, heavily guarded institution. I used the content and structure of the document to help *guide* readers (I assume not always successfully) to an understanding of the ways in which the women who participated had resisted the oppressive structures of the prison. These women, often verbal about their acceptance of the punishment for their crimes, found ways to resist what they perceived as injustices within the prison system. Although they understood the futility of their attempts, they were unwilling to be passive, accepting of their fates. As some of them sat at the computers in the school, asking for help with their writing, they constructed letters to the ombudsman about the unfair practices they were made to endure in the prison. I did not want readers of the dissertation to categorize the women participants as victims, but to see the women's subtle and *in your face* acts of resistance as reflective of their strength in the face of incarceration. I used my writing choices and decisions to help me accomplish this goal, knowing that readers would ultimately decide what sense they would make of what I had written.

In my dissertation, I wrote about the ways participants created space in the prison where they could be free for small periods of time from the all-observing, invisible, punishing eyes embedded in the prison structures. The following is an example:

> There are windows from the top to about two feet off the floor, windows along the wall that are to the left as I walk down the centre of the class-room, windows dividing classroom from rotunda. There are blinds, those that open and close sideways, attached to the windows. They are sup-posed to be kept open so that people can see in. A very large blackboard, fifteen feet wide and nine feet high, almost as long as the window, is kept in front of the window. Although the blinds are open, people cannot see in through the blackboard. The view from outside to inside is disrupted. (Tilley 1998a: 11)

I was teaching in the school for a while before I began to understand the ritual of the women closing the blinds whenever the opportunity arose. The guards noticed, interrupted class to make the women open them and then gave them (and the teachers) a lecture.

Surprisingly, no cameras were embedded in the ceilings and walls of the classrooms. The large windows were there to provide guards with a view inside the school. The women were pleased to have the blackboard placed in front of the window, even though it blocked their vision of what was happening outside in the rotunda. They valued the board that obstructed the guards' view into the classroom and closed the blinds whenever possible, knowing full well that a total blackout of the school from those in control was unacceptable. Initially, I thought the women's persistence was a childish act of petulance, but when considered in light of what I learned as I spent time in the context, I understood their actions as a form of resistance. Closing the blinds was very important to the women. Their actions of resistance were carefully thought through.

When student researchers practise a critical reflexivity, they ask questions such as this: Why include this data and not that data? By asking themselves critical questions, they can better work with the complexities of their choices of which representations find their way into the research texts they construct. Most often, the choices are obvious, the data are essential and there is no question of their inclusion. However, occasions arise when researchers have to reflect critically on why they chose certain data as important to represent or why other data are left to rest on the cutting board.

The research process includes moments of excitement as well as experiences of the mundane, of "dull moments." The importance of mundane occurrences and details related to the research focus is not always obvious when student researchers are collecting their data; in fact, these dull moments may not contribute to understanding the research focus more fully. However, mundane occurrences and details are often important data that help build the researchers' and audience's knowledge of the research context and understandings of the findings.

Kari Dehli (2008: 55–56) describes her reflexive thoughts on her decisions of what to write and make public in relation to observations made in school council meetings:

> Much of the time I was not at all sure what to write; nor could I see what kind of sense could be made of our observation. What if the subjects of our ethnographic stories were not as transparent and rational as critical ethnographies would assume? Some of the time, there seemed to be very little if anything worth noting in meetings we observed. Could the narrative be one where boredom was the central theme? Isn't it the ethnographer's task to craft stories from the "field" that are not only truthful but engaging and interesting? ... I sometimes felt that there were many "dull moments" in our research into school council meetings.

While collecting and analyzing data, student researchers may find it difficult to keep their focus on the everyday and often repetitive occurrences that seem insignificant in the grander scheme of the research project. In my doctoral research, mundane details were essential to include for the reader to understand the everyday life in prison that influenced the women's schooling experiences. For instance, I wrote fieldnotes *ad infinitum* that described the classrooms and spaces where I worked with the women. At times, I suffered boredom as I recorded specifics of the physical structures, often wondering whether it was time well spent. I remember in particular the bathroom scene I documented, including the minutiae of measurement: "The washroom was a room six feet long and five feet wide, and was to the left as I walked into the teachers' office."

> As you go through the doorway off the office, to the left, there is a bathroom. It is a fairly small bathroom. Just standard size with a toilet and sink. The garbage can is overflowing with hand towels. There's a hand towel container on the right hand side. There are in the corner, to the left, as you walk into the bathroom, a fresh supply of sanitary napkins and tampons [are] piled up high. There is a broom and dustpan just leaning against the wall. There are two rolls of toilet paper. (Fieldnote, Tilley 1998a: 13–14)

It was not until later in the research process that I recognized the value of the mundane data to understand the participants and their gendered experiences, and the importance of them finding a modicum of privacy within the prison context:

> It is a woman's bathroom. No attempt is made to hide the tampons. The washroom sometimes becomes the centre of arguments when the cleanliness does not hold up to many of the students' or teachers' expectations. But having access to a washroom inside the school is important to both teachers and students because it contributes to the sectioning off of the education program from the rest of the prison. Women do not have to leave the school to go to a washroom. They remain inside. (Tilley 1998a: 14)

Other data may be considered exotic/explosive because of their shock power, data that can appeal to reluctant readers or those with voyeuristic tendencies who are attracted to the inconceivable comparisons between their lives and those of the participants. Student researchers will need to consider the value of the data represented in their final documents. Does the inclusion lead to voyeurism or continued exploitation of participants or does it contribute to something very necessary that is related to the research questions and findings? There were data that provided a window into explosive moments in the prison school that I chose not to include when writing my dissertation; those representations, decontextualized and used by a reader, might do more harm than good. I perceived the risk to be greater than the possible benefits.

As Van Maanen (1988: 25) suggests, "Meanings are not permanently embedded by an author in the text at the moment of creation. They are woven from the symbolic capacity of a piece of writing and the social context of its reception." Student researchers can make choices to work against the tendency toward the voyeuristic through the choices they make, while knowing that ultimately they have no control over how readers/audiences will choose to engage with their representations, print, visual or otherwise. Even when student researchers have the best of intentions, other people can use their data in unintended ways.

Researchers, particularly those who situate themselves within critical frameworks, have a responsibility to offer critique based on the study's data, even when such critique may at times contradict the understandings of individuals, communities or institutions who participated. How they decide to represent data that participants may not easily welcome being made public will be very important in terms of the credibility of their findings. Participants' responses will be based not only on what student researchers have constructed and they have read/viewed but also on the trust that has been built between researcher and participants over the life of the study. Researchers need to account for differences in interpretations/ representations, alternate readings of data. In actual text, this might mean indicating disagreement between themselves and the participants, explaining the different ways in which data can be interpreted. Although findings may not coincide with participant expectations (or desires), those findings should not fall so far outside of expectations as to lack credibility or be perceived as totally unfounded by the majority of those involved.

Sometimes at the conclusion of the research, student researchers are not forgiven for what they have produced and made public, but they need to be able to stand by their decisions. Arguing the sense of their decisions is made easier when they have carefully documented the rationale for their choices. When organized well, the research journal can prove useful at this stage of the process as students revisit the reasoning they documented in their journals for decisions they made while collecting and analyzing their data. If the reasoning for their decisions is recorded, they can consider their rationale for including or dismissing certain aspects of the data (for example, part of a conversation recorded during an interview or an interaction observed when in the field). The following questions are useful to contemplate when considering the inclusion/exclusion of data:

- Are mundane data — the everyday data — being excluded because those data may not hold the attention of the readers? What purpose might the mundane data be serving?
- Are data represented in ways that may contribute to the participants' or communities' exploitation?
- Are data that smack of voyeurism included?
- What harm or good can participants or communities experience because of the release of research texts, visuals or artistic data representations to the public?

Student researchers may not be able to determine the answer to each of these questions, but they are responsible for at least spending time considering these and similar questions. When possible, interacting with participants is useful to become more informed about the not-so-obvious implications of representational decisions.

USING PARTICIPANTS' WORDS: QUOTING AS A PROBLEMATIC PROCESS

In qualitative research, using participants' recorded words to support a researcher's analysis and findings is common practice. Student researchers construct representations of participants' lives and experiences by quoting from data or using visuals produced or collected. Using direct quotes can draw readers into the research and introduce them to the participants, a way for readers to get to know people and contexts, to understand data. However, students need to keep a critical eye on their use of direct quotations. In the same way, student researchers need to question the assumption that data transcribed into verbatim text capture the truth of an interview conversation or observation; they must also critique the assumption that direct quotes reflect the participants' truths in the text constructed. What is direct about a direct quote?

Before a quote finds itself on the page, it has gone through multiple layers of processing. The raw data is distanced an additional degree as it is represented in the public texts using words/images captured in transcripts/fieldnotes/journals or camera/video. A quote placed on the page has been carefully staged through its juxtaposition in relation to the surrounding texts and/or visuals. Representations of data are constructed as researchers clip, snip and juxtapose quotes that document their participants' retelling of their experiences. When writing my dissertation, I struggled with questions related to how to use the women's words, to represent my participants in respectful ways in the texts I constructed:

> As I read them [the interview transcripts and those based on observations], I consider the women's words. I read and decide what pieces I will quote in my dissertation. I consider why some words jump out at me as quotable and others do not. Is it because the words ground some theoretical point I want to develop? And/or is it because of the actual words that women choose to use? Do I find them powerful, hard-hitting, for some reason? (Tilley 1998a: 54)

Decisions about how researchers might represent data are often made in the early stages of the research process, but plans change as a result of the actual writing experience. Documenting decisions that influence what is represented in the thesis or dissertation contributes to a transparency of research process as well as a rationale for decisions that can be used in research documents at the latter stages. When grappling with how to use recorded data in the form of quotations, I wrote the following two journal entries:

> I decide to use what I call slice chapters, small chapters that include only excerpts of the women's words. As I begin the process of organizing women's words, I am left wondering/wandering. I have tried to let their words guide the framing of my research; that is why I keep returning to the transcripts. However, once I try to piece together such a slice chapter I understand how difficult that is. What words? Around which theme? What is important? I realize that these slices may be disruptive to the readers of academic dissertations. Too many different voices, words, may interfere with their readings. I laugh to myself as I think about this. On the one hand I talk/write about allowing the women's words to guide my writing/analysis and on the other hand question how those words might disrupt. Isn't that exactly what I want to happen? Disruptions of all kinds. The women who speak have been continually silenced because their voices disrupted the norm, the status quo. So am I to silence them too? (Journal entry, Tilley 1998a: 56)

Eight months later, I wrote this:

> I am re-considering my original plan to have slice chapters of the women's words fronting the academic analyses. This is partly in response to my advisor's comments around placing a large volume of de-contextualized words as chapters. Initially, the quotes may be read with interest but because of the volume, as people continue reading, quotes may be treated in a superficial manner. Maybe I should try to make sure that each woman is quoted somewhere in the document. I am no longer sure that using chapters of the women's words, totally de-contextualized is any better at re-presenting what they told me than inserting quotes inside the academic analyses. Maybe I will use extensive quotes within the text as a means of attempting to use a large number of the women's words, not be afraid of having long paragraph quotes instead of two-liners. I will make a final decision as the dissertation writing and format unfold. (Journal entry, Tilley 1998a: 56–57)

The shape of the thesis or dissertation emerges over time. Students will make decisions about what to include or not, and at another point (possibly after more time with the data or returning to the participants, the literature and/or additional theories) realize the limitations of their initial choices. Decisions should not be taken lightly nor considered unalterable later in the research or writing process. Writing is an act of inquiry (Richardson 2000, 2001; Richardson and St. Pierre 2005), a time during which researchers engage with data on multiple levels, often developing additional understandings.

It is important for students to understand that direct quotes cannot strengthen weakly constructed arguments or surface readings of data. They do not reflect or take the place of deep analysis As Loutzenheiser (2007: 114) suggests, "Using student [participant] words does not absolve the researcher from understanding the role of power and power relations in research, nor does it abdicate analytic responsibility." Although readers can be drawn to the romance of hearing from participants, they can also quickly lose interest when quoted material is disconnected from critical analysis and the purpose of the words chosen is not evident. Too long and too many direct quotes that are only loosely connected tend to lose their power.

When working cross-culturally, students may not have the knowledge to understand when something they have chosen is not theirs to share. Words/images quoted or represented can also reflect a form of cultural appropriation on the part of the researcher. Celia Haig-Brown (2010), informed by her long history working and researching with Indigenous peoples as a non-Indigenous person, addresses various forms of cultural appropriation, including the use of postmodern quotations. Checking with individuals and communities on representational issues will provide guidance to student researchers making decisions regarding respectful representation of data.

The following questions are useful for students to consider as they make decisions on how to use the words of their participants. When working collaboratively with participants, researchers and participants can consider such questions together:

- What constitutes a verbatim quote?
- What was the process completed to produce these quotes? Is the process transparent?
- Why are certain words chosen to be included in the form of direct quotes?
- Is confidentiality breached through the use of particular words or images?
- Are participants respectfully represented in the ways that the words and images are captured in the data?
- Is cultural appropriation the result of using particular words/images?
- Are participants' words edited before using them?
- How much material is directly quoted?

- Are there too many direct quotes scattered without appropriate analysis?

When students ask critical questions about the research process in which they engage, they are more likely to produce representations they can live with and support when questioned.

REPRESENTATION ACROSS DIFFERENCE

When researching across differences, researchers need to pay attention to how these differences may influence the ways in which they choose to represent the research context and participants. When student researchers lack historical and cultural understandings and knowledge, choices they make can be problematic.

Indigenous scholars and communities worldwide have critiqued the inappropriate ways in which they have been researched and represented. They have been both exoticized and demonized over time in research projects (McCaslin and Breton 2008). First Nations scholars and others have written about the importance of decolonizing research methodologies (Battiste 1998; Kovach 2010; Smith, L. 1999, 2005), questioning the historical and often continuing colonial practices of privileged researchers accruing benefits from researching the oppressions of their participants and communities and of their misrepresentation of First Nations peoples. "[Decolonizing research] neither parasites on the oppression experienced as everyday life by colonized/oppressed people nor does it extrematize/exoticize those experiences or minimize their lives of oppression as most giving voice/colonizing research has tended to do" (Mutua and Swandener 2004: 14). Although care must be taken in the case of all researchers, Indigenous and otherwise, student researchers need to be informed about the historical past of participants and communities when researching across difference. They should ask central questions related to issues of representation and whether they are contributing to voyeurism and exploitation. For example, when researching from a decolonizing stance, researchers will question whether what they are engaging in is cultural appropriation. Are Indigenous concepts and artifacts used improperly or borrowed/stolen for research purposes? If student researchers are distanced (geographically and otherwise) from the culture and context of the research, they need to spend the time and energy ascertaining what respectful practice might look like in this unfamiliar location working with unknown populations.

Sophie McCall (2011: 213) suggests the possibilities arising from respectful collaborations between Indigenous and non-Indigenous researchers while issuing this warning: "Collaborative authorship remains an uneasy and volatile process."

Collaboration may also give rise to a new model of understanding and honouring Indigenous sovereignty, as well as conveying a sense of historical accountability that, as a non-Indigenous person of the "Second Nations," I am implicated within. A diversity of forms of affiliation is possible and indeed necessary to recognize the struggle of writing and of telling a more just story of Indigenous presence in North America, through the mode of cross-cultural collaboration.

It is at the planning and research design stage when students need to assess whether they have the contextual, cultural and historical knowledge to make decisions on how to conduct respectful research and to represent the data collected. Students trying to be helpful to marginalized communities need to find nonpatronizing and respectful ways to accomplish that. For many racialized and minority individuals and communities, the respectful practice for researchers who are situated within the dominant group includes collaboratively researching with individuals from and within the community, and possibly waiting to be invited into the context, rather than repeating old harms.

For racialized minority researchers who may have some of the contextual, historical and cultural knowledge needed, but are not members of the participant community, issues of representation may also be difficult. Carl James (2012), a Canadian researcher of Black Caribbean descent, describes the ethical issues he faced when researching in a mostly Black racial minority and marginalized community in Canada that had already been stigmatized and characterized as "troubled" through media discourse. He checked back with community members regarding issues of anonymity and representation, asking for guidance in decisions related to the appropriate means of representing the community. His research involved instances of collaboration of various sorts throughout the life of the project.

Language issues also complicate matters of representation. Canadian students come from a variety of backgrounds and are often fluent in multiple languages, whether English is their first language or not. The participant base chosen will dictate the language used in data collection. Researchers need to have the capacity to conduct the research within the language group or have constructed a process that enables them to solicit the assistance of others with knowledge of the language; the former always preferable. Translation work will add additional complexities, not only to the data collection but also to the construction and representation of data. To produce English language representations, strategies have to be in place to account for the distance that lengthens between the researchers and the data as others translate, transcribe or do both. When multiple languages are involved in data-collection and analysis, additional critical attention needs to be paid to the research process and issues of representation. When students, who do not have the same resources or experience as established researchers or their advisors, make the choice to conduct research that involves multiple languages, they need to have the knowledge and resources necessary to support the challenges of the research process. Most importantly, serious consideration of the language challenges needs to precede the actual data collection, inform the analysis and be accounted for in representation decisions.

Snezana Ratković (2014: 111) uses bilingual research texts through the various stages of the research process: interviewing, transcribing, analyzing and representing the data collected. She had the knowledge to engage with the multiple languages at various stages of the research process:

> For those women who were interviewed in the Serbo-Croatian language, I presented bilingual quotations and transcript poems in two parallel columns ... the left column represents original conversations conducted in the Serbo-Croatian language, while the right column provides English translation of the left column. I use this bi-lingual form of data representation to honour participants' cultural identities, to keep the accuracy of the Serbo-Croatian word, and to invite the reader to enter the messiness and the beauty of our trans/lingual worlds. Blank spaces occasionally emerged within this bi-lingual landscape:

Jos jedna godina suza	Another Year of Tears
Bilo je tesko,	It was another year of tears;
Beograd su bombardovali,	Belgrade under the fire,
a ucenici moji	My students cried,
u Beogradu rodbinu imali,	those moments were hard,
meni dolazili i plakali,	hardest than ever before.
Teski su to momenti bili,	
najtezi u karijeri.	
Daleko sam bila,	I was far away from the bombs,
ali i na daljinu pogodi.	yet the bombs got to me
Trebalo je preziveti.	through the worries and the tears,
	through my people's destiny.

The blank spaces indicate that even those poems that are translated with linguistic accuracy might become vulnerable to losing their poetic expressions and sentiments.

Although having the necessary language capacity to work across participants, complete data analysis and make representational decisions made Ratković's research possible, student researchers who choose to work across multiple languages when conducting research must also factor in the additional challenges they will face, including the possibility of having to extend their timelines to complete their research.

Questions that student researchers might consider with issues of representation in mind include these:

- Considering all the data sets analyzed, have the data been represented in ways that capture their intended meanings?
- Are the representations contradictory to what is known of the participants and context?
- Has communication occurred in any way with participants or their communities during the construction of representations?

ARTICULATING RESEARCH FINDINGS

At different junctures in their research, student researchers think about the research findings and have to construct a formal articulation of their findings in their final documents. Similar to decisions on how to represent the data they analyze, students have to decide how they want to represent their findings. Findings reflect knowledge constructed as a result of their research process and data analysis, and are part of the picture they present of their participants and their research context.

Students ultimately decide what the results of their research are, at times in consultation with participants and communities. What are their findings? How do they relate to the research focus and questions? How did the research process shape the findings? What findings are pertinent to which participants and audiences? They have to choose what will be included in their final research documents and what will be left out. The findings will be a formal response to the research questions, informed by the literature in the field and the theoretical framework embedded in the study, as well as demonstrated and supported in/by the data collected and analyzed. Significant findings will be given more space than other results deemed not so important.

In qualitative research, the findings may be represented in a variety of ways connected to the qualitative methodology and methods. Findings will be constructed through language/images, rather than sophisticated quantitative measures. Findings often include knowledge that is not too surprising as well as knowledge that startled the researcher and participants, and ultimately surprises readers. Based on the degree level, expectations will vary as to the depth and breadth and originality of the research findings (the higher the degree, the greater the expectations: undergraduate, master's and PhD). When students research from critical perspectives, an aim of their research findings is often to make a contribution to the world outside academe, useful to their specific research participants and contexts, as well as inform the literature and discussions in the field; the aim is to hopefully also produce fodder for future research.

THE FINAL PROGRAMMATIC REPRESENTATION: THESIS, MRP AND DISSERTATION

> As researcher I acknowledge that the final text evolved in a particular way because I created it. Regardless of my intent to assist in the documentation of the stories of others it is my story, influenced by those tellings that emerged…. The words do not stand alone on the page but are contextualized and situated by me. I juxtaposed the chosen words in a particular way on the page. I created another text from pieces of texts recorded from interview conversations with the women. (Journal entry, Tilley 1998a: 58)

While writing my dissertation, I documented thoughts related to the representation and writing process in my research journal. I was aware of the power of authorship in my hands as the researcher and writer. Along with incorporating data representations into the research text, I was also deciding what the meta-narrative would include and how the dissertation would be shaped through my writing and representational choices. I was also aware that what I crafted as a research text would be evaluated.

Although degrees of freedom exist for researchers to construct final documents, as researchers and writers completing degree requirements, students must also pay attention to the institutional requirements. What is important to include in the institutional documents that serve as criteria for their degree program and will be available to the public? The content to be included in a thesis, MRP and dissertation, as well as the layout of the documents, are dictated by the discipline and degree program and influenced by the methodology chosen.

Although program guides and documents may have relevant information about the expectations for final documents that will be evaluated and possibly defended in a public venue, advisors will be the main guides in such questions. They not only have the formalized programmatic knowledge but also an awareness of the cultural, disciplinary norms and the possibilities of pushing the boundaries if that is the student's desire and/or need (or the advisor's).

DECISIONS ABOUT WRITING

Student researchers need to be strategic, not only about what they write but also about the language and style and choice of visuals they make. Although readers/viewers of their texts will make sense of what students have constructed based on the readers' identities and backgrounds and relevant connected knowledge, the language and visuals student researchers choose to use to represent their research will contribute to the ways in which their audiences understand the research contexts and participants, the research process and findings. When students are applying a critical lens, they are questioning their choices on a variety of levels. Sometimes these choices are strategic and connected to the student researchers' efforts to ensure as much as possible that the reader/viewer interprets the work in the ways the student researchers intended.

While teaching and researching in the prison, I became aware of the ways in which the experience of incarceration and the descriptions of the prison structures were being advanced through media discourse, the implications of the language chosen. For example, prisons were called *correctional centres*, guards referred to as *correctional officers*, cells labelled *living units*, prisoners identified as *inmates*. This softening of language supported the discourse of prisons and prisoners as places where people were enjoying free room and board and recreational facilities. In news media, prisoners were shown playing ping-pong and watching television. Decontextualized snippets of data were given as representations of the easy life lived out in prison; a lifestyle for which the citizen viewer was paying. In my dissertation, I strategically chose to make visible this softening process and use language that I understood as more reflective of the life most prisoners lived within the multimillion-dollar security protected buildings. I used the words *prisoners* and *prisons*, *guards* and *cells*. I identified the problematics of the media discourse sold to the public to convince them to support, with enormous amounts of capital, the incarceration of women who posed no harm and were often not able to recover from being criminalized and objects of derision.

Student researchers will return to the question of what is reasonable to include in the final research documents many times. They will often experience challenges when constructing a document that cannot include everything they believe is essential. At some institutions, page limits are applied, whereas in others the number of pages required is open to interpretation. The shape of content can also be dictated. Some programs encourage innovation; others are not so accepting of modes of representation too far afield of the traditional written documentation. Students need to ensure that repetition is not the cause of an unreasonably long document that may frustrate their readers, especially those evaluating their thesis or dissertation. This is a time when students who have maintained healthy and effective communication with their advisors, and especially those without extensive research experience, can reap the rewards of their advisors' expertise in their decision-making.

The audiences that decide whether they can trust the findings claimed based on the research conducted will pay attention to a variety of aspects of the document, including whether the research process is transparent (including important moments of decision-making). The complexities of an emergent design need to be demonstrated, most likely included in the methodology chapter/explanation. What challenges were faced when collecting data? Interviewing? Observing? Collecting data in collaborative ways with participant involvement? What were the ethical issues arising in the moments of research, not identified in the ethical review process? Complexities of process are described and discussed openly in various relevant sections of the qualitative thesis or dissertation (e.g., the methodology chapter).

A qualitative thesis or dissertation that presents a flawless, easy-flowing research process will provoke many questions and (in the end) perhaps create doubt in the readers' minds as to the credibility of the research findings. Qualitative researchers are expected to make their quandaries available to their readers/audiences, but also need to take care they do not question themselves so intently as to create readers' mistrust of the process (see Pillow 2003 for discussion of reflexivity/ uncomfortable reflexivity).

From the early stages, students can benefit from reading other qualitative theses and dissertations that provide models of what is acceptable (and also what is left wanting!). They can read award-winning theses and dissertations to understand what is judged as credible research at the level of their degree program (e.g., the American Educational Research Association [AERA] and the Canadian Society for the Study of Education [CSSE] provide awards for student research at various levels and across multiple disciplines).

Tradition holds great sway in institutional settings like universities, even when students delve into innovative methodologies and methods. What is acceptable at the institutional level will influence content and formatting choices. Changes in criteria for such documents happen when traditional conservative norms are challenged. This is particularly evident in the variety of forms of work finding their way into academic spaces (Bosco and Herman 2010; Browne and Nash 2010; Conrad and Wallis 2009; Finley 2011; Gallagher et al. 2013; Goldstein 2008; Irwin and Springgay 2008; Krieg and Roberts 2010; Olesen 2011; Prosser 2011; Roland 2013; Wilson 2008).

Sandra Weber (2008: 49) writes of the necessity of using visuals in the presentation of research findings. Describing a study in which the visual details were immense, she explains how data "refused to be flattened onto a page of scholarly text" and how the researchers "turned to artistic visual modes to theorize and represent some of our findings." She reminds readers (2008: 49) that "as the norms and expectations for communicating research results change, a growing number of scholars are turning to image-based modes of representation, *creating art* [italics in original] to express their findings and theories."

Qualitative methodologies are pushing boundaries in the twenty-first century that are slowly shaping what is acceptable as culminating research documents such as theses and dissertations (Schostak and Schostak 2013).

Questions of representation intersect with decisions regarding respectful dissemination of research during and after the completion of the study. (Chapter 8 focuses on the topic of dissemination, considering possibilities at the early stages of student researchers' programs, as well as exploring dissemination experiences that may occur intermittently as the research process unfolds.) How invested students become in the various dissemination activities available to them will be tied to their degree program level, the individual goals they have for completing the program they have chosen and, as always, their initiative. The thesis or dissertation defence, a culminating and important activity, and often a public affair, is discussed in relation to dissemination in the next chapter.

Annotated Bibliography

Carter, Stacie M., and Miles Little. 2007. "Justifying Knowledge, Justifying Method, Taking Action: Epistemologies, Methodologies, and Methods in Qualitative Research." *Qualitative Health Research* 17, 10: 1316–1328.

Stacie M. Carter and Miles Little indicate that when researchers write up their findings, they often do not include enough information regarding their guiding assumptions and beliefs about knowledge, as well as their methodological decision-making. Although the authors recognize that researchers must abide by publication guidelines, they feel that the integrity of the research is also at stake. They encourage researchers to a) be transparent, b) engage with key research concepts early and repeatedly, c) ensure that harmony exists among key dimensions of the research (both process- and product-related) and d) be open to negotiating and readjusting strategies as needed. They suggest that researchers will attend to and privilege different details in their written documents based on their particular beliefs and methodological orientations.

Cole, Peter. 2002. "Aboriginalizing Methodology: Considering the Canoe." *Qualitative Studies in Education* 15, 4: 447–459.

Peter Cole offers a powerful, poetic, Aboriginal perspective around the complexities of the research process. He critiques Western practices and advocates for culturally respectful and sensitive approaches to researching and representing, particularly within Aboriginal contexts. With reference to his experiences writing a doctoral dissertation, Cole describes moments of tension when Western academic ways of writing clashed up against Aboriginal oral traditions and storytelling. He considers the disconnect between Western frameworks and discourses, as well as words and their meanings, which do not always map out onto Aboriginal concepts and practices. While exploring themes of colonization, relationship-building and environmental awareness, Cole strives to make meaning of the world and his experiences in a manner that is in keeping with Aboriginal ways of knowing and observing. Yet he articulates a necessity to navigate academic terrain and adhere to Western practices to gain acceptance and credibility in these spaces, which in turn will enable him to make important contributions to his own community.

Collier, Diane. 2013. "Being Tough, Staying Good, and Playing Inside the Box: An Ethnographic Case Study of One Boy's Multimodal Textmaking." Unpublished doctoral dissertation, University of British Columbia, Vancouver, BC.

This dissertation is an ethnographic case study that followed one child, Kyle, across home and school as he created and drafted texts. The data generated consisted of notes from participant-observation, informal interviews, artifacts (photos, photocopies, drafts), audio recordings and transcriptions of audio recordings, and video recordings with their transcriptions. Although data were generated in a conventional manner, the dissertation was written as a series of manuscripts. Although separate framings of the data, the individual manuscripts were developed chronologically, and each one built upon the ideas developed in the previous framing. This approach to dissertation writing can provide graduate students with the opportunity to develop skills for writing journal articles, as well as innovative ideas for collecting and representing data.

Davison, Colleen M. 2007. "Engagement and the Northern School Setting: A Critical Ethnography among the Tlicho First Nation of Behchoko, NWT." Unpublished doctoral dissertation, University of Calgary, Calgary, AB.

For this critical ethnography, Colleen M. Davison spent six months living in an Aboriginal community in Northwest Territories and employed qualitative and quantitative strategies (e.g., participant observation, interviewing, focus groups, journaling, document analysis) to understand Aboriginal youth engagement in school. She carefully describes the community and school, situating the research within particular theoretical perspectives (critical, social and ecological understandings). Her use of pictures, tables, summary and flowcharts, timelines and models provide a powerful representation of different aspects of her research process. Davison also draws the reader's attention to twelve publications and presentations that have emerged from her doctoral work.

Halifax, Nancy V.D., and Gail J. Mitchell. 2013. "(Nurse) — Writing with the Wolves." *Qualitative Inquiry* 19, 5: 349–352.

In this article, an interdisciplinary team of health care workers create a poetic and visual representation of their experiences in the professional field. The researchers choose this method of inquiry and representation as a means to express their commitment to social justice issues surrounding the lack of spaces within health care institutions for bearing witness to suffering or responding ethically to the suffering of others. They argue that creating art reveals other ways of understanding "truths" about human care in hospital settings and that art, not only as a product but also as a process, has a vital role to play in modern health care services.

Hole, Rachelle D. 2007a. "Working between Languages and Cultures: Issues of Representation, Voice, and Authority Intensified." *Qualitative Inquiry* 13, 5: 696–710.

In Rachelle Hole's (2007a: 703) research with deaf women, she candidly acknowledges some of the difficulties she experienced during the analysis and representation stages:

> *To minimize the issues of representation that were evident as a result of working across languages and cultures, I made the methodological decision to treat the videotaped research interview as a textual performance. Rather than coding a transcript, I returned to the performed text and analyzed the videotapes when conducting the analytic readings.*

She focused on visual cues to inform her understandings and sometimes found it difficult to move between words and signs, especially when the two did not always align. For instance, Hole (2007a: 706) indicates that "I made my position as a hearing researcher and my previous connections to the Deaf community explicit, and I journaled my thoughts about how my hearingness influenced the process of data collection, analysis, and the writing up of the findings."

Leggo, Carl, Anita E. Sinner, Rita L. Irwin, Kathy Pantaleo, Peter Gouzouasis and Kit Grauer. 2011. "Lingering in Liminal Spaces: A/r/tography as Living Inquiry in a Language Arts Class." *International Journal of Qualitative Studies in Education* 24, 2: 239–256.

This article presents readers with an innovated approach to gathering, analyzing and writing up data in poetic form. In their study of teachers' beliefs and teaching practices at five different arts programs, Carl Leggo and his colleagues explore the liminal spaces between ethnographic research methods (which they had initially intended to use) and a/r/tography (the approach they ended up using instead) to raise questions about "the dynamics of research processes and practices" (2011: 250). The authors concluded that to create a representation of the data that best opened up possibilities for constructing meaning and understanding, an a/r/tographic approach of living inquiry was the most appropriate to their study. The article includes several poems created during the time of the study to represent their research findings.

Lewis, Patrick J. 2008. "A Good Teacher." *Forum Qualitative Sozialforschung / Forum: Qualitative Social Research* 9, 2, Art. 41.

Patrick J. Lewis explores how film can transcend text-based data and reform participant stories. The author resisted interpreting participants' stories and invited them to tell their stories through a filmed interview. He recognized, however, that his editing and framing of the film did influence the participant story: "In film I have captured one iteration, removed from the natural flow of time, however, not even that keeps the story from being reworked, reinterpreted and re-performed each time the listener-viewer turns her gaze toward it" (paragraph 15). A link to the video is found at the end of the article.

Moffatt, Jessica, Maria Mayan and Richard Long. 2013. "Sanitoriums and the Canadian Colonial Legacy: The Untold Experiences of Tuberculosis Treatment." *Qualitative Health Research* 23, 12: 1591–1599.

Jessica Moffat and her colleagues use a postcolonial theoretical framework in their community-based participatory research project as a means to share the perspectives of First Nations people and their experiences of health sanitoriums. They chose to disseminate the findings with the community in the form of an educational health video intended to fulfil their obligation to create a sustainable project with benefits that would outlast the research process as well as highlight social inequity in an effort to initiate change. With the intention to ensure that the cultural values of the community were respected and that the project moved forward in a culturally sensitive manner, the authors established a community advisory board made up of Elders, lay community members and health care staff who work in the First Nations community. Data-collection procedures and the steps taken to establish trustworthiness and rigour of the data are described in great detail.

Sethi, Bharati. 2012. "Searching for Self in a World of Labels." *Disability and Society* 27, 5: 717–722.

This article reflects issues related to one of the main themes of this chapter: representation across difference. Bharati Sethi draws on her experiences in the various identities she holds (an immigrant, victim and survivor of post-traumatic stress disorder, social worker and a client of social services, among others) and uses them as the material to create two pieces of performance poetry. Sethi states that for her, performance poetry is a means to "confront otherness as disability and as alien." The author suggests that performance poetry can be an effective approach to challenge those in the social work profession to confront their own assumptions of "difference" and to encourage her coworkers to truly accept Sethi as a colleague with a disability (2012: 717).

Chapter 8

DISSEMINATION: MOVING INTO THE PUBLIC DOMAIN

Although dissemination activities occur at various points in the research process (e.g., during the construction of a conference presentation or public performance piece based on preliminary analysis), this aspect of the research process is emphasized at the latter stages. The project is completed, and it is time to report findings to audiences interested in the research. Plans for dissemination will be addressed at the research design stage. For example, during the consent-gathering process, student researchers will describe for the participants their plans to include data representations and findings in their MRP, thesis or dissertation, and in other forms and venues useful for disseminating research findings and other aspects of the research. On occasion, student researchers may have to return to participants (or the institutional ethics review board) to gain permission to use the data in ways not agreed upon originally (i.e., when publication plans are made late in the process and not discussed in consent materials or when a desire to share raw data with individuals not named originally in consent documents arises). With permissions in place, students can move forward with the dissemination and publication activities that they have planned. Based on the comprehensiveness of the study, the expectations of participants and communities, and the public interest in the topic, students may disseminate their research beyond the documents that are regularly housed in institutional libraries. Dissemination involves spreading the news and ensuring that the results of the completed research do not remain on a shelf or in a file on a computer.

The form the dissemination takes will be tied to the methodology and types of data collected. In the case of data collected through traditional methods of interviews and observations, dissemination may follow the conventional route of presentation and publication, especially dissemination at the conclusion of the research project. In the case of arts-based research, data representations may be shaped as visuals, performance and literary texts (e.g., poetic representations). Research findings may be disseminated in venues open to the public and in local public space (local galleries, theatres) and through technologies to reach wider audiences in cyberspace (video and blogs). Visual and arts-based data can sometimes speak more easily to a wider audience that crosses local and activist communities than more traditional forms can. Student researchers may want to explore possibilities for dissemination that will take on a multiplicity of forms to reach the appropriate audiences for their research. Dissemination plans are made early in the process, but many things can happen as the research unfolds that will influence those plans.

Researchers who conduct critical qualitative research make dissemination decisions based on many factors, often wanting to ensure that findings move beyond the typical terrain of academic contexts. If the intention of the research is to contribute to social change and to be of benefit to individuals and communities, researchers will need to be strategic in their decisions while keeping in mind the welfare of their participants or collaborating communities. What they will be disseminating and how they will make public aspects of the research is a discussion they will have with their participants throughout the research process, including the latter stages.

When contemplating dissemination, students might want to consider the following questions:

- What purposes are served through publication and presentation of the research?
- What do student researchers have a responsibility to make public?
- What do students have a strong desire to make public?
- To whom are students obligated to report? Which individuals and groups/communities will be interested in the students' research?
- What forms can dissemination take to move the research beyond the typical academic presentation and publication?
- How will findings reach the policy-makers?

Generally speaking, the work of dissemination can be seen as related to three areas: what is required (degree expectation), what is expected and/or given back (requirement and reciprocity) and what is desired (academic/personal goals). Each of these areas is discussed in the following sections.

REQUIRED: CONSTRUCTING AND DEFENDING A FINAL DOCUMENT

Students produce research texts of various formats and contents to meet the program's research exit requirement. Master's- and doctoral-level students, depending on their program, will be expected to successfully complete an oral defence as a culminating task. At this point, the completed research is officially moving beyond the realm of a student's advisory committee and is being shared with others, including internal and external examiners. The evaluation of these texts is part of the process of going public. The organization of a defence will differ across universities, so students need to be clear about the expectations of their institutions. For example, the defence is an avenue through which student research is made public, but whether this process is open to a wide audience will be based on the practices of the institutions/faculty granting the degrees.

Although the defence and its organization is context-specific, students often have a degree of freedom to make the defence their own. For example, they are often able to decide on what to include in the initial time allotted (often between twenty to forty minutes) for their *talking piece* when they introduce their research at the beginning of the defence process. A common practice is to provide an overview referencing the research focus/questions, theoretical framework, methodology, important findings and implications, and the common areas included in theses and dissertations. With more innovative methodologies making their way into graduate student research, this introduction may take other forms that are representative of the methodology and methods used (e.g., arts-inspired presentation, text with video clips, performance piece). The question to ask is this: What purpose is the introductory piece to serve in relation to the research conducted?

My doctoral defence was an open defence, and those who attended included faculty, graduate students, a participant in the research, my sister and a friend who travelled from the east to the west coast of Canada to attend. I decided that my defence was an opportunity to educate the audience about women imprisoned in general, but also more specifically as a venue to emphasize issues related to the challenges of conducting respectful research in a prison institution with a captive, vulnerable population. I focused specifically on methodology and ethical research practices, knowing that the examining committee would have all read and been familiar with the dissertation content. Luckily, my advisor was in agreement with my preferences.

Although defences vary across institutions, common elements are embedded in the experience. The following lists some general advice I give to students to consider.

Before the defence:

- Communicate with advisors about the expectations of the process well in advance of the defence. Take the initiative to contact advisors with questions and concerns.

- Attend multiple defences at institutions prior to the defence. Pay attention to how other students choose to introduce their work, the questions posed, the student responses to the questions asked and the roles of the individuals on the examining committees.
- Participate in a mock defence in advance of the defence, early enough in the process to make changes to presentation plans. Start by asking advisors about organizing a mock defence in which you can practise your presentation. Invite other students to attend. Ask individuals beforehand to read your document and play the role of committee members asking questions related to your research. Time your introduction and ensure that you do not go over the time limit given. Be prepared to receive feedback from the audience members and be willing to incorporate the constructive feedback given. If your advisor does not see this activity as necessary or cannot participate, organize on your own. If possible, hold the mock defence in the room in which the official defence is planned to take place.
- Before the defence date, check the technology in the room in which you will defend using the materials you plan to use in your defence.

During the defence:

- Have a copy of your thesis/dissertation in front of you with pen and paper in hand.
- Stick to the time limit for your introduction. The committee members can become very frustrated when students stretch out the introduction, preventing the questioning process from beginning. What students do not get to include can sometimes be incorporated during the question period. The advisor can often find a way to direct students to something important missed when it is his/her time to ask questions.
- Write down the multilevel questions asked; refer to them to make sure all parts of the question were answered. If you do not understand a question, ask to have it repeated.
- Questions often begin with the external and internal-external examiners and then move to the other committee members, ending with the student's advisor. There may be one or more rounds of questioning. In some circumstances, after the committee has finished questioning, others in the room may be invited to ask questions based on the research presented. Be calm and provide succinct responses to the best of your ability.

- Do not pretend to know an answer when you are unsure. One question usually leads to another, and it does not take long to dig and fall into a deep hole from which it may be difficult to recover.
- Areas that were not an emphasis of the research may be discussed; suggest that the area may be a focus for future research.
- Check arrogant tendencies at the door. Recognize the limitations of your knowledge and use this opportunity to learn from others present.

After the defence:

- There will be multiple outcomes possible at the conclusion of the defence, ranging from no revisions, minor revisions, major revisions or failure. The most common result falls within the minor revision category. Work with the advisor to ensure you know what is being asked of you in terms of revisions.
- Make the revisions requested within the specified time period.
- Remember that the texts that emerge at the conclusion of the evaluation and defence process will be available to a wider public. For instance, in the Canadian context, theses and dissertations are automatically housed in a national archive and can be accessed electronically (<collectionscanada.gc.ca/thesescanada/index-e.html>). They will be of interest to other researchers and may serve as models for other students.
- Have a celebration!

Advisors often remind students that the students are the research experts. They will know their research better than anyone else in the room. Advisory committee members and external examiners have agreed that the thesis/dissertation is ready for defence. The outcome is expected to be positive. The defence is an opportunity for students to share what they have learned and to be centre stage after the conclusion of a great deal of work of which they should be proud. There is some truth in all this. However, be aware of the context-specific information (and idiosyncrasies) related to oral defences in your faculty/department/program; use this information and the knowledge of your advisor to guide preparation.

Although students may have been working with their advisors long before a final draft is submitted and a defence is planned, this is the stage when a breakdown in the relationship can occur. Sometimes students are misinformed as to the time that it takes to complete a draft that is acceptable to the advisor and committee members and is ready to send to an external examiner. Multiple people (advisor and committee members) are involved in this stage of the process and they all have many other responsibilities. They will not necessarily be ready to read and respond to drafts at the time the student produces them. Students may expect a quick return when this is not a possibility. Relationships can also break down when students believe they are ready for the defence when advisor or committee members do not. Moving forward before their document is ready can result in major revisions or failure. It is important not to underestimate the advisory committee's expertise and experience.

Time is needed for students to produce the document, but also for meeting the institutional requirements involved in organizing the defence (e.g., time requirements for identifying and retaining an external examiner). The process for organizing a defence needs to be discussed at the beginning stages and reiterated as the student moves through the research steps. Time requirements are specific to institutions and they often have *normal* timelines articulated in program guidelines. Two to three months for setting up a doctoral defence after advisor and committee members indicate that the document is ready was the most recent timeline quoted to me in regards to my institution. Students need to remember that these logistics are often out of the hands of the advisor.

On the other hand, it is possible that the timelines for the student receiving feedback are not reasonable because of unforeseeable circumstances, but there is little that can be changed about this. When students have made it this far in the process with their advisory committee, it is wise to practise patience as the process heads toward completion.

EXPECTATION: ENGAGING IN RECIPROCITY

Human participants and/or communities involved in students' research projects have committed time and energy of varying degrees to the research. There is a general expectation that researchers will share their findings with research partici-pants and communities. Students will have articulated plans for dissemination in their ethics applications. When the student researcher is involved in participatory or community research initiatives, plans for dissemination may have been made jointly with the participants, many of whom may be part of the activities. Regardless of early planning, possibilities for dissemination will also emerge as the research process progresses.

When writing ethics applications, students often describe a dissemination process that includes the promise of an executive/final report, a short report with a list of findings upon participant request (upon request; the responsibility is left with participants) and a thank-you to participants. They might also offer to provide a copy of their MRP, thesis or dissertation. Although an interesting read for some, participants may find it difficult and time-consuming to cull these large documents for the pieces they find relevant and useful. The promise of making these docu-ments available to participants often meets the institutional requirements. However, when conducting critical qualitative research, student researchers are expected to move beyond what is often the bare minimum of institutional requirements to disseminate findings through making available culminating reports and final research documents. When students (with or without contributions from participants) give serious consideration to the possible benefits of dissemination activities that can accrue for participants and communities that move beyond what is required, they are at a point at which dissemination and reciprocity intersect.

Plans for reciprocity through dissemination activities may mean more one-on-one connections with individuals and communities, and sharing results, theoretical frameworks and methodological knowledge with participants during and after the research is completed. In addition to sharing knowledge accrued and elements of the research process with individuals and communities, student researchers can target policy-makers who have the power to initiate change based on the findings.

Student researchers can give back to the participant and communities locally; for example, students conducting educational research may have the expertise to provide professional development for teachers involved in the research and more generally. They might also be able to help parents who permitted their children to participate (or participated themselves in the research) to understand new programs or new school board initiatives (e.g., literacy programming).

For some researchers, it is difficult to give back to the specific people or communities who participated (e.g., patients, prisoners). However, reciprocity also constitutes benefits shared with a broader community of people and institutions not directly involved in the research. Student researchers can present their work in meeting contexts, institutional and activist-oriented. I have presented research findings related to ethics at school board meetings as well as academic conferences that have a social justice focus with a variety of people attending. I have been able to translate what I learned from the women in the prison into courses I instruct and then hopefully through the teachers completing the courses, back into public school classrooms — those classrooms similar to the ones the women in my study described as having no space or place for them to learn. Student researchers and participants can discuss the possibilities for and shaping of reciprocity together; participants often know more about what is needed and possible than the student researchers.

Participants with the desire can be involved in the presentation and dissemination of the research in workplace, community-based and academic contexts. Their involvement may be of individual benefit (e.g., lead to work promotion or a desired change in work focus) as well as contribute to the construction of respectful representations of participants and research contexts. Participants can be involved in multiple ways, including collaborative writing of various forms (news articles, blogs, community reports, academic manuscripts) with the researcher and co-participants. Whether participants will want (or be able) to participate in the dissemination of research will not be known if student researchers do not discuss the possibilities with participants in the early stages.

Ultimately, individuals and communities who have provided data may just want to move on. I asked one of the women participants, who would have served out her term during the writing of my dissertation, if she would like to be part of that final process in some capacity, but she declined, explaining that she did not want to be reliving her experience of prison life ever again, even in writing about it, within the context of my study or on her own with support I could have provided.

DESIRED: ACADEMIC AND PERSONAL GOALS

The choices students make in terms of dissemination and publication are also connected to their academic and personal goals; their desires. Doctoral students with plans to compete for academic positions at the completion of their programs will have different goals than students completing master's or undergraduate degrees with no plans or aspirations to continue graduate work in the future. Master's students who want to continue and enrol in another degree will think differently from a student who envisions the current degree as a final one. Those who want to return quickly to the workforce at the completion of their degrees may not be interested in spending time and effort presenting at conferences or building a publication record connected to their research. I caution students that plans change, and that it is most important to finish strong — with an MRP, undergraduate or graduate thesis, or dissertation that they can be proud of and that can open doors into a future not imagined at the time of degree completion. Not only will the students' academic work be considered when they apply for positions in the workforce, graduate programs or academic positions; strong references will also be an important consideration, along with a CV that includes accomplishments over the time of their studies. The important piece is for students to give their goals serious thought in the early stages of their program and to plan their research journey accordingly: to make the most of the opportunities available to them while living their student status.

DISSEMINATION VENUES

There are myriad ways in which students can disseminate and publish their work. They will need to plan the logistics of moving their work into a context larger than their program and university. Such planning should occur in the early stages of research and continue after the research is concluded.

Graduate students are encouraged to attend conferences at which they can present on various aspects of their research. Conferences provide students with the chance to present their work to academics and other students interested in their research topic, to individuals who can offer constructive criticism and provide helpful suggestions. In a conference setting, they can discuss preliminary findings based on a portion of the data analyzed at an early stage of the analysis process. Presenting their work in this venue is good practice for students who will eventually have to present and defend their thesis or dissertation. As well, during conferences students have the opportunity to hear experienced academics and other students present their research.

Conference venues are also open to undergraduate students, but they may not be encouraged to attend as much as their graduate counterparts are. It is often assumed that if undergraduate students are interested in such activities, they will pursue the opportunity when possible. They will ultimately apply for a graduate degree at a later time and will then be more involved in conferences. I urge all interested students to take advantage of the experience regardless of their program's degree level. Advisors may encourage students to present at conferences; if not, students can also take the initiative to explore the opportunities available.

Various conferences exist that are graduate student–focused specifically or open to the academic community in general. Students can also submit proposals to present at major conferences such as the annual conference of academic and professional societies. Many conference venues offer discounted registration costs for students. Websites of these associations provide the logistical information, including proposal content and deadline requirements. Institutional supports are available for students, to varying degrees, through a student's faculty or department as well as a university's faculty of graduate studies, including grants to support conference travel and registration fees. Students need to search out the existing resources available through their institutions.

Academic associations often have graduate student divisions that look for student participation. Students may want to become involved in local, national or international associations related to their disciplinary and other affiliations (e.g., serving on a student executive). The key is to measure the degree of involvement that makes sense in light of the time and resources students have to complete their research and degree program. Benefits (connection to other students and first-hand involvement in a subsection of the academic culture) and risks (extended or interference to time to program completion) of the activities students choose to become involved in throughout their program need to be weighed.

Successful dissemination activities are often collaborative. Students can plan a panel or symposium on a particular topic that intersects with their research interests; each individual presents a paper. Conferences are often publicized, and proposals are due months before the actual conference and sometimes before students have their research fully completed. For example, the AERA (<aera.net>)

conference asks for proposal submissions in July, and the conference takes place the following April. Individuals submitting proposals do not find out whether their proposals have been accepted until late fall. It is not unusual in some venues for students to submit a conference proposal based on research not completed, but which they plan to complete and write about before the conference takes place. To fulfil the desire to present at a conference takes extensive, time-sensitive planning. Part of the challenge for students is to appropriately estimate the timelines so that if accepted, they will be able to deliver as promised.

There are numerous conferences from which to choose. Graduate student conferences that are in-house or offered at local universities are numerous. These conferences might also have specific journals associated with the hosting association, and students can develop their paper presentations into manuscripts for publication to the conference journal.

There are many presentation formats: posters, round tables, single paper and panels. Students can become familiar with the formats available for specific conferences and then follow the guidelines given. There will be disciplinary expectations of oral presentations that are designated as acceptable, and information will be available via websites. When it is a paper presentation, the organizers will often put four or five papers around a theme in a session block, allowing a portion of time to each presenter — sometimes as low as ten minutes, or up to thirty or forty minutes, based on the conference.

The following points guide students with preparatory considerations:

- There are disciplinary styles attached to presenting, so students need to be aware of what is acceptable in their field of study. Presenters are often warned not to read directly from a paper; however, if the paper is written to be read, this may be the best option. In other instances, presenters may depend on visuals, speaking to slides with text and fleshing out the details. The downside of this approach is that if the content is poorly organized and presenters are ad libbing, the audience may not follow, and presenters might be over time and rushing to the finish.
- If students read from their text, write the text to be read, not as a paper submission. There is a difference. Remember that people are listening, not reading along. Choices of content and delivery should be made to hold the audience's attention. Talk slowly so that the audience can follow along. Time is needed for listeners to digest what they are hearing.
- Based on the audience, there may be people attending with a different first language from the language of the presentation. This may also be the case for the student presenter. There will be individuals with varying degrees of fluency. Be mindful of language choices, words and phrases.

- Practise reading out loud while timing the length of the presentation. If students ad lib while reading, the timing from the practice may be inaccurate. Either write asides into the actual text or stick to what is written. Students may have time in the discussion/question period to add details they were not able to include in their presentation. They may actually do all the proper preparation and timing but then have to contend with other presenters who have not been thinking of the shared time of the presentation format. Often there will be a chair who controls these matters, but if students are unlucky and are the last presenters whose time has become cut from twenty to ten minutes, for example, they need to act as graciously as possible and cut back to the main points they want to leave with the audience. Those attending will be very aware of what has happened and be impressed if the student calmly deals with the matter. The audience will find ways to connect with students' work, even within the shortened time limit, if what they hear piques their interest.
- Talking faster as time runs out is a very poor strategy to complete a presentation. Not only will the audience miss most of the hurried content but they also will become very irritated. If students have prepared, but for some reason have miscalculated the time, they need to stop when they should and state that they will end on the point being discussed, but will remain at the close of the session to discuss their work further if anyone is interested.
- When students use visuals in their presentation, they need to remember that the visual display does not replace critical content. Visuals can be outstanding, but they do not compensate for weak arguments or lack of substantive content. The production of an effective visual presentation requires basic decisions to be made about amount of content (not too much text or too many visual representations; the purpose is to guide the presentation) and size of words and images included (text and images large enough so the audience can read or view them from a distance).
- Students need to be respectful to other presenters as well as their audience. This means sticking to allocated timelines but also paying attention to others when they are presenting. When people in the audience observe that students waiting their turn work on their computer or phone when others are presenting, they may be left with this image of the students, not the content of the students' actual presentation.
- Be prepared to respond to questions as much as possible and not be defensive when answering.

Panels are often organized around topics with individual speakers. The points listed previously also relate to this form of presentation. The panel offers a level of security when a group of students familiar with one another plans together. Students do not have to be in close proximity; they can choose to work together, even if located at different campuses and institutions.

Posters are well-developed visual representations of the research and take a lot of time, thought and much creativity to develop. Posters are often organized in spaces in which attendees can go to view them and talk to the researchers on a one-to-one basis. Students often start conferencing through poster sessions.

The round table (which may not actually be a round table!) is another format often available for presentations at conferences. The researcher is stationed at a table in a given time slot, and those interested can come and sit together. More recently, the round table sessions have become more popular. Some conferences have time slots when only round table sessions are available. The format's small group setting provides time for researchers to present and talk about their work and for attendees to ask questions. Student researchers need to come prepared with copies of their papers to distribute. One of my first experiences was a round table session with six people who were very interested in my doctoral research. I offered a discussion based on preliminary analysis and findings. They asked constructive questions and gave very helpful feedback that helped move my work forward.

Currently, the downside of the conference world is its money-making agenda: More people presenting means additional money. This emphasis has a ripple effect on the organization of the conference sessions. For example, less time is given to individuals to present, and as a result of the enormous number of choices, fewer people are present in each session. At the last conference I attended, I was the only person besides the four presenters in one of the sessions. The presenters were very disappointed, but ultimately we had a very interesting and informed discussion. Be prepared; at large conference settings it is not a rare occurrence to have only a few people attending, regardless of presenter, format and research emphasis.

Also, be aware of the politics influencing the choices made regarding research dissemination and conference attendance. As reflected in many aspects of academe, conferences are embedded in a hierarchical structure, and certain conferences are deemed most important. The large national and international conferences in a field are often the places where well-known people are found. These people draw large crowds while attendance numbers may be low at other sessions. For many students, these are the conferences they often have the greatest desire to attend, hoping to put faces to the academic sources they have been reading. However, as students gain experience, this desire might lessen, and more time can be spent at smaller venue conferences at which they have reasonable time slots, and intense discussions and a wider dissemination of ideas is possible.

Before presenting their work, students can acquire conference experience through an RA position with their advisors or other faculty members. It might be wise to accept a contract with a faculty member who has a history of involving students in all aspects of research projects, including presentation and publication. The very lucky students are the ones able to obtain a research assistantship that is connected to their own research interests or specifically develops research skills that they will need to conduct their research later. Although these rich experiences will further develop the students' skills, they might also drain time away from the students' focus on their research; students need to be strategic and not overcommit so that their research is put at risk as it waits for attention.

Based on future plans, conferences can be an essential part of the graduate student experience, both as a venue for students to present their work as well as a means to becoming familiar with the field and people in it. Many of the large conferences have a student emphasis, with training and mentoring sessions available. With graduate student associations, opportunities to learn from other students in a similar graduate program or otherwise is very important. As well, many conference venues include opportunities to discuss new positions opening up in universities, which will be of great interest to students planning an academic career. It is not unusual for students completed or near completion of a PhD to be formally or informally interviewed for a position while attending a national conference.

If students have the goal of becoming an academic, they need to build the knowledge and experience and connections through networking that will put them on the short list for academic positions. Remember that advisors have knowledge and experience that can be shared with students when planning for the future. Although the program content and successful completion are primary criteria, they are only partly responsible for students attaining a future position in the field or at an academic institution.

GOALS FOR COMPLETING THE PROGRAM

The goals students want to achieve as a result of completing their degrees should be articulated and considered at the initial stages of the program. Do not keep them a secret. I ask students to consider their goals in light of their CVs and to strategize, early in their studies, the ways to develop their CVs in areas needed for them to achieve the goals articulated. I ask them to consider the following questions:

- Have they considered what their CV needs to demonstrate for their future work applications?
- Have they worked as a TA?
- Have they been a course instructor?
- Have they worked as an RA?

- Have they presented at conferences and other venues?
- Have they participated in publication activities?
- Have they worked for or been involved with activist organizations and community groups?
- Have they worked for community agencies?

Based on what students want to pursue at the completion of their programs, there will be other questions to reflect on and answer. The strategy of critiquing their CVs at an early stage of the program is useful no matter the plans for future employment. Students need to consider what is missing and build this experience and knowledge to strengthen their CVs and work applications.

Connected to the particular institution and program, new students will be moving into an institutional climate within which they will have to find a *way to be* that will ultimately lead to successfully completing their program. Institutional practices can support a negative competitive climate, but students can contribute to working against this climate and the level of competition embedded in their everyday program experiences. Although it is true that grant money and many privileges are awarded for competing successfully against peers in the program, students have some choice in how they decide to compete, conduct themselves and treat their peers through to program completion. They need to start early and be strategic in their plans to successfully complete their goals, but not so strategic that they show a lack of respect and care for others, including taking credit when not due and withholding support for peers when it is easily given.

FROM PRESENTATION TO PUBLICATION

A paper presented at a conference is very different from a manuscript ready to be submitted for publication. Although one can be seen as a stepping-stone to the other, multiple rewritings are often required.

I pass on to my students the advice one of my professors gave in a doctoral class when I was a student. He was well-established in his field and had published a number of books and articles in various journals. He described how before writing a manuscript he would choose three journals for which he thought the manuscript might be considered. He would prioritize them from first to third choice of venue. He would shape the article in terms of focus and length to fit (as much as possible) the criteria of the journals, emphasizing the first choice initially. He would submit the manuscript and wait for the review and feedback. When received, if it was accepted with minor revisions, he would work on those revisions and resubmit. If feedback suggested that he make major revisions, he would consider the revisions and, if he agreed with them, revise and resubmit. If not in agreement, he would make the changes that made sense and then submit the newly revised manuscript to the next journal on his list. He would follow a similar process based on the response of the journal. He explained to the class that he always found a home for his manuscripts, even if it took a lengthy time period. Although at times I have faltered in following his directions, I think it is a good formula that can lead to a healthy publication record.

Another important aspect of the publication process is for students to take the feedback of reviewers and editors seriously; address the revisions requested, but when revisions are not appropriate, take the time to articulate a rationale for the lack of revision in a response letter to the editor. Even though students may not have completed all the requested revisions, they may be able to convince the editor that there were good reasons for their resistance. Although the people reviewing are not always experts in the areas the manuscript covers, often the reviewers' suggestions, when applied, can strengthen a paper.

Appendix D contains portions of a letter written to the editor of a journal that accepted (with revisions required) a paper that two doctoral students and I wrote related to graduate studies. The letter is comprehensive, addressing all reviewer comments the editor provided. Students need to spend the time and effort necessary to complete the appropriate revisions required and to articulate that clearly in the letter and ultimately to convince the editor that the manuscript is ready for publication.

Before beginning the writing, students need to be informed about the submission rules for the journals they are considering. Some general rules are applied broadly; for example, a manuscript can be under review with only one journal. Before submitting the manuscript elsewhere, it has to be withdrawn formally from the first journal. A withdrawal can happen on occasion when unreasonable time lengths have passed and no decision is made, and there is no sign of a decision being made in the near future. The specific rules (e.g., acceptable style) are provided on journal websites, often under headings such as *Notes to Authors*.

Students can visit the journal websites and determine the number of times the journal is published each year and the rate of acceptance for manuscripts submitted. Information on the journal's preferred format (citation format, word count) and submission procedures are available. Following a journal's guidelines may not directly translate into an acceptance; however, not following directions will leave a negative impression in the early stage of the process and may lead to the manuscript not leaving the editor's office. Remember, the manuscript that is sent for review should be as good a copy as possible. A well-written manuscript will result in feedback on content rather than on format and writing conventions.

The response wait time for the completion of the full review process will vary, depending on the journal, but expect at least ten to twelve weeks as an average. Journal websites might provide the specific timelines to be expected. Most often, a confirmation that the manuscript was received (electronically generated) will be sent to the author. If time passes with no acknowledgement, sending a polite e-mail asking for confirmation is acceptable. The same process can be followed when no news on the manuscript review has been received after a reasonable time period passes. Sending a polite e-mail asking for an update regarding timelines for the review process to be completed is not unreasonable. For many journals, the turn-around times for manuscript review has been shortened with the introduction of electronic submissions and review processes.

WHERE TO PUBLISH?

Numerous venues exist for manuscript submission, and the numbers keep growing:

- Professional and activist publications interested in research findings or connected to the research
- Chapters in edited books
- Journals connected to academic conferences
- Journals connected to professional associations
- Journals and books with book review sections
- Specially themed journal issues

Publications grow out of a variety of circumstances:

- A course paper developed into a publication
- A comprehensive, critical literature review connected to a research topic
- A methodology paper based on research conducted
- Conference paper revised and edited to submit for publication
- Collaborative research paper connected to RA work or advisor research
- Collaborations with individuals and communities engaged in activism
- Internet activities (e.g., blogs and video posting)

Journal and book publishers have the necessary information on their websites for students to consider when choosing where to submit their work. The following lists additional information that might influence student researchers' decisions:

- The hierarchical assessment of *quality* journals: first tier is often touted as the ultimate achievement. Acceptance rates are inversely related to the tier of the journal (the lowest acceptance rate for top-tier journals).
- Time to review manuscripts can vary greatly across journals.
- Open access journals can provide access to a larger population at no cost.
- Choices differ based on intended audience: a university press publication (journal or book) versus a professional journal or trade book publication.

- Internet online publications can have short timelines to move findings into a public arena.

Power and politics circulate around publication issues; philosophical-political perspectives and ethical commitments shape dissemination decisions. Student researchers' choices about what to write and publish and where to disseminate their research will be influenced by their activism. For instance, open access journals provide research publications to a wider population and to individuals not necessarily connected to academic institutions in which libraries pay the fees for access. Visual and video data can be made public in venues that include community centres, libraries, theatres and other local spaces. Community and local newspapers may be the most relevant places for disseminating certain findings.

Seeing a manuscript through to publication requires elements of the following:

- Organization
- Time (lots!) carved out of a schedule for writing
- Strong work ethic
- Connection of publication to works in progress
- Friendly and knowledgeable critics to read and provide feedback
- Control of perfectionist tendencies
- Good judgment of manuscript readiness
- Reasonable deadlines (that are met successfully)
- Small-scale start (e.g., book review as publication)
- Big-scale goals (e.g., publishing thesis or dissertation as a book)

Students need to take an honest look at their writing abilities and work on strengthening any areas in need of improvement. What I noticed both as an instructor and advisor is that students do not always realize the time it takes to write something well or the degree of revision and editing needed to produce work ready for publication.

AUTHORING WITH OTHERS

When students have worked closely with their advisors, they may to want to publish work related to their research thesis or dissertation with their advisor (see Gilbar et al. 2013 for guidelines). Student researchers can learn much working side-by-side with advisors through the publication process. To avoid conflict that can arise as a result of the power issues embedded in advisor-student relations, universities have policies in place to protect students (for example, in terms of ownership when students write a manuscript based on their research with their advisors). It is important for students to be familiar with university regulations before beginning the writing collaboration. In many disciplines, the current acceptable practice is for students to be first authors on research publications related to their thesis or dissertation.

Coauthorship can entail the student and advisor constructing a manuscript together or occur as a result of a student's collaborations with faculty members, student peers or others from the wider community, including individuals who participated in the research (see Yu et al. 2013 for academic collaborations; McGinn et al. 2005 for collaboration and research teams).

I encourage students to consider writing a manuscript related specifically to issues of methodology and methods. If they decide to do this at the beginning of their research process, they can document their ideas as they conduct their research. An informed critique of context-specific research can make a contribution to the field that offers other researchers an in-depth look at someone else's research process, the methodological challenges and experiences of methods (for example, Watt 2007). Many venues for such manuscripts exist through the growing number of journals focused on qualitative methodologies and methods, specialty journals (*Qualitative Research*, *Qualitative Inquiry*, *International Journal of Social Research Methodology* and *Cultural Studies – Critical Methodologies*, to name only a few). In these journals, students also learn about current methodological practices and dilemmas, and find some of the content that is included in methodology chapters in theses and dissertations. Such manuscripts are also useful to journals that are not specifically focused on methodology, but are connected to the research focus. It was very important for me to publish "Conducting Respectful Research: A Critique of Practice," an article developed from my dissertation and written during the last stages of my program. Although it was a first step for me in beginning a publication record (and a help to starting my academic career), this critique of methodology was also a form of reciprocity, a way of giving back to the women in prison, with its focus on exploring how to conduct respectful research in a prison context.

BEYOND THE BOOK AND JOURNAL ARTICLE

The intended audience will influence the choices that student researchers make in terms of what and where to publish. The different audiences interested in the research might require different forms of representation and writing in the dissemination activities. Popular culture venues and technology are accessed to find ways to spread the word not only within academic contexts but also to people outside of academe. Patti Lather (1995) presented her research with women living with HIV/AIDS at academic conferences and published in academic journals, but also wrote a book to provide access to the study to a wider nonacademic audience and for the participants (Lather and Smithies 1997). Films and artwork are produced to share research with a larger audience and community members. Celia Haig-Brown and Helen Haig-Brown (2009) created a documentary film called *Pelq'ilc: Coming Home*, which was connected to Celia Haig-Brown's (1988) earlier master's degree research documented in *Resistance and Renewal: Surviving the Indian Residential School*.

Jon D. Prosser (2011: 482) explores the challenges for visual researchers to publish their work in appropriate ways; however, he also points to the opening of "new methodological possibilities for visual researchers" through the advance and use of "innovative technology and software."

When conducting critical qualitative research with social justice goals in mind, researchers often access venues that will best support the dissemination of findings across multiple audiences that include the participants and communities, activists and their associations, and policy-makers of all kinds. Gaile S. Cannella and Yvonna S. Lincoln (2009: 69) suggest that "strategic forms of dissemination" are needed to support the public's knowledge and critique of the privileging of particular individuals and communities and the marginalization of others:

> Networks, collaborations, and strategic forms of dissemination are necessary that address foundationally issues like: enlarging the public's understanding of the research imaginary, generating unthought discursive spaces, and public critique of the ways that groups are privileged and silenced by various forms of research, science, and academic practice.

CHECKING BACK AGAIN

Even if plans for dissemination are articulated in the information letter, participants may not have fully understood the implication of publication at the initial stages of the research. Keeping participants fully informed can mean returning to issues of dissemination at the conclusion of the research so that participants are not surprised to find themselves represented in publications later. When student researchers have completed writing their final documents, they will have hopefully decided what they want and are able to make public. They will have an idea of the degree to which participants will be comfortable with their decisions of what to tell and what to exclude from publication. However, based on participant requests, sometimes student researchers must decide not to present or disseminate aspects of their research outside the institutional requirements.

The following are questions related to dissemination students may want to consider:

- Is it important for them to disseminate aspects of their research and findings beyond the defence? Why or why not?

- How will they share the knowledge of the research experience? Findings produced?
- How can they give back to the participants and research communities and contexts? Provide reciprocity? If student researchers do not fulfil dissemination promises made, they may leave disappointed people who value research less as a result of their experience.

A REMINDER

Student researchers need to take the work of dissemination and publication seriously. What they construct to represent their research and send out into the public, although related to their goals, can have major implications for the participants and the research contexts. Wise ethical choices need to be made at all stages of the research, but especially when disseminating research to a greater public than the participants and communities who made the research possible. Situations can be created when access closes down for other researchers based on the previous researcher's behaviour. The aftermath of the research, which includes the relationship maintained (or not) between the researcher and the researched will influence whether participants and their communities support future research endeavours, including those they might consider to be in their best interests.

Annotated Bibliography

Boise, Robert. 1990. *Professors as Writers: A Self-Help Guide to Productive Writing.* Stillwater, OK: New Forums Press.

This book provides a timeless practical framework for productive writing. Though somewhat dated, the advice, strategies and writing exercises that Robert Boise provides are still highly effective and relevant to the challenges professional writers face today, from new graduate students to experienced researchers and professors. Boise discusses the challenging nature of writing to help readers gain insight into their personal difficulties with the process. He then provides practical solutions in the form of a systematic yet flexible approach to help writers generate and organize their ideas and their environment to be most conducive to the spontaneous and creative process of writing. The author's approach to writing, along with companion writing exercises, provide the tools writers need to make writing a habitual, creative and productive process.

Broad, Gail, and Jose Reyes. 2008. "A Colombia-Canada Research Collaboration." *Action Research* 6, 2: 129–147.

An assistant professor from Algoma University College and a leader of a nonprofit community organization from Colombia describe their alliance and involvement in a PAR project with Indigenous peoples. Coming together, Gail Broad and Jose Reyes are able to demonstrate respect and reciprocity amid difference, and share and mutually benefit from the research collectively undertaken. They value different types of knowledge (e.g., "applied," "practical," "theoretical" and "historical"), considering and integrating them in meaningful ways. Focusing on similarities as a way to move forward, they adopt an ethical stance for collaboration built upon open lines of communication with all stakeholders, confronting and dispelling "misconceptions" when needed for the benefit of all. Broad and Reyes pose many useful questions that have helped them think through the complexities of cross-cultural work. They attempt to consider community welfare ahead of institutions' and prospective funders' agendas whenever possible.

Castleden, Heather, Vanessa Sloan Morgan and Aelita Neimanis. 2010. "Researchers' Perspectives on Collective/Community Co-Authorship in Community-based Participatory Indigenous Research." *Journal of Empirical Research on Human Research Ethics* 5, 4: 23–32.

Heather Castleden and her colleagues discuss the benefits of coauthorship in this article. They describe the sharing of power, pride and sense of accomplishment that comes from authorship of work that is made public. They promote coauthorship as a means of recognizing and openly acknowledging participants' intellectual contributions and a way of demonstrating researchers' respect for Indigenous participants and their communities. The authors argue that when used to promote understandings of Indigenous worldviews and ways of knowing, coauthorship benefits both Indigenous and academic communities.

Haig-Brown, Celia (Producer), and Helen Haig-Brown (Director). 2009. *Pelq'ilc: Coming Home.* (Documentary film). Vancouver: University of British Columbia Press.

Film can be a productive way to disseminate research. This 33-minute documentary film explores the intergenerational transmission of the Secwepemc peoples' culture and language. The film takes up this question: "What role does education play in the renewal of culture?" It draws from and expands on interview data from a study that Celia Haig-Brown conducted in the mid-1980s. She interviewed former students of the Kamloops Indian Residential School to learn about their experiences at the school, as well as their resistance toward the institution that nearly destroyed the Secwepemc culture and language. The film, shot nearly twenty years after the participants were interviewed, engages with the former participants' children and grandchildren. The film shows that the former participants have taken up many of their traditional ways once again as they continue their journey through resistance to the regeneration of their native language and culture, allowing them to pass on what they learn to future generations.

Hall, Wendy, Bonita Long, Nicole Bermbach, Sharalyn Jordan and Kathryn Patterson. 2005. "Qualitative Teamwork Issues and Strategies: Coordination through Mutual Adjustment." *Qualitative Health Research* 15, 3: 394–410.

While conducting research as part of a team, Wendy Hall and her colleagues identified the need to have immediate and thoughtful conversations about how they would report on their future research findings. It was paramount for all those involved to reach consensus and develop a shared understanding, despite their differing backgrounds, positions, roles and goals. After examining a range of possible strategies, the primary investigator drew on existing materials to create a working document that was brought forward to the group for their consideration. This document articulated a "publication agreement" and provided a space for open discussions about a range of issues, including academic currency, professional aspirations, ethics and varying degrees of contributions (see Hall et al. 2005: 408–409 for details). The group established a process to be followed and various mechanisms for obtaining feedback, which supported them to move forward and ensure that important information would be circulated to others.

Jalongo, Mary R., Wanda Boyer and Marjory Ebbeck. 2014. "Writing for Scholarly Publication as 'Tacit Knowledge': A Qualitative Focus Group Study of Doctoral Students in Education." *Early Childhood Education Journal* 42: 241–250.

Through the use of focus group data from doctoral students in Canada, Australia, and the United States, Mary Jalongo and her colleagues explore a student perspective on the process of writing for publication. Excerpts from the interviews highlight four main themes or concerns that doctoral students have with the process: a) a need for writing for publication to be integrated into doctoral-level curriculum; b) more opportunities provided for peer and faculty review of doctoral writing for publication; c) a need to acquire a "constellation" of abilities, skills, habits, attitudes and values associated with successful publication; and d) concerns about the value of publication now and in the future.

Rivière, Dominique. 2005. "Identities and Intersectionalities: Performance, Power and the Possibilities for Multicultural Education." *Research in Drama Education* 10, 3: 341–354.

Dominique Rivière, a doctoral student and research assistant from the Ontario Institute for Studies in Education, is carving out her dissertation research from part of a bigger study that she is involved in. In a peer-reviewed publication, she shares "emergent findings" from her critical ethnographic case study of high school students' identity negotiations in a drama classroom, framed in the context of "multicultural education." It is clear that her doctoral study is an extension of her master's research and is connected to her paid work. She shares only a portion of the findings related to a specific subset of participants. Reading this article helps novice researchers understand how to frame a work-in-progress, including how to write up preliminary findings while providing clear connections to a research question, relevant historical background, theoretical and conceptual frameworks, a description of the context and key players, methodological details, a description of the methods, identification of relevant themes, appropriate participant quotes and significance for various stakeholders. She strategically uses critical questions to shift direction while maintaining flow and coherence. She acknowledges that parts of this paper were presented at an international and local conference, at which she was able to elicit feedback on her developing understandings.

Sethi, Bharati. 2014. "A Grand Erie Photovoice Community Report 'Do You See What I See?' Community-based Participatory Research with Immigrant/Refugee KAAJAL Women Using Photovoice," 1–40.

With this report, Bharati Sethi found an innovative way to disseminate knowledge gained during her doctoral work to the broader community beyond the academy. Her dissertation and this report that subsequently followed were created using a visual qualitative research method called photo-voice. Sethi provided immigrant and refugee women with digital cameras to record their Canadian experiences. She then theorized the data using an intersectional approach to explore how factors of nationality, immigrant status, geography, age, ability, sexuality, race and socioeconomic status impact her participants' health and employment. Sethi's findings, based on her interpretations of the photographs as well as diary entries and in-depth interviews of her participants, were written up as a report for members of the Fort Erie community as a means to give marginalized women a voice to bring public awareness to the impact these markers of difference have on their mental and physical health within the workplace as they adjust to being new Canadians.

Shearer, Kathleen, and William F. Birdsall. 2005. "A Canadian Strategy for the Dissemination of Research Knowledge." *Feliciter* 4: 192–194.

This article outlines five major concerns regarding the dissemination of research knowledge in Canada: a) ensuring access to and the preservation of creative, diverse and unique forms of scholarly research; b) concerns about digital preservation issues of data and knowledge to ensure long-term accessibility; c) the current academic merit system, which is primarily based on publication output and its impact on researchers' motivation to disseminate their findings to a broader social community beyond the institution; d) uneven distribution of power and infrastructure within the academy that impacts access to information resources across universities and even across disciplines; and e) recent copyright and intellectual property issues in the digital age of research. The authors conclude that as awareness about the importance of research contributions to our society increases, greater consideration may be given to the process and channels through which research findings are disseminated.

Chapter 9

CONCLUSION

The linearity of this text following from research plan to dissemination is meant to assist readers to become familiar with and prepare for the multiple intersecting aspects of the research process. However, I want to remind readers that the appearance of this textual representation does not do justice to the messy, back-and-forth, cyclical and iterative reality of conducting qualitative research. Hopefully, the contents of the book, the discussions and illustrations will have met that goal.

I imagine that many readers of this book are students energized and excited about the prospects of conducting qualitative research and completing their degrees, students who exude passion for the research focus they have chosen. Passion can play an important role in student researchers' experiences of conducting critical qualitative research. The passion can sustain them through critical moments, including unanticipated events and disappointments, and the lengthy time period they will be involved in their research projects — often more of a time commitment than they originally imagined. Passion of various degrees may be what fuels individuals' and communities' decisions to participate in the research, to continue through to completion.

My hope is that after students engage with this text, they will be more informed about the complexities of conducting qualitative research and better prepared to address the challenges that arise as they research with human participants. Regardless of their choice of qualitative methodologies and methods, whether conservative or on the innovative side, students will need to think broadly about the responsibilities that come with the privilege of conducting research with real people and communities who will experience the research in a variety of ways.

Conducting critical qualitative research can be exciting, exhilarating and exhausting; it can also be fraught with complications and sometimes unimagined repercussions. Respectful research praxis requires students to pay close attention to the decisions they make and their actions, maintaining an awareness of the ethical implications of their research process and the ripple effects possible.

FINAL REFLECTIONS

I learned many things from my experience conducting research in the prison, knowledge that was transferable to other research contexts that on the surface seem very different from prisons, but connect in the realm of research. No matter the context or participants and communities involved, to conduct respectful research, researchers have to think deeply about issues of power and privilege and the implications of both to the research planned and conducted.

Although power issues are magnified in a context such as a prison, power circulates in various ways in all research contexts and is embedded in the research process. Power influences the shaping of researcher-researched relationships, sometimes ameliorated to various degrees based on the participatory or collaborative elements of the research process, but always present. Who is positioned as researcher and participant? Who is involved in what ultimately serves as the knowledge produced and shared as a result of research? Who decides what form this knowledge takes? What is sanctioned? What is dismissed and never shared? Who benefits from the knowledge produced? Foucault (1979, 1980) writes of power/knowledge as being in relation, a relation that can be seen reflected in the process of knowledge construction and dissemination as a result of research conducted.

In the case of critical qualitative research, it is a given that researchers acknowledge the influence of power in the conduct of research, that they continuously apply a critical reflexivity to the research process that unfolds and to their decision-making, informed by input from individual and community participants and collaborators whenever possible. Student researchers who are aware of the complexities of power and its influence on the research process will be better able to appreciate the resistance that individuals and communities demonstrate toward research, to understand resistance as more than a negative force — as a force that can lead to productive relationships and respectful research.

It is not surprising that as the distance between researcher and participants lessens, the ways in which privilege and power intersect and influence the research experience become more visible. In the context of the prison, I was faced with questioning how privilege was exercised in the embedded institutional practices but also in relation to the research conducted, research that I (as well as that of other researchers) was involved in. I was forced to consider the ways in which privilege contributed to my positioning as researcher and to the women's roles as participants. I carried privilege in my white, middle-class, heterosexual body; a formally educated body that had reaped the benefits of fitting into the dominant groups and structures that influenced what happened in schools and the larger society. Although individuals (including student researchers) experience degrees of privilege/marginalization at various junctures and in life situations, researching in that context made me aware that privilege had afforded me great protection throughout my social/institutional/political interactions, and it was not too surprising that I was able to position myself as researcher. Although I was protected, many of the women, based on their classed, raced, gendered and socially constructed identities, were left to fend for themselves, often fighting for the opportunity to receive an education. It was not surprising that I found my place as researcher and they were positioned as participants.

Engaging a critically reflexive stance can help student researchers uncover the ways in which privilege and power intersect and influence the research process, including the data collected, analyzed and disseminated. When student researchers understand how privilege and power influence what is researched and to whose benefit, they can better articulate relevant questions at the beginning stages of the process to apply to the research they plan. What makes research worthwhile? Who has access to resources and who doesn't? Whose knowledge is privileged? Whose voices are loud or only a whisper? Heard or silenced? Will the researcher or those in charge benefit more from the research than participants and their communities? Answers to such questions can assist students in designing research that has the potential to contribute to social, institutional and community change.

In the same way that a qualitative research design is not a plan once and for all, but instead is revised as process influences plan, the knowledge students need to conduct the research they plan will also become more apparent at multiple junctures in the research process, and especially in the context of the research and through involvement with their individual and community participants. Students' willingness to acknowledge and question the limitations of their knowledge and to work against those limitations as they collect and analyze data, grapple with questions of representation, articulate findings and decide venues for dissemination will contribute to the credibility of the study and its outcomes.

A LOOK FORWARD

> Actively engaging established traditions in debate with recent innovations leads to a research practice that is more rigorous, methodologically robust, theoretically sophisticated and politically relevant." (Ezzy 2002: xiv)

The qualitative research world has been and continues to be an exciting world for researchers, student and otherwise; conversations that intersect across various disciplinary fields have been and continue to be lively and engaging. Whether one falls into the camp of excitement or suspicion of the proliferation of perspectives and methods, the debates have been critical and educational (Wright 2006). Whether researchers engage with the new modes of representation, move more fully into the electronic age, or take advantage of the growing visual and performance arts' influences on qualitative methodologies and methods, they still need to consider to what good they put their time and resources and to ask critical questions: How does the research contribute to the lives of participants and their communities, to the broader field in general? Who benefits from the research and who may be harmed? Is reciprocity an aspect emphasized in the design?

In institutional contexts, however, the willingness to explore and adopt the myriad of methodologies and methods available to qualitative researchers can be slow. Universities continue to be conservative places driven by a neoliberalism that influences program decisions and possibilities available to students who want to push boundaries. For now, student researchers need to challenge the "taken-for-grantedness" of what is possible in terms of their choice of methodologies and methods, sometimes pushing the boundaries successfully and other times making the best of their choices, imagining another time when they might explore in ways they had envisioned. For those who can make choices of where to complete their degrees and with whom, they can make smart decisions about searching to find a good match with their needs and also their desires. However, as always, conditions exist that will make choice a possibility for some individuals but not for others. For those privileged with choice, maybe they can make it a visible matter — discussed in the open in their university context. The upside of the downside is that hard times are often also exciting times when resistance takes many shapes and change can actually happen.

Students who engage with the debates in the field have the opportunity not only to strengthen the research they produce as students but also to educate themselves better. This is important for those who choose to move into academic contexts, who will become the researchers and advisors to others, as well as for those individuals who return to their previous or newly acquired professional and working lives with an informed critical lens they can apply to question decisions made in the social and political realms outside the academy.

> For those who want their research to have a more direct social relevance, the critical and *post* [italics in text] traditions offer myriad opportunities to critique contemporary social structures and envision alternative institutional formations. Thus, in many ways, a number of the qualitative traditions offer the excitement of intellectual vigor without the seclusion

of the ivory tower. For those of us who love the challenge of academic discourses but want to remain a part of the so-called real world, qualitative research may well be the answer. (Prasad 2005: 292)

For researchers who want their research to have a more direct relevance, to "remain part of the so-called real world," finding ways to work respectfully with others and to collaborate across contexts and communities will be important. Participatory research and transnational feminist research has provided many models from which to learn how to move forward. Collaboration in current times will be shaped by various factors, but ultimately this may mean researchers engaged in an informed decolonizing research praxis, working in partnerships across difference, First Nations, transnational, racialized and non-Indigenous researchers working collaboratively inside and outside of the academy.

POSTSCRIPT

If research doesn't change you as a person, then you haven't done it right. (Wilson, S. 2008: 135)

I return to the prison world and women incarcerated to write this postscript. Chapter 1 began with a journal entry that described my first walk through the prison and the pivotal moments I constructed to explain the impetus that led to me conducting research with women in a prison school. The research I describe influenced and continues to influence my trajectory as researcher and teacher (reflecting Shawn Wilson's words, that research did change me). However, rather than concluding it was "done right," I expect that individuals (myself included) who have conducted critical qualitative research will often be left questioning how we could have done it better.

In this text, I revisit my doctoral research for two reasons. The first is as an illustration of the complexities of conducting respectful research. The women who participated in that research taught me much of what I know about engaging in respectful research praxis, and they continue to teach me today; their voices influenced the shaping of the chapters. Although many of the readers of this text will not be researching in contexts like prisons, they will conduct critical qualitative research that they feel passionate about and hopefully make a contribution to individuals and communities with whom they research.

A second reason to connect this exploration of the qualitative research process specifically to my doctoral experience was to bring readers into what for many will be the distanced world of incarceration. While engaged in thinking about the complexities of conducting respectful research, readers will also have learned (at least a little) about women incarcerated in prisons; perhaps they will then be more willing to engage critically in the future with others in the discourse circulating in the everyday about incarceration. Perhaps readers may point the conversation to a more comprehensive consideration of whose bodies are imprisoned and why, and the falsity of claims that somehow such a punishing regime is the answer to rehabilitating prisoners. At the least, readers might begin to question the media and other representations of women in prisons.

In Canada, not much has changed over the last few decades for those women who find themselves imprisoned in multimillion-dollar secured institutions. Disturbing images and narratives of what is happening to people who are incarcerated are more recently part of the media coverage. Very few people in Canada do not know of Ashley Smith (even though they may have forgotten her name) and the terrible circumstances of her history of incarceration and her demise in that system (UCCO 2008). Debates on the use of segregation are currently a focus of Canadian media, with descriptions of the impact on those who are given often lengthy periods of time isolated from others. I am reminded of what I learned about segregation and the misleading rationales in support of its use across multiple situations. Ashley's death has contributed to pushing this debate further, but at a very high cost to her and her family.

> [A person's] hope is necessary, but it is not enough. Alone, it does not win. But without it, my [their] struggle will be weak and wobbly. We need critical hope the way a fish needs unpolluted water. (Freire 1994: 8)

Although the past should not dictate the future, it should at least inform it. I think about Paulo Freire's words in relation to the continued incarceration of women and their struggles for an education. In light of what is happening in current times, hope (critical or otherwise) is difficult to maintain. The extensive statistical data about women in prisons, taken in isolation of contextual knowledge and an informed critical analysis, is difficult to read beyond a surface level. Currently, the number of women incarcerated is increasing in the Canadian context and in other contexts (Statistics Canada 2010). Statistics continue to show an overrepresentation of Aboriginal/Indigenous peoples in prisons in general, and Indigenous women specifically. The number of female youth admitted to sentenced custody is also increasing; many of these young women are Aboriginal and members of minority and marginalized populations. A high percentage of women in prison have not completed high school and before incarceration were poor and unemployed; many struggled with mental health issues and drug addictions (Mahony 2011; Statistics Canada 2010). The majority of these women continue to be no danger to the public. The media discourse, however, persists in emphasizing the stereotypes of the dangerous female offender. Erica R. Meiners (2007: 34) explains, "As prisons are an institution where access is deeply regulated, few alternative media sources, or representations that challenge the dominant stereotypes about violent and crazed 'felons,' get to emerge."

The increase in individuals incarcerated is in line with the growth of the *prison industrial complex* (Davis 2003; Meiners 2011). Prisons and detention centres have become big business, contributing to the growth of the economy in a time of deindustrialization. Embedded in the prison industrial complex is "a set of symbiotic relationships among correctional communities, transnational corporations, media conglomerates, guards' unions and legislative and court agendas" (Davis 2003: 107). This industry growth is not surprising considering the increased fear for safety in the West (including of one's belongings) and the belief that incarceration ensures the protection of law-abiding citizens: "The prevailing contemporary carceral logic recycles the false notion that safety can be achieved through essentially more of the same: more guards, fences, surveillance, suspensions, punishment" (Meiners 2011: 559).

While incarceration grows in popularity, support for prisoners' access to educational opportunities for purposes of rehabilitation has lessened, even as the statistical data supports education (higher education in particular) as a means of decreasing the numbers of prisoners reoffending (Fine et al. 2001; Sims 2008; Steurer et al. 2001). Among other factors, the more recent social and political climate appears to be emphasizing punishment over rehabilitation. As Chris Sims (2008: 2) reminds us:

> Policy approaches to education and training in prisons are, however, vulnerable to changes in the political climate, as prevailing views about the core purposes of prison change. In the 1970s, views emphasizing the rehabilitative role of prison — offenders to return to society — began to give way to a more punitive view in many developed countries, particularly the USA.

The women participating in my doctoral research exhibited a strong desire to become better educated. They believed that receiving their General Education Development (GED) diploma or being further schooled in what they had not learned in public school classrooms (e.g., math and English grammar) was their ticket to a better life; even those who had left the prison and later returned to pick up their books and to continue their schooling. However, the actual successful completion of an examination for the GED, although useful for lifting the women's spirits, did not do much in terms of securing the future they were promised. The opportunity for postsecondary education in prisons that was available in earlier years held some possibilities, but it is now discontinued.

The official prison agenda was for students to upgrade their public school knowledge, learn the sanctioned knowledge. When I explained to my friend that I felt I had the freedom to teach in the prison, I was not referring to the times when I was teaching students to do mathematical percentages. It was during our morning meetings when we had student-led discussions in which women chose the focus and whether they would participate. Although I questioned the ethics of engaging in critical pedagogical moments in a prison institution, participants in those moments educated each other and their teachers.

Students in prison classrooms (similar to those in public school classrooms) were schooled in knowledge embedded in hegemonic disciplines rather than encouraged to develop capacities to critique such knowledge (Davidson 1995; Faith 1993). Although many of the participants spoke of having deep regrets for terminating their public education, they also narrated incidents that spoke to the marginalizing and often degrading experiences that occurred in schools and classrooms they attended. Life circumstances that were at times out of their control also contributed to their departure. These women had a sharp critique that they often could not silence when sitting in public school classrooms.

Many of these women had travelled the school-to-prison pipeline (Kim et al. 2012; Meiners 2011; Winn 2010) as part of the flow of young people who left (and are continuing to leave) public school systems and are eventually imprisoned, sometimes hindered on their travels by a sentence in a detention centre. Michelle Fine (1991) writes of youth being institutionally framed as dropouts, even though many of them made conscious decisions to leave public school institutions. She describes secondary school culture with its lack of support for critique from students (or teachers, for that matter); those who offered institutional/social/political critique were often the ones leaving. In school, students who did not *fit in* resisted through silence, whereas others left the school system; resistance was marked by their absence (Fine 1991; see Dei et al. 1997). The youth that Fine describes remind me of the women I taught in the prison.

> Geraldine: One of the things that I like about the women we work with is that they're rebels. In some way, they have stepped out against society, that's why they're [in prison]. They've gone against something that's very powerful in this society ... many of them have been incredibly courageous in doing what they did ... if they were willing to take that kind of risk, they might take a risk about learning. They might take a risk and step outside the kind of paradigms they've been offered in the past and look at the world another way. (Tilley 1998a: 175)

Critical hope might be kept alive if student researchers and others "take a risk about learning," as Geraldine was suggesting the women do. Researchers might take a risk and step outside of the kind of perspectives they have been offered in the past. For those individuals currently involved in prison research, this might mean moving beyond advocating for change, that although important in the material reality of the everyday, does not push the question "why prisons at all?" Perhaps the focus can emphasize the possibilities of abolition. This was not part of my mindset at the time of my study, but it is today.

LINKS

For those readers interested in pursuing resources related to women and girls and incarceration, the following links connect to books and other resources:

- AK Press. <akpress.org/captivegenders.html>.
- Davis, Angela Y. *Disability Incarcerated: Imprisonment and Disability in the United States and Canada.* 2014. <amazon.ca/gp/product/1137404051/ref=ox_sc_sfl_title_7?ie=UTF8&psc=1&smid=A3DWYIK6Y9EEQB>.
- Faith, Karlene and Anne Near (eds.). 2006. *13 Women: Parables from Prison.* <douglas-mcintyre.com/book/13-women>.
- Leverentz, Andrea. *The Ex-Prisoner's Dilemma: How Women Negotiate Competing Narratives of Reentry and Resistance.* 2014. <rutgerspress. rutgers.edu/product/Ex-Prisoners-Dilemma,5109.aspx>.
- PM Press. <secure.pmpress.org/?l=product_detail&p=91>.
- Ross, Richard. 2015. *Girls in Justice.* <juvenile-in-justice.com/shop/girls-in-justice>.

REFERENCES

Absolon, Kathy, and Cam Willett. 2005. "Putting Ourselves Forward: Location in Aboriginal Research." In Leslie Brown and Susan Strega (eds.), *Research as Resistance: Critical, Indigenous, and Anti-Oppressive Approaches* (pp. 97–126). Toronto: Canadian Scholar's Press.

Acker, Joan, Kate Barry and Johanna Esseveld. 1991. "Objectivity and Truth: Problems in Doing Feminist Research." In Mary Fonow and Judith Cook (eds.), *Beyond Methodology: Feminist Scholarship as Lived Research* (pp. 133–153). Bloomington: Indiana University Press.

Acker, Sandra. 2000. "In/out/side: Positioning the Researcher in Feminist Qualitative Research." *Resources for Feminist Research* 28, 1/2: 189–208.

Agee, Jane. 2009. "Developing Qualitative Research Questions: A Reflective Process." *International Journal of Qualitative Studies in Education* 22, 4: 431–447.

Aguiar, Luis, and Christopher J. Schneider (eds.). 2012. *Researching Amongst Elites: Challenges and Opportunities in Studying Up.* Farnam, UK: Ashgate Press.

Aitken, Stuart C. 2010. "'Throwntogetherness': Encounters with Difference and Diversity." In Dydia DeLyser, Steve Herbert, Stuart C. Aitken, Mike Crang and Linda McDowell (eds.), *The Sage Handbook of Qualitative Geography* (pp. 46–68). London: Sage.

Altheide, David L., and Christopher J. Schneider. 2013. *Qualitative Media Analysis*, 2nd ed. London: Sage.

Alvesson, Mats, and Kaj Sköldberg. 2009. *Reflexive Methodology: New Vistas for Qualitative Research*, 2nd ed. Los Angeles: Sage.

Anfara, Vincent A., and Norma T. Mertz (eds.). 2014. *Theoretical Frameworks in Qualitative Research*. London: Sage.

____. 2006. *Theoretical Frameworks in Qualitative Research*. London Sage.

Angrosino, Michael V., and Judith Rosenberg. 2011. "Observations on Observation: Continuities and Challenges." In Norman K. Denzin and Yvonna S. Lincoln (eds.), *The Sage Handbook of Qualitative Research*, 4th ed. (pp. 467–478). London: Sage.

Archibald, Jo-ann. 2008. *Indigenous Storywork: Educating the Heart, Mind, Body, and Spirit*. Vancouver: University of British Columbia Press.

Atkinson, Paul, and Sara Delamont. 2005. "Analytic Perspectives." In Norman K. Denzin and Yvonna S. Lincoln (eds.), *The Sage Handbook of Qualitative Research*, 3rd ed. (pp. 821–840). London: Sage.

Avni, Anoosha E. 2012. "Skilled Worker Immigrants' Pre-Migration Occupation: Re-Entry Experiences in Canada." Unpublished doctoral dissertation, University of Alberta, Edmonton, AB.

Bakhru, Tanya S. 2008. "Negotiating and Navigating the Rough Terrain of Transnational Feminist Research." *Journal of International Women's Studies* 10, 2: 198–216.

Bailey, Julia. 2008. "First Steps in Qualitative Data Analysis: Transcribing." *Family Practice* 25, 2: 127–131.

Banks, James. 1998. "The Lives and Values of Researchers: Implications for Educating Citizens in a Multicultural Society." *Educational Researcher* 27, 7: 4–17.

Barbour, Rosaline. 2007. *Doing Focus Groups*. London: Sage.

Barnes, Benita J., and Ann E. Austin. 2009. "The Role of Doctoral Advisors: A Look at Advising from the Advisor's Perspective." *Innovative Higher Education* 33: 297–315.

Barrett, Margaret, and Janet Mills. 2009. "The Inter-Reflexive Possibilities of Dual Observations: An Account from and through Experience." *International Journal of Qualitative Studies in Education* 22, 4: 417–429.

Battiste, Marie. 2008. "Research Ethics for Protecting Indigenous Knowledge and Heritage: Institutional and Researcher Responsibilities." In Norman K. Denzin, Yvonna S. Lincoln, and Linda Tuhiwai Smith (eds.), *Handbook of Critical Indigenous Methodologies* (pp. 497–510). London: Sage.

____. 1998. "Decolonizing the University: Ethical Guidelines for Research Involving Indigenous Populations." Plenary address at the Canadian Society for the Study of Education annual conference. May. Ottawa, ON.

Baumbusch, Jennifer. L. 2010. "Conducting Critical Ethnography in Long-term Residential Care: Experiences of a Novice Researcher in the Field." *Journal of Advanced Nursing* 67, 1: 184–192.

Bell, Kirsten, and Amy Salmon. 2011. "What Women Who Use Drugs Have to Say about Ethical Research: Findings of an Exploratory Qualitative Study." *Journal of Empirical Research on Human Research Ethics* 6, 4: 84–98.

Bird, Cindy. 2005. "How I Stopped Dreading and Learned to Love Transcription." *Qualitative Inquiry* 11, 2: 226–248.

Bloor, Michael, Jane Franklin, Michelle Thomas and Kate Robson. 2001. *Focus Groups in Social Research*. Thousand Oaks, CA: Sage.

Bogdan, Robert, and Sari K. Biklen. 2003. *Qualitative Research for Education: An Introduction to Theories and Methods*, 4th ed. New York: Pearson.

Boise, Robert. 1990. *Professors as Writers: A Self-Help Guide to Productive Writing*. Stillwater, OK: New Forums Press.

Boote, David N., and Penny Beile. 2005. "Scholars Before Researchers: On the Centrality of the Dissertation Literature Review in Research Preparation." *Educational Researcher* 34, 6: 3–15.

Bosco, Fernando J., and Thomas Herman. 2010. "Focus Groups as Collaborative Research Performances." In Dydia DeLyser, Steve Herbert, Stuart Aitken, Mike Crang and Linda McDowell (eds.), *The Sage Handbook of Qualitative Geography* (pp. 193–207).

London: Sage.

Bose, Christine E. 2012. "Intersectionality and Global Gender Inequality." *Gender & Society* 26, 1: 67–72.

Bourdieu, Pierre. 1984. *Distinction: A Social Critique of the Judgement of Taste* (R. Nice, Trans.). Cambridge, MA: Harvard University Press.

Brady, Jennifer. 2011. "Cooking as Inquiry: A Method to Stir Up Prevailing Ways of Knowing Food, Body, and Identity." *International Journal of Qualitative Methods* 10, 4: 321–334.

Brannen, Julia. 2004. "Working Qualitatively and Quantitatively." In Clive Seale, Giampietro Gobo, Jaber Gubrium, and David Silverman (eds.), *Qualitative Research Practice* (pp. 282–296). London: Sage.

Breidenstein, George. 2007. "The Meaning of Boredom in School Lessons: Participant Observation in the Seventh and Eighth Form." *Ethnography and Education* 2, 1: 93–108.

Britzman, Deborah P. 1991. *Practice Makes Practice: A Critical Study of Learning How to Teach*. Albany: State University of New York Press.

Broad, Gail, and Jose Reyes. 2008. "A Colombia-Canada Research Collaboration." *Action Research* 6, 2: 129–147.

Brook, Julia, Susan Catlin, Christopher DeLuca, Christine Doe, Alyson Huntly and Michelle Searle. 2010. "Conceptions of Doctoral Education: The PhD as Pathmaking." *Reflective Practice* 11, 5: 657–668.

Browne, Kath, and Catherine Nash. 2010. "Queer Methods and Methodologies: An Introduction." In Kath Browne and Catherine Nash (eds.), *Queer Methods and Methodologies: Intersecting Queer Theories and Social Science Research* (pp. 1–24). Surrey, UK: Ashgate.

Burbules, Nicholas C., and Rupert Berk. 1999. "Critical Thinking and Critical Pedagogy: Relations, Differences and Limits." In Thomas S. Popkewitz and Lynn Fendler (eds.), *Critical Theories in Education: Changing Terrains of Knowledge and Politics* (pp. 45–66). New York: Routledge.

Burgos-Debray, Elizabeth. (ed.). 1984. *I Rigoberta Menchu: An Indian Woman in Guatemala*. London: Verso.

Burles, Meredith. 2010. "Negotiating Serious Illness: Understanding Young Women's Experiences through Photovoice." Unpublished master's thesis, University of Saskatchewan, Saskatoon, SK.

Caelli, Kate, Lynne Ray and Judy Mill. 2003. "'Clear as Mud': Toward Greater Clarity in Generic Qualitative Research." *International Journal of Qualitative Methods* 2, 2: 1–24.

Cahnmann-Taylor, Melisa, and Richard Siegesmund (eds.). 2008. *Arts-Based Research in Education: Foundations for Practice*. New York: Routledge.

Cannella, Gaile S., and Yvonna S. Lincoln. 2009. "Deploying Qualitative Methods for Social Purposes." In Norman K. Denzin and Michael D. Giardina (eds.), *Qualitative Inquiry and Social Justice* (pp. 53–72). Walnut Creek, CA: Left Coast Press.

Carlson, Julie A. 2010. "Avoiding Traps in Member Checking." *The Qualitative Report* 15, 5: 1102–1113.

Carnevale, Franco A., Mary Ellen Macdonald, Myra Bluebond-Langner and Patricia McKeever. 2008. "Using Participant Observation in Pediatric Health Care Settings: Ethical Challenges and Solutions." *Journal of Child Health Care* 12, 1: 18–32.

Carter, Stacie M., and Miles Little. 2007. "Justifying Knowledge, Justifying Method,

Taking Action: Epistemologies, Methodologies, and Methods in Qualitative Research." *Qualitative Health Research* 17, 10: 1316–1328.

Castleden, Heather, Vanessa Sloan Morgan and Christopher Lamb. 2012. "'I Spent the First Year Drinking Tea': Exploring Canadian University Researchers' Perspectives on Community-based Participatory Research Involving Indigenous Peoples." *The Canadian Geographer* 56, 2: 160–179.

Castleden, Heather, Vanessa Sloan Morgan and Aelita Neimanis. 2010. "Researchers' Perspectives on Collective/Community Co-authorship in Community-based Participatory Indigenous Research." *Journal of Empirical Research on Human Research Ethics* 5, 4: 23–32.

Charmaz, Kathy. 2011. "Grounded Theory Methods in Social Justice Research." In Norman K. Denzin and Yvonna S. Lincoln (eds.), *The Sage Handbook of Qualitative Research*, 4th ed. (pp. 359–380). London: Sage.

____ (ed.). 2006a. *Constructing Grounded Theory: A Practical Guide through Qualitative Analysis*. Thousand Oaks, CA: Sage.

____. 2006b. "Gathering Rich Data." In Kathy Charmaz (ed.), *Constructing Grounded Theory: A Practical Guide through Qualitative Analysis* (pp. 13–41). Thousand Oaks, CA: Sage.

____. 2000. "Grounded Theory: Objectivist and Constructivist Methods." In Norman K. Denzin and Yvonna S. Lincoln (eds.), *Handbook of Qualitative Research*, 2nd ed. (pp. 509–536). Thousand Oaks, CA: Sage.

Chase, Susan E. 2011. "Narrative Inquiry: Still a Field in the Making." In Norman K. Denzin and Yvonna S. Lincoln (eds.), *The Sage Handbook of Qualitative Research*, 4th ed. (pp. 421–435). London: Sage.

Cho, Sumi, Kimberlie W. Crenshaw, and Leslie McCall. 2013. "Intersectionality Studies: Theory, Applications, and Praxis." *Signs: Journal of Women in Culture and Culture in Society* 38, 4: 785–810.

Choo, Hae Yeon. 2012. "The Transnational Journey of Intersectionality." *Gender and Society* 26, 1: 40–45.

Clandinin, D. Jean (ed.). 2007. *Handbook of Narrative Inquiry: Mapping a Methodology*. Thousand Oaks, CA: Sage.

Clandinin, D. Jean, and F. Michael Connelly. 2000. *Narrative Inquiry: Experience and Story in Qualitative Research*. San Francisco: Jossey-Bass.

Clifford, James. 1990. "Notes on (Field)notes." In R. Sanjek (ed.), *Field Notes: The Making of Anthropology* (pp. 47–70). Ithaca, NY: Cornell University Press.

____. 1988. *The Predicament of Culture: Twentieth Century Ethnography, Literature, and Art.* Cambridge, MA: Harvard University Press.

Clifford, James, and George E. Marcus. 1986. *Writing Culture: The Poetics and Politic of Ethnography*. Berkeley: University of California Press.

Coffey, Amanda, and Paul Atkinson. 1996. *Making Sense of Qualitative Data: Complementary Research Strategies*. Thousand Oaks, CA: Sage.

Cole, Peter. 2002. "Aboriginalizing Methodology: Considering the Canoe." *International Journal of Qualitative Studies in Education* 15, 4: 447–459.

Collier, Diane. 2013. "Being Tough, Staying Good, and Playing Inside the Box: An Ethnographic Case Study of One Boy's Multimodal Textmaking." Unpublished doctoral dissertation, University of British Columbia, Vancouver, BC.

Collins, Patricia Hill. 2012. "Social Inequality, Power, and Politics: Intersectionality and American Pragmatism in Dialogue." *Journal of Speculative Philosophy* 26, 2: 442–457.

____. 2000. *Black Feminist Thought*, 2nd ed. New York: Routledge.

____. 1991. "Learning from the Outsider Within: The Sociological Significance of Black Feminist Thought." In Joan E. Hartman and Ellen Messer-Davidow (eds.), *(En) Gendering Knowledge(s): Feminists in Academe* (pp. 40–65). Knoxville: University of Tennessee Press.

Conn, Lesley G. 2008. "Ethics Policy as Audit in Canadian Clinical Settings: Exiling the Ethnographic Method." *Qualitative Research* 8, 4: 499–514.

Conrad, Diane. 2004. "Exploring Risky Youth Experiences: Popular Theatre as a Participatory, Performative Research Method." *International Journal of Qualitative Methods* 3, 1: 12–25.

Conrad, Diane, and Kendal Wallis. 2009. "Making Space for Youth: iHuman Youth Society and Arts-Based Research with Street-Involved Youth in Canada." In Dip Kapoor and Steven Jordan (eds.), *Education, Participatory Action Research, and Social Change: International Perspectives* (pp. 251–264). New York: Palgrave & Macmillan.

Cook, Catherine. 2011. "Email Interviewing: Generating Data with a Vulnerable Population." *Journal of Advanced Nursing* 68, 6: 1330–1339.

Cook, Judith A., and Mary Margaret Fonow. 1990. "Knowledge and Women's Interests: Issues of Epistemology and Methodology in Feminist Sociological Research." In Joyce Nielsen (ed.), *Feminist Research Methods: Exemplary Readings in the Social Sciences* (pp. 69–93). Boulder, CO: Westview Press.

Cotnam-Kappel, Megan. 2014. "Tensions in Creating Possibilities for Youth Voice in School Choice: An Ethnographer's Reflexive Story of Research." *Canadian Journal of Education* 37, 1: 140–162.

Daiute, Colette, and Cynthia Lightfoot. 2004. *Narrative Analysis: Studying the Development of Individuals in Society*. Sage: London.

Damianakis, Thecia, and Michael R. Woodford. 2012. "Qualitative Research with Small Connected Communities: Generating New Knowledge While Upholding Research Ethics." *Qualitative Health Research* 22, 5: 708–718.

Davidson, Christina. 2009. "Transcription: Imperatives for Qualitative Research." *International Journal for Qualitative Methods* 8, 2: 35–52.

Davidson, Howard (ed.). 1995. *Schooling in a "Total Institution": Critical Perspectives on Prison Education*. Westport, CT: Bergin & Garvey.

Davidson, Judith, and Silvana di Gregorio. 2011. "Qualitative Research and Technology: In the Midst of a Revolution." In Norman K. Denzin and Yvonna S. Lincoln (eds.), *Collecting and Interpreting Qualitative Materials*, 4th ed. London: Sage.

Davies, Bronwyn, Jenny Browne, Susanne Gannon, Eileen Honan, Cath Laws, Babette Mueller-Rockstroh ... Eva Bendix Petersen. 2004. "The Ambivalent Practices of Reflexivity." *Qualitative Inquiry* 10, 3: 360–389.

Davis, Angela. 2003. *Are Prisons Obsolete?* New York: Seven Stories Press.

Davis, Mark, Graham Bolding, Graham Hart, Lorraine Sherr and Jonathan Elford. 2004. "Reflecting on the Experience of Interviewing Online: Perspectives from the Internet and HIV Study in London." *AIDS Care* 16, 8, 944–952.

Davison, Colleen M. 2007. "Engagement and the Northern School Setting: A Critical

Ethnography among the Tlicho First Nation of Behchoko, NWT." Unpublished doctoral dissertation, University of Calgary, Calgary, AB.

Dehli, Kari. 2008. "Coming to Terms: Methodological and Other Dilemmas in Research." In Kathleen Gallagher (ed.), *The Methodological Dilemma: Critical, Creative and Post-Positivist Approaches to Qualitative Research* (pp. 46–66.) New York: Routledge.

Dei, George J. Sefa, Josephine Mazzuca, Elizabeth McIsaac and Jasmin Zine. 1997. *Reconstructing "Dropout": A Critical Ethnography of the Dynamics of Black Students' Disengagement from Schools*. Toronto: University of Toronto Press.

DeLyser, Dydia, Steve Herbert, Stuart C. Aitken, Mike Crang and Linda McDowell (eds.). 2010. *The Sage Handbook of Qualitative Geography*. London: Sage.

Denzin, Norman K. 1997. *Interpretive Ethnography: Ethnographic Practices for the 21st Century*. Thousand Oaks, CA: Sage.

____. (ed.). 1978. *The Research Act: A Theoretical Introduction to Sociological Methods*. Thousand Oaks, CA: Sage.

Denzin, Norman K., and Yvonna S. Lincoln (eds.). 2011. *The Sage Handbook of Qualitative Research*, 4th ed. London: Sage.

____. 2005a. "Introduction: The Discipline and Practice of Qualitative Research." In Norman K. Denzin and Yvonna S. Lincoln (eds.), *The Sage Handbook of Qualitative Research*, 3rd ed. (pp. 1–20). London: Sage.

____. 2005b. *The Sage Handbook of Qualitative Research*, 3rd ed. London: Sage.

____. 2000. *The Handbook of Qualitative Research*, 2nd ed. London: Sage.

DeVault, Marjorie L. 1999. *Liberating Method: Feminism and Social Science Research*. Philadelphia: Temple University Press.

Dey, Ian. 1993. *Qualitative Data Analysis: A User-Friendly Guide for Social Scientists*. London: Routledge.

Dhamoon, Rita Kaur. 2011. "Considerations on Mainstreaming Intersectionality." *Political Research Quarterly* 64, 1: 230–243.

Dillard, Cynthia Band, and Chinwe Okpalaoka. 2011. "The Sacred and Spiritual Nature of Endarkened Transnational Feminist Praxis in Qualitative Research." In Norman K. Denzin and Yvonna S. Lincoln (eds.), *The Sage Handbook of Qualitative Research*, 4th ed. (pp. 147–162). London: Sage.

Dion, Susan. 2009. *Braiding Histories: Learning from Aboriginal Peoples' Experiences and Perspectives*. Vancouver: University of British Columbia Press.

Dlamini, Nombuso S., Eleanor Maticka-Tyndale, Francisca Omorodion, Uzo Anucha and Adrianne J. Lowick. 2012. "What Does a Decolonizing/Decentralizing Methodology in Examining Sexual Lives Entail?" *African Journal of Reproductive Health* 16, 2: 55–70.

Doucet, Andrea. 2008. "'From Her Side of the Gossamer Wall(s)': Reflexivity and Relational Knowing." *Qualitative Sociology* 31: 73–87.

Doyle, Susanna. 2007. "Member Checking with Older Women: A Framework for Negotiating Meaning." *Health Care for Women International* 28, 10: 888–908.

Duggleby, Wendy. 2005. "What About Focus Group Interaction Data?" *Qualitative Health Research* 15, 6: 832–840.

Eaton, Mary. 1993. *Women After Prison*. London: Open University Press.

Edgington, Kristine, and Jillian Roberts. 2005. "Serving Youth with Physical Deformity in Canadian Schools: Ethical Guidelines for Non-Discriminatory Practice." *Forum*

Qualitative Sozialforschung/Forum: Qualitative Social Research 6, 2, Art. 44.

Edwards, Judith A., and Martin D. Lampert (eds.). 1993. *Talking Data: Transcription and Coding in Discourse Research*. Hillsdale, NJ: Lawrence Erlbaum.

Ellingson, Laura L. 2011. "Analysis and Representation Across the Continuum." In Norman K. Denzin and Yvonna S. Lincoln, *The Sage Handbook of Qualitative Research*, 4th ed. (pp. 595–610). London: Sage.

Ells, Carolyn, and Shawna Gutfreund. 2006. "Myths about Qualitative Research and the Tri-Council Policy Statement." *Canadian Journal of Sociology* 31, 3: 361–373.

Emerson, Robert M., Rachelle I. Fretz and Linda L. Shaw. 2001. "Participant Observation and Fieldnotes." In Paul Atkinson, Amanda Coffey, Sara Delamont, John Lofland, and Lyn Lofland (eds.), *Handbook of Ethnography* (pp. 352–369). Thousand Oaks, CA: Sage.

Eyre, Linda. 2010. "Whose Ethics? Whose Interests? The Tri-Council Policy Statement and Feminist Research." *Journal of Curriculum Theorizing* 26, 3: 75–85.

Ezzy, Douglas. 2002. *Qualitative Analysis: Practice and Innovation*. Crows Nest, Australia: Allen and Unwin.

Faith, Karlene. 1993. *Unruly Women: The Politics of Confinement and Resistance*. Vancouver: Press Gang Publishers.

Farrar, Joyce P.J. 2004. "Troubling Talk, Unsettling Silence: The Discourse of an Inclusive Community Planning Group." Unpublished doctoral dissertation, University of Calgary, Calgary, AB.

Fine, Michelle. 1994. "Working the Hyphens: Reinventing Self and Other in Qualitative Research." In Norman K. Denzin and Yvonna S. Lincoln (eds.), *Handbook of Qualitative Research*, 2nd ed. (pp. 70–82). Thousand Oaks, CA: Sage.

____. 1991. *Framing Dropouts: Notes on the Politics of an Urban Public High School*. Albany: State University of New York Press.

Fine, Michelle, Maria Torre, Kathy Boudin, Iris Bowen, Judith Clark, Donna Hylton ... Debora Upegui. 2001. *Changing Minds: The Impact of College in a Maximum-Security Prison*. <prisonpolicy.org/scans/changingminds.pdf>.

Fine, Michelle, and Lois Weis. 1996. "Writing the 'Wrongs' of Fieldwork: Confronting Our Own Research/Writing Dilemmas in Urban Ethnographies." *Qualitative Inquiry* 2, 3: 251–274.

Fine, Michelle, Lois Weis, Susan Weseen and Loonmung Wong. 2000. "For Whom? Qualitative Research, Representations, and Social Responsibilities." In Norman K. Denzin and Yvonna S. Lincoln (eds.), *Handbook of Qualitative Research*, 2nd ed. (pp. 167–207). Thousand Oaks, CA: Sage.

Finley, Susan. 2011. "Critical Arts-Based Inquiry: The Pedagogy and Performance of a Radical Ethical Aesthetic." In Norman K. Denzin and Yvonna S. Lincoln (eds.), *The Sage Handbook of Qualitative Research*, 4th ed. (pp. 435–450). London: Sage.

Fitzgerald, Maureen H. 2005. "Punctuated Equilibrium, Moral Panics and the Ethics Review Process." *Journal of Academic Ethics* 2, 4: 315–338.

Fontana, Andrea, and James H. Frey. 2005. "The Interview: From Neutral Stance to Political Involvement." In Norman K. Denzin and Yvonna S. Lincoln (eds.), *The Sage Handbook of Qualitative Research*, 3rd ed. (pp. 695–727). London: Sage.

____. 2000. "The Interview: From Structured Questions to Negotiated Text." In Norman K. Denzin and Yvonna S. Lincoln (eds.), *Handbook of Qualitative Research*, 2nd ed. (pp.

645–672). Thousand Oaks, CA: Sage.

Fontana, Andrea, and Anastasia H. Prokos. 2007. *The Interview: From Formal to Postmodern*. Walnut Creek CA: Left Coast Press.

Foucault, Michel. 1980. "Prison Talk." In Colin Gordon (ed.), *Michel Foucault: Power/ Knowledge, Selected Interviews, 1972–1977* (pp. 37–54). Brighton, UK: Harvester Press.

____. 1979. *Discipline and Punish: The Birth of the Prison*. New York: Vintage Books.

Fraser, Heather. 2004. "Doing Narrative Research: Analysing Personal Stories Line by Line." *Qualitative Social Work* 3, 2: 179–201.

Freeman, Donald. 2000. "'To Take Them at Their Word': Language Data in the Study of Teachers' Knowledge." In Barbara M. Brizuela, Julie Pearson Stewart, Romina G. Carrillo, and Jennifer Garvey Berger (eds.), *Acts of Inquiry in Qualitative Research* (pp. 293–320). Cambridge, MA: Harvard Educational Review.

Freire, Paulo. 2008. *Pedagogy of the Oppressed*. New York: Continuum Publishing.

____. 1994. *Pedagogy of Hope: Reliving Pedagogy of the Oppressed*. New York: Continuum Publishing.

Frey, James H., and Andrea Fontana. 1991. "The Group Interview in Social Research." *Social Science Journal* 28, 2: 175–187.

Gallagher, Kathleen. 2008. "Introduction." In Kathleen Gallagher (ed.), *The Methodological Dilemma* (pp. 1–8.) New York: Routledge.

____. 2007. *The Theatre of Urban: Youth and Schooling in Dangerous Times*. Toronto: University of Toronto Press.

Gallagher, Kathleen, and Isabelle Kim. 2008. "Moving Towards Postcolonial, Digital Methods in Qualitative Research." In Kathleen Gallagher (ed.), *The Methodological Dilemma: Critical, Creative and Post-Positivist Approaches to Qualitative Research* (pp. 103–120). New York: Routledge.

Gallagher, Kathleen, Anne Wessels, and Burcu Yaman Ntelioglou. 2013. "Becoming a Networked Public: Digital Ethnography, Youth and Global Research Collectives." *Ethnography and Education* 8, 2: 177–193.

Ganga, Deianira, and Sam Scott. 2006. "Cultural 'Insiders' and the Issue of Positionality in Qualitative Migration Research: Moving 'Across' and Moving 'Along' Researcher-Participant Divides." *Forum Qualitative Sozialforschung/Forum: Qualitative Social Research* 7, 3, Art. 7.

Gannon, Susanne, and Bronwyn Davies. 2012. "Postmodern, Post-structural, and Critical Theories." In Sharlene Nagy Hesse-Biber (ed.), *Handbook of Feminist Research: Theory and Praxis*, 2nd ed. (pp. 65–91). London: Sage.

Garcia, Angela C., Alecea I. Standlee, Jennifer Bechkoff and Yan Cui. 2009. "Ethnographic Approaches to the Internet and Computer-Mediated Communication." *Journal of Contemporary Ethnography* 38, 1: 52–84.

Geertz, Clifford. 1973. *The Interpretation of Cultures: Selected Essays*. New York: Basic Books.

Gilbar, Ora, Zeev Winstok, Mickey Weinberg and Orit Bershtling. 2013. "Whose Doctorate Is it Anyway? Guidelines for an Agreement Between Advisor and Doctoral Student Regarding the Advisement Process and Intellectual Property Rights." *Journal of Academic Ethics* 11: 73–80.

Goldstein, Tara. 2008. "Performed Ethnography: Possibilities, Multiple Commitment and the Pursuit of Rigor." In Kathleen Gallagher (ed.), *The Methodological Dilemma:*

Critical, Creative and Post-Positivist Approaches to Qualitative Research (pp. 85–102). New York: Routledge.

Gorelick, Sherry. 1991. "Contradictions of Feminist Methodology." *Gender and Society* 5, 4: 459–477.

Gormley, Louise. 2006. "A Case Study of Issues of Success in Four Public Primary Schools in a Low-Income Region of Northern Mexico." Unpublished doctoral dissertation, University of Toronto, Toronto, ON.

Graham-Marrs, Holly Ann. 2011. "Narrative Descriptions of Miyo-Mahcihoyan (Well-Being) from a Contemporary Nehiyawak (Plains Cree) Perspective." Unpublished doctoral dissertation, University of Saskatchewan, Saskatoon, SK.

Grayson, J. Paul, and Richard Myles. 2005. "How Research Ethics Boards Are Undermining Survey Research on Canadian University Students." *Journal of Academic Ethics* 2, 4: 293–314.

Guba, Egon G., and Yvonna S. Lincoln. 2005. "Paradigmatic Controversies, Contradictions, and Emerging Confluences." In Norman K. Denzin and Yvonna S. Lincoln (eds.), *The Sage Handbook of Qualitative Research*, 3rd ed. (pp.163–188). London: Sage.

Gubrium, Jaber, and James Holstein (eds.). 2001. *Handbook of Interview Research: Context and Method*. London: Sage.

Guillemin, Marilys, and Lynn Gillam. 2004. "Ethics, Reflexivity, and 'Ethically Important Moments' in Research." *Qualitative Inquiry* 10: 261–280.

Hagens, Victoria, Mark J. Dobrow and Roger Chafe. 2009. "Interviewee Transcript Review: Assessing the Impact on Qualitative Research." *BMC Medical Research Methodology* 9, 1: 47.

Haggerty, Kevin D. 2004. "Ethics Creep: Governing Social Sciences Research in the Name of Ethics." *Qualitative Sociology* 27, 4: 391–414.

Haig-Brown, Celia. 2010. "Indigenous Thought, Appropriation, and Non-Aboriginal People." *Canadian Journal of Education* 33, 4: 925–950.

____. 1992. "Choosing Border Work." *Canadian Journal of Native Education* 19, 1: 96–116.

____. 1988. *Resistance and Renewal: Surviving the Indian Residential School*. Vancouver: Arsenal Pulp Press.

Haig-Brown, Celia, and Jo-Ann Archibald. 1996. "Transforming First Nations Research with Respect and Power." *International Journal of Qualitative Studies in Education* 9, 3: 245–267.

Haig-Brown, Celia (Producer), and Helen Haig-Brown (Director). 2009. *Pelq'ilc: Coming Home*. (Documentary film.) Vancouver: University of British Columbia Press.

Haley, Janice. 2006. "The Voices of Warriors: Urban Girls Unite to Address Violence and Victimization." Unpublished master's thesis, Simon Fraser University, Burnaby, BC.

Halifax, Nancy V.D., and Gail J. Mitchell. 2013. "(Nurse) — Writing with the Wolves." *Qualitative Inquiry* 19, 5: 349–352.

Hall, Wendy, Bonita Long, Nicole Bermbach, Sharalyn Jordan and Kathryn Patterson. 2005. "Qualitative Teamwork Issues and Strategies: Coordination through Mutual Adjustment." *Qualitative Health Research* 15, 3: 394–410.

Hammersley, Martyn. 1992. "The Paradigm Wars: Reports from the Front." *British Journal of Sociology of Education* 13, 1: 131–143.

Haraway, Donna. 1991. *Simians, Cyborgs and Women: The Reinvention of Nature*. London:

Free Association.

Harding, Sandra (ed.). 1993. *The Racial Economy of Science: Toward a Democratic Future.* Bloomington: Indiana University Press.

____. 1987. *Feminism and Methodology: Social Science Issues.* Bloomington: Indiana University Press.

Harding, Sandra, and Kathryn Norberg. 2005. "New Feminist Approaches to Social Science Methodologies: An Introduction." *Signs* 30, 4: 2009–2015.

Harper, Lynette A. 2006. "A Multi-Site Ethnography Exploring Culture and Power in Post-Secondary Education Partnerships." Unpublished doctoral dissertation, University of British Columbia, Vancouver, BC.

Hart, Chris. 2009. *Doing a Literature Review: Releasing the Social Science Imagination.* London: Sage.

Heath, Christian, Jon Hindmarsh and Paul Luff. 2010. *Video in Qualitative Research.* London: Sage.

Hennink, Monique M. 2008. "Emergent Issues in International Group Discussions." In Sharlene Nagy Hesse-Biber and Patricia Leavy (eds.), *Handbook of Emergent Methods* (pp.189–205). New York: Guilford Press.

____. 2007. *International Focus Group Research: A Handbook for the Health and Social Sciences.* Cambridge, UK: Cambridge University Press.

Henry, Marsha G. 2003. "Where Are You Really from? Representation, Identity and Power in the Fieldwork Experiences of a South Asian Diasporic." *Qualitative Research* 3, 2: 229–242.

Hergenrather, Kenneth C., Scott D. Rhodes, Chris A. Cowan, Gerta Bardhoshi and Sara Pula. 2009. "Photovoice as Community-Based Participatory Research: A Qualitative Review." *American Journal of Health Behavior* 33, 6: 686–698.

Herron, Rachel, and Mark Skinner. 2013. "Using Care Ethics to Enhance Qualitative Research on Rural Aging and Care." *Qualitative Health Research* 23, 12: 1697–1707.

Hesse-Biber, Sharlene Nagy (ed.). 2012. *Handbook of Feminist Research: Theory and Praxis,* 2nd ed. London: Sage.

Hesse-Biber, Sharlene Nagy and Patricia Leavy (eds.). 2004. *Approaches to Qualitative Research: A Reader on Theory and Practice.* New York: Oxford University Press.

Hewson, Claire, Peter Yule, Dianna Laurent, and Carl Vogel. 2003. *Internet Research Methods.* London: Sage.

Hine, Christine. 2012. *The Internet: Understanding Qualitative Research.* New York: Oxford University Press.

Hole, Rachelle D. 2007a. "Working between Languages and Cultures: Issues of Representation, Voice, and Authority Intensified." *Qualitative Inquiry* 13, 5: 696–710.

____. 2007b. "Narratives of Identity: A Poststructural Analysis of Three Deaf Women's Life Stories." *Narrative Inquiry* 17, 2: 259–278.

Holt, Amanda. 2010. "Using the Telephone for Narrative Interviewing: A Research Note." *Qualitative Research* 10, 1: 113–121.

Ibanez, Francisco. 1997. "From Confession to Dialogue." In Suzanne de Castell and Mary Bryson (eds.), *Radical in<ter>ventions: Identity, Politics, and Difference/s in Educational Praxis* (pp. 107–130). Albany: State University of New York Press.

Inckle, Kay. 2010. "Telling Tales? Using Ethnographic Fictions to Speak Embodied 'Truth.'"

Qualitative Research 10, 1: 27–47.

Irwin, Lori, and Joy Johnson. 2005. "Interviewing Young Children: Explicating Our Practices and Dilemmas." *Qualitative Health Research* 15, 6: 821–831.

Irwin, Rita, Barbara Bickel, Valerie Triggs, Stephanie Springgay, Ruth Beer, Kit Grauer … Pauline Sameshima. 2009. "The City of RichGate: A/r/tographic Cartography as Public Pedagogy." *International Journal of Art & Design Education* 28, 1: 61–70.

Irwin, Rita, and Stephanie Springgay. 2008. "A/r/tography as Practice-based Research." In Melisa Cahnmann-Taylor and Richard Siegesmund (eds.), *Arts-Based Research in Education: Foundations for Practice* (pp. 103–124). New York: Routledge.

Jackson, Peter, and Polly Russell. 2010. "Life History Interviewing." In Dydia DeLyser, Steve Herbert, Stuart Aitken, Mike Crang, and Linda McDowell (eds.), *The Sage Handbook of Qualitative Geography* (pp.172–192). London: Sage.

Jaggar, Alison M., and Scott Wisor. 2014. "Feminist Methodology in Practice: Learning from a Research Project." In Allison M. Jaggar (ed.), *Just Methods: An Interdisciplinary Feminist Reader* (pp. 498–518). London: Paradigm Publishers.

Jalongo, Mary Renck, Wanda Boyer and Marjory Ebbeck. 2014. "Writing for Scholarly Publication as 'Tacit Knowledge': A Qualitative Focus Group Study of Doctoral Students in Education." *Early Childhood Education Journal* 42: 241–250.

James, Carl. 2012. *Life at the Intersection: Community Class and Schooling*. Halifax, NS: Fernwood Publishing.

James, Carl, and Leanne Taylor. 2013. "'Talk to Students About What's Really Going On': Researching the Experiences of Marginalized Youth." In Tricia Kress, Curry Malott and Brad Porfilio (eds.), *Challenging Status Quo Retrenchment: New Directions in Critical Qualitative Research* (pp. 147–167). Charlotte, NC: Information Age Publishing.

James, Nalita, and Hugh Busher. 2009. *Online Interviewing*: London: Sage.

Janesick, Valerie, J. 1999. "A Journal about Journal Writing as a Qualitative Research Technique: History, Issues, and Reflections." *Qualitative Inquiry* 5, 4: 505–524.

Jesson, Jill, Lydia Matheson and Fiona Lacey. 2011. *Doing Your Literature Review*. London: Sage.

Johnson, Barbara, and Jill Clarke. 2003. "Collecting Sensitive Data: The Impact on Researchers." *Qualitative Health Research* 13, 3: 421–434.

Johnson, Holly, and Karen Rodgers. 1993. "A Statistical Overview of Women and Crime in Canada." In Ellen Adelberg and Claudia Currie (eds.), *In Conflict with the Law: Women and the Canadian Justice System*. Vancouver: Press Gang Publishers.

Jordan, Steven. 2009. "From a Methodology of the Margins to Neoliberal Appropriation and Beyond: The Lineages of PAR." In Dip Kapoor and Steven Jordan (eds.), *Education, Participatory Action Research, and Social Change: International Perspectives* (pp. 15–27). New York: Palgrave & Macmillan.

Kamberelis, George, and Greg Dimitriadis. 2013. *Focus Groups: From Structured Interviews to Collective Conversations*. New York: Routledge.

_____. 2011. "'Focus Groups: Contingent Articulations' of Pedagogy, Politics and Inquiry." In Norman K. Denzin and Yvonna S. Lincoln, *The Sage Handbook of Qualitative Research*, 4th ed. (pp. 545–561). London: Sage.

_____. 2005. "Focus Groups: Strategic Articulations of Pedagogy, Politics and Inquiry." In Norman K. Denzin and Yvonna S. Lincoln (eds.), *The Sage Handbook of Qualitative*

Research, 3rd ed. (pp. 887–907). Thousand Oaks, CA: Sage.

Kanuha, Valli K. 2000. "'Being' Native versus 'Going Native': Conducting Social Work Research as an Insider." *Social Work* 45, 5: 439–447.

Kanuka, Heather, and Terry Anderson. 2015. "Ethical Issues in Qualitative e-Learning Research." *International Journal of Qualitative Methods* 6, 2: 20–39.

Kapoor, Dip, and Steven Jordan (eds.). 2009. *Education, Participatory Action Research, and Social Change: International Perspectives.* New York: Palgrave & Macmillan.

Kezar, Adrianna. 2003. "Transformational Elite Interviews: Principles and Problems." *Qualitative Inquiry* 9, 3: 395–415.

Khan, Shahnaz. 2005. "Reconfiguring the Native Informant: Positionality in a Global Age." *Signs* 30, 4: 2017–2037.

Kilbourn, Brent. 2006. "The Qualitative Doctoral Dissertation Proposal." *Teachers College Record* 108, 4: 529–576.

Kim, Catherine Y., Daniel J. Losen and Damon T. Hewitt. 2012. *The School-to-Prison Pipeline: Structuring Legal Reform.* New York: New York University Press.

Kindon, Sara, Rachel Pain and Mike Kesby. 2010. "Participatory Action Research: Origins, Approaches and Methods." In Sara Kindon, Rachel Pain and Mike Kesby (eds.), *Participatory Action Research Approaches and Methods: Connecting People, Participation and Place* (pp. 9–18). London: Routledge.

Kirsch, Gesa. 2005. "Friendship, Friendliness, and Feminist Fieldwork." *Signs* 30, 4: 2163–2172.

Knowles, J. Gary, and Ardra L. Cole. 2008. *Handbook of the Arts in Qualitative Research.* London: Sage.

Kovach, Margaret. 2010. "Conversational Method in Indigenous Research." *First People Child and Family Review* 5, 1: 40–48.

Kreuger, Richard A. 1994. *Focus Groups: A Practical Guide for Applied Research*, 2nd ed. Thousand Oaks, CA: Sage.

Krieg, Brigette, and Lana Roberts. 2010. "Insights into Marginalisation Through a 'Community Lens' in Saskatchewan, Canada." In Sara Kindon, Rachel Pain, and Mike Kesby (eds.), *Participatory Action Research Approaches and Methods: Connecting People, Participation and Place* (pp. 150–159). London: Routledge.

Kuoch, Phong. 2013. "Hip Hoe to Hip HoPe: Hip Hop Pedagogy in a Secondary Language Arts Curriculum," Unpublished doctoral dissertation, Simon Fraser University, Burnaby, BC.

Kvale, Steinar. 1996. *InterViews: An Introduction to Qualitative Research Interviewing.* Thousand Oaks, CA: Sage.

Lafreniere, Darquise, and Susan M. Cox. 2013. "'If You Can Call it a Poem': Toward a Framework for the Assessment of Arts-based Work." *Qualitative Research* 13, 3: 318–336.

Lapadat, Judith, and Anne Lindsay. 1999. "Transcription in Research and Practice: From Standardization of Technique to Interpretive Positionings." *Qualitative Inquiry* 5, 1: 64–86.

Lather, Patti. 1995. "Troubling Angels: Interpretive and Textual Strategies in Researching the Lives of Women with HIV/AIDS." *Qualitative Inquiry* 1, 1: 41–68.

____. 1991. *Getting Smart.* New York: Routledge.

Lather, Patti, and Chris Smithies. 1997. *Troubling Angels: Women Living with HIV/AIDS.* Boulder, CO: Westview/HarperCollins.

Lau, Sunny Man Chu, and Saskia Stille. 2014. "Participatory Research with Teachers: Toward a Pragmatic and Dynamic View of Equity and Parity in Research Relationships." *European Journal of Teacher Education* 37, 2: 156–170.

Lave, Jean, and Etienne Wenger. 1991. *Situated Learning: Legitimate Peripheral Participation.* Cambridge, UK: Cambridge University Press.

Lawrence, Bonita. 2002. "Rewriting Histories of the Land: Colonization and Indigenous Resistance in Eastern Canada." In Sherene H. Razack (ed.), *Race, Space, and the Law: Unmapping a White Settler Society* (pp. 21–46). Toronto: Between the Lines.

Leggo, Carl, Anita E. Sinner, Rita L. Irwin, Kathy Pantaleo, Peter Gouzouasis and Kit Grauer. 2011. "Lingering in Liminal Spaces: A/r/tography as Living Inquiry in a Language Arts Class." *International Journal of Qualitative Studies in Education* 24, 2: 239–256.

Lewis, Magda. 2008. "New Strategies of Control: Academic Freedom and Research Ethics Boards." *Qualitative Inquiry* 14, 5: 684–699.

Lewis, Patrick J. 2008. "A Good Teacher." *Forum Qualitative Sozialforschung /Forum: Qualitative Social Research* 9, 2, Art. 41.

Lincoln, Yvonna S., and Egon G. Guba. 1985. *Naturalistic Inquiry.* Newbury Park, CA: Sage.

Lincoln, Yvonna S., Susan A. Lynham and Egon G. Guba. 2011. "Paradigmatic Controversies, Contradictions, and Emerging Confluences, Revisited." In Norman K. Denzin and Yvonna S. Lincoln (eds.), *The Sage Handbook of Qualitative Research*, 4th ed. (pp. 97–128). London: Sage.

Longboat, Catherine. 2008. "Ethical Space in a Secondary School: A Case Study." Unpublished master's thesis, Brock University, St. Catharines, ON.

Lopez, Gerardo R., and Laurence Parker. 2003. "Conclusion." In Gerardo R. Lopez and Laurence Parker (eds.), *Interrogating Racism in Qualitative Research* (pp. 195–225). New York: Peter Lang.

Loppie, Charlotte. 2007. "Learning from the Grandmothers: Incorporating Indigenous Principles into Qualitative Research." *Qualitative Health Research* 17, 2: 276–284.

Lorenzetti, Liza. 2013. "Research as a Social Justice Tool: An Activist's Perspective." *Affilia: Journal of Women and Social Work* 28, 4: 451–457.

Loutzenheiser, Lisa W. 2007. "Working Alterity: The Impossibility of Ethical Research with Youth." *Educational Studies* 41, 2: 109–127.

MacLean, Lynne, Mechtild Meyer and Alma Estable. 2004. "Improving Accuracy of Transcripts in Qualitative Research." *Qualitative Health Research* 14, 1: 113–123.

Mahoney, Dan. 2007. "Constructing Reflexive Fieldwork Relationships: Narrating My Collaborative Storytelling Methodology." *Qualitative Inquiry* 13, 4: 573–594.

Mahony, Tina H. 2011. "Women and the Criminal Justice System." Catalogue no. 89-503-X. Ottawa, ON: Statistics Canada.

Maiter, Sarah, Laura Simich, Nora Jacobson and Julie Wise. 2008. "Reciprocity: An Ethic for Community-Based Participatory Action Research." *Action Research* 6, 3: 305–325.

Malinowski, Bronislaw. 1961. *Argonauts of the Western Pacific.* New York: E.P. Dutton.

Mann, Chris, and Fiona Stewart. 2000. *Internet Communication and Qualitative Research: A Handbook for Researching Online.* London: Sage.

Markham, Annette N. 2005. "The Methods, Politics, and Ethics of Representation in Online

Ethnography." In Norman K. Denzin and Yvonna S. Lincoln (eds.), *The Sage Handbook of Qualitative Research*, 3rd ed. (pp. 247–284). London: Sage.

Markle, D. Thomas, Richard E. West and Peter J. Rich. 2011. "Beyond Transcription: Technology, Change, and Refinement of Method." *Forum Qualitative Sozialforschung/ Forum: Qualitative Social Research* 12, 3, Art. 21.

Marshall, Catherine, and Gretchen Rossman. 1989. *Designing Qualitative Research*. Newbury Park, CA: Sage.

Mazzei, Lisa A. 2003. "Inhabited Silences: In Pursuit of a Muffled Subtext." *Qualitative Inquiry* 9, 3: 355–368.

McCall, Leslie. 2005. "The Complexity of Intersectionality." *Signs* 30, 3: 1771–1800.

McCall, Sophie. 2011. *First Person Plural: Aboriginal Storytelling and the Ethics of Collaborative Authorship*. Vancouver: University of British Columbia Press.

McCaslin, Wanda D., and Denise C. Breton. 2008. "Justice as Healing: Going Outside the Colonizers' Cage." In Norman K. Denzin, Yvonna S. Lincoln, and Linda Tuhiwai Smith (eds.), *Handbook of Critical Indigenous Methodologies* (pp. 511–529). London: Sage.

McCosker, Heather, Alan Barnard and Rod Gerber. 2001. "Undertaking Sensitive Research: Issues and Strategies for Meeting the Safety Needs of all Participants." *Forum Qualitative Sozialforschung/Forum: Qualitative Social Research* 2, 1, Art. 22.

McGinn, Michelle K., Carolyn Shields, Michael Manley-Casimir, Annabelle L. Grundy and Nancy Fenton. 2005. "Living Ethics: A Narrative of Collaboration and Belonging in a Research Team." *Reflective Practice* 6, 4: 551–567.

McKenzie, Holly Ann. 2012. "The Different Stories of Cree Woman, Daleen Kay Bosse (Muskego) and Dakota-Sioux Woman, Amber Tara-Lynn Redman: Understanding Their Disappearances and Murders Through Media Re-presentations and Family Members' Narratives." Unpublished master's thesis, University of Regina, Regina, SK.

Mead, Margaret. 1923. *Coming of Age in Samoa*. New York: William Morrow.

Meiners, Erica R. 2011. "Ending the School-to-Pipeline/Building Abolition Futures." *The Urban Review* 43, 4: 547–565.

____. 2007. "Life after OZ: Ignorance, Mass Media, and Making Public Enemies." *The Review of Education, Pedagogy, and Cultural Studies* 29, 1: 23–63.

Mero-Jaffe, Irit. 2011. "'Is That What I Said?' Interview Transcript Approval by Participants: An Aspect of Ethics in Qualitative Research." *International Journal of Qualitative Methodology* 10, 3: 231–247.

Merriam-Webster Online Dictionary. 2013. "Distance." <merriam-webster.com/info/ copyright.htm>.

Miles, Matthew B., and Michael Huberman. 1994. *Qualitative Data Analysis: An Expanded Sourcebook*, 2nd ed. Thousand Oaks, CA: Sage.

Mishler, Elliot. G. 1991. "Representing Discourse: The Rhetoric of Transcription." *Journal of Narrative and Life History* 1, 4: 255–280.

Mishna, Faye, Beverly Antle, and Cheryl Regehr. 2004. "Tapping the Perspectives of Children: Emerging Ethical Issues in Qualitative Research." *Qualitative Research* 3, 4: 449–468.

Mitchell, Claudia, and Susan Allnut. 2008. "21 Photographs and/as Social Documentary." In J. Gary Knowles and Ardra L. Cole (eds.), *Handbook of the Arts in Qualitative Research* (pp. 251–264). London: Sage.

Moffatt, Jessica, Maria Mayan and Richard Long. 2013. "Sanitoriums and the Canadian Colonial Legacy: The Untold Experiences of Tuberculosis Treatment." *Qualitative Health Research* 23, 12: 1591–1599.

Moletsane, Relebohilie, Naydene de Lange, Claudia Mitchell, Jean Stuart, Thabsile Buthelezi and Myra Taylor. 2007. "Photo-voice: A Tool for Analysis of Activism in Response to HIV and AIDS Stigmatisation in a Rural KwaZulu-Natal School." *Journal of Child and Adolescent Mental Health* 19, 1: 19–28.

Morgan, David, Collin Fellows, and Heather Guevara. 2008. "Emergent Approaches to Focus Group Research." In Sharlene Nagy Hesse-Biber and Patricia Leavy (eds.), *Handbook of Emergent Methods* (pp.189–205). New York: Guilford Press.

Morrison, Connie. 2011. "Avatars and the Cultural Politics of Representation: Girlhood in Social Networking Spaces." Unpublished doctoral dissertation, Memorial University, St. John's, NL.

Morrison, Zachary James, David Gregory and Steven Thibodeau. 2012. "'Thanks for Using Me': An Exploration of Exit Strategy in Qualitative Research." *International Journal of Qualitative Methods* 11, 4: 416–427.

Morse, Janice. 2005. "Ethical Issues in Institutional Research." *Qualitative Health Research* 15, 4: 435–437.

Mosselson, Jacqueline. 2010. "Subjectivity and Reflexivity: Locating the Self in Research on Dislocation." *International Journal of Qualitative Studies in Education* 23, 4: 479–494.

Mullings, Beverly. 1999. "Insider or Outsider, Both or Neither: Some Dilemmas of Interviewing in a Cross-cultural Setting." *Geoforum* 30, 4: 337–350.

Mutua, Kagendo, and Beth Blue Swandener. 2004. "Introduction." In Kagendo Mutua and Beth Blue Swandener (eds.), *Decolonizing Research in Cross-Cultural Contexts: Critical Personal Narratives* (pp. 1–26). Albany: State University of New York Press.

Nash, Jennifer, C. 2008. "Re-thinking Intersectionality." *Feminist Review* 89: 1–15.

Norris, Sigrid. 2002. "The Implication of Visual Research for Discourse Analysis: Transcription Beyond Language." *Visual Communication* 1, 1: 97–121.

O'Connell, Daniel C., and Sabine Kowal. 1999. "Transcription and the Issue of Standardization." *Journal of Psycholinguistic Research* 28, 2: 103–120.

Oakley, Ann. 1981. "Interviewing Women: A Contradiction in Terms." In H. Roberts (ed.), *Doing Feminist Research* (pp. 30–61). London: Routledge.

Ochs, Eleanor. 1979. "Transcription as Theory." In Eleanor Ochs and B.B. Schieffelin (eds.), *Developmental Pragmatics* (pp. 43–72). London: Academic Press.

Oki, Gwenn, and John Zaia. 2006. "Expedited Institutional Review Board Review." In Elizabeth Bankert and Robert J. Amdur (eds.), *Institutional Review Board: Management and Function*, 2nd ed. (pp. 97–100). Boston: Jones and Bartlett.

Olesen, Virginia. 2011. "Feminist Qualitative Research in the Millennium's First Decade." In Norman K. Denzin and Yvonna S. Lincoln (eds.), *The Sage Handbook of Qualitative Research*, 4th ed. (pp. 235–278). Thousand Oaks, CA: Sage.

Olson, Karin. 2011. *Essentials of Qualitative Interviewing*. Chicago: Left Coast Press.

Onwuegbuzie, Anthony, Wendy Dickinson, Nancy Leech and Annmarie Zoran. 2015. "A Qualitative Framework for Collecting and Analyzing Data in Focus Group Research." *International Journal of Qualitative Methods* 8, 3: 1–21.

Orbach, Susie. 1986. *Hunger Strike: The Anorectic's Struggle as a Metaphor for Our Times.*

London: Karnac Books.

Owen, Michael. 2004. "Conflict and Convergence: The Ethics Review of Action Research." *Journal of Research Administration* 35, 2: 21–30.

Paechter, Carrie. 2013. "Researching Sensitive Issues Online: Implications of a Hybrid Insider/Outsider Position in a Retrospective Ethnographic Study." *Qualitative Research* 13, 1: 71–86.

Palys, Ted, and Chris Atchison. 2012. "Qualitative Research in the Digital Era: Obstacles and Opportunities." *International Journal of Qualitative Methods* 11, 4: 352–367.

Parnis, Deborah, Janice Du Mont and Brydon Gombay. 2005. "Cooperation or Co-Optation? Assessing the Methodological Benefits and Barriers Involved in Conducting Qualitative Research through Medical Institutional Settings." *Qualitative Health Research* 15, 5: 686–697.

Patai, Daphne. 1994. "U.S. Academics and the Third-World Women: Is Ethical Research Possible?" In Sarah O. Weisser and Jennifer Fleischner (eds.), *Feminist Nightmares: Women at Odds* (pp. 21–43). New York: New York University Press.

Patterson, Donna. 2008. "Research Ethics Boards as Spaces of Marginalization: A Canadian Story." *Qualitative Inquiry* 14, 1: 18–27.

Patton, Michael Quinn. 2002. *Qualitative Research and Evaluation Methods*, 3rd ed. London: Sage.

Peshkin, Alan. 2001. "Angles of Vision: Enhancing Perception in Qualitative Research." *Qualitative Inquiry* 7, 2: 238–253.

Peters, Evelyn J. 2011. "Emerging Themes in Academic Research in Urban Aboriginal Identities in Canada, 1996–2010." *Aboriginal Policy Studies* 1, 1: 78–105.

Piquemal, Nathalie. 2001. "Free and Informed Consent in Research Involving Native American Communities." *American Indian Culture and Research Journal* 25, 1: 65–79.

Plett Martens, Vonda L. 2007. "Moving between Opposing Worlds: The Moral Experiences of White, Anti-Racism Educators in Saskatchewan." Unpublished doctoral dissertation, University of Saskatchewan, Saskatoon, SK.

Poland, Blake. 1995. "Transcription Quality as an Aspect of Rigor in Qualitative Research." *Qualitative Inquiry* 1, 3: 290–310.

Power, Elaine M. 2004. "Toward Understanding in Postmodern Interview Analysis: Interpreting the Contradictory Remarks of a Research Participant." *Qualitative Health Research* 14, 6: 858–865.

Power, Nicole, Edward N. Moss and Kathryn Dupre. 2014. "Rural Youth and Emotional Geographies: How Photo-voice and Words-alone Methods Tell Different Stories of Place." *Journal of Youth Studies* 17, 8: 1114–1129.

Powick, Kelly D. 2004. "Conversations with ESL Teachers: Toward an Understanding of Whiteness in the Classroom." Unpublished master's thesis, Brock University, St. Catharines, ON.

Prasad, Pushkala. 2005. *Crafting Qualitative Research: Working in the Postpositivist Traditions*. New York: M.E. Sharpe.

Pratt, Geraldine, in collaboration with the Philippine Women Centre of BC and Ugnayan ng Kabataang Pilipno-Canadian Youth Alliance. 2010. "Working with Migrant Communities: Collaborating with the Kalayaan Centre in Vancouver, Canada." In Sara Kindon, Rachel Pain, and Mike Kesby (eds.), *Participatory Action Research*

Approaches and Methods: Connecting People, Participation and Place (pp. 95–111). London: Routledge.

Prendergast, Monica, Peter Gouzouasis, Carl Leggo and Rita L. Irwin. 2009. "A Haiku Suite: The Importance of Music Making in the Lives of Secondary School Students." *Music Education Research* 11, 3: 303–317.

Prosser, Jon D. 2011. "Visual Methodology: Toward a More Seeing Research." In Norman K. Denzin and Yvonna S. Lincoln (eds.), *The Sage Handbook of Qualitative Research*, 4th ed. (pp. 479–496). London: Sage.

Psathas, George, and Timothy Anderson. 1990. "The 'Practices' of Transcription in Conversation Analysis." *Semiotica* 78, 1–2: 75–99.

Quint-Rapoport, Mia. 2010. "Open Source in Higher Education: A Situational Analysis of the Open Journal Systems Software Project." Unpublished doctoral dissertation, University of Toronto, Toronto, ON.

Rallis, Sharon F. 2010. "'That Is NOT What's Happening at Horizon': Ethics and Misrepresenting Knowledge in Text." *International Journal of Qualitative Studies in Education* 23, 4: 435–448.

Rapley, Tim. 2004. "Interviews." In Clive Seale, Giampietro Gobo, Jaber Gubrium and David Silverman (eds.), *Qualitative Research Practice* (pp. 15–33). London: Sage.

Ratković, Snezana. 2014. "Teachers without Borders: Exploring Experiences, Transitions and Identities of Refugee Women Teachers from Yugoslavia." Unpublished doctoral dissertation, Brock University, St. Catharines, ON.

Raynor, Margaret E. 2012. "Salves and Sweetgrass: Singing a Metis Home." Unpublished master's thesis, York University, Toronto, ON.

Reason, Peter, and Hillary Bradbury. 2006. *Handbook of Action Research*. London: Sage.

Reid, Jo-Anne, Barbara Kamler, Alyson Simpson and Rod Maclean. 1996. "'Do You See What I See?' Reading a Different Classroom Scene." *International Journal of Qualitative Studies in Education* 9, 1: 87–108.

Reinharz, Shulamit. 1992. *Feminist Methods in Social Research*. Oxford, UK: Oxford University Press.

Richardson, Laurel. 2001. "Getting Personal: Writing-stories." *International Journal of Qualitative Studies in Education* 14, 1: 33–38.

____. 2000. "Writing: A Method of Inquiry." In Norman K. Denzin and Yvonna S. Lincoln (eds.), *Handbook of Qualitative Research*, 2nd ed. (pp. 923–948). Thousand Oaks, CA: Sage.

Richardson, Laurel, and Elizabeth A. St. Pierre. 2005. "Writing: A Method of Inquiry." In Norman K. Denzin and Yvonna S. Lincoln (eds.), *The Sage Handbook of Qualitative Research*, 4th ed. (pp. 959–978). London: Sage.

Rivière, Dominique. 2011. "Looking from the Outside/In: Re-thinking Research Ethics Review." *Journal of Academic Ethics* 9: 193–204.

____. 2005. "Identities and Intersectionalities: Performance, Power and the Possibilities for Multicultural Education." *Research in Drama Education* 10, 3: 341–354.

Rolling, James Haywood Jr., 2013. *Arts-Based Research: Primer*. New York: Peter Lang.

Rose, Gillian. 2007. *Visual Methodologies: An Introduction to the Interpretation of Visual Materials*, 2nd ed. London: Sage.

Rosell, Lourdes R., Isabel Martinez, Ainhoa Flecha and Pilar Alvarez. 2014. "Successful

Communicative Focus Group With Teenagers and Young People: How to Identify the Mirage of Upward Mobility." *Qualitative Inquiry* 20, 7: 863–869.

Roth, Wolff-Michael. 2005. *Doing Qualitative Research: Praxis of Method.* Rotterdam: Sense Publishers.

Sanjek, Roger. 1990. "Examples of Fieldnotes." In Roger Sanjek (ed.), *Fieldnotes: The Makings of Anthropology* (pp. xi–xviii). London: Cornell University Press.

Schnarch, Brian. 2004. "Ownership, Control, Access, and Possession (OCAP) or Self-Determination Applied to Research: A Critical Analysis of Contemporary First Nations Research and Some Options for First Nations Communities." *Journal of Aboriginal Health* 1, 1: 80–95.

Schostak, John, and Jill Schostak. 2013. *Writing Research Critically: Developing the Power to Make a Difference.* New York: Routledge.

Schroeter, Sara. 2013. "'The Way It Works'" Doesn't: Theatre of the Oppressed as Critical Pedagogy and Counternarrative." *Canadian Journal of Education* 36, 4: 394–415.

____. 2008. "Theater in My Toolbox: Using Forum Theatre to Explore Notions of Identity, Belonging and Culture with Francophone Secondary Students in a Context of Diversity." Unpublished master's thesis, York University, Toronto, ON.

Schwandt, Thomas A. 1996. "Farewell to Criteriology." *Qualitative Inquiry* 2, 1: 58–72.

Scott, Shannon, Heather Sharpe, Kathy O'Leary, Ulrike Dehaeck, Kathryn Hindmarsh, John Moore and Martin Osmond. 2009. "Court Reporters: A Viable Solution for the Challenges of Focus Group Data Collection?" *Qualitative Health Research* 19, 1: 140–146.

Seale, Clive, Giampietro Gobo, Jaber Gubirum and David Silverman (eds.). 2004. *Qualitative Research Practice.* London: Sage.

Sethi, Bharati. 2014. "'Do You See What I See?' A Grand Erie Photovoice Community Report: Community-based Participatory Research with Immigrant/Refugee KAAJAL Women using Photovoice." <sociology.uwo.ca/cluster/en/documents/reports/PhotovoiceCommunityReport.pdf>

____. 2012a. "From a Maid to a Researcher: A Story of Privilege and Humility." *Canadian Social Work Review* 29, 1: 87–100.

____. 2012b. "Searching for Self in a World of Labels." *Disability & Society* 27, 5: 717–722.

Shearer, Kathleen, and William F. Birdsall. 2005. "A Canadian Strategy for the Dissemination of Research Knowledge." *Feliciter* 51, 4: 192–194.

Sherif, Bahira. 2001. "The Ambiguity of Boundaries in the Fieldwork Experience: Establishing Rapport and Negotiating Insider/Outsider Status." *Qualitative Inquiry* 7, 4: 436–447.

Silverman, David. 2012. *Interpreting Qualitative Data*, 4th ed. London: Sage.

Sims, Chris. 2008. *Briefing Note: Education and Training in Prisons* (pp. 1–6). London: City & Guilds Centre for Skills Development.

Sinding, Christina, and Jane Aronson. 2003. "Exposing Failures, Unsettling Accommodations: Tensions in Interview Practice." *Qualitative Research* 3, 1: 95–117.

Sinner, Anita, Carl Leggo, Rita Irwin, Peter Gouzouasis and Kit Grauer. 2006. "Arts-based Educational Dissertations: Reviewing the Practices of New Scholars." *Canadian Journal of Education* 29, 4: 1223–1270.

Skorobohacz, Christina. 2008. "Exploring Female Graduate Students' Multifaceted and

Intersecting Roles and Identities in a Complex Educational Milieu." Unpublished master's thesis, Brock University, St. Catharines, ON.

Skukauskaite, Audra. 2012. "Transparency in Transcribing: Making Visible Theoretical Bases Impacting Knowledge Construction from Open-Ended Interview Records." *Forum Qualitative Sozialforschung/Forum: Qualitative Social Research* 13, 1, Art. 14.

Smith, Dorothy E. 1987. *The Everyday World as Problematic: A Feminist Sociology.* Toronto: University of Toronto Press.

Smith, John K., and Phil Hodkinson. 2005. "Relativism, Criteria, and Politics." In Norman K. Denzin and Yvonna S. Lincoln, (eds.), *The Sage Handbook of Qualitative Research,* 3rd ed. (pp. 915–932). London: Sage.

Smith, Linda Tuhiwai. 2014. "Research through Imperial Eyes." In Alison M. Jagger (ed.), *Just Methods: An Interdisciplinary Feminist Reader* (pp. 58–67). London: Paradigm.

____. 2005. "On Tricky Ground: Researching the Native in the Age of Uncertainty." In Norman K. Denzin and Yvonna S. Lincoln (eds.), *The Sage Handbook of Qualitative Research,* 3rd ed. (pp. 85–108). Thousand Oaks, CA: Sage.

____. 1999. *Decolonizing Methodologies: Research and Indigenous Peoples.* Dunedin, NZ: University of Otago Press.

Social Sciences and Humanities Research Ethics Special Working Committee. 2004. *Giving Voice to the Spectrum.* Ottawa, ON: Interagency Advisory Panel and Secretariat on Research Ethics. <ethics.gc.ca/policy-politique/initiatives/docs/SSHWCVoiceReportJune2004_EN.pdf>.

Spivak, Gayatri. 1993. *Outside in the Teaching Machine.* New York: Routledge.

St. Denis, Verna. 2007. "Aboriginal Education and Anti-racist Education: Building Alliances Across Cultural and Racial Identity." *Canadian Journal of Education* 30, 4: 1068–1092.

St. Pierre, Elizabeth Adams. 2011. "Post Qualitative Research: The Critique and the Coming After." In Norman K. Denzin and Yvonna S. Lincoln (eds.), *The Sage Handbook of Qualitative Research,* 4th ed. (pp. 611–626). London: Sage.

Stacey, Judith. 1988. "Can There Be a Feminist Ethnography?" *Women's Studies International Forum* 11, 1: 21–27.

Stack, Carol. 1996. "Writing Ethnography: Feminist Critical Practice." In Diane Wolf (ed.), *Feminist Dilemmas in Fieldwork* (pp. 96–106). Boulder, CO: Westview Press.

Stanger-Ross, Jordan. 2008. "Municipal Colonialism in Vancouver: City Planning and the Conflict Over Indian Reserves, 1928–1950s." *The Canadian Historical Review* 89, 4: 541–580.

Statistics Canada. 2010. "Women in Canada! A Gender-based Statistical Report." Catalogue no. 89-503-X. <statcan.gc.ca>.

Steurer, Steven, Linda Smith and Alice Tracy. 2001. *Three State Recidivism Study.* Lanham, MD: Correctional Education Association.

Stonebanks, Christopher D. 2008. "An Islamic Perspective on Knowledge, Knowing, and Methodology." In Norman K. Denzin, Yvonna S Lincoln, and Linda Tuhiwai Smith (eds.), *Handbook of Critical Indigenous Methodologies* (pp. 293–321). London: Sage.

Strega, Susan. 2005. "The View from the Post-Structural Margins: Epistemology and Methodology Reconsidered." In Leslie Brown and Susan Strega (eds.), *Research as Resistance: Critical, Indigenous, and Anti-Oppressive Approaches* (pp. 199–254). Toronto: Canadian Scholar's Press.

Styres, Sandra, and Dawn Zinga. 2013. "The Community-First Land-Centred Theoretical Framework: Bringing a 'Good Mind' to Indigenous Education Research?" *Canadian Journal of Education* 36, 2: 284–313.

Swarr, Amanda, and Richa Nagar. 2010. *Critical Transnational Feminist Praxis*. New York: State University of New York Press.

Tang, Shang. 2006. "The Research Pendulum: Multiple Roles and Responsibilities as a Researcher." *Journal of Lesbian Studies* 10, 3–4: 11–27.

TCPS (Canadian Institutes of Health Research, Natural Sciences and Engineering Research Council of Canada, and Social Sciences and Humanities Research Council of Canada. 2014. *Tri-Council Policy Statement: Ethical Conduct for Research Involving Humans*.

____. 2010. *Tri-Council Policy Statement: Ethical Conduct for Research Involving Humans*.

____. 1998. *Tri-Council Policy Statement on Ethical Conduct for Research Involving Humans*.

Teeuwsen, Phil, Snezana Ratković and Susan A. Tilley. 2014. "Becoming Academics: Experiencing Legitimate Peripheral Participation in Part-Time Doctoral Studies." *Studies in Higher Education* 39, 4: 680–694.

Tessier, Sophie. 2012. "From Field Notes, to Transcripts, to Tape Recordings: Evolution or Combination?" *International Journal of Qualitative Methods* 11, 4: 446–460.

Thomas, Robina Anne. 2005. "Honouring the Oral Traditions of My Ancestors Through Storytelling." In Leslie Brown and Susan Strega (eds.), *Research as Resistance: Critical, Indigenous, and Anti-Oppressive Approaches* (pp. 237–254). Toronto: Canadian Scholar's Press.

Tilley, Susan A. 2008. "A Troubled Dance: Doing the Work of Research Ethics Review." *Journal of Academic Ethics* 6: 91–104.

____. 2003a. "Challenging' Research Practices: Turning a Critical Lens on the Work of Transcription." *Qualitative Inquiry* 9, 5: 750–773.

____. 2003b. "Transcription Work: Learning Through Coparticipation in Research Practices." *International Journal of Qualitative Studies in Education* 16, 6: 835–851.

____. 1998a. "Becoming Familiar: Exploring Stories of Schooling with Women in Prison." Unpublished doctoral dissertation, Simon Fraser University, Burnaby, BC.

____. 1998b. "Conducting Respectful Research: A Critique of Practice." *Canadian Journal of Education* 23, 3: 316–328.

Tilley, Susan A., and Louise Gormley. 2007. "Canadian University Ethics Review: Cultural Complications Translating Principles into Practice." *Qualitative Inquiry* 13, 3: 368–387.

Tilley, Susan A., Kelly Powick-Kumar and Snezana Ratković. 2009. "Regulatory Practices and School-Based Research: Making Sense of Research/Ethics Review." *Forum Qualitative Sozialforschung/Forum: Qualitative Social Research* 10, 2, Art. 32.

Tilley, Susan A., and Kelly D. Powick. 2002. "Distanced Data: Transcribing Other People's Research Tapes." *Canadian Journal of Education* 27, 2/3: 291–310.

Tilley, Susan A., and Snezana Ratković. 2009. *School District Research Review Procedures: State of the Art in Ontario. Report on Findings*. Report to Ontario School Boards. St. Catharines, ON: Brock University. <brocku.ca/webfm_send/26512>.

Tjora, Aksel H. 2006. "Writing Small Discoveries: An Exploration of a Fresh Observers' Observations." *Qualitative Research* 6, 4: 429–451.

Tolich, Martin, and Maureen H. Fitzgerald. 2006. "If Ethics Committees Were Designed for Ethnography." *Journal of Empirical Research on Human Research Ethics* 1, 2: 71–78.

Tomkinson, Sule. 2015. "Doing Fieldwork on State Organizations in Democratic Settings: Ethical Issues of Research in Refugee Decision-making." *Forum Qualitative Sozialforschung/Forum: Qualitative Social Research* 16, 1. Art. 6.

Townsend, Anne, and Susan M. Cox. 2013. "Accessing Health Services through the Back Door: A Qualitative Interview Study Investigating Reasons Why People Participate in Health Research in Canada." BMC *Medical Ethics* 14, 40: 1–11.

Twine, France Winddance, and Jonathan Warren (eds.). 2000. *Racing Research Researching Race: Methodological Dilemmas in Critical Race Studies.* New York: New York University Press.

Tyson, Cynthia A. 2003. "Research, Race, and Epistemology of Emancipation." In Gerardo R. Lopez and Laurence Parker (eds.), *Interrogating Racism in Qualitative Research Methodology* (pp.19–28). New York: Peter Lang.

UCCO (Union of Canadian Correctional Officers). 2008. "A Rush to Judgment: A Report on the Death in Custody of Ashley Smith, an Inmate at Grand Valley Institution for Women." <ucco-sacc-csn.ca/wp-content/uploads/2015/05/Full-Report-A-Rush-to-Judgment1.pdf>.

University of Texas. Intellectual Entrepreneurship. *Sample Dissertation Proposals.* <ie/sample_diss.html>.

van den Hoonaard, Will C. 2011. *Seduction of Ethics: Transforming the Social Sciences.* Toronto: University of Toronto Press.

____. 2002. *Walking the Tightrope: Ethical Issues for Qualitative Researchers.* Toronto: University of Toronto Press.

van den Hoonaard, Will C., and Martin Tolich. 2014. "The New Brunswick Declaration of Research Ethics: A Simple and Radical Perspective." *Canadian Journal of Sociology* 39, 1: 87–97.

Van Maanen, John. 1988. *Tales of the Field: On Writing Ethnography.* Chicago: University of Chicago Press.

Walford, Geoffrey. 2009. "The Practice of Writing Ethnographic Fieldnotes." *Ethnography and Education* 4, 2: 117–130.

Walsh, Susan C., and Susan M. Brigham. 2007. "Internationally Educated Female Teachers Who Have Immigrated to Nova Scotia: A Research/Performance Text." *International Journal of Qualitative Methods* 6, 3: 1–28.

Walton, Ginger, Stuart J. Schleien, Lindsey R. Brake, Catharine Trovato and Tyler Oakes. 2012. "Photovoice: A Collaborative Methodology Giving Voice to Underserved Populations Seeking Community Inclusion." *Therapeutic Recreation Journal* XLVI, 3: 168–178.

Watt, Diane. 2007. "On Becoming a Qualitative Researcher: The Value of Reflexivity." *The Qualitative Report* 12, 1: 82–101.

Weber, Sandra. 2008. "Visual Images in Research." In Gary L. Knowles and Ardra L. Cole (eds.), *Handbook of the Arts in Qualitative Research* (pp. 41–53). London: Sage.

Weis, Lois, and Michelle Fine. 2004. *Working Method: Research and Social Justice.* New York: Routledge.

Wiebe, Natasha. 2013. "Mennonite Memories of Pelee Island, Ontario, 1925–1950: Toward a Framework for Visual Narrative Inquiry." *Narrative Inquiry* 23, 2: 405–423.

Wilson, Dana Helene and Nancy A. Ross. 2011. "Place, Gender and the Appeal of Video

Lottery Terminal Gambling: Unpacking a Focus Group Study of Montreal Youth." *GeoJournal* 76: 123–138.

Wilson, Shawn. 2008. *Research Is Ceremony: Indigenous Research Methods.* Halifax, NS: Fernwood Publishing.

Winn, Maisha. 2010. *Girl Time: Literacy, Justice, and the School-to-Prison Pipeline.* New York: Teacher's College Press.

Witcher, Chad S.G. 2010. "Negotiating Transcription as a Relative Insider: Implications for Rigor." *International Journal of Qualitative Methods* 9, 2: 122–132.

Wolf, Margery. 1992. *A Thrice Told Tale: Feminism, Postmodernism, & Ethnographic Responsibility.* Stanford, CA: Stanford University Press.

Wright, Handel K. 2006. "Qualitative Researchers on Paradigm Proliferation in Educational Research: A Question-and-Answer Session as Multi-Voiced Text." *International Journal of Qualitative Studies in Education* 19, 1: 77–95.

Wright, Lisa L. 2009. "Leadership in the Swamp: Seeking the Potentiality of School Improvement through Principal Reflection." *Reflective Practice* 10, 2: 259–272.

Yon, Daniel A. 2000. *Elusive Culture: Schooling, Race, and Identity in Global Times.* Ithaca, NY: State University of New York Press.

Yosso, Tara, J. 2006. *Critical Race Counterstories Along the Chicana/Chicano Educational Pipeline.* London: Routledge.

____. 2005. "Whose Culture Has Capital? A Critical Race Theory Discussion of Community Cultural Wealth." *Race, Ethnicity, and Education* 8, 1: 69–91.

Yu, Wai-ming, Chun-kwork Lau, and John Chi-kin Lee. 2013. "Into Collaborative Research and Co-authorship: Experiences and Reflections." *Reflective Practice* 14, 1: 31–42.

Zeni, Jane. (ed.). 2001. "A Guide to Ethical Decision-making for Insider Research." In Jane Zeni (ed.), *Ethical Issues in Practitioner Research* (pp. 153–165). New York: Teachers College Press.

Zhou, Ally A. 2004. "Writing the Dissertation Proposal: A Comparative Case Study of Four Nonnative- and Two Native-English-Speaking Doctoral Students of Education." Unpublished doctoral dissertation, University of Toronto, Toronto ON.

INFORMATION LETTER AND INFORMED CONSENT FORM

Appendices A and B provide examples of documents required in the REB applications researchers submit to conduct research involving human participants. Although these forms are connected to a specific study (Ratković 2014), they may be useful for students to consider when constructing their REB applications to conduct qualitative research. Permission was given for use of student work found in the appendices and body of the text.

INFORMATION LETTER

Title of Study: Creating a Life in a Foreign Space: Refugee Women Teachers from the Former Yugoslavia Reclaiming Professional Identities in Ontario, Canada
Researcher: Snežana Ratković
Date

Dear Participant,
The purpose of this study is to deepen understanding of women's professional identity construction within the landscape of exile. The study will also examine the broader experience of exile and settlement, as well as the barriers and supports to refugee women teachers' integration into the teaching profession in Ontario.

You are invited to participate in this study if you are a refugee woman teacher from the former Yugoslavia who immigrated to Ontario between 1991 and 2000 and have had at least 2 years of teaching experience in your home country. Your fluency in speaking, reading, and writing English and your availability and willingness to meet the scheduled timeline for the research study, are also important.

Your participation in this study will be greatly appreciated. As a participant, you will be invited to participate in two in-depth, open-ended individual interviews over a 3-month period at a site convenient for you. Each individual interview will last approximately 2 hours. After each interview, you will receive several story titles and an interpretative story of your interview. You will be asked to read and comment on both, a task that should take approximately 30 minutes. You will also be asked to send your comments related to your first interpretative story to me by e-mail or mail prior to your second interview (and your comments related to your second interpretative story prior to our focus group interview). Questions to be addressed in the individual interviews include:

- Tell me your story of exile.
- How have the experiences of exile and settlement influenced your teacher identity; your professional goals and expectations?

You will also be invited to take part in a focus group interview lasting approximately 2 hours. The focus group interview will involve approximately 4–5 women. I will moderate the interview by asking questions and keeping notes/charts of points raised. At the end of the focus group interview, I will facilitate a short debriefing session. The focus group debriefing will be used as a form of member checking; you will be invited to comment on story titles and the interpretative story constructed from the focus group conversations which will take approximately 30 minutes. The focus group procedures will include an opening discussion of the purpose of the focus group; description of ethical considerations related to confidentiality of data; explanation of focus group process and expectations; focus group discussion; and debriefing session. Questions to be addressed in the focus group interview include:

- What effective strategies could policy-makers and teachers' associations use to integrate refugee women teachers into the teaching profession in the province?

You will also be asked to read and comment on the personal experience narrative constructed from the interpretative stories of your first interview and your second interview, a task that should take approximately 30 minutes. I will keep fieldnotes during the focus group and interview sessions.

Participation in this study is voluntary, and you are free to withdraw at any time and for any reason without any consequences. There is no obligation to answer any questions that you may consider invasive, offensive, or unsuitable. If you withdraw from the study and request your individual interview data to be withdrawn, the data will be destroyed, hard copies shredded, audio tapes erased, and electronic copies deleted. However, if you should choose to withdraw your focus group data, I will not be able to extract your individual data from the focus group transcript or destroy audio recording of the focus group interview. Requests for withdrawal made after the completion of the study and/or publication of the findings will not be possible to meet.

You will have an opportunity to share your story; learn from other participants' stories; record and reflect on your strengths and concerns; and promote critical dialogue and knowledge about exile, settlement, and professional identity construction in exile.

To ensure confidentiality, you will be invited to choose a pseudonym for yourself and this pseudonym will be used throughout the project (e.g., in transcripts). I will create and secure a master list that includes all the participants' names and pseudonyms, and only my supervisor and I will have access to this list.

You will be asked to sign an Informed Consent Form and a Focus Group Participant Confidentiality Agreement Form before beginning participation in the study. Keeping focus group discussions confidential means keeping confidential any information about any participant in the focus group that is not currently in the public domain or readily available to the public.

If you would like to address any concerns regarding the focus group discussion, you may remain after the focus group interview and we can discuss your concerns.

If you prefer to be interviewed in Serbian or Croatian, I have the ability to do so.

I will mail or e-mail a copy of the final report to you upon your request. I will disseminate findings of the study through conference presentations, research papers in peer reviewed journals, and reports to the government agencies and educational authorities who influence integration of refugee women teachers in the teaching profession in Ontario. My doctoral dissertation will be available through the university library system.

Data (audio tapes, hard copies of transcripts, as well as electronic files) will be stored in my locked university office or home office. This study is focused on Ontario but may serve as a starting point for a study with a more national focus. Data will be kept indefinitely to ensure its availability if the study is extended to include other provinces.

INFORMED CONSENT FORM

I understand that: This study, in which I have agreed to participate, will involve:

- two digitally recorded individual interviews approximately 2 hours each and 1 month apart;
- review of story titles, two interpretative stories, and a personal experience narrative constructed by the researcher approximately;
- an audio taped focus group interview approximately 2 hours long and 1 month apart from the second individual interview.

I understand that primary data in this study will be collected through two individual interviews and a focus group interview. The researcher will keep fieldnotes. My personal identifiers will be collected to return interview transcripts to me. To ensure confidentiality, I will choose a pseudonym and this pseudonym will be used throughout the project (e.g., in transcripts). The researcher will create and secure a master list that includes all the participants' names and pseudonyms and only she and her supervisor will have access to this list. I recognize that anonymity and confidentiality cannot be guaranteed in the case of the focus group interview, but participants will be asked to sign a Focus Group Interview Participant Confidentiality Agreement Form and respect the privacy of other participants. My participation in the study will take approximately 7.5 hours of my time over a 3-month period.

Data will be stored in the researcher's locked university office or home office.

This study is focused on Ontario but may serve as a starting point for a study with a more national focus. The data will be kept indefinitely to ensure its availability if the study is extended to include other provinces.

Contact: If I have any questions or concerns about my participation in this study, I can contact Snežana Ratković (telephone and e-mail); Ethics Officer (telephone and e-mail) or the researcher's Faculty Supervisor (telephone and e-mail address).

Consent: I understand that my participation in this study is voluntary and that I may choose to withdraw from the study at any time and for any reason without any consequences. I understand that there is no obligation to answer any question or participate in any aspect of this project that I consider invasive, offensive or unsuitable. If I withdraw from the study and request my individual interview data to be withdrawn, the data will be destroyed. I understand, however, that if I withdraw from the study and request my focus group data to be withdrawn, the researcher will not be able to extract my individual data from the focus group transcript or destroy audio recording of the focus group interview. I am aware that the researcher will not be able to meet any requests for data withdrawal made after the completion of the study or publication of the findings.

I agree to participate in this study described above. I have made this decision based on the information I have read in the Information Letter and Informed Consent Form. I have had the opportunity to receive any additional details I wanted about the study and understand that I may ask questions in the future. I understand that I may withdraw this consent at any time.

I have read and understood the above information. I reserve the right to ask questions about the project at any time. By signing this document, I am indicating free consent to research participation in a focus group interview and two individual interviews.

Participant Signature: _____   Date:_____

The Research Ethics Board has officially given clearance for this study (File #).

Thank you for your help!

Please take one copy of this form with you for further reference.

I have fully explained the procedures of this study to the above participant.

Researcher Signature: _____ Date: _____

Appendix B

FOCUS GROUP
INTERVIEW SCRIPT

Title of Study: Creating a Life in a Foreign Space: Refugee Women Teachers from the Former Yugoslavia Reclaiming Professional Identities in Ontario, Canada
Researcher: Snežana Ratković

I would like to remind you that our conversations during this focus group interview must be kept confidential. Keeping our conversations confidential means keeping confidential any information about any participant in the focus group that is not currently in the public domain or readily available to the public; any participant's personal information that might reasonably allow identification of the person; as well as any and all information concerning participants' personal and professional lives that is disclosed during this focus group interview.

I would also like to discuss the ground rules for this focus group interview: (a) everyone is encouraged to engage in the conversation, (b) there are no correct or incorrect answers to any of the questions, (c) everyone's opinion is valuable and will be respected, and (d) a specific amount of time will be allocated to each question. The session will be recorded so that all your ideas and thoughts can be captured.

I invite you to stay after each focus group interview if you would like to talk about any potential concerns regarding the focus group discussion. If you need support working through any challenging circumstances faced during the focus group interview and/or individual interview you may consult the Human Rights and Equity Officer at the University, or the Research Ethics Officer and/or Distress Centre.

I also want to remind you that your participation in the study is voluntary. You do not have to answer any question you do not wish to answer. You also may leave the interview at any time you wish.

Today, I want us to spend some time discussing your experiences of exile, settlement, teacher identity construction and negotiation in the Ontario context, and the ways in which your gender may have influenced these experiences. Specifically, I want to hear your views of exile and settlement in Ontario, as well as challenges you have faced and opportunities you have embraced in your attempt to reclaim your professional status in the province. I would also like to hear from you how people — including policy-makers, government officials, researchers, and yourselves — can work to support the integration of refugee women teachers in the teaching profession in Ontario. Over the next 2 hours, I'm going to ask you 8–10 questions. Please share your opinions and thoughts on each of the questions. Your input is an important part of developing a better understanding of how you, and other women in similar situations to you, feel about exile and settlement issues, and the experience of professional identity construction and negotiation in Ontario.

Appendix C

MOVING FROM TRANSCRIPTS TO (BILINGUAL) TRANSCRIPT POEMS (SAMPLE)

Title of Study: Creating a Life in a Foreign Space: Refugee Women Teachers from the Former Yugoslavia Reclaiming Professional Identities in Ontario, Canada
Researcher: Snežana Ratković

As I was transcribing my conversations with Jagoda, I was creating transcript poems from Jagoda's transcripts by selecting only meaningful, powerful and rhythmical words. While analyzing Jagoda's second transcript recorded in the Serbo-Croatian language, for example, I selected a paragraph that spoke to Jagoda's decision to give up education in Canada:

> Pa … Ne bih ja to nazvala žrtvom, ali recimo … ja sam se odrekla škole pošto sam ja (um) kad sam pokupila sve informacije shvatila da ulagati u sebe nema nikakvog smisla, jer moja djeca rastu i ako treba u nekoga ulagati, onda treba [ulagati] u njih…ja sam se odrekla [škole], jer ja sam shvatila da ja (zveckanje šoljica za kafu) ne bih imala kontrolu nad mojom djecom da sam pristala da se doškolujem. Ja jednostavno ne bih imala vremena ni da ih vidim. (Jagoda, Konverzacija 2, Maj 2010)

Next, I translated this paragraph to English:

> Well … I wouldn't call it sacrifice, but let's say … I gave up school because (um) once I gathered all the information needed, I realised that investing

in my education does not make any sense anymore; my children were growing up and it was time to invest in them [in their education] ... I gave up [school], because I realised that I would lose control over my children if I continued my education. I wouldn't even have time to see them. (Jagoda, Conversation 2, May 2010)

Then, I moved from a field text (i.e., Conversation 2 Transcript) to a research text (i.e., transcript poem) by trimming the paragraph down for meaning and rhyme. I was committed to keeping Jagoda's words intact as much as possible:

Odrekla sam se škole	I gave up school
Ulagati u sebe nema smisla,	Investing in me didn't make any sense;
jer moja djeca rastu	my children were growing up and
i u njih ulagati treba.	it was time to invest in them.
Odrekla sam se škole i ne žalim,	I gave up school,
ne, ne žalim,	I had no regrets,
jer da sam bila okupirana sobom	I wasn't the centre of the universe,
tko zna kakva bi se nevolja zbila.	my children's future was at stake.

Finally, I sent the poem together with the rest of the preliminary analysis (i.e., conversation subtitles, interpretative stories, metaphors and participants' views of me as researcher) to Jagoda for member check. Once Jagoda approved this poem, I added the poem to my research text.

Appendix D

RESPONSE TO THE EDITOR REGARDING MANUSCRIPT SUBMITTED FOR PUBLICATION

Included in this appendix are excerpts from a letter to the editor in which we respond to reviewers' comments on a manuscript we submitted for publication. We received three reviews that varied in length, number and types of recommendations. We include excerpts to illustrate the types of comments received and how we dealt with them. Reviewers gave surface and substantive comments that we incorporated. We hope the excerpts illustrate to students the level of detail we provided to the editor to explain the changes made. In our response, we included actual text to make it very easy for the editor to connect reviewer comments with changes made. Our goal was to show the seriousness with which we engaged the task of addressing reviewers' concerns. When we did not change, we explained why not (e.g., contradictory comments, and we chose what we thought to be most appropriate change to make). We believe that responding to reviewers' comments in such detail contributes to a positive reading of the revised version. The letter and a revised manuscript were sent June 28, 2012. The paper, "Becoming Academics: Experiencing Legitimate Peripheral Participation in Part-Time Studies," was published in 2012.

EXCERPTS

We would like to thank the Reviewers for their detailed and constructive comments on our manuscript. We carefully considered and responded to each of their comments, queries and suggestions. We have created a comprehensive document/

letter clearly indicating the changes we made to the text. We list the reviewers' suggestions/questions in order and provide an explanation of how we addressed each in the text.

Comments to the Authors

Reviewer 1

1. There is really nothing new here. The recommendations with which you end, in particular, are the kinds of things that I and others have read — and probably also written — many times.

- We have refined the paper to make our focused analysis of the experience of legitimate peripheral participation (LPP) through a socio-cultural lens much clearer and revised the conclusion to reflect this emphasis.
- LPP addresses the movement toward a greater identification within a community of practice. It does not discuss in detail the complexities and contradictions of such identity development. We have interpreted the development of a researcher identity within the LPP framework through a socio-cultural lens. We explore the role of hybrid socio-cultural identities in the process of LPP.
- Lave and Wanger address power relations. We extend their notion of power relations by exploring how such relations are embedded in socio-cultural identity and exercised by the newcomer/oldtimer binary.

Reviewer 2

1. Some of the paragraphs are too short and could be linked for better flow.

- We have revised sentences and edited the manuscript for clarity and consistency throughout.

2. You should also consider whether you can update the LPP model rather than just test it for fit — an amendment to your discussion section perhaps?

- In this paper we examine LPP specifically through a critical socio-cultural lens. We explore the experience of part-time education PhD students becoming researchers and developing a sense of belonging to the academic research community using Bhabha's (1994) concepts of "hybrid identities" and "Third Space."

We are arguing the need for those of us using LPP as a model for graduate student development to take more seriously the role individual socio-cultural identities play in that process.

As an illustration from the revised manuscript:

"LPP defines learning not as the acquisition of knowledge by individuals, but rather as a process of social co-participation. The meaning of this social co-participation or social learning is configured through the process of observing and practising expected socio-cultural activities, belonging to a community of practice, and becoming a legitimate participant in that community. However, LPP fails to address in significant ways the influence of the individual socio-cultural identities on the individual's and group's experiences." (24)

We then summarize how individual socio-cultural identities impacted learning and growth as researchers in the discussion.

3. Otherwise I find this 'text-book' perfect. For those in education doctoral supervision and their students, it is helpful to realize they are not alone in their challenges. You have made good use of the literature, kept the methodology to a manageable length, extracted the voices of the participants allowing both supervised and supervisors to speak and rounded off with reasonable recommendations.

Reviewer 3

1. I enjoyed reading this paper, the Authors present a case, which will interest readers of this journal, and think it has potential for shedding light on the part-time student experience. However, I think it needs major revisions. I detail the reasons why below but, in essence, I felt it was theoretically under-developed and there were some significant omissions.

- We have made many revisions to address this reviewer's concerns as can be seen below in our response to this reviewer's comments and suggestions.

2. Theoretical Framework (pp. 3–6) This gave an excellent, if perhaps overly detailed, explication of LPP. However, this, I felt needed to be given a) a more critical and analytical cast by including sources which problematize L and W's framework, and b) used to situate the current study more concretely i.e. what does this research contribute which is new/ different/ takes the field forward?

- We have expanded on the LPP framework by showing how in our study, the socio-cultural identity theory (Bhabha 1994; Said 1994) informs the process of becoming an academic in this specific community of practice. We address this in earlier comments.

We write in the revised manuscript:

"As well, even if not intended, the language associated with LPP reflects a straight path, a trajectory, from newcomer to oldtimer, periphery to center. The lived-experience of such learning is generally not experienced as such an uncomplicated journey. Communities of practice are more than sites where specific skills and discourse are mastered and implemented. They are also complex and often problematic sites in which power circulates (Foucault 1980), and where boundaries between participants are constructed based on individuals' acquired skill, years of practical experience, and professional credentials. Socially constructed differences such as race, ethnicity, gender, religious-affiliation, (dis)ability, and sexual orientation, social constructs that influence how we identify and are often ascribed identities by others (Hall 2000), also influence the shape the learning trajectory takes. The networks of power operating within any community of practice will be influenced by these socially constructed differences." (8)

6. I also felt the paper could benefit from reference to a much broader literature on identity, researcher reflexivity and learning processes — as these issues emerge later as crucial in the 'Findings' section, and could do with being signalled and contextualized in a more substantive literature review at this point.

- We have revised sections and now have a Discussion section and Conclusion. We have broadened the literature to support the revisions made. Page limitations dictated the degree to which we could expand the literature.

8. Methodology (pp. 7–8) This is too brief. Authors need to justify why they chose these particular methods. The data analysis explains the procedures that were followed. I was more curious about the '*a priori*' and 'emergent' codes, what these were, and how the analysis process 'worked' in terms of relationships, given the point already acknowledged concerning variations in research experiences and power relations.

- We received a contradictory comment from Reviewer 2 regarding the methodology who stated that we kept it at a "manageable length." We did expand the methodology, however, to meet the request of this Reviewer.
- We write:

"We collaboratively designed an interpretive qualitative study (Coffey and Atkinson 1996; Freeman 2000; Lincoln & Guba 1985) to explore our learning experiences. The critical socio-cultural perspective embedded in the course content also informed our research process and the critical lens we applied to the data. Data included four digitally recorded course sessions approximately 3.5 hours each, weekly written responses to assigned readings, final papers, minutes of meetings, and reflexive journals." We included more details on the development of *a priori* and emergent codes."

We write:

"After extensive discussion, we coded the first interview transcript individually using 10 *a priori* codes connected to the course content (e.g., deep learning, difficult knowledge, distance, part-time status, personal narrative, power issues, time). We came back together to reflect on our prior codes and those that emerged through our readings (e.g., critical pedagogy, multiple roles, and supervisor as learner). We compared and contrasted our coding work as we analyzed various data. Using this approach, we were able to code each data source systematically supporting the emergence of relevant categories and themes (e.g., part-time status, third space, and power relations). We selected specific examples from the data analyzed to illustrate emergent themes and to construct our personal narratives (For extended discussion related to themes see Authors 2010)."

9. Participants (pp. 8–9) The implication is that Author 3 was consciously working to 'produce' Authors 1 and 2 as 'future colleagues' and academics. Why? How explicit was this? To what extent did Authors 1 and 2 share this goal? What does this tell us about power, identity, etc.?

- We have addressed this aspect of the experience in Margaret's section of the paper. In it we indicate the reasoning behind Margaret's suggestion that we structure the Directed Study the way we did. The two students were explicit in their goal of becoming academics in the educational research community. This blended well with their supervisor's feelings about the legitimacy of student-research and the view to students as future colleagues.
- We explain the attention that was paid to the identities of the participants and the need for authentic research participation. We discuss how Margaret was challenged balancing the role of the supervisor/learner and supervisor/expert and the power that circulates through the balancing act. We also point out the important learning that Margaret experienced in the process. We write:

"What Margaret had not considered was the way in which the combination of identities created a space for learning that would not likely have happened in another context. In particular, Milka's experiences as refugee and English language learner continually created a backdrop for considering LPP not only as a theoretical concept but also as lived experience connected to individual socio-cultural identities. Margaret had to consciously consider how her identity, particularly as a white woman and part of the dominant group, influenced the experiences she had in the academy and often differed from Milka's experiences. As discussions focused on Othering, Whiteness and Eurocentrism, Margaret experienced an uncomfortable knowledge of how these theoretical concepts were related to institutional and pedagogical practices. Although in the context of the Directed Study she could be positioned as the oldtimer, she continued to identify as someone who had not completed her journey, continually learning through the powerful group interactions. Balancing the tensions between the role of supervisor/expert and supervisor/learner was a place of struggle for Margaret. At times, she wondered how each of these positionings influenced the opportunities for Jim and Milka to engage in meaningful learning opportunities. Mackenzie and Ling (2009) view the supervisor/student relationship as dialectical in nature. For Margaret, this dialectical relationship was foundational to her learning as well as to the learning Milka and Jim experienced." (21, 22)

11. Where is Author 3's narrative? Although I see that this paper is predominantly about 'experiencing' and 'becoming' from a p/t student perspective I think it would be stronger if Author 3's perspective were included. As it is, I am bothered that its omission seems to re-inscribe power differentials by implying that Authors 1 and 2 are 'junior partners' in this relationship and only they must write about their learning journey. Author 3 was surely a key part of the other two Authors' 'becomings' in moving from periphery to participation? Author 3's narrative could be included to draw through some points about 'community of practice' (Wenger again), as well as explicating their own reflexive researcher stance, particularly as the next section points out that LPP is about social co-participation.

- Author 3's narrative is included in this revised version of the paper. This section addresses the complex situation a supervisor faces when positioned both as learner and as supervisor (Margaret learns with students but also grades them).

13. Discussion (pp. 20–22) This section raises important points about p/t students. However, it is theoretically insubstantial. Reflection back to a much more

substantial literature review of L and W, critiques of L and W, etc is needed to contextualize and explore the key findings from the previous section. It is not at all clear how the codes, *a priori* and emergent, referred to earlier relate either to the findings or the discussion. It may be a good idea to integrate the Guiding Principles, which follow into the Discussion section, and again to substantiate these Principles with reference to relevant studies?

- We have revised the discussion and focused it more clearly on the implications of looking at LPP and the "becoming and belonging" of part-time students to the academy through a critical social-cultural lens. The appropriate Guiding Principles have been integrated into this discussion as suggested.

AUTHOR INDEX

Absolon, Kathy, 16
Acker, Joan, 8–9
Acker, Sandra, 30
Aguiar, Luis, 104
Aitken, Stuart C, 177
Allnut, Susan, 124
Altheide, David L., 62, 153
Alvarez, Pilar, see Rosell, et al. 2014
Alvesson, Mats, 39
Anderson, Terry, 88
Anderson, Timothy, 131
Anfara, Vincent A., 27
Angrosino, Michael V., 54, 56, 178–9
Antle, Beverly, see Mishna et al. 2004
Anucha, Uzo, see Dlamini et al. 2012
Archibald, Jo-ann, 28, 31
Aronson, Jane, 123
Atchison, Chris, 174
Atkinson, Paul, 61–2, 154, 157, 270–1
Austin, Ann E., 22
Avni, Anoosha E., 67

Bahkru, Tanya S., 9
Bailey, Julia, 148
Barbour, Rosaline, 115
Bardhoshi, Gerta, see Hergenrather et al. 2009
Barnard, Alan, see McCosker et al. 2001
Barnes, Benita J., 22
Barrett, Margaret, 126
Barry, Kate, 9, see Acker et al. 1991
Battiste, Marie, 12, 42, 71, 85, 158, 190
Baumbusch, Jennifer L., 22–3
Bechkoff, Jennifer, see Garcia et al. 2009
Beile, Penny, 67
Bell, Kirsten, 95
Berk, Rupert, 13–14
Bermbach, Nicole, 223

Bershtling, Orit, see Gilbar et al. 2013
Biklen, Sari K., 1
Bird, Cindy, 132, 143, 148–9
Bloor, Michael, 114
Bluebond-Langner, Myra, 96
Bogdan, Robert, 1
Boise, Robert, 221
Bolding, Graham, see Davis, M. et al. 2004
Boote, David N., 67
Bosco, Fernando J., 52, 196
Bose, Christine E., 9
Boudin, Kathy, see Fine et al. 2001
Bowen, Iris, see Fine et al. 2001
Boyer, Wanda, 223
Bradbury, Hillary, 28
Brady, Jennifer, 23
Brake, Lindsey R., see Walton et al. 2012
Brannen, Julia, 157
Breidenstein, George, 127
Breton, Denise C., 12, 190
Brigham, Susan M., 46
Britzman, Deborah P., 11
Broad, Gail, 221–2
Brook, Julia, 23
Browne, Jenny, see Davies et al. 2004
Browne, Kath, 28, 196
Burbules, Nicholas C., 13
Burgos-Debray, Elisabeth, 92–3
Burles, Meredith, 96
Busher, Hugh, 49
Buthelezi, Thabsile, see Moletsane et al. 2007

Caelli, Kate, 125
Cahnmann-Taylor, Melisa, 46
Canadian Institutes of Health Research, 72
Cannella, Gaile S., 220
Carlson, Julie A., 136–7, 149
Carnevale, Franco A., 96

Carter, Stacie M., 29, 197
Castleden, Heather, 96–7, 222
Catlin, Susan, 23
Chafe, Roger, see Hagens et al. 2009
Charmaz, Kathy, 28, 38, 54, 62, 124, 153
Cho, Sumi, 9
Choo, Hae Yeon, 9
Clandinin, D. Jean, 28, 132
Clark, Judith, see as Fine et al. 2001
Clarke, Jill, 101
Clifford, James, 62, 118, 176–7
Coffey, Amanda, 61–2, 154, 157, and see Emerson et al. 2001
Cole, Ardra L., 46
Cole, Peter, 197–8
Collier, Diane, 198
Collins, Patricia Hill, 9, 14, 31, 164, 166, 168
Conn, Lesley G., 72–3
Connelly, Michael F., 28, 132
Conrad, Diane, 8, 28, 46, 50, 196
Cook, Catherine, 127
Cook, Judith A., 8
Cotnam-Kappel, Megan, 112
Cowan, Chris A., see Hergenrather et al. 2009
Cox, Susan M., 46, 99
Crang, Mike, see DeLyser et al. 2010
Crenshaw, Kimberlie W., see Cho et al. 2013
Cui, Yan, see Garcia et al. 2009

Daiute, Colette, 62, 153
Damianakis, Thecia, 97
Davidson, Christina, 132
Davidson, Howard, 233
Davidson, Judith, 153–4
Davies, Bronwyn, 7–8, 14
Davis, Angela, 232

Davis, Mark, 49
Davison, Colleen M., 51, 198
Dehaeck, Ulrike, see Scott et al. 2009
Dehli, Kari, 8–9, 11, 171, 184
Dei, George J. Sefa, 233
Delamont. Sara, 62, 157
de Lange, Naydene, see Moletsane et al. 2007
DeLuca, Christopher, 23
DeLyser, Dydia, 28
Denzin, Norman K., 8, 28, 62, 132, 156, 176–7
DeVault, Marjorie L., 9
Dey, Ian, 62, 153
Dhamoon, Rita Kaur, 9
di Gregorio, Silvana, 154
Dickinson, Wendy, see Onwuegbuzie et al. 2015
Dillard, Cynthia B., 9
Dimitriadis, Greg, 48, 51–2
Dion, Susan, 161
Dlamini, Nombuso S., x, 33
Dobrow, Mark J., see Hagens et al. 2009
Doe, Christine, 23
Doucet, Andrea, 171–2
Doyle, Susanna, 149
Duggleby, Wendy, 172
Du Mont, Janice, see Parnis et al. 2005
Dupre, Kathryn, see Power et al. 2014

Eaton, Mary, 167–8
Ebbeck, Mary, 223
Edwards, Judith A., 131
Elford, Jonathan, see Davis, M. et al. 2004
Ellingson, Laura L., 152–4, 176
Ells, Carolyn, 73
Emerson, Robert M., 57
Esseveld, Johanna, see Acker et al. 1991
Estable, Alma, see MacLean et al. 2004
Eyre, Linda, 9, 16, 72–3
Ezzy, Douglas, 10, 61–2, 153, 228

Faith, Karlene, 233
Farrar, Joyce P.J., 59
Fellows, Collin, see Morgan et al. 2008
Fenton, Nancy, see McGinn et al. 2005
Fine, Michelle, 8, 31, 34, 62, 232–3
Finley, Susan, 196
Fitzgerald, Maureen H., 72–3, 85–6
Flecha, Ainhoa, see Rosell, et al. 2014
Fonow, Mary Margaret, 8
Fontana, Andrea, 47–8, 51–2, 138
Foucault, Michel, 10–11, 113, 164–6, 168, 227
Franklin, Jane, see Bloor et al. 2001
Fraser, Heather, 172–3
Freeman, Donald, 154–5, 270–1
Freire, Paulo, 10, 231
Fretz, Rachelle I., see Emerson et al. 2001
Frey, James H., 47–8, 51–2, 138–9

Gallagher, Kathleen, 8, 46, 56–7, 64, 82, 119, 196
Ganga, Deianira, 32
Gannon, Susanne, 7 and see Davies et al. 2004
Garcia, Angela C., 56
Geertz, Clifford, 54, 157, 175, 177
Gerber, Rod, see McCosker et al. 2001
Gilbar, Ora, 218
Gillam, Lynn, 93
Goldstein, Tara, 46, 50, 196
Gombay, Brydon, see Parnis et al. 2005
Gorelick, Sherry, 8
Gormley, Louise, 75, 85
Gouzouasis, Peter, 68, 150, 199–200
Graham-Marrs, Holly Ann, 23–4
Grauer, Kit, 68, 199

Grayson, J. Paul, 72
Gregory, David, 97–8
Grundy, Annabelle L., sees McGinn et al. 2005
Guba, Egon G., 1, 8, 58, 63, 123, 145
Gubrium, Jaber, 47
Guevara, Heather, see Morgan et al. 2008
Guillemin, Marilys, 93
Gutfreund, Shawna, 73

Hagens, Victoria, 132, 146
Haggerty, Kevin D., 72
Haig-Brown, Celia, x, 31, 189, 219–20, 222
Haig-Brown, Helen, 220, 222
Haley, Janice, 51, 89–90
Halifax, Nancy V.D, 199
Hall, Wendy, 223, 270
Hammersley, Martyn, 63
Haraway, Donna, 9
Harding, Sandra, 8–9, 34
Harper, Lynette A., 59–60
Hart, Chris, 27
Hart, Graham, see Davis, M. et al. 2004
Heath, Christian, 52, 119,141, 143–4, 154
Hennink, Monique M., 53, 101
Henry, Marsha G., 9
Herbert, Steve, see DeLyser et al. 2010
Hergenrather, Kenneth C., 50
Herman, Thomas, 52
Herron, Rachel, 127–8
Hesse-Biber, Sharlene Nagy7–8, 28–9
Hewitt, Damon T., see Kim et al. 2012
Hewson, Claire, 39, 46–7, 56
Hindmarsh, Jon, 52, 119,141, 143–4, 154, see Heath et al. 2010
Hindmarsh, Kathryn, see Scott et al. 2009
Hine, Christine, 26, 39, 46–7, 153
Hodkinso, Phil, 63

Hole, Rachelle D., 101–2, 123, 199
Holstein, James, 47
Holt, Amanda, 128
Honan, Eileen, see Davies et al. 2004
Huberman, Michael, 154–5
Huntly, Alyson, 23
Hylton, Donna, see Fine et al. 2001

Ibanez, Francisco, 8
Inckle, Kay, 178–9
Irwin, Lori, 110
Irwin, Rita, 47, 68, 150, 196, 199–200

Jackson, Peter, 47
Jacobson, Nora, 97
Jaggar, Alison M., 28, 43
Jalongo, Mary Renck, 223
James, Carl, ix–x, 128–9, 191
James, Nalita, 49
Janesick, Valerie, J., 58
Jesson, Jill, 27
Johnson, Barbara, 101
Johnson, Holly, 108–9
Johnson, Joy, 110
Jordan, Sharalyn, see Hall et al. 2005
Jordan, Steven, 12, 28–9

Kamberelis, George, 48, 51–2
Kamler, Barbara, see Reid et al. 1996
Kanuha, Valli K., 34
Kanuka, Heather, 88
Kapoor, Dip, 28–9
Kesby, Mike, sees Kindon et al. 2010
Kezar, Adrianna, 104
Khan, Shahnaz, 30, 33–4
Kilbourn, Brent, 24, 26
Kim, Catherine Y., 223
Kim, Isabelle, 56–7, 82, 119
Kindon, Sara, 28
Kirsch, Gesa, 47
Knowles, J. Gary, 46
Kovach, Margaret, 28, 190
Kowal, Sabine, 131

Kreuger, Richard A., 114
Krieg, Brigette, 196
Kuoch, Phong, 129
Kvale, Steinar, 47, 137

Lacey, Fiona, see Jesson et al. 2011
Lafreniere, Darquise, 46
Lamb, Christopher, 96
Lampert, Martin D., 131
Lapadat, Judith, 131, 136, 148
Lather, Patti, 7–9, 12–14, 44, 92, 219
Lau, Chun-kwork, see Yu et al. 2013
Lau, Sunny Man Chu, 67–8
Laurent, Dianna, see Hewson et al. 2003
Lave, Jean, 150–1, 268
Lawrence, Bonita, 12, 31
Laws, Cath, see Davies et al. 2004
Leavy, Patricia, 8, 29
Lee, John Chi-kin, see Yu et al. 2013
Leech, Nancy, see Onwuegbuzie et al. 2015
Leggo, Carl, 68, 150, 199–200
Lewis, Magda, 72
Lewis, Patrick J., 200
Lightfoot, Cynthia, 62, 153
Lincoln, Yvonna S., 1, 7–8, 28, 58, 62–3, 123, 132, 145, 177, 220
Lindsay, Anne, 131–2, 136, 148
Little, Miles, 29, 197
Long, Bonita, see Hall et al. 2005
Long, Richard, 200
Longboat, Catherine, 85
Lopez, Gerardo R., 12
Loppie, Charlotte, 173
Lorenzetti, Liza, 24, 35
Losen, Daniel J., see Kim et al. 2012
Loutzenheiser, Lisa W., 12, 32–3, 189
Lowick, Adrianne. J., see

Dlamini et al. 2012
Luff, Paul, 52, 119,141, 143–4, 154, see Heath et al. 2010
Lynham, Susan A., see Lincoln et al. 2011

Macdonald, Mary Ellen, 96
MacLean, Lynne, 143
Maclean, Rod, see Reid et al. 1996
Mahoney, Dan, 59, 123
Mahony, Tina H., 231–2
Maiter, Sarah, 97, 105, 158
Malinowski, Bronislaw, 54
Manley-Casimir, Michael, see McGinn et al. 2005
Mann, Chris, 46
Marcus, George E., 62–3, 176–7
Markham, Annette N., 46
Markle, D. Thomas, 149
Marshall, Catherine, 152–3
Martinez, Isabel, see Rosell, et al. 2014
Matheson, Lydia, see Jesson et al. 2011
Maticka-Tyndale, Eleanor, see Dlamini et al. 2012
Mayan, Maria, 200
Mazzei, Lisa A., 122
Mazzuca, Josephine, see Dei et al. 1997
McCall, Leslie, 9
McCall, Sophie, 190
McCaslin, Wanda D., 12, 190
McCosker, Heather, 77–8
McDowell, Linda, see DeLyser et al. 2010
McGinn, Michelle K., 219
McIsaac, Elizabeth, see Dei et al. 1997
McKeever, Patricia, 96
McKenzie, Holly Ann, 24–5
Mead, Margaret, 54
Meiners, Erica R., 231–3
Mero-Jaffe, Irit, 132, 146
Mertz, Norma T., 27
Meyer, Mechtild, see MacLean et al. 2004
Miles, Matthew B., 154–5

Mill, Judy, 125
Mills, Janet, 126
Mishler, Elliot. G., 130–1, 138
Mishna, Faye, 77
Mitchell, Claudia, *see* Moletsane et al. 2007
Mitchell, Gail J., 199
Moffatt, Jessica, 200
Moletsane, Relebohilie, 50
Moore, John, *see* Scott et al. 2009
Morgan, David, 52, 115
Morgan, Vanessa Sloan, 96, 222
Morrison, Connie, 129
Morrison, Zachary James, 97–8
Morse, Janice, 80–1
Moss, Edward, N., *see* Power et al. 2014
Mosselson, Jacqueline, 173–4
Mueller-Rockstroh, Babette, *see* Davies et al. 2004
Mullings, Beverly, 33
Mutua, Kagendo, 28, 190
Myles, Richard, 72

Nagar, Richa, 9
Nash, Catherine, 28, 196
Nash, Jennifer, C., 9
Natural Sciences and Engineering Research Council of Canada, 72
Neimanis, Aelita, 222
Norberg, Kathryn, 8, 34
Norris, Sigrid, 141
Ntelioglou, Burcu Yaman, *see* Gallagher, et al. 2013

Oakes, Tyler, 50, *see* Walton et al. 2012
Oakley, Ann, 9, 47
Ochs, Eleanor, 130
O'Connell, Daniel C., 131
Oki, Gwenn, 75
Okpalaoka, Chinwe, 9
O'Leary, Kathy, *see* Scott et al. 2009
Olesen, Virginia, 9, 196

Olson, Karin, 47–8
Omorodion, Francisca, *see* Dlamini et al. 2012
Onwuegbuzie, Anthony, 52, 114
Orbach, Susie, 178–9
Osmond, Martin, *see* Scott et al. 2009
Owen, Michael, 73

Paechter, Carrie, 30–1, 42, 46–7, 78, 153
Pain, Rachel, *see* Kindon et al. 2010
Palys, Ted, 174
Pantaleo, Kathy, 199–200
Parker, Laurence, 12
Parnis, Deborah, 73
Patai, Daphne, 9, 34, 47, 112
Patterson, Donna, 73
Patterson, Kathryn, *see* Hall et al. 2005
Patton, Michael Quinn, 28, 55, 63, 116–17, 156–7
Peshkin, Alan, 116
Peters, Evelyn J., 12
Petersen, Eva Bendix, *see* Davies et al. 2004
Piquemal, Nathalie, 85
Plett Martens, Vonda L., 129–30
Poland, Blake, 136, 140–1
Power, Elaine M., 174
Power, Nicole, 50
Powick, Kelly D., 39–40, 98–9, 133–4, 143
Prasad, Pushkala, 8, 230
Pratt, Geraldine, 40–1
Prendergast, Monica, 150
Prokos, Anastasia H., 47–8
Prosser, Jon D., 46–7, 196, 220
Psathas, George, 131–2
Pula, Sara, *see* Hergenrather et al. 2009

Quint-Rapoport, Mia, 174–5

Rallis, Sharon F., 175
Rapley, Tim, 101
Ratković, Snezana, ix, 71, 90,

98–9, 124, 146, 192, and *see* Teeuwsen et al. 2012
Ray, Lynne, *see* Caelli, Ray and Mill 2003
Raynor, Margaret E., 68
Reason, Peter, 28
Regehr, Cheryl, *see* Mishna et al. 2004
Reid, Jo-Anne, 116–17, 119
Reinharz, Shulamit, 8–9
Reyes, Jose, 221–2
Rhodes, Scott D., *see* Hergenrather et al. 2009
Rich, Peter J., *see* Markle, D. Thomas, Richard Edward West and Peter J. Rich. 2011
Richardson, Laurel, 189
Roberts, Lana, 196
Robson, Kate, *see* Bloor et al. 2001
Rodgers, Karen, 108
Rolling, James Haywood Jr., 46
Rose, Gillian, 46, 50, 124
Rosell, Lourdes R., 52
Rosenberg, Judith, 54, 56
Ross, Nancy A., 130
Rossman, Gretchen, 152–3
Roth, Wolff-Michael, 8
Russell, Polly, 47

St. Denis, Verna, 12
St. Pierre, Elizabeth A., 9, 188–9
Salmon, Amy, 95
Sanjek, Roger, 57, 118
Schleien, Stuart J., *see* Walton et al. 2012
Schnarch, Brian, 85, 158
Schneider, Christopher J., 62, 104, 153
Schostak, Jill, 197
Schostak, John, 197
Schroeter, Sara, 50, 130
Schwandt, Thomas A., 63
Scott, Sam, 32
Scott, Shannon, 138–9
Searle, Michelle, 23
Sethi, Bharati, 25, 158, 200–1, 224

Sharpe, Heather, *see* Scott et al. 2009
Shaw, Linda L., *see* Emerson et al. 2001
Sherif, Bahira, 30–1
Sherr, Lorraine, *see* Davis, M. et al. 2004
Shields, Carolyn, *see* McGinn et al. 2005
Siegesmund, Richard, 46
Silverman, David, 153 and *see* Seale et al. 2004
Simich, Laura, 97
Simpson, Alyson, *see* Reid et al. 1996
Sims, Chris, 232
Sinding, Christina, 123
Sinner, Anita E., 68, 199–200
Skinner, Mark, 127–8
Sköldberg, Kaj, 39
Skorobohacz, Christina, ix, 60
Skukauskaite, Audra, 132
Smith, Dorothy E., 8
Smith, John K., 63
Smith, Linda Tuhiwai, 42, 190
Smithies, Chris, 219
Social Sciences and Humanities Research Council of Canada (sshrc), 72
Social Sciences and Humanities Research Ethics Special Working Committee, 73, 85–6
Spivak, Gayatri, 182
Springgay, Stephanie, 47, 196
Stacey, Judith, 9, 177
Stack, Carol, 182
Standlee, Alecea I., *see* Garcia et al. 2009
Stanger-Ross, Jordan, 12
Statistics Canada, 231–2
Steurer, Steven, 232
Stewart, Fiona, 46
Stille, Saskia, 67–8
Stonebanks, Christopher D., 12
Strega, Susan, 9
Stuart, Jean, *see* Moletsane et al. 2007

Styres, Sandra, 42
Swandener, Beth Blue, 28, 190
Swarr, Amanda, 9

Tang, Shang, 31–2
Taylor, Leanne, 128–9
Taylor, Myra, *see* Moletsane et al. 2007
Teeuwsen, Phil, ix, 21
Tessier, Sophie, 150
Thibodeau, Steven, 97–8
Thomas, Michelle, *see* Bloor et al. 2001
Thomas, Robina Anne, 160–1
Tilley, Susan A., 4, 16, 21, 31, 44, 71, 74–5, 78, 80–1, 85, 92–3, 98–9, 103, 108–9, 112–15, 117–21, 133–6, 138–40, 143, 151–2, 156–8, 162–3, 166–8, 180–8, 194, 233
Tjora, Aksel H., 118
Tolich, Martin, 72–3, 85–6
Tomkinson, Sule, 16
Torre, Maria, *see* Fine et al. 2001
Townsend, Anne, 99
Tracy, Alice, *see* Steurer et al. 2001
Trovato, Catherine, *see* Walton et al. 2012
Twine, France Winddance, 12
Tyson, Cynthia A., 12

Union of Canadian Correctional Officers (ucco), 231
University of Texas, Intellectual Entrepreneurship, 27
Upegui, Debora, *see* Fine et al. 2001

van den Hoonaard, Will C., 72–3, 85–6
Van Maanen, John 13, 177, 185–6

Vogel, Carl, *see* Hewson et al. 2003

Walford, Geoffrey, 118
Wallis, Kendal, 28–9, 196
Walsh, Susan C., 46
Walton, Ginger, 50
Warren, Jonathan, 12
Watt, Diane, 219
Weber, Sandra, 19, 46, 82, 19
Weinberg, Mickey, *see* Gilbar et al. 2013
Weis, Lois, 8, 34
Wenger, Etienne, 150–1, 272
Wessels, Anne, 46, 196
Weseen, Susan, *see* Fine et al. 2000
West, Richard E., 149
Wiebe, Natasha, 50
Willett, Cam, 16
Wilson, Dana Helene, 130
Wilson, Shawn, 12, 28, 196, 230
Winn, Maisha, 233
Winstok, Zeev, *see* Gilbar et al. 2013
Wise, Julie, *see* Maiter et al. 2008
Wisor, Scott, 28
Witcher, Chad S.G., 151
Wolf, Margery, 8–9, 54, 176–7
Wong, Loonmung, *see* Fine et al. 2000
Woodford, Michael R., 97
Wright, Handel K., 229
Wright, Lisa L., 69

Yon, Daniel A., 54
Yosso, Tara, J., 10, 12
Yu, Wai-ming, 219
Yule, Peter, *see* Hewson et al. 2003

Zaia, John, 75
Zeni, Jane, 72
Zhou, Ally A., 69
Zine, Jasmin, *see* Dei et al. 1997
Zoran, Annmarie, *see* Onwuegbuzie et al. 2015

SUBJECT INDEX

advertising, 51, 101

advisor's expertise, 73–5, 98, 125, 159, 195, 207

alternative institutional formations, 229

analysis, 2, 30, 66, 69, 118, 131–2, 135, 141–2, 152–75
  decisions, 71, 138, 148–9, 153
  justify, 164, 197
  process, 15, 37, 47, 64, 105, 124, 130, 143–5, 154–8, 191–2
    analytic perspectives and related themes, 38, 158–9, 163–4, 166–8
    consider before the research begins, 36
    four Cs of analysis, 61–2
    surface analysis, 164, 167
    systematic analysis process, 60, 62, 169–70
  representation overlap, 176–7

analyzed transcripts, 69, 108–9, 126, 131–48, 155–9, 182

annotated bibliographies, ix, 21–2

appropriateness of the use of technological assistance, 120–1, 154
  ethical issues, 119–20

articulating qualitative research questions, 15–16, 26, 37–9, 66–7, 228

arts-based methodologies, 25, 46–7, 50–1, 68, 108, 199–200, 203–4, 228–9

ask critical questions, 1, 8, 11, 16–17, 22, 69, 159–60, 190, 224, 229

asking why, 5–6, 10, 17, 22, 26, 122–3, 155, 169, 184, 267

assumptions,
  critique of, 54, 160, 187
  epistemological, 107
  ontological , 54, 53, 107, 149
  philosophical, 47–8, 107

audience, an intended, 179, 217–20

auto-ethnography, 23

below the surface disruptions, 121

bilingual
  quotations, 192, 265–6
  research texts, 192

binary categories, 25, 31, 33

boredom, 127, 134, 184–5

breach ethical respectful praxis, 178

breakdown in relationship, 206–7

CBPAR, *see* community-based participatory research

challenges (in conducting respectful research), 2–3, 9, 13–15, 100, 107, 177, 204, 219, 230–2

checking back process, 36, 63, 84, 88, 111, 137, 145-9, 158, 180–1, 220–1, 259
  introduce complications, 181

choice of participants and research contexts, 7–8, 14, 33–4, 37, 43–4, 48, 53–4, 61, 95, 107, 119–20,

choice of research focus, 2, 14–18, 26, 28–30, 35–40, 45, 67
  passion, 30, 37, 39, 41, 226, 230
  responsibilities, 2, 10, 13, 22, 43, 45, 66, 68, 70, 81, 85, 93, 95, 96, 98, 107, 133, 144, 157, 177, 179, 186, 189, 203, 206, 207, 226

closeness, 14–15, 172–3

co-authorship, 219, 222

code for units of meaning, 143–4, 154–5, 270–3

collaborative authorship, 190–1, 208–10, 217

collective biography, 23

colonialism
  de-colonization, 33, 190, 230
  effects of, 42, 97
  embedded, 42
  post-, 25

community-based participatory research (CBPAR), 50, 96–7, 105, 200, 222, 224

community-based research, 29, 158, 177, 208

complexities of race, 6, 9 ,12, 30, 32, 34, 107, 128–9, 161, 166, 168–9, 177, 224, 228

conclusion of the research, 44, 103, 108, 147, 186, 203, 220

conducting research in small communities, 6, 25, 85, 97, 174

conferences, 22, 65, 202, 208–19, 224
  downside, 211, 213
  experience, 22, 65, 202, 208–17

confidentiality, 53, 63, 70–1, 74, 83, 86–91, 95–7, 109–10, 144, 147, 174, 178–9, 189, 259–61, 263
  anonymity, 82, 86–7, 127, 191, 261

assigning pseudonyms, 31, 87–8, 178,
260–1
breach, 189
risk and vulnerability, 6, 17, 80–2, 104,
128, 178
consent, 70–1, 74, 77, 80–91, 94–106, 110,
125, 141, 178, 202, 258–62
continuous (process), 70–1, 81–6,
124–5, 178, 261–2
contextual sensitivity, 16
continuous process of sensitization, 158
continuously aware of the messiness, 35,
154–5
continuously question, 93, 163
contradict the understandings, 157–8, 173,
186
contradictions, 5, 123, 157–8, 165, 268
contribute new knowledge, 97, 163, 170
contribution to the literature, 40, 92, 170,
269
correct and full information, 101
consent form, 77, 82–5, 88, 89, 96, 101,
258–62
information letter, 77, 83, 101, 220,
258–62
credibility, 15, 36, 63–4, 145, 148, 153, 156,
177, 186, 196, 228
crisis of representation, 177
critical ethnographic research, 2, 6, 49, 157,
164, 184, 198, 224
critical feminist researchers, 2, 6–13, 34–5,
47, 49, 63, 92, 107, 157, 169, 177
critical lens, 13–17, 61, 64, 66, 107–9,
116–17, 154–5, 157–9, 163–4, 169,
194–5, 229–30
critical qualitative perspectives, 35
critical qualitative research plan, 100
critical, questioning stance, 38, 48, 62, 159
critical race theory, 128
critical reflexivity, 2, 13–17, 24, 35, 39–40,
63–4, 88, 93, 114, 121-3, 158–9, 169,
175, 177, 184, 227
critical theoretical frameworks, 6–13, 21, 24,
35, 38, 47–8, 63, 128, 130, 148, 152,
159, 163–6, 169, 193, 198, 208, 224
critical youth studies, 128
critically reflexive lens, 2, 13–14, 16–17, 24,
35, 39, 63–6, 88, 92–4, 114, 121–3,
148–9, 158–9, 169, 177, 184, 227–8
critique based on the study's data, 186
critique of methodology, 8–9, 34, 219

form of reciprocity, 219
critique of the privileging, 220
critique their institutional experiences, 10,
164, 168, 171, 229
critiquing and learning from the experience,
35, 38, 107, 122, 223
cross-cultural collaboration. 33, 41–2,
190–1
culminating research documents, 197, 208
cultural appropriation, 189–90
cultural complications that influence
interpretive research traditions, 33, 171

data
alternate readings, 7, 160, 164, 186, 189
amount, 46–7, 53, 55, 107–8, 15, 143,
153–4
artifacts, 15, 29, 50, 59, 198
collecting data, 2, 8, 15, 37–9, 46–7,
60–4, 79, 89–91, 100–30, 156–8, 179,
191–2
found photographs, 50, 124
interviewing, 47–53, 89–90, 109–14,
124–30, 141–6, 160–1
observing, 7–8, 54–8, 90–1, 107–9,
116–22, 141–2
photographing, 29, 50, 56, 61, 64, 82,
88, 91, 120, 124, 176, 224
videotaping, 29, 51–53, 56–7, 64–5,
82, 103–4, 109, 119–20, 127, 141–2,
187, 204
convenience sampling, 101
creating artistic representations, 15, 29,
51, 64, 82, 91, 107, 124, 126, 176, 186,
196
data representation, 2, 50, 62–4, 71,
77, 87–8, 91, 131–51, 161–3, 171,
176–201, 202–3, 212–13, 219, 228
documents, 29, 59–60, 88, 124, 156–7
informed explanations, 14, 123, 163–4
made meaning, 169, 185–6
mundane, 109, 138, 184–6
organization, 47
purpose and type of research, 24, 26, 28,
36, 46, 81, 91, 103, 104–5, 115, 143,
153, 186
rich data, 29, 49–51, 53, 127
shock power, 185
tangentially connected, 155–6, 158
too little, 46–7, 61
too much, 46–7, 60–1

types, 29, 46, 154–6, 202–3, 222
    withdrawal, 83, 89, 181–2, 260–1
debate, 1, 9, 72, 150, 154, 176–7, 228–9, 231
deception, 104
deeper meanings, 28, 58, 160, 172–3
defence,
    culminating task, 204
    degree expectation, 20, 170, 193–4,
        203–4
    oral defence, 204, 206
    oral presentations, 87, 211,
    paper presentation, 60, 65, 210–15, 260
degree of interpretive and analytic work,
    134, 143, 177
degree of involvement, 210
demographic information, 108–9, 128,
    178–9
dignity, 86, 95, 104–5
disclosure, 83, 86, 104–5, 108–9
dissemination, 15, 170, 193–7, 202–225
    academic/personal goals, 203, 209, 215,
        218, 221, 223
    activities, 220
    collaborative, 210–11
    decisions, 218
    early, 65
    going public, 88, 176, 180, 204
    respectful, 145, 197
    strategic forms of, 203, 220
dissertation, 24, 27, 61–2, 64, 67–9, 123,
    157, 163, 176, 187–8, 194–7, 206
    proposal writing, 24, 26–7, 51, 63, 69
    writing and format unfold, 61–2, 188
distance dynamic, 2, 13–15, 17, 23–4,
    158–9
documenting decisions
    assumptions, 12–13, 35
    effective search skills, 46, 59, 105–6, 214
    historical and/or contextual knowledge,
        10, 26, 59, 94, 141, 160–1, 170–1, 191,
        222
    plans for the future, 60, 156, 193–4
    rationale, 186–8
    transparency, 64, 123, 143, 156, 171–2,
        187–8
dominant groups and structures, 6–7,
    10–12, 25, 35, 38, 40–2, 161–3, 182,
    191, 228, 272
dropouts,
    youth being institutionally framed as,
        233,

dull moments, 184

emotional involvement, 15, 140
empathic communication skills, 5, 112, 127
ethics
    application, 66, 70–83, 86, 88–99, 178,
        207
        processing of, 76
    assessed level of risk, 75
    educational function, 74
    in situ, 66, 71, 93, 103, 178
    international students, 75, 78
    interpretive research, 72–3, 79–80
    level of vulnerability, 24, 66–7, 77, 80–3,
        95, 99 103–4, 112, 127, 178, 204
    minimal risk, 75, 79–80, 82, 104–5
    minors, 80
    overestimate, 80–1
    terminal patients, 96
ethnographic fiction, 179
exploitation, 12, 71, 92–3, 185–6, 190

feedback, 66–7, 87, 128, 205, 213, 223–4
    from advisor, 19–20, 76, 207
    from First Nations, 85
    from participants, 36, 137, 146, 179–82
    from reviewers/editors, 215–16, 218
female drug users, 95, 231–2
feminist care ethics, 96, 127–8
feminist perspective, 1, 6–13, 34–5, 47, 96,
    107, 177
feminist poststructuralist lens, 129
field
    communication, 95, 103, 125–6, 195
    notes, 57, 61, 85, 90, 102, 113, 117–19,
        129, 150–1, 155–8, 176, 182, 184–5,
        187
    work, 54, 59, 123
films, 57, 82–3, 91, 103, 107, 120, 122, 200,
    220–1, 222–3
focus groups,
    challenges, 114, 125, 138–9, 172
    complexities, 52
    confidentiality, 89–90
    contribution to social justice, 52
    cross-cultural, 52–3
    emergent options, 52, 115
    ethics, 53, 89–90, 258–62
    extensive explanations, 130
    group dynamics, 53, 114–16, 138–9,
    interpreting, 52, 90, 138, 140, 143, 147,

interviews, 47, 51–3
  planning, 35–6
  positivist orientation, 51–2
  postmodern, post-structural orientations, 52
  role of moderator, 52, 115, 129
  transcript, 138–144
  video, 51–2, 141, 143
freedom to teach, 5, 38, 233,

goals,
  emancipatory, 28, 38, 46
governmentality, 11, 172
graduate student experience, 18, 20, 64, 65, 122, 133, 148, 204–5, 209–10, 214
grounded theory, 28, 62, 153, 175

hermeneutics, 10
hierarchical structure, 167–8, 213
human
  instrument, 58, 156

identities
  differences, 33, 161–3, 201
  intersecting, 29, 35, 161, 170,
  multiple shifting, 14, 29, 30, 33
incarceration, see prison
incentives, 92, 126
inconsistency of "seeing," 119
informed critical lens, 17, 107, 229–30
inspecting gaze, 164–5
institutional board decisions, 98–9
institutional case study, 14–15
institutional critique, 164, 167, 233
institutional practices, 215, 227–8
institutional whiteness and racism, 162
integrity,
  of researchers, 70, 92, 94
interlocking nature of oppressions, 13–14, 164, 166
interpretive epistemology, 129
intersections, 9, 32–3, 157–8, 163–8
interviews
  assess knowledge, 47, 53
  assumptions, 8, 47–50, 54, 96, 107, 113, 187
  basic supplies, 109
  computer-based technologies, 47, 56–7
  expectations, 47–8, 83, 135, 145, 174, 186
interviewee transcript review, 84

kinetic conversations, 110
multiple truths, 7–8, 10, 48, 119, 187
naturalistic contexts, 110
online, 29, 46–52, 78–9, 127–9
pilot study, 111, 149
power, 2, 9, 48, 53–5, 98, 113–16, 128, 271
preparatory interviews, 111
types of,
  focus group, 47–51, 130, 147
  gendered, 47–8
  open-ended-in-depth, 6, 15, 22, 48–9, 84, 96–9, 113, 130, 142, 174
  postmodern interviews, 7, 47–8, 51, 116, 174
  semi-structured, 47–8, 130
  structured, 47–51, 96 113, 142
  telephone, 47, 49, 128
  unstructured, 47–9

jotnotes, 113, 118–21
journal,
  entries, 176,
  organization, 58–60, 123, 186
  publication, 215–16, 219–20,
  research journal, 67, 69, 122–4, 155–6,
  writing, 4, 58–60, 63–4, 123–4, 188, 194,

language challenges, 14, 53, 136–7, 146, 151, 191–2, 195, 199, 211, 265, 272
legitimation crisis, 177
literature review,
  comprehensiveness, 24, 27–29, 63, 67, 114, 153, 161, 163, 170–1, 217
  return to, 27, 160–1, 163, 171, 188–89

manuscript, 63, 198, 208–9, 211, 215–19
marginalization, 7, 12, 33, 42, 104, 163–4, 166, 220, 228
matrix of domination, 166
media discourse, 6, 159, 180, 182–3, 191, 195, 231–2
Mestizaje approach, 25
meta-narrative, 176, 194
methodology,
  of a/r/tography, 47, 68, 199–200
  decisions, 16, 24, 28–30, 35–8, 49–50, 55, 58, 62–64, 111, 122–3, 143, 153, 177, 182, 194–9, 226, 229
  feminist, 9, 28, 96, 107
  hybrid, 46

Indigenous, 12, 24–5, 28, 33, 158, 173, 190
innovative, 196, 204, 220, 224, 226–7
practices and dilemmas, 2, 54, 218–19
queer, 28, 32–3
Metis epistemology, 68
minority populations, 42, 231–2
misrepresentation,
of First Nations peoples, 190

narrative inquiry, 23–4, 28, 62, 149, 150, 153, 177
neo-liberalism, 11, 229
new ethnography, 129
nuance, 56, 61–2, 164, 167, 170

observation, 31, 46, 49–51, 54–8, 86–7, 90–1, 107–8, 116–27, 131, 135, 141–144, 156–7, 180, 184, 198, 202–3
dual, 126

panoptic architecture, 164–5
paradigm, 8, 33, 63, 233
qualitative, 46, 149
interpretivist , 159–60
participants
may change their minds, 104, 124–5
participant observation, 55–6, 96, 117–18, 127, 168, 198
recruitment, 41, 43, 67, 77, 79, 81–2, 89–91, 101–2, 104, 106, 127, 129, 161, 174
surprised, 126, 145, 159, 180–1, 220
theorizing, 164, 168–9
Participatory Action Research (PAR), 67–8, 97, 105, 125, 130, 141, 158, 177, 222
participatory research (PR), 28, 50, 55, 57, 67–8, 81, 96–7, 115, 154, 200, 224, 230
participant-researcher, 98
partnership, 97
pathmaking, 23
personal details, 102, 108–9
policies and procedures (ethics review), 72–3, 93–4, 100
politics,
of access, 40
cultural, 129
of dissemination, 213, 218
feminist, 9
gender, 23

positivism, 8–9, 48
posters, 101, 211, 213
post-positivist stance, 48
preparation, 45, 65, 67, 100, 109, 111, 115–16, 132, 152, 169, 206, 212
principal reflection, 69
prison,
Aboriginal/Indigenous peoples, 160, 231–2
all-observing, invisible, punishing eyes embedded in, 119–20, 183
distanced world of, 230–1
industrial complex, 232
injustices, 183
minority and marginalized populations, 5, 7, 103–5, 204, 231
official prison agenda, 233
school-to-prison pipeline, 233
structure, 164–9, 182–5, 195
struggles for an education, 5–7, 38, 78, 102, 185, 208, 231, 232
women prisoners, 2, 4–9, 15–17, 30–1, 38, 40–1, 46, 49, 60–1, 78, 80–1, 88, 92, 102–105, 108–9, 111–13, 117–18, 120-1, 145–6, 151, 159–60, 163–9, 180–5, 195, 204, 208–9, 219, 230–4
privileged
with choice, 229
population, 42
privileging, 1, 38, 163–4, 169, 220
researchers, 3, 30, 123, 190
promises, 63, 88–9, 178–9, 221
protective custody, 166–8

quality issues, 72, 144
quoting as problematic, 187–190

racialized and minority individuals and groups, 25, 129, 169, 191, 230
racialized minority researchers, 191
racism, 42, 83, 129, 162, 168–9
rapport, 31, 36, 39–40, 42, 98, 102–3, 145, 179, 181
rationale, 26, 39, 58, 154, 186-8, 216
REBs, see ethics; research ethics boards.
reciprocity, 9, 36, 44, 63, 68, 90, 92, 97, 99, 105–6, 123, 128–9, 158, 203, 207–9, 219, 221–2, 229
rehabilitation, 38, 122, 160, 168, 231–2
relational power and identity, 23

report
  executive / final, 27, 87, 178, 180, 207–8, 260
  expectations, 170, 202–3, 207–8
representation
  constructed, 108, 135–6, 146, 180, 187
  crisis, 176–7
  essentialist claims, 182
  image-based modes, 141, 196
  neutrality, 7–9, 11, 35, 176–7
request for clarifications, 75–8, 87, 98–9
request for withdrawal, 83, 89, 125, 181–2, 216, 260–1
Research Assistant (RA), 65, 69, 214
research ethics boards (REBs), 65, 70–81, 84, 92–99, 105–6, 258
resistance, 107–9, 165, 183–4, 216, 222–3, 227, 229, 233
round-table, 213

schools (as research location), 16–17, 34, 41, 43, 80, 83, 98–9, 104, 175
segregation,
  misleading rationales, 231
Serbo-Croatian language, 146, 192, 260, 265
social change, 22–3, 25, 35–8, 104–5, 203
social context, 185–6
social justice, 1, 3, 24–5, 28–9, 35–6, 38, 46, 52, 130, 161, 199, 208, 220
student-advisor relationship, 17–22, 62–66, 206–7, 218–19
studying up, 104–5
surveillance, 61, 164–6, 232

teaching
  and observing simultaneously, 121
  theatre techniques, 130
technology, 50–3, 56–7, 75, 119, 129, 149–50, 205, 219–20
themes,
  intersecting, 17, 158–9
theoretical framework,
  constructed, 27–8, 170–1
  needing adjustments, 163–4
theories
  feminist, 1, 6–7, 9–13, 25, 28, 35–7, 63, 127, 169
  intersectional, 35–7, 163–8, 224
  postmodern, 1, 7, 9, 12, 35–7, 48, 51–5, 63, 116, 119, 169, 177
  post-structural, 7, 12–13, 25, 52, 127, 129

theorizing, 143, 163–9
timelines
  challenges, 15, 45, 100, 125, 211
  deadlines, 45, 218
  plan backwards, 45
  revisit regularly, 45
trans/lingual worlds, 192
transcription
  conventions, 132–3, 142–3, 198
  image-based transcription, 141
  as a key phase of data analysis, 132
  maximizing quality, 111–12, 141–4, 149, 151
  multi-modal, 141–2, 198
  multiple languages, challenges, 136–7, 151, 172, 191–2, 199
  verbatim, 131–3, 136–7, 141, 145–6, 187, 189
transformational potential of qualitative research, 24
translation, 82, 137, 191–2
transnational feminist research, 9, 33–4, 146, 230
Tri-Council Policy Statement on Ethical Conduct for Research Involving Humans (TCPS), 66, 70–72
triangulation, 156–7

university regulations, 73–4, 98–9, 218–19

voyeurism, 71, 185–6, 190
vulnerable groups, 5, 40, 82, 95, 98–9, 103–4, 112, 126–7, 150–1, 161, 204, 232
  coercion of, 80
  participants, 24, 67, 77, 83
  senior citizens, 80,

White, anti-racism educators, 129
writing
  abilities, 36
  collaboration, 33, 40–1, 105, 189–91, 208–9, 218–19

young offenders, 128